A Lawyer Writes

A Lawyer Writes

A Practical Guide to Legal Analysis

Third Edition

Christine Coughlin
Joan Malmud Rocklin
Sandy Patrick

CAROLINA ACADEMIC PRESS
Durham, North Carolina

.

Library of Congress Cataloging-in-Publication Data

Names: Coughlin, Christine Nero, author. | Rocklin, Joan Malmud, author. | Patrick, Sandy, author.
Title: A lawyer writes : a practical guide to legal analysis / Christine Coughlin, Joan Malmud Rocklin, and Sandy Patrick.
Description: Third edition. | Durham, North Carolina : Carolina Academic Press, LLC, [2018] | Includes bibliographical references and index.
Identifiers: LCCN 2018014390 | ISBN 9781531008765 (alk. paper)
Subjects: LCSH: Legal composition. | Law--United States.
Classification: LCC KF250 .C683 2018 | DDC 808.06/634--dc23
LC record available at https://lccn.loc.gov/2018014390

Carolina Academic Press, LLC
700 Kent Street
Durham, NC 27701
Telephone (919) 489-7486
Fax (919) 493-5668
www.cap-press.com

Printed in the United States of America
2020 Printing

Dedication

To the family I was born to and the family I was blessed with—
Rick, Jacob, Jonathan, Addison, and Isabelle.
CNC

To my parents, who were my first editors, and to Bob Rocklin,
my co-editor and partner in all that I do.
JMR

To Shawn, Anna Blake, and MacLean,
who teach me new things every day.
SCP

Contents

Acknowledgments

We are keenly aware that we could not have written this book without the time, talents, and wisdom of our national and institutional colleagues, students, and families. We are grateful for the steadfast support each group has given to us.

Our legal writing colleagues have provided invaluable insights as the pages of this book took shape. Special thanks go to Steve Johansen, Toni Berres-Paul, Bill Chin, Rebekah Hanley, Lance Long, Megan McAlpin, and Lia Miles, who bravely field-tested the first draft of this book. Thanks also go to Suzanne Rowe, Anne Villella, Daryl Wilson, Debbie Parker, and Miles Foy who cheerfully read and critiqued portions of the book despite their busy schedules. Angus Nesbit helped us research details for the chapter on Sources and Systems of the Law. Other colleagues routinely gave us ideas, materials, support, and encouragement as we worked through countless drafts including Tracey Coan, Luellen Curry, Beth Enos, Judy Giers, Miki Felsenburg, Steve Garland, Russell Gold, Laura Graham, Heather Gram, Sue Grebeldinger, John Korzen, Barbara Lentz, Judith Miller, Ruth Morton, David Olsson, Linda Rogers, Donna Williamson, Judith Miller, Vanessa Zboreak, and Aliza Kaplan. Thanks to Connery Wilson for helping us capture our graphic vision on the page. The Deans and Associate Deans at our individual law schools also supported us immeasurably through research grants, funding for this project, and sabbaticals. Alumni, such as Norm Wiener and Don Walker, also provided financial support for our endeavors. We are fortunate to teach at such wonderful schools.

Our heartfelt thanks also go out to all our colleagues in the legal writing community from whom we have drawn ideas and inspiration. While we have attempted to individually acknowledge everyone whose work and ideas have shaped this book, that task is nearly impossible given the many ideas we have obtained through conferences, listservs, blogs, the Legal Writing Institute's Idea Bank, and its Writer's Workshop. If we have somehow missed someone, we apologize for our unintentional oversight.

We would also like to thank the students who helped us in so many ways. Our research assistants unfailingly read, edited, and commented on numerous versions of text, tables, and call outs. We especially thank Alexis Baello, Steven Bell, Laura Carlsen, Mieke de Vrind, Erin Gould,

Erin Hartnett, Christine Meier, Ryan Orr, Stephen Pritchard, Austin Saylor, Stephen Schima, Erin Smith, Jarrad Smith, and Maggie Walter for helping us refine each version and remember our audience. We also thank our teaching assistants including Evan Andersen, Megan Bode, Jessica Breuer, Crystal Chase, Matthew Clark, Sarah Einowski, Madeline Engel, Dale Fujimoto, Lauren Goldberg, Brooks Hanner, Gema Junco, Lauren Trask Millovitsch, and Raife Neuman for endorsing our efforts and convincing our students that reading this textbook was a worthwhile endeavor. Great thanks also go to our wonderful students; we could not have contemplated such a book without their suggestions. The students unabashedly shared what worked and what did not, yet they critiqued our work gently. They have been teachers to us. Special thanks go to Katy Aultman, Alicia Bettenburg, Marco Boccato, Sarah Brandenburg, Erin Farris, Starla Hargita, Teresa Jacobs, Jennifer Prince, Katrina Schaffhouser, Matthew Schroettnig, Matthew Rowan, Youngki Sohn, Alison Torbitt, Evan Wickersham, and Mariko Yoshioka.

Finally, we would like to thank Carolina Academic Press for giving us the opportunity to create a different kind of legal writing text—one we hope will inspire and be accessible to all the different types of learners and writers that make up the future of the legal profession. In particular, we would like to thank Tim Colton of Carolina Academic Press for his dedication and patience in helping us publish this text.

Perhaps the greatest thanks go to our families who backed us throughout this endeavor. They read chapters and gave us feedback. They adjusted schedules so that we could write and rewrite, patiently adapted to conference calls during family vacations, and kept daily life afloat so that we could review another chapter one more time. Without their time and sacrifice, this book surely would not have been possible.

Introduction

Imagine that you are a lawyer in the middle of your first day on the job. You have completed your W-4 forms, taken a tour of the office, and shaken hands with new colleagues. Finally, you walk into your office.

At that moment, the phone rings. A senior partner asks that you come to her office. When you arrive, she explains that the firm has a new client who has been arrested and charged with robbing a local bank. She explains that the client's guilt hinges on a statement he made to an undercover police officer. She wants to know whether the client's statement can be excluded from the trial. She asks that you research the problem and get back to her with your analysis.

Your legal career will get off to a much better start if you know *how* to "get back to her with your analysis." We have written this book for that reason. This book will teach you how to assess the merits of a legal problem and how to communicate your assessment to other attorneys. Those two skills—the ability to assess a legal problem and to communicate your assessment to others—will form the cornerstone of your work as an attorney.

To develop those skills, it will help to imagine that you are a new attorney working in a law office, perhaps a private law firm or a public agency. Your client faces either civil litigation or a criminal trial. Your job is to assess the strength of your client's legal position—one of the most typical tasks asked of a new attorney.

We know that not all of you plan to be trial attorneys. Some of you may not even plan to practice law after you graduate. This book, however, will be useful no matter what field you choose. As you read this book, you will be developing fundamental skills of analysis and communication.

To learn those skills, you will have to be open to a new way of thinking, organizing, and explaining. Each professional discipline has its own way of analyzing a problem and communicating that analysis. The tools and language that a doctor would use to explore and discuss a problem are different from the tools and language that an engineer would use or that an English professor would use.

Our job is to teach you how an *attorney* would explore and discuss a legal problem. Although you bring with you a great many skills from your previous academic and professional disciplines—most notably a keen intellect—you have never before been an attorney.

In this book, we will take you step-by-step through the process of developing and presenting a legal analysis. To prepare you to analyze your client's legal question, we will describe the sources of law and how to weigh, synthesize, and organize those sources. Then, we will show you how to construct a variety of legal arguments, from the simple to the more sophisticated. Finally, we will discuss how to present your legal analysis, whether in an office memorandum or in a professional email.

And that brings us to the first chapter. That chapter explains how attorneys in an office communicate with each other and what it will look like when you get back to that partner with your legal analysis.

A Lawyer Writes

Chapter 1

How Attorneys Communicate

When you are asked to provide a legal analysis to a senior attorney, you will typically provide that analysis in writing, either in an office memorandum or in an email. That analysis must do two things: It must present an objective analysis of the client's legal question *and* convince the senior attorney that the analysis is sound. This chapter explains what an objective analysis is, how to present that analysis in a memorandum or email, and how to convince an attorney that the analysis is sound. Finally, this chapter will explain a bit more about what happens with your legal analysis after you have submitted it to the senior attorney.

I. What Is an Objective Analysis?

When a senior attorney asks you to get back to her with your analysis, the senior attorney is asking for an "objective analysis." An "objective analysis" is a neutral assessment of a client's legal problem. An objective analysis overtly discusses both the strengths and weaknesses of a client's legal position and predicts the most likely outcome. For that reason, "objective writing" is also referred to as "predictive writing."

3

Objective writing is distinct from "persuasive writing." When an attorney writes persuasively, the attorney urges the reader to focus on those arguments that support the client's preferred outcome and minimizes any weaknesses in those arguments. In both objective and persuasive writing, the attorney accurately presents the law, applies the law to the client's case, and makes a recommendation about how to proceed. The difference between the two is in how explicitly the writer explores weaknesses. In objective writing, an attorney specifically and thoroughly explores and evaluates weaknesses.

II. How Do I Present My Analysis?

An objective analysis can be presented to a colleague in either an office memorandum or an email. Of those two methods, an office memorandum is more appropriate if your legal analysis will fill more than one computer screen. Since most of your legal analyses will fill more than one computer screen, this book will look first at how to develop an office memorandum. Later, this book will look at presenting a legal analysis in an email. Once you know how to present your legal analysis in an office memorandum, it is fairly easy to scale back and present a shorter analysis in an email.

A. An Office Memorandum

You can see how you might present an analysis in an office memorandum in Example 1-A. In that memorandum, an attorney answers the question posed in the Introduction: Will a client's statement be admissible at trial? As you read the memorandum, look first at the substance of the memorandum; then look at the form in which it is communicated.

1. The substance of a memorandum

With respect to the substance, the attorney will explain the law and then apply the law to the facts of the client's case. Those two components—an explanation of the law and then an application of the law to the client's facts—are the core components of a legal argument.

Look also at the conclusion the attorney reaches. The attorney explains that the client's statement will be admissible. Since the statement, if admitted at trial, will likely send the client to jail, the attorney is predicting an unwelcome outcome. He explains other alternatives, but ultimately he has to acknowledge that a bad outcome is likely.

Honestly assessing and clearly stating the real likelihood of success is critical to providing sound legal advice; an honest assessment is the purpose of writing an objective legal analysis. Your research and analysis will not always lead you to a result that is bad for your client, but when it does, you must acknowledge the bad news and consider alternative strategies. Doing so allows you, your colleagues, and your client the opportunity to realistically assess the available strategies *before* investing thousands (and sometimes millions) of dollars on a business decision or litigation.

2. The form of a memorandum

After reading the substance of the memo, consider its form. Although every law office has its own style, a memo typically has five parts: (1) an introductory statement that briefly lays out the questions the memo addresses, (2) concise answers to those questions, (3) a statement of facts, (4) a discussion that analyzes those questions, and (5) a conclusion. You can see each of these parts in Example 1-A.

Example 1-A • Memorandum

MEMORANDUM

TO: Rita Zal

FROM: Theo Thomas

DATE: August 24, 2018

RE: Paul Adams – Admissibility of evidence

QUESTION PRESENTED

Under Oregon law, which allows a defendant's statement into evidence if the statement was made during "mere conversation" with an officer, will Mr. Adams's statement be admissible when it was made after the undercover officer parked an unmarked police car behind Mr. Adams's car and Mr. Adams told the officer he was not yet planning to leave?

The **Question Presented** describes the legal questions the memo will address. (Ch. 13)

BRIEF ANSWER

Yes. The statement will be admissible against Mr. Adams. Evidence is admissible against a defendant if it is gathered during "mere conversation" rather than during a stop. An officer stops another individual only if that individual could reasonably believe that his liberty was being restrained. Mr. Adams could not reasonably believe that his liberty was being restrained. Therefore, Mr. Adams's statement likely will be admissible.

The **Brief Answer** tells the senior attorney the author's bottom line. (Ch. 13)

STATEMENT OF FACTS

The **Statement of Facts** tells the client's story; however, the story is limited to the facts that will be relevant to the author's legal analysis. (Ch. 14)

On August 15, 2018, police officer Ephgrave spoke with Paul Adams, a suspect in a local bank robbery. During that conversation, Paul Adams revealed information that implicated him in the bank robbery.

Earlier that day, Officer Ephgrave saw a white Ford Probe pull into a parking lot. The car looked similar to the car involved in the Davinsk Mutual Bank robbery, and Officer Ephgrave decided to investigate. At the time, Officer Ephgrave was working undercover and was wearing ordinary street clothes and driving an unmarked car.

Officer Ephgrave pulled into the parking lot and parked behind the Ford Probe. As the officer got out of the car, Mr. Adams yelled at the officer to move his car. Officer Ephgrave walked over to the bench where Mr. Adams was sitting and asked if he was planning to leave. According to the officer, Mr. Adams said, "No, I'm going to sit a little longer." Officer Ephgrave pointed out that there was nowhere else to park because all the other spaces were full and told Mr. Adams he would move his car before Mr. Adams had to leave. According to Officer Ephgrave, Mr. Adams said, "Oh, okay. No problem."

Officer Ephgrave and Mr. Adams began chatting. Officer Ephgrave steered the conversation to the recent bank robbery. As they spoke, Officer Ephgrave remarked that the bank teller had said that the robber was very polite. Mr. Adams added, "Yeah, I heard he even gave a strawberry lollipop to a kid in the bank." Officer Ephgrave knew that the media had reported that the bank robber had given a child a lollipop, but not its flavor. Officer Ephgrave then arrested Paul Adams.

Mr. Adams was arraigned on August 20, 2018. He pleaded not guilty to the charges. He is now awaiting trial.

DISCUSSION

The first paragraph is an **introductory roadmap** (Ch. 12). It states the conclusion to the question being asked, explains the rule that governs that question, and identifies the argument that will be analyzed below: whether Paul Adams's interaction with the officer was "mere conversation" or a "stop."

Paul Adams's incriminating statement about the flavor of the lollipop will be admissible. Whether a defendant's statement to a police officer is admissible depends upon the circumstances under which the statement was made. Oregon courts distinguish between statements that were "mere conversation" and statements that occur during a "stop." *State v. Warner*, 585 P.2d 681, 689

(Or. 1991). Statements that were made during mere conversation with a police officer are admissible. *State v. Shelton*, 796 P.2d 390, 392 (Or. Ct. App. 1990); *State v. Spenst*, 662 P.2d 5, 6 (Or. Ct. App. 1983). By contrast, statements made by a person during a stop are admissible only if the stop was justified by reasonable suspicion. *Spenst*, 662 P.2d at 6. As explained below, Mr. Adams made his incriminating statement during "mere conversation," and not during a stop. Accordingly, his statement will be admissible without any further justification by the officer.

Mr. Adams's statement was mere conversation because he could not ◄——— reasonably believe his liberty was restrained during his encounter with Officer Ephgrave. Whether an encounter with a police officer is "mere conversation" ◄— or a "stop" depends upon the extent to which the person's liberty is restrained. If a person's liberty has not been restrained, then the encounter is "mere conversation." *See, e.g., State v. Smith*, 698 P.2d 973, 975 (Or. Ct. App. 1985). By contrast, a "stop" occurs if a person's liberty is restrained by a police officer lawfully present in any place. Or. Rev. Stat. § 131.605(6) (2017); *State v. Warner*, 901 P.2d 940, 942 (Or. Ct. App. 1995). A person's liberty may be restrained if that person believes that his liberty has been restrained and that belief is objectively reasonable. *Warner*, 901 P.2d at 942. To determine whether a person reasonably believes his liberty has been restrained, a court will consider the totality of the circumstances. *State v. Wenger*, 922 P.2d 1248, 1251 (Or. Ct. App. 1996).

A police officer may request information without restraining a person's liberty. *State v. Gilmore*, 860 P.2d 882, 883 (Or. Ct. App. 1993). In *State v. Gilmore*, a uniformed officer requested identification from three people who were sitting in a truck. *Id.* When the defendant opened the glove compartment to retrieve his identification, the officer saw a gun and arrested the defendant for illegal possession of a firearm. *Id.* Although the defendant argued he had been illegally stopped and, therefore, evidence of the gun should be excluded from trial, the trial court admitted the gun into evidence. *Id.* In upholding the trial court's decision, the court of appeals explained that, even if the defendant felt he was not free to leave, that belief was not objectively reasonable. *Id.* The court of appeals noted that, although the officer requested identification, the

The legal argument addressing whether the interaction was "mere conversation" or a "stop" begins in the second paragraph.

The legal argument begins with a **Conclusion** (Ch. 9) to that question.

After stating the conclusion, the attorney **explains the law** (Ch. 7). The explanation of the law begins with the sentence, "Whether an encounter with a police officer is 'mere conversation' . . . ."

The explanation of the law includes both rules and case illustrations. Here, the writer provides *State v. Gilmore* and *State v. Wenger* as case illustrations.

officer did not require the defendant to alter his course, nor did the officer prevent the defendant from leaving. *Id.*

By contrast, a person may reasonably believe his liberty has been restrained if a police officer blocks that person's car. *Wenger*, 922 P.2d at 1251-52. In *Wenger*, the defendant was intending to leave a parking lot when uniformed officers parked their patrol car and blocked in the defendant's car. *Id.* After noting that a stop occurs when an officer prevents a vehicle from being driven away, the court held that the defendant reasonably believed his liberty had been restrained. *Id.* at 1251-52.

The explanation of the law ends here. ⟶

After explaining the law, the attorney **applies the law** *to the client's case.* (Ch. 8)
The application does not include any new law. The attorney relies on law that has been explained above in the explanation of the law.

In this case, Mr. Adams's encounter with Officer Ephgrave was mere conversation rather than a stop because he could not reasonably believe his liberty was being restrained. Mr. Adams's encounter is similar to the encounter in *Gilmore*. In both cases, an officer approached the defendant seeking information. In *Gilmore*, the officer asked for identification, and in Mr. Adams's case, the officer wanted to learn whether the defendant was involved in the bank robbery.

However, seeking information is not enough to convert their conversation to a stop. In Mr. Adams's case, as in the *Gilmore* case, the officer did not alter the defendant's course or prevent him from leaving. Officer Ephgrave asked Mr. Adams whether he was planning to leave. Mr. Adams said he was not. In addition, Officer Ephgrave said that he would move his car before Mr. Adams had to leave. According to Officer Ephgrave, Mr. Adams agreed, saying "Oh, okay. No problem." Therefore, Officer Ephgrave did not prevent Mr. Adams from leaving nor did the officer alter Mr. Adams's course. Thus, a court should follow the reasoning in *Gilmore* and conclude that Mr. Adams could not reasonably believe his liberty was restrained.

In fact, a court is likely to conclude that Mr. Adams's encounter with the officer was even less restrictive than the encounter in *Gilmore*. In addition to not altering Mr. Adams's course and not preventing him from leaving, Officer Ephgrave was not in uniform. Because Mr. Adams believed he was talking to a civilian, Mr. Adams should have felt even more free to leave than did the defendant in *Gilmore*, who knew he was talking to a uniformed officer. Thus, a court is likely to hold that Mr. Adams's encounter with the officer was mere conversation.

Even though Officer Ephgrave's car did block Mr. Adams's car, a court is likely to distinguish Mr. Adams's case from the *Wenger* case. In the *Wenger* case, the court noted that the defendant was intending to leave at the time his car was blocked. By contrast, Mr. Adams told Officer Ephgrave that he was "going to sit a little while longer," suggesting that he was not intending to leave. Because he was not intending to leave, a court is less likely to conclude that Mr. Adams reasonably felt his liberty was restrained. Accordingly, a court will likely determine that Mr. Adams was not stopped, but rather, that his encounter with the officer was "mere conversation."

The application of the law to the client's case ends with a **Conclusion**. (Ch. 9)

CONCLUSION

The evidence against Mr. Adams is likely admissible because Mr. Adams was engaged in mere conversation when he spoke with the officer. Accordingly, we should discuss with Mr. Adams the risks associated with going to trial, the costs and benefits of pleading guilty, and plea bargains he might be willing to make.

In the **Conclusion to the Memorandum,** *the attorney includes practical suggestions about the next steps to be taken.* (Ch. 15)

B. An Email

Although longer analyses should be presented in an office memorandum, shorter analyses can be quickly conveyed in an email. Example 1-B shows a typical inter-office email. In substance and in form, emails are similar to office memoranda.

Example 1-B · Email

From: Gail Mosse [gmosse@zalassociates.com]
Sent: Friday, September 8, 2018
To: Dina Wong [dwong@zalassociates.com]
Subject: Oursine Living Will

Dina –

You asked whether Tom and Kitty Oursine's living will would be enforceable in Oregon. The answer is that it will not be enforceable.

The Oursines drafted their living will on their computer and signed it themselves without any witnesses. Under Oregon Revised Statutes § 127.531, living wills "must be the same as the form set forth in this section to be valid." That section also requires that two witnesses sign the form. *Id.*

As a result, the Oursines will need to re-draft their living will. The Oursines can access the correct form at http://egov.oregon.gov/DCBS/SHIBAadvanced directives.shtml.

Please let me know if you have any further questions.

Gail

___

1. The substance of an email

In an inter-office email, as in a memorandum, attorneys seek to give an honest assessment of their legal analysis and provide practical solutions for their clients. In Example 1-B, the attorney explains that Oregon courts will not enforce a living will as the clients have currently written it, but the attorney also explains how to create an enforceable living will.

2. The form of an email

An email will often have the same five parts that are in an office memorandum. If you look closely at the email in Example 1-B, you will see that the first paragraph states (1) the question the email addresses and (2) the answer to that question. The second paragraph (3) states the facts and (4) analyzes the question. The last paragraph (5) concludes and offers practical advice.

III. How Do I Convince an Attorney My Analysis Is Sound?

Whether your analysis is in an office memorandum or an email, you will have to convince another attorney that your analysis is sound. Convincing an attorney that your analysis is sound takes work. Attorneys are skeptical readers. They question. They test each statement as they read. The steps below describe the process you will follow to create that sound analysis.

A. Know Your Client and Your Client's Question

Your work begins with your client. Law offices maintain files about each client and the legal matters the clients have brought to the office. Even though the senior attorney may have provided you with background about the client, ask for the client's file. Review it and all the documents in it. Clients' legal questions typically turn on the facts, so you must have a comprehensive understanding of the facts before you begin researching.

Make sure you understand the question that your client needs answered. Likely, when the senior attorney described the legal question, it seemed clear enough. Sometimes, though, as you learn more about your client, you realize that you actually have questions about the question being asked. Don't waste time researching if you are unclear about the question. Go back to the senior attorney and ask.

B. Research Thoroughly

Once familiar with your client's facts and clear about the legal question, you are ready to research. Researching is itself an analytical process that goes beyond merely gathering different legal authorities. You must make choices. You will have to read each authority critically, weed out the irrelevant, and from amongst the relevant, consider *how* relevant each will be. As you research and read, you'll begin developing theories about your client's legal question.

C. Organize

When you are done researching, you will likely have a stack of legal documents and a variety of books piled up around you. From those stacks, you will have to coax a clear explanation of how the law will respond to your client's problem.

Creating a clear explanation from a variety of legal authorities is no easy feat. A clear explanation of the law requires you to see the legal principles each authority represents. Therefore, you will have to re-organize those stacks around the legal principles relevant to your client's question. You can create a chart and draft an outline to understand the major legal principles, supporting authorities, and how the pieces of the law fit together. In whatever form, re-organizing the authorities around legal points will allow you to see themes in the law, and you will develop a more nuanced understanding for how the law might affect your client.

D. Draft and Revise

Next, you will begin writing. Writing involves numerous drafts and re-drafts. As you write, you should re-read the authorities to ensure that your analysis is consistent with the law. At this point, you should still be open to revising everything about your analysis and its organization. Ultimately, after re-writing and re-thinking, you will settle on an analysis and an organization that work.

E. Edit and Polish

After drafting and revising, the editing and polishing begin. You must take a step back from your work and see it as your reader will. As an

Sidebar

Although previously you may have been a one-draft wonder when writing papers, legal writing requires more. Attorneys who communicate their analysis most clearly and precisely typically spend more than half their time re-drafting, revising, and editing.

attorney, you will be dealing with complex ideas. Your job as a writer is to make those complex ideas easy to understand.

When you edit, you will not simply proofread for typos. Rather, you will check that the content is complete and logically ordered. Then, you will tweak transitions and topic sentences so that your discussion flows well. Finally, you will polish, looking for any words that might cause confusion and hunting for any errors in punctuation, grammar, citation, and format.

At the end, you will have a clearly organized, analytically correct, polished discussion of your client's legal problem. Table 1-C charts the five basic stages a lawyer goes through to answer a legal question.

Table 1-C · The legal thinking process

Stage of the Process	Steps of the Stage
I. Understand your client's problem and the question being asked	1. Understand your client's factual situation. 2. Determine the legal question(s) being asked.
II. Research the law	1. Research • to find the governing rule. • to find legal authorities that interpret the governing rule. 2. Critically read the relevant authorities.
III. Organize	Organize to understand the relationship among the relevant authorities: 1. Use a case chart or other method • to reconcile cases. • to identify the best cases to illustrate the governing rule. 2. Outline the legal principles at issue and the legal authorities that will guide your analysis of the client's legal question.
IV. Draft and revise your memorandum	1. After understanding the law and determining the governing rule(s), draft. 2. Review the relevant authorities to ensure your analysis is consistent with the law. 3. Revise the memo to make sure it is organized well (around legal principles).
V. Edit and polish	1. Edit the substance of the draft to ensure your argument is complete and logically ordered. 2. Polish to weed out words that might confuse and to eliminate errors in grammar, punctuation, and citation. 3. Re-read one last time carefully before submitting to your senior partner.

F. Think Recursively

Although we have laid out five neat and distinct stages of legal writing, you will likely revisit stages as you work through your project. At each stage, you learn more about the law and how it applies to your client's problem. Knowing more, you may want to return to an earlier stage and re-think a decision based on the knowledge you've gained.

For example, once you begin researching, you may realize that you don't know a key fact. You'll have to go back, investigate that fact, and then return to your research. Similarly, as you begin to write, you may identify a gap in your legal analysis. You'll have to go back and conduct additional legal research to fill that gap.

Especially as you write, stay open-minded to changing earlier decisions. Writing clarifies thoughts. As you write, you will better understand the law and how it will affect your client. You may see better ways to organize your discussion; you may see that a case originally put to the side is more important than you thought. You may even change your conclusion.

In fact, "legal writing" is almost a misnomer. Legal writing is really about committing to paper something much more complex—legal thinking. That legal thinking is the end result of a recursive process that repeatedly looks back on itself and asks whether previous decisions still stand. Expert legal writers allow themselves the time to re-think and revise so that their readers see—not the thinking process—but a complex analysis, clearly explained.

IV. What Happens Next?

After you submit a legal memorandum or send an email to a senior attorney, the attorney may use it in a variety of ways. The attorney might pick up the phone and call the client to advise the client of your analysis. The analysis might be revised and sent to the client. Alternatively, your analysis might be incorporated into a brief that will be submitted to a court. Depending on the law office, your memorandum or email might also be logged into a document retrieval system so that other attorneys who are working on similar legal questions can build from the legal research that you have already conducted. In that case, your analysis becomes a permanent part of the office's legal database.

In all cases, your goal is to provide your supervisor with a thorough legal analysis so she can provide sound legal advice to your client. The rest of this book will take you step-by-step through the process of developing and communicating that objective legal analysis.

Practice Points

- The most basic type of legal analysis, an "objective analysis," allows an attorney to neutrally evaluate the strengths and weaknesses of any legal claim.

- An objective analysis is most typically communicated in one of two ways: a legal memorandum or an email.

- Good attorneys know that revising, editing, and polishing can take as much time, if not more time than, drafting the initial document.

Chapter 2

Sources and Systems of the Law

The last chapter showed you the path ahead. Now, we must go back and look more closely at the steps you will take to develop that analysis.

After learning about your client and the problem that brought your client to your office, you will begin to research. To answer your client's legal question, you will need to know the universe of law that might govern and choose from that universe. To choose well, you will need to determine which law is relevant and assess the impact it is likely to have on your client's case. That is, you will need to evaluate the "weight" of each legal authority. As you select relevant authority and assess the weight of each, you will begin to develop an answer to your client's question.

This chapter is about how to select and weigh legal authority. It will introduce the most common sources of law in our legal system and explain some basic principles that will guide you in determining the use and relative importance of those legal authorities.

I. Sources of the Law

A law is any binding custom or practice of a community. In the United States, each branch of government has authority to create and publish law: The legislative branch enacts statutes; the executive branch issues regulations and executive orders; and the judicial branch produces case law.

Law from any branch of government is primary authority. The word "primary" refers to authority that the government creates and publishes. In other words, primary authority *is* the law. "Secondary" authority is commentary about the law and is not binding on anyone. Secondary authority can provide you with an overview of an area of law or a critique of the law. Examples of secondary authority are legal encyclopedias, law review articles, and treatises.

Secondary authority is helpful when you are researching an unfamiliar area of the law and need to quickly understand its broad contours. Primary authority, however, has more weight because it is the law. Thus, in your memorandum to the senior partner, you will typically rely on primary authorities.

The Federal Constitution, which is primary authority, is the highest law of the land. It establishes the three branches of the federal government, each of which creates law. Each state also has its own state constitution, which likewise establishes the branches of state government.

A. The Legislature

Legislatures create two types of authority frequently relevant to analyzing a client's legal question: statutes and legislative history.

1. Statutes

A statute is simply a law enacted by a legislature. Under the Federal Constitution, Congress has sole authority to enact statutes for the nation. Similarly, the legislature of each state is responsible for enacting statutes that regulate conduct in that state.

Typically, statutory sections are grouped into a statutory scheme. For instance, Washington State prohibits bribery in baseball through a series of statutory sections (Example 2-A). Similarly, the Federal Clean Air Act is a statutory scheme composed of more than 150 sections (Example 2-B). Together, those sections seek to reduce air pollution in the United States.

Example 2-A · A series of statutory sections creates a statutory scheme

67.04.010. Penalty for bribery in relation to baseball game
Any person who shall bribe or offer to bribe, any baseball player with intent to influence his play, action or conduct in any baseball game, or any person who shall bribe or offer to bribe any umpire of a baseball game, with intent to influence him to make a wrong decision or to bias his opinion or judgment in relation to any baseball game or any play occurring therein, or any person who shall bribe or offer to bribe any manager, or other official of a baseball club, league or association, by whatsoever name called, conducting said game of baseball to throw or lose a game of baseball, shall be guilty of a gross misdemeanor.

67.04.020. Penalty for acceptance of bribe

Any baseball player who shall accept or agree to accept, a bribe offered for the purpose of wrongfully influencing his play, action or conduct in any baseball game, or any umpire of a baseball game who shall accept or agree to accept a bribe offered for the purpose of influencing him to make a wrong decision, or biasing his opinions, rulings or judgment with regard to any play, or any manager of a baseball club, or club or league official, who shall accept, or agree to accept, any bribe offered for the purpose of inducing him to lose or cause to be lost any baseball game, as set forth in RCW 67.04.010, shall be guilty of a gross misdemeanor.

67.04.030. Elements of offense outlined

To complete the offenses mention in RCW 67.04.010 and 67.04.020, it shall not be necessary that the baseball player, manager, umpire or official, shall, at the time, have been actually employed, selected or appointed to perform their respective duties; it shall be sufficient if the bribe be offered, accepted or agreed to....

Example 2-B · Statutory sections from the Federal Clean Air Act

§ 7401. Congressional findings and declaration of purpose
(a) Findings

The Congress finds—

(1) that the predominant part of the Nation's population is located in its rapidly expanding metropolitan and other urban areas, which generally cross the boundary lines of local jurisdictions and often extend into two or more States;

(2) that the growth in the amount and complexity of air pollution brought about by urbanization, industrial development, and the increasing use of motor vehicles, has resulted in mounting dangers to the public health and welfare, including injury to agricultural crops and livestock, damage to and the deterioration of property, and hazards to air and ground transportation....

§ 7407. Air quality control regions
(a) Responsibility of each State for air quality; submission of implementation plan

Each State shall have the primary responsibility for assuring air quality within the entire geographic area comprising such State by submitting an implementation plan for such State which will specify the manner in which national primary and secondary ambient air quality standards will be achieved and maintained within each air quality control region in such State....

§ 7408. Air quality criteria and control techniques
(a) Air pollutant list; publication and revision by Administrator; issuance of air quality criteria for air pollutants

(1) For the purpose of establishing national primary and secondary ambient air quality standards, the Administrator shall within 30 days after December 31, 1970, publish, and shall from time to time thereafter revise, a list which includes each air pollutant—

(A) emissions of which, in his judgment, cause or contribute to air pollution which may reasonably be anticipated to endanger public health or welfare; (B) the presence of which in the ambient air results from numerous or diverse mobile or stationary sources; and (C) for which air quality criteria had not been issued before December 31, 1970, but for which he plans to issue air quality criteria under this section....

2. Legislative history

Legislative history is the record that develops as an idea makes its way through the legislative process and becomes a statute. Attorneys use legislative history to determine the intended purpose of a statute when the language of the statute is unclear.

When a legislator has an idea for a new law, the legislator drafts what is called a bill. The legislator then introduces the bill to the legislature. Typically, the bill will be considered by a committee in each house[1] and, if each committee approves the bill, the bill will be considered by the full legislative body of each house. Along the way, the bill is debated and amended. If the bill is approved by both houses and signed into law by the President (in the case of a federal bill) or by a governor (in the case of a state bill), the bill becomes a statute.

If the language of the statute is unclear and a court is asked to interpret the meaning of the statute, the court may look to the debate that surrounded the statute's enactment and the history of amendments to the statute to interpret the statute's meaning. Because legislatures enact so many statutes, not every statute is subject to formalized, recorded debates.

As an attorney, if your client's legal question involves an ambiguous statute, you will have to determine the extent to which a legislative history exists and assess how that history would affect a court's interpretation of the statute. Example 2-C shows an excerpt of the legislative history to the Federal Clean Air Act.

Example 2-C · Clean Air Act legislative history

CLEAN AIR ACT

Senate Report No. 638, Nov. 7 1963 [To accompany S. 432]
House Report No. 508, July 9, 1963 [To accompany H.R. 6518]
Conference Report No. 1003, Dec. 5, 1963 [To accompany H.R. 6518]
The House bill was passed in lieu of the Senate bill. The House Report and the Conference Report are set out.

---

1. Except in Nebraska, which does not have a bicameral legislature.

House Report No. 508

The Committee on Interstate and Foreign Commerce, to whom was referred the bill (H.R. 6518) to improve, strengthen, and accelerate programs for the prevention and abatement of air pollution, having considered the same, report favorably thereon with amendments and recommend that the bill as amended do pass.

HISTORY OF LEGISLATION

Air pollution is a serious national problem. It is probable that it will increase greatly, unless appropriate action is taken, owing to further industrial growth and the concentration of population in urban areas. The Nation's rapid progress in technological development has made possible a high level of material benefits for the people, but has also generated, as byproducts of such development, a high level of existing and potential problems of contamination of our environment....

B. The Executive Branch

The executive branch also creates law. For example, agencies within the executive branch can create regulations, and the President can issue executive orders.

1. Regulations

Although Congress has sole authority to enact statutes, once it has enacted a statute it often delegates to the executive branch the responsibility for creating regulations that will implement the statute. For example, although Congress passed the Clean Air Act, it delegated to the Environmental Protection Agency, an agency within the executive branch, the responsibility for promulgating regulations to implement the Act (Example 2-D).

If the legal question you are researching involves a statute, you will need to determine if that statute also has accompanying regulations. Some statutes do. Some do not. If the statute is implemented through regulations, you will have to research those regulations to determine how the statute will be applied to your client's case.

Example 2-D · Excerpt from the Code of Federal Regulations showing regulations implementing the Federal Clean Air Act

§ 50.2 Scope.

(a) National primary and secondary ambient air quality standards under section 109 of the [Clean Air] Act are set forth in this part.

(b) National primary ambient air quality standards define levels of air quality which the Adminis-trator judges are necessary, with an adequate margin of safety, to protect the public health. National secondary ambient air quality standards define levels of air quality which the Administrator judges necessary to protect the public welfare from any known or anticipated adverse effects of a pollutant....

§ 50.4 National primary ambient air quality standards for sulfur oxides (sulfur dioxide).

(a) The level of the annual standard is 0.030 parts per million (ppm), not to be exceeded in a calendar year....

(b) The level of the 24-hour standard is 0.14 parts per million (ppm), not to be exceeded more than once per calendar year....

§ 51.40 In what form should my state report the data to EPA?

You must report your emissions inventory data to us in electronic form. We support specific electronic data reporting formats and you are required to report your data in a format consistent with

these. Because electronic reporting technology continually changes, contact the Emission Factor and Inventory Group (EFIG) for the latest specific formats. You can find information on the current formats at the following Internet address: *http://www. epa.gov/ttn/chief*. You may also call our Info CHIEF help desk at (919)541-1000 or e-mail to *info.chief @epa.gov*.

§ 51.45 Where should my State report the data?

(a) Your state submits or reports data by providing it directly to EPA.

(b) The latest information on data reporting procedures is available at the following Internet address: *http://www.epa.gov/ttn chief*....

---

2. Executive orders

In addition to regulations, the executive branch can issue executive orders. Executive orders are policy directives that implement or interpret a statute, a constitutional provision, or a treaty.[2] For example, President Kennedy used an executive order to eliminate racial discrimination in federally funded housing,[3] and President George W. Bush used an executive order to permit the federal government to freeze the assets of any person or entity providing financing to a terrorist organization (Example 2-E).[4] Although executive orders can govern a legal question, executive orders play a less active role in governing peoples' day-to-day lives and are, therefore, less likely to be relevant to your legal analyses.

Example 2-E · Executive Order 13224 of September 23, 2001

Blocking Property and Prohibiting Transactions With Persons Who Commit, Threaten to Commit, or Support Terrorism

By the authority vested in me as President by the Constitution and the laws of the United States of America, including the International Emergency Economic Powers Act (50 U.S.C. 1701 *et seq.*) (IEEPA), the National Emergencies Act (50 U.S.C. 1601 *et seq.*) ... and in view of United Nations Security Council Resolution (UNSCR) 1214 of December 8, 1998, ... and the multilateral sanctions contained therein, and UNSCR 1363 of July 30, 2001, establishing a mechanism to monitor the implementation of UNSCR 1333,

---

2. 4 West's Ency. of Am. L. *Executive Order* 273 (2005).

3. Exec. Order No. 11,063, 3 C.F.R. 652, *reprinted in* 42 U.S.C. § 1982 app. at 6-8.

4. Exec. Order No. 13224, 66 Fed. Reg. 49079 (Sept. 23, 2001).

I, GEORGE W. BUSH, President of the United States of America, find that grave acts of terrorism and threats of terrorism committed by foreign terrorists, including the terrorist attacks in New York, Pennsylvania, and the Pentagon committed on September 11, 2001 … I also find that because of pervasiveness and expansiveness of the financial foundation of foreign terrorists, financial sanctions may be appropriate for those foreign persons that support or otherwise associate with these foreign terrorists.…

I hereby order:

Section 1.… [A]ll property and interests in property of the following of the following persons that are in the United States or that hereafter come within the United States, or that hereafter come within the possession or control of United States persons are blocked:

(a) foreign persons listed in the Annex to this order;

(b) foreign persons determined by the Secretary of State, in consultation with the Secretary of the Treasury and the Attorney General, to have committed, or to pose a significant risk of committing, acts of terrorism that threaten the security of … the United States.

C. The Judiciary

Finally, courts also create law. When a judge issues an opinion, that opinion becomes a part of the law. A judicial opinion can add to the body of law in several ways.[5]

First, a judicial opinion can announce a new principle of law. When a body of law is wholly developed by judicial decisions, that body of law is called "common law." For example, without any enacted statute, courts have allowed individuals to recover for emotional distress after witnessing injuries to close family members; courts have imposed duties on psychiatrists to warn people about dangerous patients; and courts have created defenses such as "entrapment," which allows a defendant to argue that he would not have committed a crime but for a police officer's encouragement. In each of these situations the courts and not the legislature created rights and duties; thus, these situations are examples of the common law.

Second, a judicial opinion can create law by interpreting a constitution, statute, or regulation. If the language of any of these authorities can be understood in more than one way, a court can clarify how the language should be understood. To do this, a court would consider the language

Sidebar

Attorneys sometimes confuse "common law" with "case law." "Case law" includes *any* judicial decision. "Common law" is a subset of case law and refers to only those areas of case law that developed in the absence of a statute.

---

5. *See* David S. Romantz & Kathleen Elliott Vinson, *Legal Analysis: The Fundamental Skill* 5-6 (discussing common law, precedent, and stare decisis).

in question and how that language fits within the rest of the constitutional, statutory, or regulatory scheme. The court would then announce how the particular language should be understood.

Finally, a judicial opinion can create law by applying the law to a new set of facts. Each time a court considers how the law applies to a particular set of facts, it creates a precedent to be followed in future, factually similar cases. Thus, even when the court is not announcing a new principle of law or clarifying the language of a law, the court adds to the body of law by providing examples of how the law applies to individual cases.

II. Weave a Tapestry of Law

The many sources of the law will create challenges for you as you research and analyze your client's legal question. You will likely never find a single document with a neatly typed, clearly explained summary of the law relevant to your client's question. Rather, you will have to find all the possibly relevant sources, then *choose* the actually relevant sources, and finally *create* that neatly typed, clearly explained summary of the relevant law.

Creating that summary of the relevant law will require you to synthesize a variety of authorities into a seamless explanation of the law that governs your client's case. If you do your job well, your synthesized explanation of the law will look like a beautiful tapestry that clearly displays the intricate patterns of the law. If you do your job poorly, you'll have a fist full of loose threads, but no cohesive, well-woven explanation of the law.

For example, the memorandum in the previous chapter, Example 1-A, addresses whether a client's statement will be admissible at trial. To write that legal analysis, the attorney had to research all the relevant law and then choose those authorities that were *most* relevant to answering the client's legal question. Ultimately, the discussion focuses on a statute that defines a "stop" and case law that interprets the statute. The explanation of the statute and case law is the synthesized explanation of the law.

To weave that synthesized explanation of the law, attorneys rely on a few fundamental principles of legal analysis. Those principles help an attorney sort through the various materials and carefully select the most appropriate materials for the job. Using those principles, you will also be able to weave together a cohesive, clear explanation of the law.

III. Systems of the Law

Three fundamental principles of our legal system will help you choose the materials that will be most relevant to answering your client's legal question. Those principles are jurisdiction, the hierarchical structure of courts, and stare decisis.

A. Jurisdiction

When selecting material for a legal analysis, jurisdiction is the first cut that separates the relevant from the less relevant. "Jurisdiction" is an area of authority over which a governing body has control.[6] Because a court or enforcement agency is required to follow only the laws of its jurisdiction, your research and analysis should begin with the law of the governing jurisdiction.

Although our legal system depends on many different jurisdictions,[7] for our purposes, the most important kind of jurisdiction is jurisdiction based on the geographical reach of a legislature or court.

With respect to the geographical jurisdiction of courts and legislatures, citizens of this nation are typically governed by two sovereigns.[8] The United States federal government is one sovereign jurisdiction. Its legislature, the United States Congress, has authority to enact laws that affect all the people and businesses within the United States. Its court system has the authority to interpret and apply the laws Congress has created.

Within the United States, more than fifty other jurisdictions exist.[9] Each state is its own sovereign jurisdiction with its own legislature and its own court system. Each state's legislature has authority to enact laws for that state, and courts within that state have authority to impose those laws on those people and businesses within their jurisdiction.

When you begin researching a legal question, you must first determine the jurisdiction that will govern your client's legal question. Sometimes determining the jurisdiction is easy. For example, the jurisdiction is relatively easy to determine when all parties reside in the same state and the dispute arose in that state. In that case, jurisdiction will usually be determined by whether the client's legal question is governed by state or federal law. Sometimes, however, the jurisdiction is more difficult to determine such as when the parties live in different states or the dispute crosses state lines. In those cases, determining the jurisdiction may create an entirely new question that needs to be researched. Once you have determined the governing jurisdiction, you will focus your research and analysis on that jurisdiction.

Law from within the governing jurisdiction is called mandatory authority. Mandatory authority is binding on the parties and their dispute.

> **Sidebar**
>
> **Mandatory authority** is *always* primary authority. To be mandatory, the authority must emanate from a government body.
>
> **Persuasive authority** can be primary or secondary authority.
>
> For example, a court opinion from another jurisdiction is persuasive, primary authority. It is not binding outside of its own jurisdiction, but it emanates from a government body.
>
> A law professor's law review article is persuasive, secondary authority because it is not binding and the professor is not a government body.

---

6. *Jurisdiction, Black's Law Dictionary* 980 (10th ed. 2014).

7. For example, in Civil Procedure you will learn about subject matter jurisdiction, diversity jurisdiction, and long arm jurisdiction, to name a few.

8. Tribal nations are a third sovereign in the United States, and thus some citizens are governed by three sovereigns.

9. The United States includes "more than fifty other jurisdictions" because it also includes the District of Columbia and five territories (American Samoa, Guam, the Northern Mariana Islands, Puerto Rico, and the U.S. Virgin Islands), all with their own legislatures, executives, and court systems.

Because it is binding, mandatory authority is given the most weight in a legal analysis.

Law from other jurisdictions is persuasive authority. A court deciding a legal issue may consider authority from another jurisdiction. Although a court is not required to rely on or follow case law from another jurisdiction, a court may do so if it finds the reasoning expressed in that case law to be persuasive and consistent with the law from the court's jurisdiction.

In analyzing a client's legal question, you will likely give more weight to mandatory authority than to persuasive authority. However, persuasive authority may still be helpful, especially if the binding jurisdiction does not have law addressing the issue or if you are advocating for a change in the law. Table 2-F lists some of the authorities that you might rely on when analyzing a client's legal question and describes the weight of each.

Table 2-F • Authorities and their weight

Sources of Law	Who Makes Them	Type of Authority	Weight of Authority (in governing jurisdiction)
Constitutions	Sovereigns (nations and states)	Primary	Mandatory
Statutes	Legislature	Primary	Mandatory
Regulations	Government agencies	Primary	Mandatory
Case law	Judiciary	Primary	Mandatory (depending on level of court)
Executive orders	Executive branch	Primary	Mandatory
Legislative history	Legislature	Secondary	Persuasive
Law review or journal articles	Professors, experts, students, other writers	Secondary	Persuasive
Legal encyclopedias, dictionaries	Various legal writers	Secondary	Persuasive

B. Hierarchical Court Systems

The structure of our federal and state court systems will affect how much weight you give to a judicial decision. Both the federal courts and the courts in each state are arranged hierarchically. In federal courts and in most state courts, the hierarchy is composed of three levels: a trial court, which is the "lowest court" in the hierarchy; an intermediate appellate court; and a final appellate court, which is sometimes referred to as the "court of last resort" (Figure 2-G).

Figure 2-G · Traditional court hierarchy

Litigation begins in the trial court. After a final decision is reached in the trial court, any party not satisfied with the decision may appeal to the intermediate appellate court and ask the appellate court to review the decisions of the trial court. Usually, a person may appeal to an intermediate appellate court "as of right," which means that any party who is not satisfied can have the intermediate appellate court review the decisions of the trial court.

If a party is not satisfied with the result in the intermediate appellate court, the party may appeal to the final appellate court. Typically, however, a party is not entitled to have the highest court review the intermediate court's decision. Rather, the party must petition the highest court and ask that it hear the appeal. If the highest court believes that reviewing the intermediate court's decision will resolve a novel or important legal issue, it may grant the petition, often known as "granting certiorari," and hear the appeal.

At each level, within a given jurisdiction, courts are bound by the prior decision of the courts above it. That is, the decisions of higher courts are mandatory authority for lower courts within that jurisdiction. Thus, when a trial court is deciding an issue, its decision must follow and be consistent with the decisions of the intermediate and highest appellate courts in its jurisdiction. An intermediate court must follow and be consistent with the decisions of the highest appellate court. By contrast, the decisions of a lower court are merely persuasive authority to the courts above it in the same jurisdiction.

In this hierarchical system, attorneys give greater weight to decisions from higher courts because those decisions control the decision-making in the courts below. As a result, you'll need to become familiar with the court hierarchy of the jurisdiction that governs your client's legal question.

1. Hierarchy in the federal courts

In the federal court system, trial courts are called "United States District Courts." Each state has one or more federal districts. An entire state may be designated as one federal district, or if the state is populous, the state will be divided into two or more federal districts. For example, a less populous state such as South Carolina has only one federal district—the District of South Carolina. The more populous North Carolina is divided into three federal districts: the Western District of North Carolina, the Middle District of North Carolina, and the Eastern District of North Carolina. Figure 2-H shows how South Carolina and North Carolina (along with Maryland, Virginia, and West Virginia) are divided into districts.

Each federal district has its own trial court. For example, in the District of South Carolina, the federal trial court is the United States District Court for the District of South Carolina. In the Western District of North Carolina, the federal trial court is the United States District Court for the Western District of North Carolina.

Thus, if you see a federal judicial opinion coming out of a *district* court, you know that the decision is from a trial court, and you can assess its weight accordingly.

Figure 2-H · Federal districts within a federal circuit

Next in the federal court system are the circuit courts of appeals. These intermediate courts of appeal are arranged into thirteen circuits (*see* Figure 2-I). Eleven of the thirteen circuits are numbered. Each circuit includes federal districts of a number of states. For example, the Fourth Circuit includes the federal districts of five states—West Virginia, Virginia, Maryland, North Carolina, and South Carolina. The United States Court of Appeals for the Fourth Circuit hears appeals from the district courts in each of those five states. Figure 2-H depicts the entire Fourth Circuit Court of Appeals.

Two of the thirteen circuits are special circuits. The District of Columbia has its own circuit court, the United States Court of Appeals for the District of Columbia. That court hears appeals from the United States District Court for the District of Columbia, as well as appeals from some administrative agencies and from the United States Tax Court.

The thirteenth circuit is the Federal Circuit. The Court of Appeals for the Federal Circuit, which sits in Washington D.C., is not defined by a region but instead by the kinds of appeals it hears. The court of appeals for the Federal Circuit hears appeals from specialized courts such as the Court of International Trade, United States Court of Federal Claims, and the United States Court of Appeals for Veterans' Claims. In addition, it will hear any appeal involving patent law.

Figure 2-I · Federal circuits

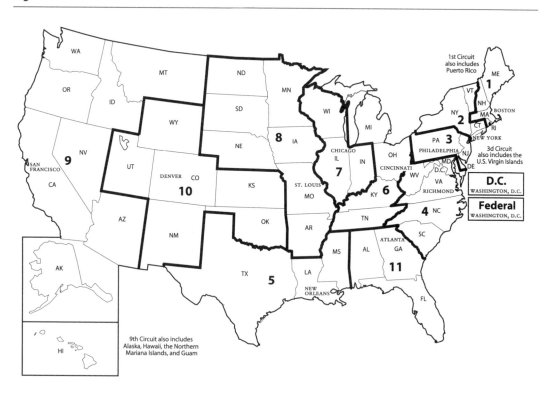

The United States Supreme Court is the highest court in the federal court system. It reviews decisions from all thirteen circuits and is the "court of last resort." Litigants unhappy with a decision from a federal court of appeals must petition the Supreme Court to hear their appeals. Of the more than 6000 petitions the Court receives each year, it usually grants certiorari to roughly one hundred cases.[10]

2. State court hierarchies

Typically, state courts have the same three-part structure, although some variety exists. For example, some states do not have any intermediate appellate court and in other states the intermediate appellate court functions very differently.[11] In North Dakota, for example, the Court of Appeals hears only those cases that are assigned to it by North Dakota's Supreme Court. And sometimes the names of courts will vary. In New York, for example, the lowest court is named the Supreme Court and the highest court is named the Court of Appeals.

Before reading state court decisions, you should be certain that you understand that state's judicial hierarchy because it affects the weight you will give to a decision. To quickly determine a state's highest and intermediate courts, you can turn to Appendix 1 in the *ALWD Citation Manual*[12] or Table 1 in *The Bluebook* citation manual,[13] which list the highest and intermediate courts in each state.

3. Side-by-side court systems

The federal court system is not hierarchically *above* the state court systems (Figure 2-J). Because a state is its own sovereign jurisdiction, state courts have final say about how to understand and apply state law.

The United States Supreme Court may review a state court decision only to determine whether it misinterprets the United States Constitution or other federal law. If the United States Supreme Court determines that the state court decision misinterprets federal law, then the Supreme Court will reverse that part of the state court decision.

Otherwise, the state court system operates independently of the federal court system, and the two systems simply co-exist in the same regions.

---

10. James C. Duff, Judicial Business of the United States: 2016 Annual Report of the Director, http://www.uscourts.gov/statistics-reports/caseload-statistics-data-tables; select Tables A-1 and B-2 (accessed July 27, 2017).

11. Delaware, Maine, Montana, New Hampshire, Rhode Island, South Dakota, Vermont, West Virginia, and Wyoming are states without typical intermediate courts.

12. ALWD & Coleen M. Barger, *ALWD Guide to Legal Citation* 359–405 (6th ed. 2017).

13. *The Bluebook: A Uniform System of Citation* 233–305 (Columbia Law Review Ass'n et al. eds., 20th ed. 2015).

Figure 2-J · The hierarchy of federal and state court systems

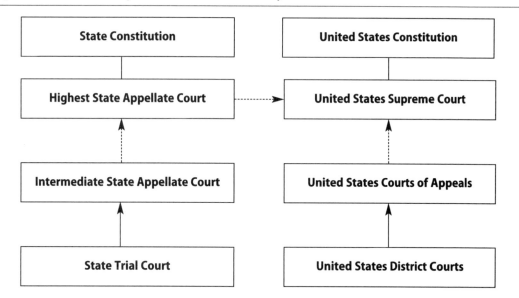

C. Stare Decisis

Finally, the principle of stare decisis will require you to look for the most factually similar cases in order to predict an outcome in your client's case. The words stare decisis are the first two words in the longer Latin phrase *stare decisis et quieta non movere*, which means "to stand by things decided and not disturb settled points."[14] Stare decisis requires a court to follow its own prior decisions when faced with the same legal issue.

Stare decisis transforms individual court decisions into law. Because a court is required to follow its own prior decisions, a single decision affects more than the parties in that case. Absent some significant change in the law or society, the court will follow that prior decision in all future cases presenting the same legal issue.

The principle of stare decisis is triggered by precedent. Precedent is a binding prior court decision. A prior decision is binding on a court only if it raises the same legal issue as the case currently before the court. To raise the same legal issue, two cases must be governed by the same law and have similar facts.

A significant amount of litigation focuses on whether a prior decision is precedent for a current case. Often, attorneys argue about whether the case currently before the court is factually similar to the prior case. If the attorney convinces a court that the current case is factually similar, then the court will be bound by the reasoning and conclusion of the prior de-

---

14. Bryan Garner, *A Dictionary of Modern Legal Usage* 841 (3d ed. 2011).

cision. If the opposing attorney convinces the court that the prior case is not factually similar, then the prior case is not precedent and the court will not be bound by the outcome of that prior case.

Because the factual similarity of a current case to a prior case generally determines whether a court will be bound by the prior case, in your research and analysis you will look for and give the most weight to those prior cases that are most factually analogous to your client's case. The precedential value of a prior case depends upon whether you can demonstrate that the facts of your case are sufficiently similar to the facts that determined the outcome in the prior case.

Stare decisis alters how we weigh case law. For example, typically, a decision from a higher court within a jurisdiction is given more weight than a decision from a lower court in that same jurisdiction. If, however, the decision of the lower court analyzes facts that are very similar to your client's facts, the factually analogous lower court decision will likely become central to your prediction about how a court in that jurisdiction will view the client's case.

For the same reason, a case that is only persuasive authority may rise in your estimation if it is factually similar to your client's case. If no case in the governing jurisdiction is factually analogous, you may look for factually analogous case law in another jurisdiction, provided that the other jurisdiction has a similar legal framework. Thus, even though the case is from another jurisdiction, and is only persuasive authority, it may be given more weight in your analysis due to its factual similarity.

D. The Effect of These Three Principles

These three principles—jurisdiction, the hierarchical court systems, and stare decisis—exert profound influences on our legal system.

First, these principles create consistency and fairness. Once a higher court reaches a decision in that case, not only will that court be bound by that decision, but so will all the lower courts within that jurisdiction. Thus, these principles ensure that two litigants will be treated the same by the courts within that jurisdiction.

Second, these principles create predictability. Attorneys can look for factually similar decisions within a jurisdiction and then predict how courts will react to future conduct. When lawyers can predict the legal consequences of future conduct, individuals can make informed choices about decisions in business or in their personal lives.

Finally, these principles allow for diversity because each jurisdiction within the United States has the opportunity to create laws appropriate to that jurisdiction, so long as those laws do not conflict with the United States Constitution. Thus, along with consistency and predictability, these principles also allow for great diversity.

The legal system, and the law it generates, is often referred to as a single, monolithic entity—"the law." "The law," however, is a synthesis of laws, often from different sources and arranged according to the weight we give each authority. As an attorney, your job is to explain the law as it will affect your client's case. To do so, you will weigh and then weave together authorities from different sources to create a legal tapestry that is unique to that client's case.

Among the many authorities you will work with, court decisions are the most challenging to weave into the pattern. To determine how a prior court decision fits within the pattern of the law, you will have to consider the prior court's jurisdiction and the court's place within the judicial hierarchy. Most importantly, whether a prior decision is featured or simply part of the pattern's background depends on a seemingly simple conclusion: Is the prior decision like your client's case or not?

Practice Points

- To determine the law that governs your client's legal question, you will have to read a variety of legal sources, assess their weight and relevance, and then synthesize those authorities to create a summary of the law relevant to your client's legal question.

- Authority comes in two forms: primary and secondary. Primary authority must be published by one of the three branches of government. Secondary authority is a legal source that describes the law.

- Case law is any judicial decision. Common law is a subset of case law. It includes only those judicial decisions made by courts in the absence of an enacted statute.

- Jurisdiction is the area of authority over which a court has control.

- Binding or mandatory authority is primary authority that controls the legal issue because it comes from the jurisdiction governing the legal dispute. Authority from other jurisdictions or secondary sources is persuasive authority.

- Federal and state court systems operate side-by-side. Each is typically a three-tiered system. Trials originate in the lowest courts. Intermediate courts generally hear appeals as of right. The highest court hears only selected appeals.

- Stare decisis requires courts to adhere to decisions of a prior court addressing the same legal issue. Whether a prior court decision addresses the same legal issue is often a matter of debate.

Chapter 3

Reading for Comprehension

---

§ 3.1   Reading Statutes
§ 3.2   Reading Judicial Opinions

Reading the law is not always a natural, intuitive process. Instead, good legal reading is a learned skill that requires you to read efficiently while deeply comprehending the materials. Getting the gist of the idea is not enough.

To deeply comprehend a legal text, you must read that text *critically*. *Critical reading* is defined as "thinking while you read."[1] Put differently, critical reading means actively engaging each bit of information and questioning it rather than passively accepting every word as written.[2]

At the same time, you must read *efficiently*. Answering a legal question often requires wading through a number of statutes, cases, and other legal authorities. Thus, reading efficiently may require you to read quickly.

Those two goals—reading for comprehension and reading quickly— are often in conflict. Generally, the faster you read, the less you will comprehend. Conversely, the more you read for comprehension, the slower you will read. At the beginning of your legal career, you must focus on comprehension. The result will be that you will read more slowly. As you gain experience, your speed will pick up, and you will be able to read more quickly while still comprehending deeply.

To read for comprehension, follow these three steps: (1) Get context; (2) skim the text; and (3) read the text critically. Those three steps are explained in more detail in Table 3-A.

The most effective legal readers will usually repeat the third step— reading the text critically—multiple times. Reading legal authority is a recursive process that builds on itself. You may read a legal authority

---

1. Debra Moss Curtis and Judith R. Karp, *In a Case, In a Book, They Will Not Take a Second Look: Critical Reading in the Legal Writing Classroom*, 41 Willamette L. Rev. 293, 296 (Spr. 2005).
2. *Id.* at 299.

Table 3-A · Three steps when reading for comprehension

1. **Get context.**	Figure out the who, what, when, where, why, and how of the material: • Who are the key parties? • What are you reading? • When was it written? • Where is its position in the body of law? • Why is the authority important—is it controlling or persuasive authority? • How does the authority analyze the issue?
2. **Skim the text.**	Get a comprehensive overview of the substance before you get into the details.
3. **Read the text critically.**	Read slowly and closely, thinking about the purpose of each word or phrase and how the substantive parts fit together. Questions that lawyers typically ask include these: • Which portions of the text are relevant to my client's legal issue and which are not? • How do those relevant portions affect my analysis? • How does this authority fit in with the other authorities I am reading? Is it consistent with those authorities? Does it expand on what other authorities have said or merely repeat the same concepts?

fairly well the first time; however, you will see things in a case or statute during your third or fourth read that you did not see the first time. As you analyze other authorities that address the same issue, you become a smarter reader. When you then return to a legal authority, you will be able to read it with greater depth and understanding.

The sections that follow—§ 3.1, *Reading Statutes*, and § 3.2, *Reading Judicial Opinions*—show how those three steps apply to reading statutes and case law (the legal authorities you are most likely to rely on in answering a client's question). By developing a systematic approach to reading statutes and case law, you will soon be reading more efficiently, and that deep comprehension will arrive more and more quickly.

Reading Statutes

I.   The Structure of a Statute
II. Reading Statutes for Comprehension
     A. Get Context
     B. Skim the Most Pertinent Statutory Sections
     C. Read the Statute Critically

To answer a client's legal question, you will often begin by researching whether a statute governs that question. This chapter explains how statutes are structured and how to read them effectively.

I. The Structure of a Statute (Title → articles / chapters → section)

To read a statute, you must first understand how statutes are structured when they are published.

In a majority of states and in federal law, statutes are organized into "titles." A "title" is simply a group of statutes organized by topic. For example, in the federal system, Title 18 includes all statutes relating to "Crimes and Criminal Procedure." Titles are then broken down into "articles" or "chapters." The articles or chapters are then broken down into "sections."

You can see this structure in the federal kidnapping statute in Example 3.1-A. Title 18, Crimes and Criminal Procedure, is broken down into chapters, and one of those chapters, Chapter 55, addresses "Kidnapping." Chapter 55 is then broken down into sections, including § 1201, which defines kidnapping and lists the elements of the crime.

In a minority of states, the statutes are first organized into "chapters," rather than "titles." The chapters are then broken down into "articles," and the articles are broken down into "sections."[3] You can see this structure in Nebraska's kidnapping statute, which is in Example 3.1-B.

---

3. A few states deviate from the patterns described in the text. In Illinois, the statutes are broken down into "chapters," then "acts," and then "sections." In Maryland, Minnesota, and Wisconsin the statutory compilations have only two divisions, in which "Titles" or "Chapters" are divided into "sections." In every state, however, "sections" are the fundamental unit of each state's statutory scheme.

Although a statute may be only one section long, typically, statutes consist of multiple related sections, as do the kidnapping statutes in Examples 3.1-A and 3.1-B. Attorneys use the word "statute" loosely. They may use the word "statute" to refer to one "section," or they may use the word "statute" to refer to multiple related sections. For our purposes, we will use the word "statute" to refer to one section and "statutory scheme" to refer to multiple interrelated sections.

Example 3.1-A · Federal kidnapping statutes

Title 18—Crimes & Criminal Procedure
Chapter 55—Kidnapping

Sec.

The list of sections at the beginning of the chapter acts as a table of contents.

1201.   Kidnapping.

1202.   Ransom Money.

1203.   Hostage taking.

1204.   International parental kidnapping.

The section title, "Kidnapping," tells you what the section is about, but it is not technically a part of the statute.

§ 1201.   Kidnapping

(a) Whoever unlawfully seizes, confines, inveigles, decoys, kidnaps, abducts, or carries away and holds for ransom or reward or otherwise any person, except in the case of a minor by the parent thereof, when—

These are subsections of § 1201.

> **(1)** the person is willfully transported in interstate or foreign commerce, regardless of whether the person was alive when transported across a State boundary, or the offender travels in interstate or foreign commerce or uses the mail or any means, facility, or instrumentality of interstate or foreign commerce in committing or in furtherance of the commission of the offense;
> ...

shall be punished by imprisonment for any term of years or for life and, if the death of any person results, shall be punished by death or life imprisonment.

...

(h) As used in this section, the term "parent" does not include a person whose parental rights with respect to the victim of an offense under this section have been terminated by a final court order....

These are historical notes to § 1201.

(June 25, 1948, ch. 645, 62 Stat. 760; Aug. 6, 1956, ch. 971, 70 Stat. 1043 ... Oct. 12, 1984, Pub. L. 98-473, title II, § 1007, 98 Stat. 2139; Nov. 10, 1986, Pub. L. 99-646, §§ 36-37(b) 100 Stat. 3599.)

§ 1202.   Ransom Money

(a) Whoever receives, possesses, or disposes of any money or other property or any portion thereof, which has at any time been delivered as ransom or reward in connection with a violation of § 1201 of this title, knowing the same to be money or property which has been at any time delivered as such ransom or reward, shall be fined under this title or imprisoned not more than ten years, or both....

(June 25, 1948, ch. 645, 62 Stat. 760....)

Example 3.1-B · Nebraska state kidnapping statutes

Chapter 28—Crimes and Punishments
Article 3—Offenses Against Persons

Section

28-301. Compounding a felony, defined; penalty.

28-302. Homicide; terms, defined.

…

28-312. Restrain, abduct; defined.

28-313. Kidnapping; penalties.

28-314. False imprisonment in the first degree; penalty.

28-315. False imprisonment in the second degree; penalty.

…

The list of sections found at the beginning of the chapter acts as a table of contents.

§28-312. **Restrain, abduct; defined.**

As used in sections 28-312 to 28-315, unless the context otherwise requires:

(1) Restrain shall mean to restrict a person's movement in such a manner as to interfere substantially with his liberty:

    (a) By means of force, threat, or deception; or

    (b) If the person is under the age of eighteen or incompetent, without the consent of the relative, person, or institution having lawful custody of him; and

(2) Abduct shall mean to restrain a person with intent to prevent his liberation by:

    (a) Secreting or holding him in a place where he is not likely to be found; or

    (b) Endangering or threatening to endanger the safety of any human being.

Source: Laws 1977, LB 38, §27

The section title, "Restrain, abduct; defined" tells you what the section is about, but it is not technically a part of the statute.

These are subsections of §28-312.

These are historical notes to §28-312.

§28-313. **Kidnapping; penalties.**

(1) A person commits kidnapping if he abducts another or, having abducted another, continues to restrain him with intent to do the following:

    (a) Hold him for ransom or reward; or

    (b) Use him as a shield or hostage; or

    (c) Terrorize him or a third person; or

    (d) Commit a felony; or

    (e) Interfere with the performance of any government or political function.

(2) Except as provided in subsection (3) of this section, kidnapping is a Class IA felony.

(3) If the person kidnapped was voluntarily released or liberated alive by the abductor and in a safe place without having suffered serious bodily injury, prior to trial, kidnapping is a Class II felony.

Source: Laws 1977, LB 38, §28.

The sections within a statutory scheme are often organized in a common pattern. The sections at the beginning of a statutory scheme will usually identify the statute's name, its purpose, any findings on which the legislation was based, definitions, and the scope of the legislation.

Operative provisions come next. Those sections explain the general rule, any exceptions to the rule, the consequences of violating the rule, and how the rule will be enforced. Some statutes also include closing provisions. Closing provisions identify the effective date of the statute and create severability, which is the idea that if one part is determined invalid, the rest will continue to operate.[4]

Some statutes may not include all of these parts; however, you can see that the Nebraska kidnapping statute, in Example 3.1-B, follows this basic pattern. Definitions, in §28-312, are described before the operative section, §28-313, which explains the prohibition against kidnapping and the consequences if someone is found guilty of kidnapping.

II. Reading Statutes for Comprehension

Reading a statute for comprehension requires the same three steps described in the introduction to this chapter: (1) Get context; (2) skim the text; and (3) read the text critically. Table 3.1-C explains these steps.

Table 3.1-C · Reading a statute for comprehension

1. Get context for the statute.	• To whom does the statute apply? • What does the statutory section govern? • In what jurisdiction does the statute apply? • What kind of statute is it—criminal or civil? • When did the statute go into effect? • Where is the statute located within the statutory scheme? • How does the statute operate—requiring behavior or prohibiting or allowing behavior?
2. Skim the most pertinent statutory sections.	• What behavior does the statute prohibit, require, or simply permit? • Does the statute have any limiting language or exceptions? • Does the relevant section cross-reference other sections? • Do any definitions from other sections in the statutory scheme control the words in the section relevant to your client? • Does the statute contain elements, factors, or both?
3. Read the text critically.	• Read carefully, slowly, and critically, marking any phrases, words, or punctuation that could affect the meaning of the statute. • Highlight every "red flag word" and understand its function in the text. • Break down the statute into its components, whether elements, factors, or both. • Think about how the statute, on its face, applies to your client's question.

---

4. The explanation in this paragraph of how a statute is organized is adopted from Christina Kunz, et al., *The Process of Legal Research* 192 (2004).

A. Get Context

Typically, to answer a client's legal question, you will focus on one or two statutory sections; however, those sections must be read in the context of the whole statutory scheme.

For example, suppose you have been asked to research whether a father can be guilty of kidnapping his stepchild. Your client has been charged under federal law, and you have identified 18 U.S.C. §1201 as the statutory section that prohibits kidnapping. Your first step in understanding that section would be to consider its relationship to other statutes within the statutory scheme that addresses kidnapping.

You can get a quick overview of a statutory scheme by reviewing the table of contents for the relevant statutory sections. In Example 3.1-A, the kidnapping statute is preceded by a list of sections that make up the statutory scheme. The list is composed of section titles. Reading those section titles shows how the section relevant to your client's question fits within the statutory scheme. Reviewing the list may also alert you to other sections that may be relevant to your client's question.

For instance, if your client had been charged under the Nebraska state kidnapping statute (shown in Example 3.1-B), you would find it very helpful to skim the sections surrounding §28-313, the section that defines "kidnapping." Skimming for context would alert you that an earlier section, §28-312, defines some of the terms used in the later section, §28-313.

After reviewing how the relevant section fits within the larger statutory scheme, you will want to gather some background information about the section most relevant to your client's question. For example, you should ask whether the statute is criminal or civil because that affects the procedural rules that will govern the litigation and the penalties that will apply if your client is held responsible.

You should also verify that the section you are reading governs your client's legal question. Of course, the statute must be from the governing jurisdiction. In addition, you should verify that the statute you have found was in effect at the time your client's legal problem arose. Sections can be added or modified at various times. Sometimes a provision within a statutory scheme will state the section's effective date. If no such provision exists, look at the section's historical notes and scan the dates. If the historical notes include any dates since the time your client's problem arose, you will know that the section has been modified in some way. A reference librarian can help you find the statute in force at the time your client's problem arose and the public laws that modified the statute.[5]

---

5. If you are using a print edition, be sure to look at the pocket parts (the paper supplement in the back of the hard copy book) for the most up-to-date version of the statute and most recent historical notes.

B. Skim the Most Pertinent Statutory Sections

Now that you have context, the next step is to get a better understanding of how the statutory section works. Skimming the relevant section will help you gain an initial understanding of how it works.

For example, skimming § 1201 (in Example 3.1-A) will allow you to see the purpose of each sub-section. Sub-section 1201(a) tells you what actions constitute kidnapping. A later sub-section, § 1201(h), defines the word "parent," a term that will be relevant to your client.

Skimming will also allow you to see the relationship among subsections within a section. For instance, think about the question you need to answer: Can a father be charged with kidnapping his step-child, or is he a "parent" and thereby exempt? You may initially examine only sub-section 1201(a), which explains that "any" person may be guilty of kidnapping; however, sub-section 1201(a) cannot be read alone. To correctly answer your client's question, you will need to note that sub-section 1201(h) defines the term "parent" and states parents who take their minor child cannot be prosecuted.

Finally, you should note whether the section cross-references any other sections. If a section cross-references another section, you will have to read the cross-referenced section as well to see how it affects the provision that governs your client's question. For instance, § 1202, Ransom Money, makes an explicit cross-reference to § 1201. The cross-reference tells you that the provision about ransom money applies only if the kidnapping charges in § 1201 have been proven.

Now that you have skimmed the statute and you understand generally how the statute works, you are ready to dig in.

C. Read the Statute Critically

To read a statute critically, you must ask yourself two fundamental questions: (1) How is this statute likely to work in my client's case? and (2) What are the component parts of this statute?

1. Investigate how the statute is likely to work

As you read a statute closely, you should develop an initial understanding of how that statute is likely to function in your client's case. However, you should be aware that, in most instances, statutory language is further explained through case law. If case law does not further explain key terms in the statute, you might need to research the statute's legislative history to better understand the legislative intent behind key statutory terms. (Chapter 11, *Statutory Analysis*, explains in more detail how to develop arguments about ambiguous statutory terms.)

As you investigate either case law or legislative history, you might discover that a statutory term that you *thought* you understood, in fact, has a different meaning. Take for example, a burglary statute, which requires a person to "enter" a building to be guilty of burglary. Would a person "enter" a building if that person used a stick or a long-reach grabber to take an item out of a building? If that person used a stick or grabber to take something from a tent, would the tent qualify as a "building"? Would a tent be more likely to qualify as a building if it were regularly used as someone's home?

In other words, read the statute carefully to ask yourself how it is *likely* to apply to your client's case, but do not become too attached to your initial assessment. Further research will bear out whether your initial understanding is accurate and complete as is or whether it needs to be adjusted and refined.

2. Identify the statute's component parts

If a statute is the governing rule for your client's problem, you will also want to break the rule down into its component parts and diagram it. As explained in Chapter 4, *Finding Your Argument*, attorneys organize their analysis of a legal issue around the elements or factors in a rule. Any attorney with whom you will work will expect you to communicate your analysis in that same way.

Thus, as you read a statute, you will want to inventory its parts. To inventory the parts of the statute, you should ask yourself these questions: (1) What are the elements or factors that comprise the statutory standard? (2) What are the red flag words that establish the relationships among the elements or factors?

Elements are requirements that must be met for a standard to be met. If one element is not met, then the standard is not met. In contrast, a factor will be considered when determining whether a standard is met. Factors are weighed, and usually no one factor is determinative. (For more detail about elements and factors, see Chapter 4, *Finding Your Argument*.)

Red flag words are words of relationship that restrict, expand, or order the elements or factors in a statute. Red flag words do not necessarily signal danger; rather, red flag words signal that you should stop and read critically to assess the meaning of a phrase or term. Because they restrict, expand, or order, you might also think of them as "operative words." Table 3.1-D lists common red flag words.

Table 3.1-D · Red flag words

• And	Requires all elements that it joins to be present for a standard to be met, or requires all factors that it joins to be considered.
• Or • Either	Only one of the elements it joins must be present for a standard to be met, or only one of the factors that it joins must be considered.
• Unless • Except • If … then	Creates an exception to the standard.
• Shall* • Must	Mandates conduct.
• Shall not • May not • Must not	Prohibits conduct.
• Provided that**	Creates a condition, an exception, or adds an additional requirement.

   * Although "shall" is typically interpreted as mandatory language, courts sometimes construe it as permissive. *See* Bryan A. Garner, *Legal Writing in Plain English: A Text with Exercises* 125-26 (2d ed. 2013).
   ** *See id.* at 128-29 (discussing the multiple meanings of "provided that" and recommending that drafters avoid the phrase).

Identifying the elements, factors, and red flag words in a statute will allow you to diagram a statute. A diagram allows you to easily see a statute's component parts and how they relate to each other. The federal kidnapping statute is diagrammed in Table 3.1-E. To prove that a person is guilty of kidnapping, a prosecutor would have to prove all three elements identified in Table 3.1-E.

Table 3.1-E · Diagramming the kidnapping statute

1. Unlawfully seizes, confines, inveigles, decoys, kidnaps, abducts, or carries away

AND

2. holds for ransom, reward, or otherwise

WHEN

3. the act is done within the federal jurisdiction through interstate commerce or to a particular group of people

EXCEPT

The act will not apply to a parent taking his or her own child.

After breaking the statute down into its parts and developing an initial understanding of how it operates, you are now ready to read cases that interpret and apply the statute.

Practice Points

- To comprehend a statute, follow these steps:

  1. Get context by asking whether the statute is civil or criminal and to whom the statute applies.

  2. Skim the statute to understand how different sections work together.

  3. Read the text critically. Your purpose is to develop an initial understanding of how the statute works in your client's case and to break the statute down into its component parts: elements, factors, and operative words.

Reading Judicial Opinions

To answer a client's question, you will also have to read cases. Often, a statute will provide the rule that governs your client's question, and case law will interpret the statute. Sometimes, however, an area of the law is governed by "common law"; that is, the area of the law is governed by case law only. Case law provides both the governing rule and interpretations of the governing rule. In either case, you will need to read, dissect, and analyze prior cases. This chapter addresses how to engage in that process as effectively as possible.

I. The Structure of a Judicial Opinion

A judicial opinion explains the dispute before the court, the legal questions the dispute raises, and the ruling the court has made on the legal questions. A judicial opinion typically contains four parts, each of which performs a function: preliminary information, the facts, the court's analysis, and any concurring or dissenting opinion. To see these parts, look at Figure 3.2-A.

45

Figure 3.2-A • A reported case*

Citation ──────────────────▶

847 A.2d 827

Caption ──────

Supreme Court of Rhode Island.
Cheryl DOWDELL
v.
Peter BLOOMQUIST.
No. 2002-630-Appeal.
March 15, 2004.

Synopsis ──────

Background: Homeowner sued neighbor for planting trees on his property in violation of spite fence statute. The Superior Court, Washington County, Gilbert v. Indeglia, J., entered injunction against neighbor. Neighbor appealed.

Holdings: The Supreme Court, Flaherty, J., held that:
(1) in a matter of first impression, row of trees was a "fence" under spite fence statute; (2) privacy was insufficient justification for presence of trees; and (3) injunctive relief was appropriate relief not prohibited by statute.

Disposition ──────────────▶ Affirmed.

Flanders, J., concurred in part, dissented in part, and filed opinion.

West Headnotes

[1] Appeal and Error
  30XVI Review
    30XVI(I) Questions of Fact, Verdicts, and Findings
      ☞ 30XVI(I)3 Findings of Court
        ☞ 30k1008 Conclusiveness in General
          ☞ 30k1008.1 In General
            30k1008.1(1) k. In General.

Preliminary information includes the caption, synopsis, and headnotes.

Factual findings are entitled to great weight and will not be disturbed by reviewing court absent proof that they are clearly wrong or that the trial justice overlooked or misconceived material evidence.

[2] Appeal and Error
  ☞ 30XVI Review
    ☞ 30XVI(I) Questions of Fact, Verdicts, and Findings
      ☞ 30XVI(I)3 Findings of Court
        ☞ 30k1008 Conclusiveness in General
          ☞ 30k1008.1 In General
            ☞ 30k1008.1(4) k. Credibility of Witnesses; Trial Court's Superior
                              Opportunity.

A headnote ──────

Credibility determinations are entitled to great weight and will not be disturbed by reviewing court absent proof that they are clearly wrong or that the trial justice overlooked or misconceived material evidence.

---

* This sample case is based on *Dowdell v. Bloomquist*, 847 A.2d 827 (R.I. 2004). It has been edited. Individual edits are not noted in the text.

...

OPINION: Flaherty, J.

The plaintiff, Cheryl Dowdell, brought this action in Superior Court alleging that the defendant, Peter Bloomquist, planted four western arborvitae trees on his Charlestown property solely to exact revenge against her, to retaliate by blocking her view, and in violation of the spite fence statute. The presiding Superior Court justice found that the trees were planted to satisfy defendant's malicious intent, not his pretextual desire for privacy. The trial justice granted plaintiff injunctive relief. We affirm the judgment of the trial justice.

The facts pertinent to this appeal are as follows. The parties' homes are on adjoining lots. Dowdell's home sits at a higher elevation than Bloomquist's and has a distant view of the ocean over the Bloomquist property. In June 2000, defendant acquired the home from his mother. Prior to that time, the Dowdell family had an amicable relationship with defendant's mother. Change was in the wind in the fall of 2000, however, when defendant petitioned for a zoning variance seeking permission to build a second-story addition to his home. The plaintiff expressed concern about the petition, anxious that the addition would compromise her view of the Atlantic Ocean. For six months the parties argued before the Zoning Board of Review as to the merits of the addition. As a result, the relationship between the neighbors became less than friendly. In March 2001, defendant began clearing land and digging holes to plant the disputed trees in a row between their homes. In April, defendant's counsel sent a letter to plaintiff warning her against trespassing onto the Bloomquist property. In May, one day after the zoning board closed its hearing on defendant's variance request, defendant began planting the four western arborvitae trees that now stand in a row bordering the property line. The forty-foot-high trees enabled little light to pass into Dowdell's second- and third-story picture windows.

The trial justice made a finding that the row of trees was a fence. He further found that the objective of privacy claimed by defendant was "no more than a subterfuge for his clear intent to spite his neighbors by erecting a fence of totally out of proportion trees." Hence, the trial justice found that the trees constituted a spite fence. He noted testimony that plaintiff's real estate values had depreciated by as much as $100,000. Bloomquist was ordered "to cut the four Western Arborvitae to no more than 6' in height and keep them at that level or remove them entirely with no more Western Arborvitae to be planted."

This is the first occasion this Court has had to address the issue of whether a row of trees may be considered a fence within the meaning of the spite fence statute, § 34-10-20. We believe the trial justice properly referred to the definition of "lawful fences" found in the statute to understand the simple meaning and legislative intent behind its use of the word "fence." Based upon the language of § 34-10-1, a fence clearly includes a hedge. And based upon the expert testimony relied on by the trial justice, a row of western arborvitae trees may constitute a hedge. However, even if the trees were not a hedge per se, the spite fence statute refers to "[a] fence or other structure in the nature of a fence." The trial justice considered the proximity of the four trees that touched one another, and the broad span of sixty feet across which they spread, and rationally interpreted that the trees were a fence. We believe that the trees, when taken as a whole, fall well within the statutory definition of a "structure in the nature of a fence." This may not be the most optimal species for the creation of a hedge owing to their enormous stature and girth. However, it is specifically because of their tow-ering presence, as well as their relative positioning on defendant's land, that we can consider the trees nothing less than a fence. What makes a spite fence a nui-sance under the statute is not merely that it blocks the passage of light and view, but that it does so "unnecessarily" for the malicious purpose of annoyance.

The court reaches a holding about whether trees can be a fence in the second to last sentence of the paragraph.

We next consider defendant's contention that the trial justice erroneously discounted defendant's testimony that the trees were erected for the beneficial purpose of privacy. Defendant relies on *Musumeci v. Leonardo*, 77 R.I. 255, 259-60, 75 A.2d 175, 177-78 (1980), for the proposition that when a fence is erected for a useful purpose, despite spiteful motive, no relief may be granted. We rec-ognize that some useful purpose for a fence may render the victim of one even maliciously erected without a remedy. In *Musumeci*, this Court determined that a fence served the useful purpose of preventing water from entering the prem-ises of the first floor of the complainant's house. Hence, because the purpose of the fence was not wholly malicious, it was not enjoined as a private nuisance. *Musumeci*, 77 R.I. at 258-59, 75 A.2d at 177.

Here, the court addresses the second issue on appeal: whether the trial court properly consid-ered an affirmative defense.

However, based on the turbulent history between the parties, the provoca-tive statements made by defendant, the notice of trespass letter sent to plain-tiff, and the size, timing, and placement of the trees, we cannot say that the trial justice was wrong to give defendant's testimony little weight and to find his claim that the fence was installed to enhance his privacy lacked credibility. In the circumstances of this case, we agree with the trial justice that defendant needed to provide more than just privacy as justification for the fence. This is especially true when a row of smaller arborvitae already stood between the homes. As the trial justice noted, "Accepting privacy alone would simply result in the statute being rendered meaningless and absurd." The very nature of a fence is such that privacy could always be given as the reason for erecting it. In an egregious case such as this, where evidence of malicious intent plainly out-weighs the discounted benefit claimed by defendant, the court correctly found defendant's actions to violate the spite fence statute.

The court reaches a holding about the second issue on appeal.

Conclusion

For the reasons set forth above, we affirm the judgment of the Superior Court. The record shall be remanded to the Superior Court.

The court states its disposition.

A. Preliminary Information

At the outset of an opinion, you can find basic information about the case that can provide you with context for the details that will follow.

1. The caption

The caption is the case's title and sets out the parties. When listing the parties involved, the caption typically lists the full names of all the parties involved. In a civil case, the parties may be individuals, as in Example 3.2-B.

Example 3.2-B · Individuals in a civil action

Cheryl DOWDELL v. Peter BLOOMQUIST

The parties may include entities, as in Example 3.2-C.

Example 3.2-C · An entity in a civil action

WILLIAM HOWARD WEST, JR., and wife, CAROLYN SUE WEST v.
KING'S DEPARTMENT STORE, INC.

In a trial court opinion, the caption also tells which party is bringing the suit. The person instigating a civil lawsuit, known as the "plaintiff," is listed first, and the party being sued, the "defendant," is listed second. For example, in Example 3.2-B, Ms. Dowdell is the plaintiff, and Mr. Bloomquist is the defendant.

In a criminal case, the prosecutor is the party instigating the suit and the defendant is the other party. If the prosecutor is the federal government, the caption might look like Example 3.2-D.

Example 3.2-D · Parties in a federal criminal action

UNITED STATES OF AMERICA, Respondent/Appellee, v. TIMOTHY JAMES
McVEIGH, Movant/Appellant.

If the prosecutor is a state, the caption might look like the one in Example 3.2-E.

Example 3.2-E · Parties in a state criminal action

STATE OF OREGON, Appellant, v. FREDERICK WENGER, JR., Respondent.

On appeal, the caption will typically tell you which party is bringing the appeal. The terms "appellant" or "petitioner" follow the party who filed the appeal first. The terms "appellee" or "respondent" will follow the other party, who may also appeal some issues. The parties may not be listed in the same order on appeal as they were in the trial court. In

Examples 3.2-D and 3.2-E you can see captions that identify the appellant and respondent.

2. The citation

Near the case name (and at the top of the page in a reporter) you will see the official case citation. Citations are important because they explain where to find the case, the level of court deciding the case, and the age of the case.

For instance, look at the two citations below in Figures 3.2-F and 3.2-G. Each citation tells you the reporter in which the case was published, the volume of the reporter, and the page of the reporter. In parentheses, the citation tells the court that decided the case (if the reporter's title does not already do so) and the year in which the court decided the case.

Figure 3.2-F · Citation tells reader where to find the case

The citation in Figure 3.2-F explains that the case is located in volume 128 of *Oregon Reports, Court of Appeals* on page 274. The case was decided by the Oregon Court of Appeals in 1994.

Figure 3.2-G · Citation components

The next citation, in Figure 3.2-G, indicates that the case is in volume 469 of the *Federal Reporter, Third Series*, at page 572. The case was decided by the United States Court of Appeals for the Sixth Circuit in 2006.

Notice that in a citation the court can be indicated in the reporter or in the parenthetical. If the deciding court is clear from the reporter, the court will not be indicated in the parenthetical. In Figure 3.2-F, the reporter's abbreviation indicates that the court is the Oregon Court of Appeals, and so no further information about the court is necessary in the parenthetical. If, however, the reporter contains decisions from many courts and the reporter does not indicate the court and its level, the court will be indicated in the parenthetical. In Figure 3.2-G, the reporter, the *Federal Reporter, Third Series*, contains cases from many federal appellate courts; therefore, the parenthetical specifies that the Sixth Circuit decided the case.

3. The publisher's enhancements

(a) Synopsis

In case reporters, immediately after the caption and preliminary information, you will usually see a one-paragraph synopsis of the case. The synopsis describes the most basic issue and underlying facts, the disposition of the case in any lower courts, and the disposition of the case in the present court. While synopses are helpful tools for researching and selecting pertinent cases, they are *not* part of the judicial opinion and are not, therefore, law. These synopses are created by editors of the case reporters. While generally very helpful, a synopsis is not a complete summary of the case and, on occasion, can be inaccurate. You should never cite to a synopsis.

(b) Headnotes

In most reported cases, particularly all of the cases reported by the West Publishing Company, after the synopsis you will find headnotes. A headnote is a one-paragraph blurb for each point of law presented in the case. Headnotes act like a table of contents to the case and direct the reader to the portions of the case that address each point of law. Headnotes are also not part of the judicial opinion and cannot be cited. Nor should the content of the headnotes be quoted; instead, go directly to the portion of the opinion to which the headnote refers and use the official opinion.

Even after recognizing each part of an opinion mentioned above, understanding judicial opinions requires you to read critically.

4. The author of the opinion

At the beginning of the opinion, you can find the author of the opinion, noted by the author's last name, followed by the letter "J."

In federal jurisdictions, a single trial judge for a district court may issue a reported opinion. (In state trial courts, opinions are not published; instead, judges just render decisions on the record.) Appellate courts—whether state or federal—sit in panels of judges, usually consisting of three judges for intermediate appellate courts or five to nine (sometimes more) for the highest appellate courts in the jurisdiction. Judges vote on the outcome of a case, and one judge from the majority writes the opinion.

The letter "J" can stand for either justice or judge, depending on the court—usually "justice" refers to members of the highest court in a jurisdiction and "judge" refers to members of the lower intermediate and trial courts. Occasionally, you will see other letter designations such as "C.J." for Chief Judge or Chief Justice and "S.J." for Special Judge. You will not likely need to use the name of the judge in your memoranda, but opinions written by well-known or prominent jurists may sometimes be more influential. At other times, knowing the writer of the opinion can give you insight into the author's ideology.

B. The Facts

1. Historical facts

Within the first few paragraphs of the opinion, a court will set out the story, or underlying events, of the case. The depth and clarity with which courts describe the facts varies. This section is important to read carefully because most cases are fact-driven, meaning the court's decision hinges on the facts before it. As you read the facts, look for clues as to which facts the court thought were most important. Often, a court will emphasize trigger facts, those facts on which its decision turns.

When a case examines more than one legal issue, you will have to determine which facts were critical to each issue addressed. Some attorneys read the fact section once and then again after reading the court's analysis. Doing so will allow you to distinguish critical, trigger facts from background facts and match the facts relevant to each issue.

2. Procedural facts

Along with the historical facts, a judicial opinion will also usually describe the legal path the case took after the plaintiff initiated the lawsuit. This information is called "procedural history." When describing the procedural history of a case, a court may explain the claims that were filed; motions that were made before, during, or after the trial; or any appeals that were brought. Within this section, the writing judge may also include information about the arguments each party made in the lower court and the lower court's opinion.

What the parties argued and what the lower court said are not part of a court's holding unless the court indicates that it is adopting those arguments. Be sure to note whether the appellate court is merely describing or actually adopting those arguments.

C. The Court's Analysis

1. The issue or issues

In a single opinion a court may decide many legal questions. An issue is one of the legal questions the court is asked to decide. An opinion typically addresses many issues, not all of which will be relevant to your client's problem. Sometimes a court will clearly state the issues it will address and organize its opinion around those issues; other times, you will have to discern the issues the court addressed.

Take for example, Paul Adams's case, discussed in the memo in Chapter 1, *How Attorneys Communicate* (Example 1-A). If his case were to go to trial, the defendant might ask the court to decide one issue: whether Paul Adams's statement would be admissible against him.

To answer that question, the court has to answer a sub-issue: whether Paul Adams was stopped. If he was not stopped, then his statement was "mere conversation" and is admissible. Accordingly, to decide one issue, the court would have to answer at least two questions: "Was Paul Adams stopped?" and "Is his statement admissible at trial?"

Actual judicial opinions differ from the cases in law school textbooks because of the number of issues each addresses. In most textbooks, the author has edited the case so that the case describes just one legal issue illustrating one point of law. Every other part of the opinion not relevant to that one point has been edited out.

In practice, the cases you read will be unedited; they will contain multiple issues, and some of those issues may be quite long and complex. In unedited cases, you must discern which of the many issues in the opinion will be relevant to your case.

2. The rule of the case

The rule of the case is the point of law the opinion will represent to future cases.

Sometimes—over time—a case comes to represent a particular point of law. Before that time, however, attorneys may argue about the rule of law that the case represents. Only after attorneys have argued about it, and a subsequent court has stated how we should understand the case, can we be certain about the rule of the case.

Remember, too, that if a case addresses more than one issue—as most cases do—more than one rule can be derived from the case.

3. The holding or holdings

A holding of a case is the court's answer to one of the questions presented by one of the parties. Thus, for every legal issue you identify in a case, you should also find a holding.

Although the holding and the rule of the case resemble each other, the holding is tied to the facts of the case before the court. The rule of the case, on the other hand, is a general principle of law the case will represent in the greater body of law.

To make matters a little more complicated, courts often use the terms imprecisely, calling the holding a rule of the case or calling a rule of the case the holding. For example, if the court said, "We rule that Officer

James impermissibly stopped the defendant when the officer placed his hand on the defendant's shoulder and physically prevented him from leaving," the court's statement is a holding because it is tied to the particular facts of that case, even though the court used the word "rule."

On the other hand, the court may write, "We hold that a stop occurs when an officer uses a physical show of authority to keep a person from leaving." This general statement is really a rule of the case because it is not tied to the facts of the case but, instead, represents the point the case will stand for in the body of law.

Thus, to distinguish between a holding and a rule of the case, pay attention to the facts. A holding is tied to facts; a rule of the case is not.

4. Reasoning

The reasoning of the case is the analysis the court follows to get from an issue to its holding about that issue. For each issue, the opinion will assess the governing law—whether it comes from statutes, common law, policy concerns, or some combination of those authorities. Then, the court will apply that law to the facts of the case. The reasoning is the "meat" of the opinion, and it requires several careful and thorough readings.

5. Dicta

Dicta are assertions or statements by the writing judge on points that are not necessary to address an issue presented by a party. A common form of dicta is a hypothetical. Often, a court will assert that had one fact in the case been different, its holding would have been different. Since that fact was not before the court, the court's statement about that different fact is dictum. Courts have authority to decide only the issues before them; thus, dicta are not a binding part of the opinion. That said, dicta can sometimes be persuasive to a future court, and attorneys may rely on dicta as persuasive but not mandatory authority.

6. The judgment or disposition

The judgment or disposition appears at the end of the case and states the final action the court is taking on the whole case after considering all of the issues presented to it. For instance, the court may "affirm" or "reverse" the decision of any lower court in whole or in part; it could also "remand" the case back to the trial court for a new determination or further action on all or some of the issues; or, it could "dismiss" or "vacate" the case entirely.

D. Concurring and Dissenting Opinions

You will find concurring and dissenting opinions only in appellate court cases decided by a panel of judges. As noted earlier, after the judges vote on the outcome of a case, one judge from the majority will write the opinion. However, other judges may also write to express their views on the analysis or the outcome of the case. If a judge agrees with the outcome but differs in the analytical approach—that is, if the judge differs in how to interpret the law or apply the law to the facts—that judge may write a concurring opinion. If a judge disagrees with the outcome of the case, he or she may write a dissenting opinion explaining why the majority was wrong or what the proper outcome of the case may be.

Concurrences and dissents question the majority's reasoning, whether in construing the law or applying the law to the facts. These concurrences and dissents can give you insight into the flip side of an argument.

Dissenting opinions are not part of the law and should not be relied on as mandatory authority in future analyses, though they can be used as persuasive authority. Typically, a concurrence is also not a part of the law. However, if the majority needs the vote of the concurring judge to remain in the majority, the concurrence may be considered part of the decided law.

II. Reading a Judicial Opinion for Comprehension

As you dig into a client's legal problem, one particularly challenging step is reading case law efficiently and effectively. Your research will often uncover a lot of case law that may be relevant to your client's legal problem. Your challenge is to move through those cases quickly, setting aside those cases that are not relevant and focusing on those cases that are relevant.

You can use the same three steps described above to manage the cases that you are reading: (1) Get context; (2) skim the case; (3) read the judicial opinion closely with your purpose in mind. Table 3.2-H on the next page provides an overview.

A. Get Context

The very first time you encounter a case, you will want to gather basic information about the case so that you can put the opinion in context. Initially, you should note the jurisdiction and the court that issued the opinion. Doing so will help you determine whether the opinion is binding or persuasive authority.

Note the year the opinion was issued so that you have a sense of whether this case is likely to represent the court's most recent analysis of the issue or if there is likely to be more recent analysis.

You might also want to verify whether the case is civil or criminal. Occasionally, a legal issue can appear in a civil or criminal case and you

Table 3.2-H · Reading a case for comprehension*

Step	Ask these questions
1. Get context for the case.	• Who are the parties? Individuals or entities? Private parties or the government? • Is this a criminal or civil case? • What is the jurisdiction? Federal or state? • What level of court wrote the opinion? Trial? Intermediate appeals? Highest appeals court? • What year was the case decided?
2. Skim.	Glean the basic information about the case so that you will have a framework of the issues presented and how they were decided. If you get the overall framework of the case in this step, you will be able to read more slowly with greater comprehension and depth of understanding in the next step. • What is the overall structure of the case? How does the court organize the discussion of the issues in the body of the opinion? • What are the key issues? • What is the basic, underlying factual dispute? • What are the key facts? (Start to get a visual image of the factual story.) • What is the procedural path the case has taken thus far? • What did the lower courts do? • What was the disposition of the case? • Look at the structure of the opinion again. Try skimming the first sentence of every paragraph. Do these sentences give you an outline of the court's reasoning?
3. Read the case closely and question it.	Now that you have a good framework of what the case does and says, you are ready to dig into the meat of the case. For each issue presented to the court, answer the questions posed below. • What was the governing law? Is it statutory? Common law? A combination of both? • What facts did the court rely on in making its decision? • Does the issue turn on particular facts, or is the court addressing a pure question of law—that is, is the court merely explaining what the law is? • Whose argument does the court appear to be following? A party's? The lower court's? Its own? • Does the court's interpretation of the law make sense? • Does the court's application of the law to the facts make sense? • Is the court's argument flawed? On what specific points? • What is the rule of the case? How will it apply to future cases? • Does the court include policy reasons for its decision? • Any concurring opinions? On what points do the judges agree? Disagree? • Any dissenting opinions? What does the dissenting judge object to in the majority opinion? Does the dissent's argument make more sense? • How does this case fit with other cases or governing laws on the topic? • What new words should you look up?

* These steps are adapted from Mary A. Lundeberg, *supra* note 3, at 428-29, and Appendix 1; Peter Dewitz, *Legal Education: A Problem of Learning from Text*, 23 N.Y.U. Rev. L. & Soc. Change 225, 240 (1997).

will want to consider whether an analysis of a legal issue in a civil case is equally applicable to that legal issue if it appears in a criminal context (and vice versa).

This first step will likely take place as you are still researching.

B. Skim the Case

After gathering that basic information about the text, you should skim the opinion. First, you must determine whether this case still seems relevant to your client's legal question. You do not want to waste your time closely reading a case that, ultimately, is not on point. If you determine that the case does seem relevant, then print the case out and get an overview of the case.

1. Determine relevance

To assess whether a case will be relevant to your client's legal issue, go directly to that part of the case where the court discusses the issue that is relevant to your client's legal problem. You can skim the headnotes to determine which part of the case is most relevant to your client's case and jump to that part of the case.

Once you are at the correct location in the case, read the court's analysis. Ask yourself these questions:

- Does the opinion add to your understanding of rules relevant to my client's legal question?
- Do the facts that the court relied on in its analysis seem similar to the facts in my client's case?

If the answer to either of those questions is "yes," you will want to put that case aside so that you can read it in more detail. Remember, you will want to review a case that is factually similar to your client's case even if the court's conclusion in the prior case does not favor your client's interest. You must be aware of and account for *all* the relevant law, not just the law that is helpful to you.

If, however, the case does not add to your understanding of the rules and the case is not factually similar, you may not need that case for your legal analysis. Before throwing that case away or deleting that case from your file, help yourself be more efficient. Make a note—either on the case or on a list of rejected cases—explaining why you have rejected the case. Getting into the habit of noting why you think a case is not relevant will save you a lot of time in the future. Often, as you research, you will see the same case again, but with so many cases, you may not remember whether you have read it or what it said. By noting your earlier decision to reject the case, you can avoid reading the case again. So, save yourself some time down the road by making a quick note about the cases you have rejected and why.

2. Print relevant cases

Once you have determined that a case is likely relevant to your client's legal issue, you should print that case out. Reading in print and reading online are different experiences. Online reading lends itself to simply scanning the text rather than absorbing the text because you can so easily scroll through the document.[7]

On the other hand, a physical document gives you a better sense of the document's beginning, middle, and end, and how the information in one location relates to information in another. Having a physical sense of how ideas relate to each has been shown to improve people's ability to comprehend and then recall the information.[8]

Studies have also shown that students comprehend text better when they read in print. One reason is that reading in print is less draining.[9] Reading in print does not strain the eye as reading on a screen does.[10] In addition, when reading in print, you avoid the distractions of hyperlinks.[11] Finally, highlighting and taking notes on the text is still easier in print than on a screen.[12] For all of these reasons, print your most important cases.

3. Get an overview of the case

If you decide that a case will likely be useful to your analysis, it is now worthwhile to invest some time and become more familiar with the details of the case.

Begin with the court's description of the facts. Your goal is to become familiar with the parties, their conflict, and the facts that will be relevant to the legal issues you are researching. If the case is relatively simple, you will likely read the court's entire description of the facts. If the case is more complex, you may find that there are too many details to absorb right away. In that case, you may want to do a combination of skimming and reading, focusing on those facts that seem most relevant to the disputed legal issues in your client's case.

Once you have a sense of who the parties are and which facts of their case are relevant to the legal issue you are researching, consider taking quick notes about the parties and their conflict. In a more complex case, you might draw a diagram of the parties and their relationships to each other.

---

7. Ruth Ann McKinney, *Reading Like a Lawyer* 265 (2d ed. Carolina Academic Press 2012).

8. Ferris Jabr, *The Reading Brain in the Digital Age: The Science of Paper v. Screen* (Apr. 11, 2013) (accessed Aug. 13, 2014 at http://www.scientificamerican.com/article/reading-paper-screens/).

9. *Id.*

10. *Id.*

11. *Id.*; McKinney, *Reading Like a Lawyer* at 275.

12. McKinney, *Reading Like a Lawyer* at 268.

Finally, skim the rest of the judicial opinion to get a sense of the variety of issues that the court addressed and so that you can see which parts of the case will be most relevant to your client's legal question.

These steps will provide you with an understanding of the facts of the case, what the legal issues were, and how the court organized its analysis of those issues. In other words, you will have a framework within which you can begin to more closely examine the legal issues that are relevant to your client's question.

C. Read the Opinion Critically

Now, the real work begins. You must extract from the case the information that you will need to answer your client's legal question. To do so, you should ask yourself these questions:

- What rules will also govern my client's legal question?
- To what extent are the facts in this case similar to the facts in my client's case? To what extent are the facts different? Do those differences matter?
- How does this case fit in with other cases? Is the court's analysis in this case consistent with the analyses in other cases? Or does this court's analysis represent a shift in the way courts are approaching this legal issue?

As you read, you will extract that information, and that information will become the basis for your legal argument. Chapter 5, *Organizing Your Legal Authority*, explains in more detail how to extract this information in an organized and efficient way.

Practice Points

- To comprehend a case, follow these steps:

  1. Get context by determining the court, the jurisdiction, and the year in which the opinion was issued.

  2. Skim the case to determine its relevance to your client's issue and to get an overview of its structure and content.

  3. Read the case critically. Ask about the rules that will govern your client's legal question, whether the facts in the case are like the facts in your client's case, and how the case fits in with other cases you have read.

Chapter 4

Finding Your Argument

The previous chapters discussed how to read the authorities that will answer your client's legal question. Moving from a desktop of authorities to an answer to your client's question requires three initial steps:

1. **Identify the rule that will govern your client's legal question.**
2. **Inventory the governing rule's working parts.**
3. **See the governing rule as individual legal arguments.**

Those three steps will allow you to identify the individual legal arguments that, when taken together, will answer your client's legal question.

I. Identify the Governing Rule

To answer your client's legal question, you must first determine the rule that governs the question. A "rule" sets a standard by telling people what they must or can do, what they must not or should not do, or what they are entitled to do under certain conditions. Rules also describe the consequences of breaking a rule.

The "governing rule" sets the standard in your client's case. It will control the answer to your client's question and create a structure around which your argument should be organized. Think of the governing rule as the backbone of your discussion. A human backbone creates the structural foundation for the body, giving the muscles, tendons, and ligaments a rigid structure on which to hold. Likewise, the governing rule creates the structural foundation for your legal argument; thus, every piece of your argument will be connected to that governing rule.

Typically, you will find the governing rule either in a statute or in the common law, or maybe in a combination of both. Because case law is subordinate to the statute it interprets, if you do not know whether a client's question is governed by statute or by common law, begin by looking for a statute.

A. A Statute as the Governing Rule

If a statute governs your client's legal problem, identifying the governing rule is rather straightforward. For example, suppose your client has been charged with burglary. Generally, the question of whether a person has committed a burglary is controlled by statute. Example 4-A describes a typical burglary statute. This statute is the governing rule that would control whether your client will be found guilty of burglary.

Example 4-A · A governing rule from a typical burglary statute

A person commits burglary if that person knowingly and without authority enters the dwelling place of another with intent to commit therein a felony or theft.

B. Common Law as the Governing Rule

Sometimes, however, no statute governs the legal question. In that case, the governing rule will come from common law.

For example, California allows people to seek compensation for emotional distress they suffered after witnessing an injury to a family member. In California, courts have defined a governing rule for such claims. The court's description of the governing rule is provided in Example 4-B.

Example 4-B · Common law sets forth the governing rule

"[A] plaintiff may recover damages for emotional distress caused by observing the negligently inflicted injury of a third person if, but only if, said plaintiff: (1) is closely related to the injury victim; (2) is present at the scene of the injury producing event at the time it occurs and is then aware that it is causing injury to the victim; and (3) as a result suffers serious emotional distress — a reaction beyond that which would be anticipated in a disinterested witness and which is not an abnormal response to the circumstances."

Thing v. La Chusa, 771 P.2d 814, 829-30 (Cal. 1989) (footnotes omitted).

C. A Synthesized Rule as the Governing Rule

Sometimes, you may have to synthesize a governing rule. To "synthesize" means to combine or blend parts to create a whole. When you synthesize a governing rule, you combine principles from more than one authority to set forth the governing rule that controls your client's legal question.

For example, in many jurisdictions the governing rule that controls an employment discrimination claim would draw on both a statute and case law. Ohio is one such jurisdiction. An Ohio statute prohibits age-based employment discrimination (Example 4-C).

Example 4-C · Ohio's anti-discrimination in employment statute

Ohio Rev. Code § 4112.02

It shall be an unlawful discriminatory practice: (A) For any employer, because of the race, color, religion, sex, national origin, disability, age, or ancestry of any person, to discharge without just cause, to refuse to hire, or otherwise to discriminate against that person with respect to hire, tenure, terms, conditions, or privileges of employment, or any matter directly or indirectly related to employment.

The shaded text will become a part of the synthesized rule in Example 4-E.

Ohio case law, however, has explained the steps an employee must take to prove discrimination under the statute (Example 4-D).

Example 4-D · Case law explains how to implement statute

"In cases brought pursuant to R.C. 4112.02 for 'disparate treatment,' Ohio courts have adopted the three-step formula set forth by the United States Supreme Court … according to which the plaintiff must first prove by a preponderance of the evidence a prima facie case of disparate treatment. That done, the burden shifts to the defendant to provide a legal justification for the differentiation. The plaintiff must then be given the opportunity to prove that the justification was merely pretextual."

Myers v. Goodwill Indus. of Akron, Inc., 701 N.E.2d 738, 743 (Ohio Ct. App. 1997).

The shaded text will become a part of the synthesized rule in Example 4-E.

If you were working on a memorandum assessing whether a client had been subjected to age-based employment discrimination in Ohio, you might draw on both the statute and case law to state a governing rule like the one in Example 4-E.

Example 4-E · Governing rule combines language of statute and case law

The governing rule draws ⟶ Whether a court will hold that a discharge is an "unlawful discriminatory prac-
on statutory language.   tice" based on age depends on a three-step analysis. *See* Ohio Rev. Code Ann.
                            § 4112.02 (2017); *Myers v. Goodwill Indus. of Akron, Inc.*, 701 N.E.2d 738, 743
                            (Ohio Ct. App. 1997). First, the employee must establish a prima facie case of
The remainder of the   disparate treatment. *Myers*, 701 N.E.2d at 743. If the employee succeeds, then
governing rule draws   the burden shifts to the employer, who must provide a legal justification for the
on language from   disparate treatment. *Id.* If the employer does present a legal justification, then the
case law.   burden shifts back to the employee to prove that the reason was a pretext. *Id.*

Once you have found the governing rule, your next step is to inventory
its working parts.

II. Inventory the Governing Rule

Lawyers inventory the parts of the governing rule for two reasons.
First, as explained in Section 3.1, *Reading Statutes for Comprehension*,
examining each component part of a statute allows lawyers to think
critically about how a statute functions.

Second, and as discussed in more detail at the end of this chapter,
lawyers analyze legal questions part by part. They first examine each part
of the rule individually. Only then—after examining each part of the
rule individually—will a lawyer reach a conclusion about whether the
standard as a whole has been met. Lawyers with whom you work will
also expect you to analyze legal questions in this way: part by part.

Thus, your job is to figure out what parts make up each rule. Most
frequently, governing rules include some combination of elements,
factors, and red flag words. No matter the components of the rule,
breaking down the governing rule into its constituent parts is a critical
step. Doing so will allow you to organize your research and your analysis
part by part.

A. Elements

An element is a condition that *must* be proved to establish that a
standard is met. For example, the burglary statute in Example 4-F is a
governing rule composed of elements. In that statute, you might identify
five elements, all of which must be established before someone can be
found guilty of burglary.

Example 4-F · Elements in a burglary statute

A person commits the crime of burglary in the first degree if [1] the person [2] knowingly and [3] without authority enters [4] a dwelling [5] with intent to commit a felony or theft therein.

Because an element must be proved for a standard to be met, you would think that it would be easy to identify each element in a rule. Unfortunately, elements are not always so easy to isolate and identify.

Let's look again at the burglary statute in Example 4-F. Different people might identify the elements in different ways. Above, Example 4-F, identifies five elements. However, there are other ways a lawyer might break the statute down into its component elements. As you can see, in Table 4-G, Lawyer A and Lawyer B combine or separate concepts in different ways, and thus have different lists of elements. Neither is the right or wrong way to divide the statute. Rather each identifies all the conditions that must exist for a person to be guilty of burglary.

Example 4-G · Lawyers may vary in how they identify the component parts of a governing rule

---

Lawyer A	Lawyer B
1. Person	1. Person
2. Knowingly enters AND	2. Enters
3. Without authority enters	(a) Knowingly AND
4. A dwelling	(b) Without authority
5. With intent to commit a felony therein OR	3. A dwelling
6. With intent to commit a theft therein	4. With intent to commit
	(a) A felony OR
	(b) A theft
	5. Therein

Importantly, each list of elements provides a starting point for thinking about a client's legal problem. As you research your client's case, you might want to adjust your list of elements. Perhaps there is no doubt that the defendant entered a building. The only question is whether the defendant "knowingly" entered. Thus, you might decide to think about the statute in terms of whether the defendant "knowingly entered." In a different case, however, there might be a real question about whether the defendant even "entered" the building. Therefore, you would need to think separately about whether the defendant "entered" and, if so, whether he did so "knowingly." Consequently, depending on the facts of the case, you might make different decisions about how to divide the governing rule into its constituent elements.

Other times, additional legal research will lead you to adjust your list of elements. For example, the rule for adverse possession, in Example 4-H, appears to have seven elements.

Example 4-H • Identifying elements in the governing rule for adverse possession

"To succeed on their adverse possession claim, defendants must establish by clear and convincing evidence, that the use of the property was **[1]** actual, **[2]** open, **[3]** notorious, **[4]** exclusive, **[5]** continuous, and **[6]** hostile for a **[7]** 10-year period." *Hoffman v. Freeman Land and Timber, LLC.,* 994 P.2d 106, 109-10 (Or. 1999).

However, additional research reveals that all courts examine "open and notorious" as one element. You would, therefore, revise your original understanding to account for that judicial interpretation. What you thought would be two elements is actually just one.

For these reasons, you may sometimes have difficulty deciding which concepts in the governing rule constitute a single element. If so, reach a reasonable conclusion about which concepts form distinct elements. Then, be open to revising your initial understanding.

B. Factors

A factor is a condition that is weighed against another condition. Not all factors must be met for the standard to weigh in favor of one party; instead, the factors will be judged on their individual and cumulative strength.

An example of a rule composed of factors is Idaho's standard for child custody, such as the rule provided in Example 4-I. To determine who will be awarded custody, a court considers "the best interests of the children" and evaluates all of the factors listed—and potentially other factors. No one factor must exist to award custody to one parent or another. Rather, the court considers the *degree* to which each factor is present and weighs the strength of the factors on one side against the strength of the factors on the other side to reach its conclusion.

Example 4-I • Factors comprise the governing rule

32-717. CUSTODY OF CHILDREN—BEST INTEREST. (1) In an action for divorce the court may, before and after judgment, give such direction for the custody, care and education of the children of the marriage as may seem necessary or proper in the best interests of the children. The court shall consider all relevant factors, which may include:
  (a) The wishes of the child's parent or parents as to his or her custody;
  (b) The wishes of the child as to his or her custodian;

(c) The interaction and interrelationship of the child with his or her parent or parents, and his or her siblings;

(d) The child's adjustment to his or her home, school, and community;

(e) The character and circumstances of all individuals involved;

(f) The need to promote continuity and stability in the life of the child; and

(g) Domestic violence as defined in section 39-6303, Idaho Code, whether or not in the presence of the child.

C. Red Flag Words

Red flag words, which were first introduced in Section 3.1, *Reading Statutes*, are words that restrict, expand, or order the contents of a rule. These words are called "red flag words" because, when you see one, you must stop and carefully consider its impact on the content of the rule. Red flag words are also called "operative words" because they change how the substantive parts of the rule will operate in relationship to each other. Red flag—or operative words—can create exceptions, limitations, requirements, or sequences in which events must occur. Thus, when you see a red flag word, slow down, and consider its relationship to the other parts of the statute and how it will impact the statute's effect on your client.

Table 4-J lists common red flag words, and Example 4-K highlights the red flag words in a burglary statute.

Table 4-J · Red flag words

• And	Requires all elements that it joins to be present for a standard to be met, or requires all factors that it joins to be considered.
• Or • Either	Only one of the elements it joins must be present for a standard to be met, or only one of the factors that it joins must be considered.
• Unless • Except • If … then	Creates an exception to the standard.
• Shall* • Must	Mandates conduct.
• Shall not • May not • Must not	Prohibits conduct.
• Provided that**	Creates a condition, an exception, or adds an additional requirement.

* Although "shall" is typically interpreted as mandatory language, courts sometimes construe it as permissive. *See* Bryan A. Garner, *Legal Writing in Plain English: A Text with Exercises* 125-26 (2d ed. 2013).
** *See id*. at 128-29 (discussing the multiple meanings of "provided that" and recommending that drafters avoid the phrase).

In Example 4-K, the red flag word "and" signals that multiple elements must be present for a person to be guilty. The prosecutor must prove all

Example 4-K • Red flag words in a statute

A person commits the crime of burglary in the first degree if the person knowingly and without authority enters a dwelling with intent to commit a felony or theft therein.

of the conjoined elements. By contrast, the red flag word "or" signals that only one of several elements must be present. When the statute uses the word "or," the prosecutor can make choices about how to prove that a person is guilty of burglary. Finally, although the word "with" is not listed in Table 4-J, here, it adds a restriction, and thus acts as a red flag—or operative—word.

D. Diagramming the Governing Rule

After you have identified the elements or factors and operative words in a statute, you may want to diagram the governing rule. When you diagram a governing rule, you are, essentially, drawing a picture of how the rule works. A picture can help you better understand how the parts of a governing rule work together, and it can help you isolate the individual parts of a governing rule that you will need to research and analyze.

The burglary statute, first mentioned in Example 4-F, might be diagrammed as in Figure 4-L.

Example 4-L • Diagramming a governing rule

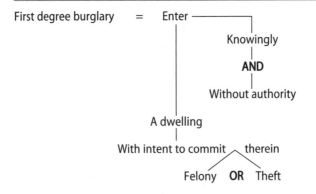

E. Tests

Elements, factors, and special operative words are the component parts of a governing rule. They combine to form different kinds of tests that courts use to determine whether the standard in the governing rule has been met.

Many kinds of tests exist, and attorneys and judges may use different names for the tests. The important thing is to recognize what kind of test is being used, how it affects the way the governing rule operates, and whether the test dictates the organizational structure of your analysis. Although the list below is not exhaustive, it names the most common tests you will see.

1. Elemental analysis

First, evaluating a rule composed of elements may be called an elemental analysis; that analysis will require each element to be met before the standard is satisfied. In an elemental analysis, you will march through an analysis of each element, usually following the same order in which that element was presented in the governing rule.

2. Balancing test

A second kind of test, a balancing test, is used to evaluate a rule composed of factors. The test is so named because the court will balance competing factors against each other to reach its conclusion.

In a balancing test, a party does not need to satisfy each factor for the court to rule in that party's favor. "The best interests of the children" example, described earlier, is a good example. Although several factors may weigh in favor of one parent, if the factor of a child's emotional ties strongly weighs in favor of the other parent, that parent may get custody of the child. So, even if a parent has only one factor weighing in that parent's favor, if the court believes that factor carries enough weight, that parent wins.

When imagining how a balancing test works, think of the traditional two-pan scale, like the scale of justice. For a party to win under a balancing test, the scale can weigh greatly in his favor or slightly in his favor. The amount of weight placed on either side of the scale depends on the court's assessment of how all the factors balance both individually and cumulatively.

In a balancing test, you will typically try to organize your analysis around the individual factors that make up the balancing test. Organizing around factors, though, is sometimes challenging. Because courts weigh factors against each other, the factors often become intertwined in a court's analysis. Thus, although you should try to organize your analysis around the individual factors, if the prior case law does not allow you to separate out the factors, you may have to examine the factors as a group.

Moreover, when the test is a balancing test, predicting an outcome in a future case may be challenging. Because balancing tests weigh a multitude of factors, the holdings that result are often case-specific. That is to say, a change in a single fact may tip the scales in the opposite way.

3. Totality of the circumstances test

Third, courts sometimes employ a "totality of the circumstances" test. When a court looks at the totality of the circumstances, it reviews all relevant facts together to determine whether the governing rule's standard is met. A totality of the circumstances test allows the court to look at a broad spectrum of facts and weigh them; however, unlike a pure factor-balancing test, the court does not have a defined list of factors to consider.[1] Rather, the court can consider any relevant fact.

4. Prong test

Finally, in a prong test, a court determines whether a standard is met by using a multi-part inquiry. Each inquiry is one prong of the test, and the court evaluates each prong in turn.

Be aware that the term "prong test" can be applied to many kinds of analyses. The name is sometimes applied to basic elemental analyses or to balancing tests. Thus, a prong can be an element, and each prong represents a requirement that must be met. Or, a prong can be a factor that must be balanced with factors in other prongs. The term can also be used when the court presents the test as a series of questions.

Ohio's test for establishing a discriminatory discharge (Example 4-E, above) is an example of a prong test. It has three prongs. The first prong requires an employee to establish a prima facie case of disparate treatment. If the employee does so, the second prong requires the employer to justify the disparate treatment. Finally, if the employer provides a justification, the employee must prove under the third prong that the justification is pretext for a discriminatory purpose.

If the governing rule in your client's question involves a prong test, such as Ohio's test for a discriminatory discharge, your analysis will be structured around those prongs, and you will evaluate each prong in turn, just as a court would.

When taking inventory of a rule's working parts, understanding the test used can show you how the rule functions and how to structure the analysis of the governing rule in your memo.

III. Think Like a Lawyer: See the Governing Rule as Individual Legal Arguments

After determining the governing rule and inventorying its working parts, the next step is to identify the individual legal arguments that you will develop. Identifiying individual arguments is an essential step in "thinking like a lawyer." To explain why, back up for a moment and remember some basic information about rules.

---

1. David Romantz & Kathleen Vinson, *Legal Analysis: The Fundamental Skill* 25-26 (1998).

As discussed above, a rule tells people what they must do, what they cannot do, or what they are entitled to do. In all cases, however, people must do something, must not do something, or are entitled to do something only under certain circumstances. Those circumstances are the various elements or factors of the rule.

To discuss a legal question, a lawyer examines each element or factor individually. Then, the lawyer structures an argument that tests for the presence of each element or factor in the client's case.[2] Only after determining whether each component is present (or the extent to which it is present) will a lawyer decide whether the standard in the governing rule has been met. The important point is that each aspect of the governing rule will likely become the subject of a single legal argument.

The senior attorney who asked you to "get back to her with your analysis" will expect you to examine each element or factor in the governing rule and develop a separate legal argument for each. Her expectation, which all attorneys share, will affect how you think about, organize, and write about your client's legal problem.

Remember, the governing rule is the backbone of your legal argument. Just as the human backbone is composed of multiple vertebrae, a complete legal discussion is usually composed of multiple legal arguments. Each element or factor in the governing rule is the source of an individual legal argument, which, similar to an individual vertebra, must support the body of the discussion.

---

2. Sometimes attorneys will analyze factors as a group rather than individually. Whether to analyze factors as a group or individually is discussed in §7.1, *Structuring Factor Analyses* in Joan Rocklin, Bob Rocklin, Christine Coughlin, and Sandy Patrick, *An Advocate Persuades* 151-160 (2016).

Practice Points

- Before you can write about your client's legal issue, you must first find the governing rule.

- The governing rule can come from a statute, case law, or any combination of sources. The rule may not be explicit, and you may have to synthesize several sources to determine the current governing rule.

- Once you have found the governing rule, take inventory of its working parts. Notice whether the standard uses elements or factors and what kind of test they form.

- A governing rule is the backbone of your analysis. It indicates the structure your argument will take. Typically, your analysis will follow the structure and order established in the governing rule. Each smaller argument, whether an element or factor, will need to be analyzed in turn.

Chapter 5

Organizing Your Legal Authority

By now, you have identified the rule that governs your client's legal question; you have inventoried that rule; you have read a lot of cases that explain how that rule has applied in the past; and perhaps you have read some additional statutory sections that relate to the governing rule. Although it is tempting at this stage to jump in and start writing, that approach is not efficient and is more likely to lead to gaps or inaccuracies in your analysis. Instead, take some time now to organize the law you have found.

Organizing is a process that often entails several rounds before you are ready to draft. As you learn more about the law and how it will apply, you will refine your organizational materials so that they can better support your writing.

Taking some time to organize is important, and different people will organize in different ways. This chapter will show you different ways to organize at various stages of your research and analysis: (1) at the outset, as you are sorting through and trying to keep track of the many legal authorities you have found; (2) next, as you are trying to get a handle on individual elements or factors in the governing rule; and (3) finally, when you are on the cusp of writing.

This chapter will give you an idea of different organizational strategies that can capture your developing analysis. As you review the text and examples, think about the efficiency of each strategy and its compatibility with your individual learning style. You can then select or imagine an organizational system that will work for you.

I. Step 1: Organize Your Research

At the outset of research and writing projects, lawyers can become overwhelmed by the number of cases they find. Thus, most lawyers develop some system—formal or informal—for keeping track of the cases that might be relevant to their analysis. At a minimum, at this stage, you should keep track of the issues each case addresses so that you do not have to re-read a case just to find out if it is addressing an issue you are interested in. A more detailed system might also help you get an overview of this area of law and a sense of how the cases work together. With those goals in mind, you might try one of two organizational systems for your cases.

A. Case Charts

First, as you research, you might chart your cases. To create a chart, as in Example 5-A, begin with the governing rule. List each element or factor of the governing rule across one axis and the cases you have found along the other axis. Then, for each case, note the most important facts. The facts will create a picture in your head and allow you to more quickly recall the case and what it was about.

Next, note which elements or factors the court analyzed and the court's conclusion about each. Doing so will help you remember which issues the court did and did not analyze in that case. In addition, by looking down the column of each element, you can begin to get a sense of how courts have approached that element or factor. This overview of an area of law is one of the great benefits of charting the cases—you can quickly see which cases address the legal arguments.

Then, note the court's overall holding about whether the standard in the governing rule was met. Although those cases that reach the outcome that your client desires are usually more favorable, cases that reach the opposite outcome may also be helpful if the rule is well stated or if the facts are easily distinguishable. Ultimately, you will want to keep track of both those cases that reached the outcome that your client desires and those that reached the opposite outcome, because your analysis will have to account for both. Again, reading down this column can give you an overview of this area of the law.

Finally, you may want to include a column that compares the case on the chart to your client's case. Doing so will jumpstart your thinking about how your client's case fits in with the prior case law.

Example 5-A · Case chart addressing burglary

CASE NAME	FACTS	KNOWINGLY	ENTERS WITH-OUT AUTHORITY	DWELLING	INTENT	HOLDING	LIKE OR UNLIKE OUR CASE
State v. Smith, 201 N.E.2d 673 (Ohio Ct. App. 1973).	Two unarmed teenagers entered the home of one of their friends.				No. Intent to commit crime therein not established. Boys were trying to play practical joke by putting friend's prize pet boa in his book bag.	No burglary. Intent element not met. Although other elements were met, boys did not enter tent with intent to commit a felony or theft.	Dwelling was a tent. Client knew it was tent of another. Client wanted to take camera to delete photographs and prevent friend from taking additional photos.
State v. Jones, 518 N.E.2d 333 (Ohio 1985).	Armed men entered vacation home of their acquaintances.	Yes. Knew it was dwelling of another: they knew home belonged to acquaintances and they often stayed there for long periods of time.	No authority to enter. Although they often stayed there, on this occasion acquaintances had not given permission.	Yes, "a dwelling of another." Vacation home. Although couple not staying there at time of alleged crime, they often stayed there for as long as three months at a time. Home was fully furnished.	Yes. Intent to commit a crime therein. Intruder was armed; evidence showed he had staked out the house to determine specific items to take.	Burglary. Even though victims were not currently in vacation home, D knew the victims frequented the home, often for long periods of time, and D planned to take valuables.	Arguably, tent is like a vacation home. Victim frequently used tent for days at a time. Accused had no authority to enter. Is tent a dwelling? D knew what specific item he wanted to take and waited until friend left to enter.
State v. Green, 988 N.E.2d 901 (Ohio Ct. App. 2000).	Unarmed man entered home; did not know whose home it was.	No. Did not know it was dwelling of another: he thought home was abandoned (no one appeared to have lived there for 8 months).		Yes, "a dwelling of another." Residential dwelling but unoccupied for 8 months.	No intent to commit a crime therein. Man not armed. Just wanted a place to sleep for the night. Thought items that he took had been abandoned.	No burglary. Even though another person owned the home, no one had lived there in 8 months, and D thought it was abandoned. D also wanted to sleep, not commit theft or felony.	*Green* case is least like client's case. *Green* def. thought house was abandoned, so no burglary. Here, accused knew that someone was staying in tent and wanted to take item from him.

If you take these steps, you will have a sense of which elements and factors each case addresses. You will also have an initial sense of the law and of how your client's case fits within it.

More importantly, charting cases can help you see gaps in the law or gaps in your research. For example, in the chart in Example 5-A, only one case addresses "enters without authority." That could mean that this jurisdiction has very little law addressing that issue, or it could mean that your research has failed to uncover the cases addressing that issue. Whatever the reason, you should be aware that you have little case law addressing that issue. A chart will reveal that gap.

B. Case Notes

You can also organize your cases by adding summary notes at the top of each case. This less formal method will allow you to keep track of which issues each case addresses and prepares you for a more in-depth look at each element or factor. Case notes have the benefit of being quick to construct; however, case notes will not provide the initial overview of an area of law that a case chart does. You can make up for the lack of depth at this point by creating a more formal organizational system around individual elements or factors, as discussed in the next section, part II, *Organize by Element or Factor*.

Case notes capture the same information as a case chart, but instead of putting that information in a chart, that information is put at the top of a case. Example 5-B shows you what a case note might look like. Case notes will help you avoid re-reading a case simply to figure out what that case is about. The facts will trigger your memory as to the underlying conflict, and the list of elements or factors analyzed will act as a table of contents. By looking at the list of elements or factors at the top, you will be able to tell whether the case is relevant to a particular issue you are thinking about.

Likewise, you might note at the top of a case why that case is not relevant to your client's issue. Doing so will limit the number of times that you will reread a case only to discover (again) that the case is not relevant.

II. Step 2: Organize by Element or Factor

At some point, you will need to adapt your initial organizational system so that it focuses on one element or factor at a time. As discussed in Chapter 4, *Finding Your Argument*, lawyers analyze a legal question part by part. If the test is composed of elements, lawyers analyze one element at a time. If the test is composed of factors, lawyers will often analyze one factor at a time. Thus, it makes sense that you organize your research in that way. Doing so will help you be more efficient when moving from the research and organization stage to the writing stage.

Example 5-B · A case note identifies key aspects of a case

187 Or.App. 152
Court of Appeals of Oregon.

Robert J. GILINSKY, Appellant,

v.

Martin L. SETHER; Samuel Groves; Bobbe Groves; Donald Joseph Hess,
and Robert W. Bucan, Trustee, Respondents.

00-0620-E-1, A114803. | Argued and
Submitted Jan. 3, 2003. | Decided April 3, 2003.

Adv. Possess. established
✓ open & notorious
✓ 10 years
✓ hostile

Ds had fence & mowed
lawn in otherwise
forested area.

Plaintiff appeals the trial court's judgment that adjudicated defendants to be the owners of certain property through adverse possession. He argues, in part, that the evidence presented by defendants at trial was insufficient to prove 10 continuous years of open, notorious, and hostile possession of the disputed strips of land before 1990 by clear and convincing evidence. We affirm.

We find the following facts on *de novo* review. ORS 19.415(3); *Brunswick v. Rundell*, 126 Or.App. 582, 585, 869 P.2d 886 (1994). All the property at issue is located in a forested rural residential area of Jackson County.

* * *

Plaintiff appeals, making several arguments. First, he argues that the evidence presented by defendants was not sufficient to establish 10 years of open and notorious possession. Second, he argues that the evidence presented by defendants did not establish the hostile intent required to obtain property by adverse possession. Next, he argues that Bucan and Groves did not prove by clear and convincing evidence that their predecessors intended to convey more property than the property described in their deed. Finally, plaintiff ***159** argues that the trial court erred in failing to enter judgment in his favor on his claims for trespass and ejectment.

[1][2][3][4][5] To establish title to the disputed property by adverse possession, defendants actual, open, notorious, exclusive, continuous, and hostile possession of the property for a 10-year period. *Hoffman v. Freeman Land and Timber, LLC,* 329 Or. 554, 559, 994 P.2d 106 (1999). A party who claims title to land by adverse possession must "use or occupy the land as an average owner of the same type of land would use it." *Nooteboom v. Bulson,* 153 Or.App. 361, 364, 956 P.2d 1042, *rev. den.,* 327 Or. 431, 966

P.2d 222 (1998). An adverse possessor's use of property is open and notorious if it "is 'of such a character as to afford the [owner] the means of knowing it, and of the claim.' *Hoffman,* 329 Or. at 560, 994 P.2d 106 (quoting *Hicklin v. McClear,* 18 Or. 126, 138, 22 P. 1057 (1889)) (alteration in *Hoffman*). Limited use can satisfy the requirement of open and notorious use if its nature would put the actual owner "on notice that his or her title is being challenged." *Id.* at 560, 994 P.2d 106; *Reeves v. Porta,* 173 Or. 147, 153, 144 P.2d 493 (1944).

[6]All the land at issue in this case was "actually" used as part of "backyard" areas for defendants' respective residences. Moreover, in our view, the mowing and maintenance of the strips, as well as their use for gardening, storage, parking, and recreation are all sufficient to show open and notorious use. Further, the placement of the fences, when taken with the testimony of all the witnesses in this case, establishes defendants and their predecessors in interest believed the fences to be boundary fences, not merely fences of convenience. The contrast between the disputed property on defendants' side of the fence and the densely wooded property on plaintiff's side of the fence corroborates our conclusions; they clearly gave any observer notice of defendants' use of and claim to the disputed strips of property. Consequently, we have no difficulty in finding under the above circumstances that defendants' use was open and notorious.

Plaintiff next argues that defendants Groves and Bucan did not receive from their predecessors in interest any property interest in the disputed areas that had vested by adverse possession. An owner who acquires title to property by adverse possession may transfer that title to third parties:

"[W]here there is evidence of intent between grantor and grantee to transfer

The first step in organizing by element or factor is to divide the case that way. This step is critical.

To read a judicial opinion correctly, take care not to confuse the court's analysis about one legal issue, element, or factor with the court's analysis about a separate legal issue, element, or factor.

Take for example *Gilinsky v. Sether*, a case that addresses not only adverse possession, but also whether a predecessor in interest actually conveyed his interest. In that case, excerpts of which are provided in Example 5-C, the court's analysis about adverse possession begins five pages into the opinion after a lengthy discussion about the facts. You would want to note where the court's analysis of adverse possession begins and then where that analysis ends. You might even cross out the portion of the opinion that addresses unrelated legal issues.

Then, for each legal issue that is relevant to your client's problem, you must identify the elements or factors that the court analyzes. For example, although a legal issue might be governed by a rule composed of many elements, parties often dispute only a subset of those elements. Accordingly, the court's opinion will analyze only the elements at issue.

As you organize your authorities, note which elements the court is analyzing and mark where the court's analysis about each element or factor begins and ends. Like Example 5-C, Example 5-D provides excerpts of *Gilinsky v. Sether*, but in Example 5-D, the excerpts allow you to see a greater portion of the court's analysis about adverse possession and how you would demarcate that analysis element by element.

By noting the beginning and end of the court's analysis for each element or factor, you can more easily identify the court's holding for that element, the facts that the court relied on, and any additional reasoning the court provided.

After noting the beginning and end of the court's analysis for each element or factor, you will want to bring that information together in one place. By bringing together all the information that relates to a single element or factor, you will be able to develop a complete and nuanced understanding of how that element or factor has functioned over time and in relation to different fact patterns.

Gathering information about a single element or factor in one place also allows you to synthesize rules that explain the element. Lawyers begin by extracting explicit rules. An explicit rule is one that the court states on the page of its opinion. For example, in Example 5-D, the court explicitly states when use of land is "open and notorious."

> An adverse possessor's use of property is open and notorious if it is "of such a character as to afford the [owner] the means of knowing it, and of the claim." *Hoffman*, 329 Or. at 560, 994 P.2d 106 (quoting *Hicklin v. McClear*, 18 Or. 126, 138, 22 P. 1057 (1889) (alteration in *Hoffman*)).

Example 5-C · Noting the beginning and end of the court's analysis about a legal issue

187 Or.App. 152
Court of Appeals of Oregon.

Robert J. GILINSKY, Appellant,
v.
Martin L. SETHER; Samuel Groves; Bobbe Groves; Donald Joseph Hess,
and Robert W. Bucan, Trustee, Respondents.

00-0620-E-1, A114803. | Argued and
Submitted Jan. 3, 2003. | Decided April 3, 2003.

Plaintiff appeals the trial court's judgment that adjudicated defendants to be the owners of certain property through adverse possession. He argues, in part, that the evidence presented by defendants at trial was insufficient to prove 10 continuous years of open, notorious, and hostile possession of the disputed strips of land before 1990 by clear and convincing evidence. We affirm.

We find the following facts on *de novo* review. ORS 19.415(3); *Brunswick v. Rundell,* 126 Or.App. 582, 585, 869 P.2d 886 (1994). All the property at issue is located in a forested rural residential area of Jackson County.

* * *

Plaintiff appeals, making several arguments. First, he argues that the evidence presented by defendants was not sufficient to establish 10 years of open and notorious possession. Second, he argues that the evidence presented by defendants did not establish the hostile intent required to obtain property by adverse possession. Next, he argues that Bucan and Groves did not prove by clear and convincing evidence that their predecessors intended to convey more property than the property described in their deed. Finally, plaintiff ***159** argues that the trial court erred in failing to enter judgment in his favor on his claims for trespass and ejectment.

Adv. Poss. begins

[1][2][3][4][5] To establish title to the disputed property by adverse possession, defendants' actual, open, notorious, exclusive, continuous, and hostile possession of the property for a 10-year period. *Hoffman v. Freeman Land and Timber, LLC,* 329 Or. 554, 559, 994 P.2d 106 (1999). A party who claims title to land by adverse possession must "use or occupy the land as an average owner of the same type of land would use it." *Nooteboom v. Bulson,* 153 Or.App. 361, 364, 956 P.2d 1042, *rev. den.,* 327 Or. 431, 966

P.2d 222 (1998). An adverse possessor's use of property is open and notorious if it "is 'of such a character as to afford the [owner] the means of knowing it, and of the claim.' *Hoffman,* 329 Or. at 560, 994 P.2d 106 (quoting *Hicklin v. McClear,* 18 Or. 126, 138, 22 P. 1057 (1889)) (alteration in *Hoffman*). Limited use can satisfy the requirement of open and notorious use if its nature would put the actual owner "on notice that his or her title is being challenged." *Id.* at 560, 994 P.2d 106; *Reeves v. Porta,* 173 Or. 147, 153, 144 P.2d 493 (1944).

[6]All the land at issue in this case was "actually" used as part of "backyard" areas for defendants' respective residences. Moreover, in our view, the mowing and maintenance of the strips, as well as their use for gardening, storage, parking, and recreation are all sufficient to show open and notorious use. * * *

Adv. Poss. ends here

Plaintiff next argues that defendants Groves and Bucan did not receive from their predecessors in interest any property interest in the disputed areas that had vested by adverse possession. An owner who acquires title to property by adverse possession may transfer that title to third parties:

> "[W]here there is evidence of intent between grantor and grantee to transfer the grantor's interest in property, the grantee may acquire the grantor's interest, vested and complete, in those situations in which the grantor has adversely possessed for the statutory period."

Evans v. Hogue, 296 Or. 745, 756, 681 P.2d 1133 (1984). We find that the requisite intent to transfer the disputed property is clearly proved by the circumstantial evidence in the record. As discussed above, the fence lines on both the Bucan and Groves properties were thought to be boundary fence lines. It is clear from the evidence that the owners of the properties

Example 5-D · Noting the beginning and end of the court's analysis about individual elements

187 Or.App. 152
Court of Appeals of Oregon.

Robert J. GILINSKY, Appellant,

v.

Martin L. SETHER; Samuel Groves; Bobbe Groves; Donald Joseph Hess,
and Robert W. Bucan, Trustee, Respondents.

00-0620-E-1, A114803. | Argued and
Submitted Jan. 3, 2003. | Decided April 3, 2003.

Plaintiff appeals the trial court's judgment that adjudicated defendants to be the owners of certain property through adverse possession. He argues, in part, that the evidence presented by defendants at trial was insufficient to prove 10 continuous years of open, notorious, and hostile possession of the disputed strips of land before 1990 by clear and convincing evidence. We affirm.

We find the following facts on *de novo* review. ORS 19.415(3); *Brunswick v. Rundell,* 126 Or.App. 582, 585, 869 P.2d 886 (1994). All the property at issue is located in a forested rural residential area of Jackson County.

* * *

Adv. Poss. begins

[1][2][3][4][5] To establish title to the disputed property by adverse possession, defendants actual, open, notorious, exclusive, continuous, and hostile possession of the property for a 10-year period. *Hoffman v. Freeman Land and Timber, LLC,* 329 Or. 554, 559, 994 P.2d 106 (1999). A party who claims title to land by adverse possession must "use or occupy the land as an average owner of the same type of land would use it." *Nooteboom v. Bulson,* 153 Or.App. 361, 364, 956 P.2d 1042, *rev. den.,* 327 Or. 431, 966 P.2d 222 (1998). An adverse possessor's use of property is open and notorious if it "is 'of such a character as to afford the [owner] the means of knowing it, and of the claim.'" *Hoffman,* 329 Or. at 560, 994 P.2d 106 (quoting *Hicklin v. McClear,* 18 Or. 126, 138, 22 P. 1057 (1889)) (alteration in *Hoffman*). Limited use can satisfy the requirement of open and notorious use if its nature would put the actual owner "on notice that his or her title is being challenged." *Id.* at 560, 994 P.2d 106; *Reeves v. Porta,* 173 Or. 147, 153, 144 P.2d 493 (1944).

Open & Notorious

[5] All the land at issue in this case was "actually" used as part of "backyard" areas for defendants' respective residences. Moreover, in our view, the mowing and maintenance of the strips, as well as their use for gardening, storage, parking, and recreation are all sufficient to show open and notorious use. Further, the placement of the fences, when taken with the testimony of all the witnesses in this case, establishes defendants and their predecessors in interest believed the fences to be boundary fences, not merely fences of convenience. The contrast between the disputed property on defendants' side of the fence and the densely wooded property on plaintiff's side of the fence corroborates our conclusions; they clearly gave any observer notice of defendants' use of and claim to the disputed strips of property. Consequently, we have no difficulty in finding under the above circumstances that defendants' use was open and notorious.

Open & Notorious

To succeed in their claims of adverse possession, defendants also must show that their open and notorious use of the land continued **590 for at least 10 years before 1990. The direct and circumstantial evidence presented by defendant *160 Sether establishes that the open and notorious use of the property he claims began by 1972, when Hendricks acquired the property, and that it continued until the time of trial, or well beyond the required 10-year period. Similarly, the testimony of defendant Bucan as to his use of the property since 1980, along with the testimony of Bobbe and Sam Groves regarding the use of the property beginning in 1948, clearly establishes the 10-year continuous use element of the test. Bobbe and Sam Groves also testified about the use of the Groves property since 1948 and 1960. That use of that property has remained the same over the 50 years preceding trial.

For 10 years

* * * We are persuaded that the requirement of at least 10 years of open and notorious possession before 1990 is satisfied.

[6] [7] To establish the element of hostility, a claimant must show that he or she "possessed the property intending to be its owner and not in subordination to the true owner." * * *

Hostile

And it provides another rule further explaining what constitutes open and notorious possession:

> Limited use can satisfy the requirement of open and notorious use if its nature would put the actual owner "on notice that his or her title is being challenged." *Id.* at 560, 994 P.2d 106; *Reeves v. Porta,* 173 Or. 147, 153, 144 P.2d 493 (1944).

Both of those rules explain when a claimant's use of property was "open and notorious." They are explicit rules because they are stated directly on the page of the opinion.

Extracting all the explicit rules and listing them in one place allows you to piece together a complete rule that accounts for any changes that have occurred over time. (If a statute adds to your understanding of how an element or factor functions, you can also include the statute in your organizational scheme.)

In addition, gathering information about a single element or factor in one place allows you to see patterns in previous cases. Sometimes, for example, when you look at the facts of a case, the court's reasoning, and the outcome, you might see that the court is heading in a new direction— perhaps expanding the rule or restricting the rule from what it once was. Other times, after reading a series of cases, you might notice a pattern in the courts' decisions. You might notice, for example, certain facts virtually guarantee success for one party while other facts tend to cause difficulties.[1]

By looking for patterns in the law, you will be able to add "implicit rules" to your explanation of the law. An "implicit rule" is a rule that emerges from a case or series of cases that explains the outcome in one or several cases but that the courts have not explicitly stated in their analyses.

To the extent that you can fit a case within the larger body of case law and state explicitly what the courts are doing implicitly, the more likely you will be able to explain the law precisely and predict accurately how that law will apply to your client's case.

You can achieve those ends in a variety of formats. Here, in Examples 5-E through 5-G, you will see a chart, an outline, and a mind map. Each examines whether a claimant "actually possessed" a disputed parcel of land. "Actual possession" is one element in a claim of adverse possession.

As you examine each format, be aware of the shift in focus. In earlier organizational efforts, shown in the chart in Example 5-A and in the case note in Example 5-B, the goal was simply to keep track of all the possibly relevant cases that you found.

Once you have gathered relevant law, the goal changes. Now, the goal is to dissect that law and bring together information about one element

---

1. Suzanne Rowe, *Oregon Legal Research* 53 (3d ed. 2014) (explaining that lawyers should "[p]ay attention to how the cases fit together").

or factor at a time. Doing so will allow you to deepen your understanding of how each part of the rule works.

A. Charts

Charts can be equally helpful when analyzing an element or factor as they were when organizing your research. Example 5-E illustrates how you can fashion a chart to gather information about a single element or factor. In that chart, the primary authorities are listed along the vertical axis. Along the horizontal axis, the chart lists the following:

- **Rules** the court explained as relevant to its conclusion about the element;
- **Facts** that the court relied on to reach its conclusion about the element;
- The court's **holding** about the element;
- Any additional **reasoning** that led to the court's conclusion about the element.

You can also include a column that allows you to compare your case to each prior authority.

Notice how you can scan down the rules column to get an overview of the rules courts rely on to reach a conclusion about the element. In Example 5-E, the courts' statements are consistent: All courts state that "actual possession" requires a claimant to use the land as an owner would. By bringing the rules together in one place, you can see that the courts have consistently applied the same rule over time. This synthesis shows a fairly clear idea of the rule that governs this element.

By scanning down the facts column you can also begin to develop a sense of what kinds of facts will lead a court to conclude that the claimant has shown actual possession.

Scanning down the courts' reasoning column will likely flesh out your understanding of how courts reach a conclusion about this element.

Thus, a chart will allow you to collect, in one place, specific information about each case, and it will allow you to see patterns or trends in the law.

B. Outlines

You can also use an outline to gather information about a single element or factor. Whether you use an outline, chart, or mind map depends on the structure that feels comfortable to you. Some lawyers like using an outline because an outline looks more like the memorandum that they will ultimately write. They like to see their work beginning to take shape.

An outline contains all the same information that a chart does, but it would look something like Example 5-F. Again, by grouping all the rules and specific information about a single element in one place, you

Example 5-E • Chart examines a single element—actual possession

Case name	RULES about Actual Possession	FACTS about Actual Possession	Court's HOLDING about Actual Possession	Additional REASONING about Actual Possession
***Davis v. Parke*, 898 P.2d 804 (Or. Ct. App. 1995).**	Requires "occupation or use of the land that would be made by an owner of the same type of land, taking into account the uses for which the land is suitable." p. 805.	Claimants bought cattle and turned it loose on the property. Fence was in some disrepair, but plaintiff had repaired it. Fence intended to keep cattle on disputed property. pp. 805-06. Claimants grazed cattle on their actual property and the disputed property. p. 806.	Yes. Actual Possession.	Claimants "used the disputed property the same way they used their adjoining land." p. 806. Claimants "maintained a fence to keep cattle in, although they were not always successful in keeping their cattle inside it." p. 806.
***Hoffman v. Freeman*, 994 P.2d 106 (Or. Ct. 1999).**	Claimant must establish "a use of the land that would be made by an owner of the same type of land, taking into account the uses for which the land is suited." p. 110.	Claimants used disputed property for occasional grazing of cattle. Testimony at trial was "undisputed" that land unsuitable for most other uses. pp. 110-11.	Yes. Actual Possession.	Occasional pasturing or grazing of livestock may be sufficient to prove actual use. p. 110. The lot in dispute was unsuitable for other purposes and grazing is one use an owner would make of the land. pp. 110-11.
***Mid-Valley v. Engelson*, 13 P.3d 118 (Or. Ct. App. 2000).**	[Actual possession not addressed. Claim failed on "Hostility" element.]			
***Slak v. Porter*, 875 P.2d 515 (Or. Ct. App. 1994).**	Requires use that an owner would make of it taking into account use for which land is suited. p. 518.	Claimants erected a fence and planted trees, shrubs and other vegetation. pp. 518-19.	Yes. Actual Possession.	Erecting a fence and planting is the type of use an owner would make of this property. p. 519.
***Zambrotto v. Superior*, 4 P.3d 62 (Or. Ct. App. 2000).**	Requires "use of the land that would be made by an owner of the same type of land, taking into account the uses for which the land is suited." p. 65. "The requirement of 'actual' use is a qualitative one, determined by reference to the type of use that would be made by an owner." p. 65.	Property was rural, mostly forested. Claimants used land to hike and hunt for rattlesnakes. Repaired fence that ran along southern boundary. p. 65.	Yes. Actual Possession.	"[T]here is evidence of actual use, not much use, to be sure, but actual use nonetheless." p. 65. "Given the nature of the land, we conclude that hiking, rattlesnake hunting, and the like, constitute actual use." p. 65.

can begin to see trends or patterns in the law. In addition, and as will be explained in Chapter 6, *One Legal Argument*, this outline takes a first step toward organizing information in the order in which it will be explained in a memorandum.

Example 5-F • An outline examines a single element—actual possession

I. **Actual Possession**

  A. **Rules re. actual possession**

    1. Requires "occupation or use of the land that would be made by an owner of the same type of land taking into account the uses for which the land is suitable." *Davis* at 805; *see also Hoffman* at 110 (using same language and quoting *Davis*); *Slak* at 518 (same); *Zambrotto* at 65 (same).

    2. The requirement of "actual" use is a qualitative one, determined by reference to the type of use that would be.

  B. **Cases that analyze actual possession**

    1. *Davis v. Park*, 898 P.2d 804 (Or. Ct. App. 1995)

      a. **Facts re. act. possess.:** Claimants bought cattle and turned it loose on the property. Fence was in some disrepair, but claimant had repaired it. Fence intended to keep cattle on disputed property. *Davis* at 805-06. Claimants grazed cattle on their actual property and the disputed property. *Davis* at 806.

      b. **Holding re. act. possess.:** Yes. Actual possession because claimants maintained the fence. *Davis* at 806.

      c. **Reasoning re. act. Possess.:** Claimants "used the disputed land in the same way they used their adjoining land." *Davis* at 804. Claimants "maintained a fence to keep cattle in, although they were not always successful in keeping their cattle in." *Davis* at 806.

    2. *Hoffman v. Freeman*, 994 P.2d 106 (Or. Ct. App. 1999)

      a. **Facts re. act. possess.:** Disputed property used for occasional grazing of cattle. Testimony at trial was "undisputed" that land unsuitable for most other uses. *Hoffman* at 110-11.

      b. **Holding re. act. possess.:** Yes. Actual possession.

      c. **Reasoning re. act. Possess.:** Occasional pasturing or grazing of livestock may be sufficient to prove actual use. *Hoffman* at 110. The lot in dispute was unsuitable for other purposes and grazing is one use an owner would make of the land. *Hoffman* at 110-11.

Don't forget to cite!

Including citations now—as you organize—will save you significant time later. As you write, you will want to return to a source to verify some piece of information. Having a citation in your outline will make that easier to do. And, of course, you will need to cite your final analysis.

Although you should include citations as you organize, your citations do not need to follow formal *Bluebook* or *ALWD* rules at this stage. For now, informal cites, as in Example 5-F, are sufficient. You will revise the citations when you polish your work.

C. Mind Maps

Information about a single element or factor can also be gathered together using a mind map. A mind map looks something like Example 5-G, on the next page. Some lawyers feel that charts and outlines are too rigid and that a more organic structure allows greater flexibility in their thinking. If that's you, try a mind map, flowchart, or some other graphic.

As you can see, a mind map will also allow you to aggregate all the information about an element so that you can see both specific information about cases and patterns in the rules and facts.

III. Step 3: Prepare to Write

The next step is to select the information that you plan to include in your written analysis. When you organize element by element or factor by factor, you gather all the information that allows you to understand how each element or factor works.

At some point, however, you must choose the most relevant law to include in your final written analysis. Chapter 7, *Explaining the Law*, provides guidance about how to choose the authorities that will appear in your final written analysis. For now, realize this: You will often want to sketch out those choices before you actually begin to draft.

Again, you can use different formats to organize the authorities you intend to include in your written analysis. Most often, those formats are either an outline or mind map. Both of those formats can display the relationship and order of ideas. Examples 5-H and 5-I demonstrate how you can use a chart or a mind map to organize your thoughts as you prepare to write.

Whatever format you choose, if you sketch out the substance of your analysis in advance, you will write more efficiently. Having decided *what* to say in advance, you can focus on *how* to say it when you actually draft.

A. Outlines

Some lawyers will feel most comfortable using an outline to sketch out their written analysis. As mentioned above, an outline most closely resembles the ultimate format of a formal memorandum.

When using an outline, lawyers vary in how much content they might include. Example 5-H shows a fairly detailed outline, called a "sentence-level outline." A sentence-level outline allows a lawyer to think about the content of each sentence of a memorandum without worrying about how polished the sentences are or the flow between sentences. As you can see in Example 5-H, the writer lists in bold, the content to be included. The bolded categories can act as a check that the lawyer has included all

Example 5-G · A mind map examines a single element—actual possession.

The requirement of "actual" use is a qualitative one, determined by reference to the type of use that would be made by an owner. Zambrotto at 65.

Requires "occupation or use of the land that would be made by an owner of the same type of land taking into account the uses for which the land is suitable." Davis at 805. See also Hoffman at 110 (using same language and quoting Davis); Slak at 518 (same); Zambrotto at 65 (same).

Reasoning: Occasional pasturing or grazing of livestock may be sufficient to prove actual use. Hoffman at 110. The lot in dispute was unsuitable for other purposes and grazing is only use an owner would make of the land. Hoffman at 110-11.

Holding: Yes. Actual possession.

Hoffman v. Freeman, 994 P.2d 106 (Or. Ct. App. 1999)

Facts: Disputed property used for occasional grazing of cattle. Testimony at trial was "undisputed" that land unsuitable for most other uses. Hoffman at 110-11.

Facts: Claimants erected a fence and planted trees, shrubs, and other vegetation. Slak at 518-19.

Holding: Yes. Actual possession.

Slak v. Porter, 875 P.2d 515 (Or. Ct. App. 1994)

Reasoning: Erecting a fence and planting is the type of use an owner would make of this property. Slak at 519.

Rules

Subtopic

Actual possession

Facts: Claimants brought cattle and turned them loose on the property. Fence was in some disrepair, but claimant had repaired it. Fence intended to keep cattle on disputed property. Davis at 805-06. Claimants grazed cattle on their actual property and the disputed property. Davis at 806.

Reasoning: Claimants "used the disputed land in the same way they used their adjoining land." Davis at 804. Claimants "maintained a fence to keep cattle in, although they were not always successful in keeping their cattle in." Davis at 806.

Reasoning: "There is evidence of actual use, not much use, to be sure, but actual use nonetheless." Zambrotto at 65.

Davis v. Park, 898 P.2d 804 (Or. Ct. App. 1995)

Holding: Yes. Actual possession.

Facts: Property was rural, mostly forested. Claimants used land to hike and hunt for rattlesnakes. Repaired fence that ran along southern boundary. Zambrotto at 65.

Holding: Yes. Actual possession. "Given the nature of the land, we conclude that hiking, rattlesnake hunting, and the like, constitute actual use." Zambrotto at 65.

Zambrotto v. Superior, 4 P.3d 62 (Or. Ct. App. 2000)

necessary information. Creating a detailed outline such as the one in Example 5-H can significantly speed up the actual writing process.

Example 5-H • An outline sketches out the final memo

I. **Roadmap**
    A. **Conclusion:** The Neros can gain ownership of the disputed property through adverse possession.
    B. **Governing rule:**
        1. To acquire property by adverse possession, plaintiffs must prove by clear and convincing evidence that their possession of the land was actual, open and notorious, exclusive, hostile, and continuous, for a ten-year period. *Hoffman* at 109.
        2. ORS § 105.620 adds a requirement that the land be possessed through an honest belief that the plaintiffs owned the land.
        3. ORS § 105.620 also requires that the land vest before 1990. *Midland* at n.2.
    C. **Dispose:** The Nero's interest vested in 1989.
    D. **Map and assess what's left:** Of the remaining elements, the most difficult to prove will be that their possession was open and notorious; however, they should ultimately be able to prove that and the remaining elements.
    E. **Conclude:** Neros can acquire title through adverse possession.

II. **Actual Possession**
    A. **Conclusion:** The Neros can prove they actually possessed the disputed land.
    B. **Rules re. actual possession**
        1. Plaintiffs can establish actual possession by showing that they used the land as an owner would use that particular type of land. *Zambrotto* at 65 (same).
        2. Courts focus on the type of use for which the land is suited and do not necessarily focus on the amount of activity on the land. *Zambrotto* at 65.
    C. **Case illustrations**
        1. *Davis v. Park*, 898 P.2d 804 (Or. Ct. App. 1995)
            a. **Hook:** Plaintiffs have shown that they used the disputed land as an owner would in a variety of ways.
            b. **Facts re. act. possess.:** Claimants used the disputed property in the same way they used their actual property, which was to graze cattle. *Davis* at 806.
            c. **Holding re. act. possess.:** Yes. Actual possession. *Davis* at 806.
            d. **Reasoning:** No additional reasoning to add.
        2. *Slak v. Porter*, 875 P.2d 515 (Or. Ct. App. 1994)
            a. **Hook:** Will share hook with *Davis*.
            b. **Facts re. act. possess.:** Claimants erected a fence and planted trees, shrubs, and other vegetation. *Slak* at 518-19.
            c. **Holding re. act. possess.:** Yes. Actual possession.

Here, the drafter sketches out the roadmap section for the memo's discussion section. Roadmap sections are described in detail in Ch. 12, *The Discussion Section: Introducing and Connecting Legal Arguments.*

In Part II, the drafter sketches out the first legal argument, which addresses the element of adverse possession.

The outline identifies all the parts of an effective argument and then sketches the content within each part.

The parts of an effective legal argument are explained in Ch. 6, *One Legal Argument.*

Similarly, part II.C, "Case illustrations," identifies each part of an effective case illustration and sketches the content of each.

The parts of an effective case illustration are explained in § 7.2, *Explaining the Law: Case Illustrations.*

Again, the writer uses cites to keep track of where information can be found, but at this stage the citations are still not in formal *Bluebook* or *ALWD* form.

Part II.D of the outline, "Application," identifies the two case comparisons the writer intends to make and sketches the content of those case comparisons.

The parts of an effective case comparison are explained in §8.2: Applying the Law: Analogical Arguments.

        d. **Reasoning re. act. possess:** No additional reasoning to add.

D. **Application**

   1. **Comparison to *Davis***

      a. **Point sentence:** The Neros should be able to prove actual possession because they used the land as an owner would.

      b. **Factual similarity:** In both cases, the claimants used the land in the same way that the used the adjoining land. In *Davis*, the claimants grazed cattle on both parcels of land. In this case, the Neros planted vegetation and maintained an orchard on both parcels.

      c. **Legal consequence:** Can show actual possession as the claimants in *Davis* did.

   2. **Comparison to *Slak***

      a. **Point sentence:** Share with *Davis*?

      b. **Factual similarity:** In this case, as in *Slak*, the claimants used the land to plant vegetation and maintained a fence

      c. **Legal consequence:** Can show actual possession as the claimants in *Slak* did.

   3. **Counter-argument:** None.

E. **Conclusion:** The Neros will be able to prove they actually possessed the land.

B. Mind Maps

You can also use a mind map to display the content you intend to include in your memorandum. In the mind map shown in Figure 5-I, the elements to be addressed in the discussion are represented as spokes coming out of a wheel. (When a mind map is represented as spokes coming out of a wheel, some call it a whirlybird.[2]) Figure 5-I shows the burglary question from Example 5-A outlined in a whirlybird mind map.

As you draft, use your outline—in whatever form it takes—to guide your writing. Typically, having spent the time to think through your organization and the relevant law and facts, the writing will proceed more smoothly.

Likewise, if you are in the midst of drafting your discussion and you realize that your organizational plan is not working, stop writing. Sometimes we are unable to see the gaps in our own logic until we actually put our thoughts onto paper. When that happens, stop writing. Revise your organizational plan. Then, try again.

---

2. Bryan A. Garner, *The Winning Brief* 33 (3d ed. 2014).

Example 5-1 • Whirlybird

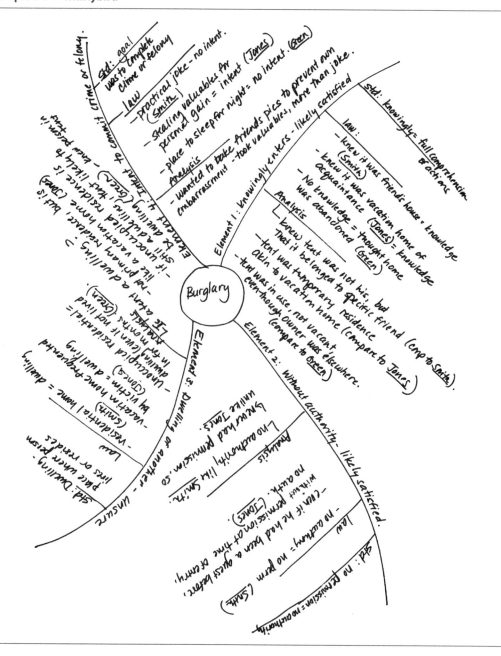

The vast majority of legal writers benefit from plotting out their arguments in advance. Some writers, however, begin drafting by "free writing." "Free writing" is simply putting down on a page all of your thoughts without any attempt to organize them. Some writers find this process avoids writer's block. They simply write information and ideas that occur to them without any criticism.

Even if you begin your draft by free writing, do not skip outlining your argument. Use your free writing to create an outline. You will, first, need to rearrange the content of your free writing so that it follows the linear analysis your colleagues will expect. As you rearrange, be prepared to discard any of the writing that does not advance your analysis. When discarding material from the outline, however, do not get rid of it entirely; instead, preserve discarded material in a separate document where it can be retrieved later if you need it. Free writing can be a great way to jump start your writing, but ultimately you will need to prune and reorganize your free writing so that it can function as an outline for your final product: a carefully organized and explained legal analysis.

IV. Write for Your Audience

As you organize, remember your intended audience. You will be writing for a reader who needs to make a legal decision based on the analysis you have done. Your audience needs to see a cogent, well-organized analysis that accurately predicts how the relevant law will apply to your client's facts.

Your audience does not need to retrace the thought process you went through to get to the answer. Organizing the memo in the same way you came to understand the information may not yield a clear organization that the attorney relying on your work product can understand. Writing and getting thoughts down onto paper without charting and outlining can be a great way to overcome writer's block or to help you understand a complex issue, but doing that should not be the final work product you provide to the attorney.

Your reader wants your argument ordered and developed around the legal points—the elements or factors—contained in the governing rule. Breaking down the governing rule into its elements or factors, charting cases to synthesize the law about each element or factor, and then outlining your argument according to those elements or factors will allow you to produce what your reader needs—a clear prediction of how the current law will apply to your client's facts. Remember, this process of finding and organizing your argument is really about good legal thinking. Without good legal thinking, your writing will not be clear.

After organizing the legal authorities, you are ready to write.

Practice Points

- Organizing your legal authorities while you research is a critical step to producing a cogent work product.

- Begin your research by keeping sources of law organized. Charting authorities can help you see the relationships among the various authorities you found as well as the patterns emerging in past cases. Charting can also help you decide the best cases to select for your memo or see holes in your research. Alternatively, you can note at the top of each case whether that case is relevant and why.

- Next, organize your ideas around the working parts of the governing rule, not around individual cases or a description of the governing rule's evolution.

- Finally, take time to outline before you write. Whether you use a traditional or non-traditional format, outlining will help you produce an analytically stronger memorandum in less time because it helps you see how the pieces of your legal puzzle will fit together.

- Give your audience what it needs. Attorneys want to see an argument arranged around the governing rule and its component parts; therefore, follow the structure the governing rule dictates. Do not simply memorialize the way you thought through the issues.

Chapter 6

One Legal Argument

After you have determined the governing rule and organized your research according to the elements or factors in the governing rule, you are ready to construct the legal arguments that will guide your prediction to your client's question.

As explained in Chapter 4, *Finding Your Argument*, you will need to construct one legal argument for each element or factor in the governing rule. Taken together, those arguments will explain why you are predicting a particular outcome to your client's question.

Over time, attorneys have established a common preference for how a legal argument is presented. Typically, a single legal argument has four components presented in the following order:

1. **A conclusion about, or statement of, the legal issue,**
2. **An explanation of the law,**
3. **An application of the law to the client's facts, and**
4. **A final conclusion.**

The initial conclusion or statement of the issue tells the reader the direction of the argument. When a reader knows where a writer is heading, the reader can more easily understand the argument that follows and why particular details are relevant. In most circumstances, a conclusion that specifies the bottom-line result of your analysis is more helpful to the reader than a general statement of the issue to be explored. For that reason, this book typically begins legal arguments with a conclusion. (Later, we will discuss instances in which an issue statement is appropriate.)

Next, attorneys explain the law. The explanation of the law educates the reader about the relevant law and shows how that law has been applied by courts in the past. In explaining how the law has been applied in the past, the attorney establishes the analytical framework that will be applied to the client's case.

After establishing that framework, an attorney then applies that law to the facts of a client's case to explain why a particular outcome is likely. In a simple case, applying the law may mean showing how an established rule of law will function in a client's case. In a more difficult case, applying the law may also mean explaining why a client's case is like or unlike previous cases and how those comparisons yield a particular legal result.

Because the application section explains why a particular outcome is likely, the application leads directly to the final part of the argument, the argument's conclusion. Although stating the conclusion at the beginning and at the end of an argument may seem repetitious, attorneys find it helpful to both tell the reader where the argument is headed and to remind the reader of the argument's point at the end.

Attorneys find that this structure is an effective way to communicate a legal argument, and they will expect you to communicate your arguments in the same way. In fact, if you look closely at the appellate court cases you are reading, you may be able to see this same structure in the courts' arguments.

Writing within this structure takes practice. As they are becoming accustomed to this structure, some attorneys use mnemonics to help them remember its components and their order. Although the mnemonics they use may differ, each mnemonic leads to the same structure. We describe some of the mnemonics commonly used in Tables 6-A through 6-C and show how they match up with the four-part structure described above.

Table 6-A · IRAC

Mnemonic	What it means	This book's analogous term
I	Issue	Conclusion or issue
R	Rule	Explain the law
A	Application	Apply the law
C	Conclusion	Conclusion

Table 6-B · CREAC

Mnemonic	What it means	This book's analogous term
C	Conclusion	Conclusion
R	Rule(s)	Explain the Law
E	Explanation of the rules	
A	Application of the law	Apply the law
C	Conclusion	Conclusion

Table 6-C · CRRPAP

Mnemonic	What it means	This book's analogous term
C	Conclusion	Conclusion
R	Rule(s)	Explain the Law
R P	Rule proof	
A	Application of the rule and rule proof	Apply the law
P	Prediction	Conclusion

No matter the mnemonic you use, and even if you use no mnemonic, the goal is the same: to explain whether each element or factor in a legal argument exists in your client's case. By constructing an argument for each element or factor and presenting it in the expected way, you will be able to effectively explain the likelihood of a particular outcome in your client's case.

You can see how these parts come together to form a legal argument in Example 6-D. Example 6-D is a single legal argument extracted from the memorandum you saw in Chapter 1. We have annotated it so you can see the parts of the legal argument.

Example 6-D · One legal argument

Mr. Adams's statement was mere conversation because he could not reasonably believe his liberty was restrained during his encounter with Officer Ephgrave. Whether an encounter with a police officer is "mere conversation" or a "stop" depends upon the extent to which the person's liberty is restrained. If a person's liberty has not been restrained, then the encounter is "mere conversation." *See, e.g., State v. Smith*, 698 P.2d 973, 975 (Or. Ct. App. 1985). By contrast, a "stop" occurs if a person's liberty is restrained by a police officer lawfully present in any place. Or. Rev. Stat. § 131.605(6) (2017); *State v. Warner*, 901 P.2d 940, 942 (Or. Ct. App. 1995). A person's liberty may be restrained if that person believes that his liberty has been restrained and that belief is objectively reasonable. *Warner*, 901 P.2d at 942. To determine whether a person reasonably believes his liberty has been restrained, a court will consider the totality of the circumstances. *State v. Wenger*, 922 P.2d 1248, 1251 (Or. Ct. App. 1996).

A police officer may request information without restraining a person's liberty. In *State v. Gilmore*, an officer requested identification from three people who were sitting in a truck. 860 P.2d 882, 883 (Or. Ct. App. 1993). When the defendant opened the glove compartment to retrieve his identification, the officer saw a gun and arrested the defendant for illegal possession of a firearm. *Id.* Although the defendant argued he had been illegally stopped and, therefore, evidence of the gun should be excluded from trial, the trial court admitted

The **conclusion** *(Ch. 9).*

The **explanation of the law** *(Ch. 7) begins here. The explanation of the law includes rules and prior cases.*

This paragraph explains the rules (§ 7.1) courts have used in the past to determine whether an encounter with police is mere conversation or a stop.

This paragraph and the next provide case illustrations (§ 7.2). The case illustrations explain how the rules, described above, were applied to cases that are factually similar to the client's case.

the gun into evidence. *Id.* In upholding the trial court's decision, the Court of Appeals explained that, even if the defendant felt he was not free to leave, that belief was not objectively reasonable. *Id.* The Court of Appeals explained that, although the officer requested identification, the officer did not require the defendant to alter his course, nor did the officer prevent the defendant from leaving. *Id.*

Notice that the explanation of the law does not mention the client.

By contrast, a person may reasonably believe his liberty has been restrained if a police officer blocks that person's car. *Wenger,* 922 P.2d at 1251. In *Wenger,* the defendant was intending to leave a parking lot when uniformed officers parked their patrol car and blocked in the defendant's car. *Id.* The *Wenger* court held that the defendant had been stopped, reasoning that a stop occurs whenever an officer prevents a vehicle from being driven away. *Id.* at 1251-52.

After explaining the law, the attorney **applies the law** (Ch. 8) to the client's case.

The signal that the writer has finished explaining the law and begun applying the law is the introduction of the client.

In this case, a court is likely to hold that Paul Adams could not reasonably believe his liberty had been restrained and that, therefore, the encounter was mere conversation. Mr. Adams's encounter is similar to the encounter in *Gilmore.* In both cases, an officer approached the defendant seeking information. In *Gilmore*, the officer asked for identification, and in Mr. Adams's case the officer wanted to learn whether the defendant was involved in the bank robbery.

However, seeking information is not enough to convert a conversation to a stop. In Mr. Adams's case, as in the *Gilmore* case, the officer did not alter the defendant's course or prevent him from leaving. Officer Ephgrave asked Mr. Adams whether he was planning to leave. Mr. Adams said he was not. In addition, Officer Ephgrave said that he would move his car before Mr. Adams had to leave. According to Officer Ephgrave, Mr. Adams agreed, saying "Oh, okay. No problem." Therefore, Officer Ephgrave did not prevent Mr. Adams from leaving, nor did the officer alter Mr. Adams's course. Thus, a court should follow the reasoning in *Gilmore* and conclude that Mr. Adams could not reasonably believe his liberty was restrained.

The application does not include any new law. The attorney relies on law that has been explained above in the explanation of the law.

In fact, a court is likely to find Mr. Adams's encounter with the officer to be even less restrictive than the encounter in *Gilmore.* In addition to not altering Mr. Adams's course and not preventing him from leaving, Officer Ephgrave was not in uniform. Because Mr. Adams believed he was talking to a civilian, Mr. Adams should have felt even more free to leave than did the defendant in *Gilmore*, who knew he was talking to a uniformed officer. Thus, a court is likely to hold that Mr. Adams's encounter with the officer was mere conversation.

Even though Officer Ephgrave's car did block Mr. Adams's car, a court is likely to distinguish Mr. Adams's case from the *Wenger* case. In the *Wenger* case, the court noted that the defendant was intending to leave at the time his car was blocked. By contrast, Mr. Adams told Officer Ephgrave that he was "going to sit a little while longer," suggesting that he was not intending to leave. Because he was not intending to leave, a court is less likely to conclude that he reasonably felt his liberty was restrained. Accordingly, a court will likely determine that Mr. Adams was not stopped, but rather, that his encounter with the officer was "mere conversation."

The application ends with a **conclusion** (Ch. 9).

Writing within this prescribed structure may seem confining at first. Over time, though, you will not only become accustomed to it, you will begin to look for it in legal arguments. You may even find yourself frustrated when a legal argument is not presented in this form.

As you are becoming accustomed to this form, you might think of it like a haiku. A haiku is a Japanese form of unrhymed poetry with a strict form. It is three lines long, with five syllables in the first line, seven syllables in the second line, and five syllables in the third. Just as a haiku must be written in this form to be a haiku, so too a legal argument must be written in its form. But within each form, there is much you can do.

The next three chapters explain each component of a single legal argument. Chapter 7, *Explaining the Law*, describes how to explain the law relevant to each element or factor. Chapter 8, *Applying the Law*, explains how to apply the law to predict outcomes about each element or factor. And Chapter 9, *Conclusions to One Legal Argument*, discusses the conclusions that will precede and sum up each argument.

Chapter 7

Explaining the Law

When writing a legal argument, you must explain the law on which your conclusion will rest. To explain the law, you will explain how the relevant authorities you located in your research fit together—that is, you will draw on all the authorities you have researched and synthesize a cohesive explanation of the law as it pertains to your client. That synthesized explanation of the law will set out the rules governing your client's legal question and will explain how courts have applied those rules in past, similar cases.

By explaining the law, you explain the legal foundation for your argument. Providing that legal foundation is the primary purpose of your explanation of the law.

In addition, your explanation of the law educates the reader about the relevant law. By explaining the rules and how courts have applied those rules in the past, you will educate the reader about the law that will apply to your client's case.

Finally, your explanation of the law previews the analytical steps you will follow in your analysis. The framework you present when you explain the law is the same framework you will later apply to your client's case in the application section of your argument.

As you explain the law, remember two things: First, an explanation of the law is a *focused* description of the law. Because the explanation is a focused description of the law, it should include only the information needed to analyze the element or factor relevant to your client's case. Your explanation of the law should not include an idea just because it is "interesting." Attorneys do not like to waste time. They do not want to read about tangential issues, nor do they want to read about how the law evolved. Attorneys want to read *only* those ideas relevant to understanding the law applicable to a client's case. Therefore, any explanation of the law that you will not rely on to analyze your client's facts should be omitted from your explanation of the law.

> ### Sidebar
>
> When you choose what to include in your explanation of the law, you should *think* about your client and the law that is relevant to your client's case; however, when *writing* the explanation of the law, do not write anything specifically about your client. Remember, your client's situation will be addressed in the application section.

Second, your explanation of the law should not mention your client's case. Attorneys prefer that their first look at the relevant law be stripped of any mention of a particular client. In that way, the attorney can absorb a clear understanding of the law without it becoming muddled with the particulars of a client's case. (You will connect the law and your client's facts later in the application section.)

In fact, one test for a well-organized argument is whether a line can be drawn that will separate your explanation of the law from your application of the law. Look at a basic explanation of the law in Example 7-A, and you can see how this line might be drawn.

Example 7-A · Basic explanation of the law

The argument begins with a **conclusion**.

Mr. and Mrs. Nero can most likely prove actual possession. Plaintiffs must establish actual possession by showing that they used the land as an owner would use that particular type of land. *Zambrotto v. Superior Lumber Co.*, 4 P.3d 62, 65 (Or. Ct. App. 2000). The courts focus on the type of use for which the land is suited and do not necessarily focus on the amount of activity. *Id.* Plaintiffs in past cases have shown that they used the disputed land as an owner would in a variety of ways. *See, e.g., Davis v. Park*, 898 P.2d 804, 806-07 (Or. Ct. App. 1995); *Slak v. Porter*, 875 P.2d 515, 518 (Or. Ct. App. 1994). In *Davis*, the plaintiffs established that they used the disputed property as an owner would by showing that they used the disputed property as they did their adjoining land. 898 P.2d at 806-07. In *Slak*, the plaintiffs built a fence and planted vegetation and, in that way, proved actual possession. 875 P.2d at 518.

The **explanation of the law** describes the rules that determine whether the element of "actual possession" is present. It then illustrates those rules by describing cases.

Notice that, after the conclusion, there is no mention of the client, the Nero family.

The **application of the law** begins here when the client is introduced.

Mr. and Mrs. Nero should be able to prove that they had actual possession of their land because they used the disputed property in a manner that an owner would. Like the landowners in *Davis*, the Neros used the disputed land exactly as they did their adjacent land: in both parcels of land, they planted and maintained a garden and fruit trees. In addition, like the plaintiffs in *Slak* who showed actual possession by building a fence and planting vegetation, the Neros built a fence and planted vegetation in their garden and orchard. The Neros should, therefore, be able to prove that they actually possessed the disputed land.

To draft an effective explanation of the law, you will need to understand its two most common components—rules and case illustrations. In this chapter, you will become more familiar with those components and how to use them to create a logical, cohesive explanation of the law.

Explaining the Law: Rules

I. The Role of Rules

When you begin explaining the law relevant to a particular element or factor, first explain the rules. As we discussed earlier, a rule sets a standard.[1] With respect to a given element or factor, rules tell a court how to determine whether that element or factor was present in your client's case. Any explanation of the law must start with the prevailing standard that controls the conduct at issue.

To explain the prevailing standard, you will usually need to explain a group of rules. Some rules will describe broad, over-arching principles. Other rules, sometimes called sub-rules, provide smaller, more specific explanations about the standard.

Example 7.1-A shows a group of rules in an explanation of the law. In that example, the rules explain what a plaintiff must do to prove he actually possessed land long enough to claim ownership in a claim for adverse possession. The first sentence is a broad rule that defines the standard for when actual possession is proven. The second sentence identifies two smaller, more specific sub-rules that describe the kinds of facts courts look for to determine actual possession. Together, these rules

---

1. The "governing rule," described in Chapter 4, *Finding Your Argument*, is one kind of rule. It describes the standard that governs one legal issue. As explained in Chapter 4, lawyers break the governing rule down into elements and factors and then develop one legal argument for each. This chapter focuses on how to explain the rules within one legal argument.

describe how a court will determine whether a person "actually possessed" the land in dispute.

Example 7.1-A · Rules describe a prevailing standard

Broad rule ⟶ Plaintiffs can establish actual possession by showing that they used the land as an owner would use that particular type of land. *Zambrotto v. Superior Lumber Co.*, 4 P.3d 62, 65 (Or. Ct. App. 2000). The courts focus on the type of
More specific rule explains ⟶ use for which the land is suited and do not necessarily focus on the amount
the broad standard. of activity. *Id.*

Table 7.1-B shows graphically the relationship amongst the rules that define "actual possession."

Table 7.1-B · Relationship of rules that define "actual possession"

Adverse Possession **Governing rule**	Is established by proving **actual**, open, notorious, exclusive, hostile, and continuous **possession** for 10 years.	
Actual Possession	Is established by proving….	
Broad rule	Plaintiffs used the land as an owner would use that particular type of land.	Broad rule and sub-rules for one element
Sub-rule 1	Courts focus on whether the plaintiff's use conforms to the uses for which the land is suited.	
Sub-rule 2	Courts do not focus on the amount of activity or use on the land.	

To explain the rules, you must first identify the rules that will be relevant to your client's case.

II. Finding the Rules

As you research the law, you will look for those rules—both broad and narrow—that will determine whether an element or factor is present in your client's case. The rules will likely come from two places: statutes and case law. Sometimes a statute or case law will clearly state the rules that govern the element or factor you are analyzing. Those rules are called explicit rules. Other times, however, finding the relevant rules requires you to sift through case law and synthesize a rule. Those rules are called implicit rules. To explain the relevant law, you will need to gather together both explicit and implicit rules relating to the element or factor being explored. (As explained in Chapter 5, *Organizing Your*

Legal Authority, case charts can help you identify both explicit and implicit rules.)

A. Explicit Rules

Statutes and case law will usually explicitly state the standards that govern an element or factor. For example, in Example 7.1-C, a statute defines when a person is "stopped."

Example 7.1-C · A statute provides an explicit rule

A "stop" occurs if a person's liberty is restrained by a peace officer lawfully present in any place. Or. Rev. Stat. § 131.605(6) (2017).

Case law may then provide sub-rules that further define when that element is met, as in the next example, Example 7.1-D.

Example 7.1-D · Rules derived from a statute and case law explaining the statute

A "stop" occurs if a person's liberty is restrained, by physical force or a show of authority, by a peace officer lawfully present in any place. Or. Rev. Stat. § 131.605(6) (2017); *State v. Warner*, 901 P.2d 940, 942 (Or. Ct. App. 1995). A person's liberty may be restrained if an individual believes that his liberty has been restrained and that belief is objectively reasonable. *Warner*, 901 P.2d at 942. To determine whether a person reasonably believes his liberty has been restrained, a court will consider the totality of the circumstances. *State v. Wenger*, 922 P.2d 1248, 1251 (Or. Ct. App. 1996). If, under the totality of the circumstances, a person could not reasonably believe his liberty was restrained, the encounter is "mere conversation." *See, e.g., State v. Smith*, 698 P.2d 973, 975 (Or. Ct. App. 1985).

◄— Broad rule

More specific sub-rules explain the broad standard.

In the absence of a statute, case law may provide all the rules you need to explain an element, as in Example 7.1-E.

Example 7.1-E · Rules derived from case law only

Plaintiffs can establish actual possession by showing that they used the land as an owner would use that particular type of land. *Zambrotto v. Superior Lumber Co.*, 4 P.3d 62, 65 (Or. Ct. App. 2000). Courts focus on the type of use for which the land is suited and do not necessarily focus on the amount of activity. *Id.*

◄— Broad rule

◄— More specific sub-rule explains the broad standard.

Usually, you will find the necessary rules explicitly stated in a statute or case law; some rules, however, are not clearly stated but implicit in the courts' decisions.

B. Implicit Rules

When courts do not state explicitly the standard they used to conclude whether an element or factor is present, you will have to explain the standard by weaving together a rule from the cases you have read. When attorneys explain a standard that courts are relying on, but which is hidden within the case law, we call the standard an "implicit rule."

Experienced attorneys read cases with an eye toward making explicit what the courts are doing implicitly. An implicit rule can explain why courts consistently reach the same decision. It can explain why seemingly inconsistent court decisions are, in fact, consistent. And it can explain a new element or factor that courts will consider when reaching a conclusion.

1. When to synthesize an implicit rule

When the standard has not been explicitly stated, you will need to synthesize cases to find that implicit rule. When you synthesize a rule, you derive one rule by looking at the principles courts relied on in a series of cases. Let's look at the three typical circumstances in which an attorney might derive an implicit rule—that is, synthesize a rule—from a series of authorities.

> **Sidebar**
>
> Synthesizing means combining principles stated in a series of authorities to form one rule.

(a) Example 1: Finding an implicit rule from consistent decisions

Sometimes after reading a series of cases, you will see that every time a certain fact is present a court will usually reach a particular conclusion. This fact is a common denominator. If you see a common denominator in a series of cases, you should identify it for your supervising attorney.

Let's assume that you have just met with a client who owns a biotechnology company in Cary, North Carolina. His ex-business partner has started a blog and published false personal statements about him. The false statements have resulted in a significant loss of business. Your client wants to know whether he can sue for intentional infliction of emotional distress.

In North Carolina, the courts have established an explicit three-element test to determine when someone may be liable for intentional infliction of emotional distress.

Example 7.1-F · North Carolina's test for intentional infliction of emotional distress

---

In North Carolina, the elements of intentional infliction of emotional distress are "(1) extreme and outrageous conduct, (2) which is intended to cause and does cause (3) severe emotional distress." *Dickens v. Puryear*, 276 S.E.2d 325, 332 (N.C. 1981).

Even though North Carolina has an explicit governing rule, it turns out that the courts have not clearly defined the first element—when someone's conduct is extreme and outrageous. As a result, you will need to extract an implicit rule to define when someone's conduct is extreme and outrageous.

Two cases appear to be relevant to your client's question. Read the synopses of the two cases in Table 7.1-G, and see if you can determine a common denominator.

Table 7.1-G · Synthesize these cases

Case	Facts	Holding
Woodruff v. Miller, 307 S.E.2d 176, 178 (N.C. Ct. App. 1983).	Defendant posted copies of warrants on a wanted board to create the impression that plaintiff had broken the law and had not been punished.	Yes. Conduct was extreme and outrageous.
West v. King's Dep't Store, Inc., 365 S.E.2d 621, 623-25 (N.C. 1988).	A store manager repeatedly accused innocent customers of shoplifting in the presence of other store patrons.	Yes. Conduct was extreme and outrageous.

The common denominator you might identify is that in both cases (1) defendants made public accusations, and (2) defendants accused plaintiffs of socially unacceptable behavior. Based on those common denominators you could now create a rule, such as the one in Example 7.1-H.

Example 7.1-H · Synthesized rule

The business partner's statements in his blog likely constitute extreme and ◄— Conclusion about the element
outrageous conduct. A public accusation of socially unacceptable behavior is ◄— Synthesized rule
evidence of extreme and outrageous conduct. *See Woodruff v. Miller*, 307 S.E.2d
176, 178 (N.C. Ct. App. 1983); *West v. King's Dep't Store, Inc.*, 365 S.E.2d 621, 623-
25 (N.C. 1988). In *Woodruff v. Miller*, for example, the defendant posted copies ◄— Beginning of a case illustration
of warrants....

This new rule would be included in your explanation of the law describing when someone's conduct is extreme and outrageous, even though no court had ever explained it that way.

Relying on your own reading and understanding of cases to create a synthesized rule can be uncomfortable at first. This task is a major part of an attorney's work, and you will get more comfortable with this process as you gain experience in reading and understanding cases.

(b) Example 2: Finding consistency in seemingly inconsistent cases

Sometimes courts will reach opposite conclusions in cases that seem to have similar facts. When that occurs, do not immediately assume that the decisions are inconsistent. Rather, look for a reason why the courts came to opposite conclusions and explain that reason to your reader.

Even when court decisions *seem* inconsistent, attorneys nevertheless assume that the decisions *are consistent*. Stare decisis requires a court to reach the same decision as a prior court given similar facts. Therefore, if two courts come to different conclusions on cases with similar facts, attorneys assume a reasoned distinction exists to explain the different outcomes. Explaining that reasoned distinction will help the senior attorney with whom you are working.

Here is a second example of synthesizing a rule, but this time the synthesized rule identifies a reasoned distinction to explain why two cases reach opposite conclusions.

A client was out bicycling in Arcata, California, with her husband. She saw him round a curve, then heard a crash and a scream. When she rounded the curve, she saw her husband had been hit by a car. You would like to consider whether your client, the wife, can sue the driver for her emotional damages after seeing her injured husband. In California, a person who witnesses an accident to a family member can sue for emotional damages if, among other things, she was "then aware" of the injury to the family member.

You need to find out more about what it means to be "then aware" of the injury. You find two relevant cases that seem factually similar in that the plaintiff in neither case actually saw the accident or the injury to the family member. Yet, in the first case, *Krouse*, the court held that the plaintiff was "then aware" of the injury, and in the second case, *Fife*, the plaintiff was not "then aware." Look at the case excerpts in Table 7.1-I and think about how the cases can be reconciled.

Table 7.1-I · Reconcile these cases

Case	Facts	Holding
Krouse v. Graham, 137 Cal. Rptr. 863 (Cal. 1977).	A husband knew his wife was standing by the trunk of his car. In his rear view mirror he saw a car approach. He then felt his car being hit by the other car. The plaintiff admitted that he did not actually see the other car strike his wife.	Yes. The husband was "then aware" of the injury to his wife.
Fife v. Astenius, 284 Cal. Rptr. 16 (Cal. App. 4th Dist. 1991).	A father heard a crash and saw debris fly over a wall. The father rushed out to the street and within seconds discovered his daughter was in the car accident.	No. Father was not "then aware."

Looking for a reasoned distinction to explain the different outcomes, you might notice that in *Krouse* the plaintiff knew the family member was in the precise location of the accident and, therefore, knew that the family member was almost certainly in the accident. By contrast, in *Fife*, although the plaintiff knew of the accident, the plaintiff did not know the family member's location prior to the accident. You might synthesize a rule that explains that whether a person is "then aware" of an injury depends on knowing the family member's location at the time of the accident, as in Example 7.1-J.

Example 7.1-J · Synthesized rule explains seemingly inconsistent cases

Gabrielle Lafille has a strong argument that she was "then aware" of her husband's injury. For a plaintiff to be then aware, a plaintiff need not see the injury occur. *Krouse*, 137 Cal. Rptr. at 871. Rather a plaintiff is then aware of a family member's injury if she was aware of the accident's location and knew the family member was in exactly that location as the accident occurred. *Krouse*, 137 Cal. Rptr. at 871; *Fife*, 284 Cal. Rptr. at 18. In *Krouse*, the court held that the plaintiff was then aware of the accident that injured a family member....

← Conclusion about the element

← Synthesized rule begins explanation of the law

← Beginning of case illustration

The synthesized rule in Example 7.1-J (shaded) refines our understanding of when someone is "then aware" by explaining that the plaintiff does not need to see a family member get injured; rather, a plaintiff can prove she was then aware if she knew the family member's location and the location of the accident as it was occurring. By identifying a reasoned distinction, you will help your reader understand how courts reach their conclusions.

(c) Example 3: Bringing parts together to form a whole

Sometimes, over time, courts add to the requirements necessary to establish an element. When you describe the law, you may need to acknowledge the additional requirements in your rules. An Oregon court did just that when it explained Oregon's standard for determining whether a stop had occurred. In Oregon, a statute defines when a stop occurs, as shown in Example 7.1-K. According to the statute, a stop occurs when a police officer restrains a person's liberty.

Example 7.1-K · Statute defines element

A "stop" is a temporary restraint of a person's liberty by a peace officer lawfully present in any place. Or. Rev. Stat. § 131.605 (2017).

When the Oregon Court of Appeals later described when a stop occurs, it reviewed the relevant case law and added that a "restraint" may be by physical force or a show of authority (Example 7.1-L).

Example 7.1-L · Case law adds to statutory definition

A "stop" is a temporary restraint, whether by physical force or a show of authority, of a person's liberty by a peace officer lawfully present in any place. *State v.
Warner*, 901 P.2d 940, 942 (Or. Ct. App. 1995).

Thus, the court reviewed prior case law, determined that prior case law
added to the statutory definition of a stop, and the court included that
information in the rule so that the reader would have a concise, complete
definition of a stop in one place. In doing so, the court helped the reader
by establishing an explicit rule that combines the statutory rule with case
law.

2. Dare to explicitly state an implicit rule

New lawyers often get nervous about explaining implicit rules. New
lawyers feel safer putting in their arguments only the language that they
have seen in cases. But remember this: An attorney adds value by making
explicit those themes that would otherwise remain obscured in a morass
of case law.

To clarify case law and add value for your client, you must read the
case law at multiple levels. To do so, ask questions:

- What are the courts *saying* the rules are?
- What are the courts actually *doing*?

By comparing what the courts are *saying* the rules are with what the
courts are *doing*, you may see unexplained areas of the law. By looking
at what courts are doing over a series of cases, you may also see themes,
which when explained will clarify the standard courts are using to reach
a decision.

You will be more valuable to other attorneys you work with and to
your client if you can see and explain both the explicit and implicit rules
in the case law. So, when you see a theme in the case law that will help
explain how courts reach their conclusions, don't be shy, share it.

Now, that doesn't mean that you can put any old thing you want into
your rules. Remember, each rule must have a basis in the case law. Any
rule that you draw out of the cases must be consistent with all the other
law that bears on the issue, including other case law, statutes, and legislative
history.

Finally, although this section spends a lot of time discussing how to
extract implicit rules from the case law, please realize that courts are
usually explicit about the rules they are relying on, so you will not always
have to dig out the implicit rules. We have spent more time discussing
implicit rules simply because it is relatively easy to find explicit rules and
relatively difficult to find implicit rules.

III. Writing the Rules

· **Write about the rules as they are today, not how they developed**

The first trick to writing the rules is knowing that attorneys typically do not care how the rules came to be the rules. Nor do they care about the mental gymnastics you went through to synthesize a rule from case law. Attorneys simply care about the rules as they are today, the rules the courts will use when analyzing your client's case.

Compare the rules in examples 7.1-M and 7.1-N. Which is the better statement of the rules?

Example 7.1-M · Rules describe current law

The business partner's statements in his blog were likely extreme and outrageous conduct. A defendant's conduct is extreme and outrageous if the conduct exceeds "all bounds usually tolerated by decent society." *Stanback v. Stanback*, 254 S.E.2d 611, 622 (N.C. 1979) (citing Prosser, The Law of Torts § 12, at 56 (4th ed. 1971)). A public accusation of socially unacceptable behavior is evidence of extreme and outrageous conduct. *West v. King's Dep't Store, Inc.*, 365 S.E. 2d 621, 623-25 (N.C. 1988).

◄— Conclusion about the element
◄— Explanation of the law begins with this rule.
◄— Synthesized rule explains what courts look for to determine extreme and outrageous conduct.

Example 7.1-N · Text describes rules' development

The business partner's statements in his blog were likely extreme and outrageous conduct. A defendant's conduct is extreme and outrageous if the conduct exceeds "all bounds usually tolerated by decent society." *Stanback v. Stanback*, 254 S.E.2d 611, 622 (N.C. 1979) (citing Prosser, The Law of Torts § 12, at 56 (4th ed. 1971)). In *Woodruff v. Miller*, 307 S.E.2d 176, 178 (N.C. Ct. App. 1983), the Court of Appeals held that extreme and outrageous conduct existed when the defendant publicly accused the plaintiff of breaking the law. Several years later, in *West v. King's Dep't Store*, 365 S.E.2d 621, 623 (N.C. 1988), the Supreme Court, following *Woodruff*, held that the defendant's conduct was extreme and outrageous because he also made a public accusation of illegal behavior in the presence of others. These cases suggest that public accusations of illegal behavior are evidence of extreme and outrageous conduct. *See Woodruff*, 307 S.E. 2d at 178; *West*, 365 S.E.2d at 625.

The writer explains the historical development of the case law.

◄— Finally, the writer explains the point: the synthesized rule.

The first statement of rules in Example 7.1-M is a better statement because it focuses on the current rules that a court will use to make a decision. By contrast, Example 7.1-N explains how the rules came into being. Notice how much more concise and direct the first statement is.

Typically, novice legal writers explain the historical development of the case law to prove that a synthesized rule is true. More experienced attorneys have more confidence. They assert their synthesized rule as a correct interpretation of the law. If a reader questions the accuracy of the synthesized rule, the more experienced attorney knows that she has provided citations that will allow the reader to find the case law and verify that the synthesized rule accurately represents the law.

Transforming a novice historical explanation of the law to a more experienced assertion of a synthesized rule is often easy to do. Notice that at the end of the historical explanation of the case law in the second example you just read, Example 7.1-N, the writer does state the synthesized rule. Simply state that final point at the outset of the discussion, as is done in the first example, Example 7.1-M, and you will explain the rule more effectively and efficiently.

· Describe broad principles before narrower principles

When an explanation of the law involves a group of rules, attorneys tend to describe a broader rule before describing a more specific rule.

Look at the rules that define "actual possession" in Example 7.1-O.

Example 7.1-O · Moving from broad rules to narrow rules

The broad rule is described first. →

More specific sub-rules are described second. →

Plaintiffs can establish actual possession by showing that they used the land as an owner would use that particular type of land. *Zambrotto v. Superior Lumber Co.*, 4 P.3d 62, 65 (Or. Ct. App. 2000). Courts focus on the type of use for which the land is suited and do not necessarily focus on the amount of activity. *Id.* Plaintiffs in past cases have shown that they used the disputed land as an owner would in a variety of ways, including by using the disputed property as they did their own land, by building a fence, or even by planting vegetation. *See, e.g., Davis v. Park*, 898 P.2d 804, 806-07 (Or. Ct. App. 1995); *Slak v. Porter*, 875 P.2d 515, 518 (Or. Ct. App. 1994).

Notice how the opening rule—explaining that a plaintiff must "use the land as an owner would"—is very broad. The rules become more specific as the discussion progresses. The sub-rules explain specific ways in which an owner can use the land as an owner would, for example, by "building a fence" or "planting vegetation." Moving from broad to narrow rules makes the discussion clearer for your reader. (Other examples in this section also show explanations of the law in which the rules move from broader to narrower rules. See the rules defining a "stop" in Oregon, Example 7.1-D, and the rules defining intentional infliction of emotional distress, Example 7.1-M.)

· Build bridges

A reader needs to know how one rule relates to the next. To help your reader see how rules relate to each other, you can create "bridges" between rules. An easy way to create a bridge is by beginning the second sentence with an idea from the prior sentence.

Look at Examples 7.1-P and 7.1-Q, and determine how the bridge helps the reader.

Example 7.1-P · A bridge connects two rules

A court determines whether a person's liberty is restrained by asking whether the individual believes that his liberty has been restrained and whether that belief is objectively reasonable. *Id.* at 942. Whether the person's belief is objectively reasonable depends on the totality of the circumstances. *See State v. Wenger*, 922 P.2d 1248, 1251 (Or. Ct. App. 1996).

Example 7.1-Q · Two unconnected rules

A court determines whether a person's liberty is restrained by asking whether the individual believes that his liberty has been restrained and whether that belief is objectively reasonable. *Id.* at 942. Courts look at the totality of the circumstances. *State v. Wenger*, 922 P.2d 1248, 1251 (Or. Ct. App. 1996).

The first example, Example 7.1-P, includes a bridge. The bridge is the repetition of the phrase "belief is objectively reasonable" at the beginning of the second sentence. The repetition helps the reader see how the idea in the first sentence (that a person's belief must be objectively reasonable) is related to the idea in the second sentence (that courts consider the totality of the circumstances). In Example 7.1-Q, however, the reader must guess the connection between those two ideas.

Don't make your reader guess how two ideas are connected. Your reader may guess wrong. And even if your reader guesses correctly, your reader will have to pause to make her guess and then pause again to wonder if she guessed correctly. Your reader should not pause. Instead, your reader should be swept along by the clarity and force of your explanation.

· Use the present tense

Always describe rules in present tense. Rules are ongoing principles of law. They were applied to past cases and they continue to apply to current cases. The present tense captures the ongoing nature of rules.

· Quote sparingly

Quotes are no substitute for analysis.[2] Too many quotations imply that either the writer either did not understand the law well enough, or worse, the writer was too lazy or timid to explain it well.

Rather than quoting, consider what the court said and explain it in your own words. Save quotations for "key language"—that is, particular phrasing or terms of art that need to be conveyed precisely as they were in the original decision. Consequently, quote only the most important sentences or phrases, those that are critical to an understanding of the

---

2. Stated by former Oregon Supreme Court Justice W. Michael Gillette to one of the authors.

case. Although judicial decisions require some deference, you can often craft a better explanation of those relevant concepts than a court did.

· **Write for a non-lawyer**

As you write the relevant rules, pretend you are explaining the rules to someone who is not involved with the practice of law. That is to say, you should try to explain the law to someone you respect, and is intelligent, but who doesn't know this topic. If you imagine that you are explaining the rules to someone unfamiliar with the law, you will probably explain the sophisticated concepts simply, step-by-step, without missing a step in between.

Practice Points

- Begin your explanation of the law by describing the rules—the standards—courts use to test for the presence of an element or factor.

- Rules are usually *explicitly* stated in statutes and case law.

- Attorneys also derive rules by looking for themes in the case law. These rules are *implicit* rules, meaning that you have to synthesize and reconcile different judicial decisions and statutory language to determine the rule.

- Describe more general principles of the law before more specific principles.

- Create bridges between rules to help your reader see the relationship between rules.

Section 7.2

Explaining the Law:
Case Illustrations

I. The Role of Case Illustrations

While rules explain how courts determine whether a particular standard is met, "case illustrations" show how those standards were met in actual cases.

In an explanation of the law, rules are generally partnered with case illustrations. In the following example, Example 7.2-A, a broad rule defines "actual possession," one element in an adverse possession claim. That broad rule—that plaintiffs can prove actual possession by showing they used the land "as an owner would"—is partnered with two short case illustrations. The two case illustrations describe the specific facts that allowed plaintiffs in different cases to prove they "used the land as an owner would."

Example 7.2-A · Explanation of the law with rules and case illustrations

Conclusion about the element

Rules begin the explanation of the law.

Two case illustrations continue the explanation of the law.

Mr. and Mrs. Nero can most likely prove actual possession. Plaintiffs must establish actual possession by showing that they used the land as an owner would use that particular type of land. *Zambrotto v. Superior Lumber Co.,* 4 P.3d 62, 65 (Or. Ct. App. 2000). Courts focus on the type of use for which the land is suited and do not necessarily focus on the amount of activity. *Id.* Plaintiffs in past cases have shown that they used the disputed land as an owner would in a variety of ways. *See, e.g., Davis v. Park,* 898 P.2d 804, 806-07 (Or. Ct. App. 1995); *Slak v. Porter,* 875 P.2d 515, 518 (Or. Ct. App. 1994). **[1]** In *Davis v. Park,* the plaintiffs established that they used the disputed property as an owner would by showing that they used the disputed property as they did their adjoining land. 898 P.2d at 806-07. **[2]** In *Slak v. Porter,* the plaintiffs built a fence and planted vegetation and, in that way, proved actual possession. 875 P.2d at 518.

Case illustrations perform a variety of functions in your explanation of the law: They can clarify rules; they can prove that you described rules accurately; and they can foreshadow the analytical framework you will use when applying the rule to your client's case.

A. Clarifying Rules

First, case illustrations add clarity and precision to the reader's understanding of the rules. The rules describe general legal principles, but at some point your reader wants to visualize how those general legal principles actually function when applied to a real set of facts.

As an example, look back to the first example, 7.2-A, which addresses when a person "actually possesses" land. The rules explain that a person actually possesses land when a person "uses the land as an owner would." But what does it mean to "use the land as an owner would"? The rule is a general principle and, therefore, unclear. Details from prior cases reveal that building a fence and planting vegetation qualify as "using the land as an owner would." Concrete details from a prior case help your reader visualize how the general legal principle described in the rule functions in real life.

B. Proving Rules

Case illustrations also "prove the rule."[1] By showing how a past court applied the rule as you described it, a case illustration proves your description of the rule is accurate.

---

1. Richard Neumann explains that case illustrations "prove the rule" in his text *Legal Reasoning and Legal Writing: Structure, Strategy, and Style* 173 (7th ed. 2013).

In the actual possession example above, Example 7.2-A, the writer asserted that courts determine whether a plaintiff actually possessed land by looking at whether the plaintiff used the land as an owner would. The case illustrations that follow prove the accuracy of that rule by providing examples of cases in which courts concluded that using land like an owner—for example, by building a fence and planting vegetation—proved "actual possession."

C. Foreshadowing the Application

Case illustrations are also the reader's first look at how a court will apply the relevant rules to a client's case. Remember, again, stare decisis. A court deciding a case today must follow the reasoning of a prior case, if the case today raises the same issue. By choosing case illustrations that are factually similar to your client's case, your case illustrations will indicate how a court is likely to rule in your client's case.

Also, remember that case illustrations set up the framework you will use later when applying the rules to your client's facts. The important points you make in the illustrations will be made again later when you apply those points to your client's facts in the application section.

D. Representing Legal Principles

In each of these roles—whether they are clarifying rules, proving a rule is true, or showing how rules will apply in the future—case illustrations represent legal principles. Writing effective case illustrations requires you to stay focused on the legal principle that each case represents. As you are working with your case illustrations, you should ask yourself the following questions:

- *Why* am I describing this prior case?
- What *legal principle* does this prior case establish?
- How is the legal principle represented by this case *relevant to my client's case*?

Answering those questions is easier when you understand what goes into a case illustration.

II. The Parts of a Case Illustration

Typically, a case illustration has four components taken from a prior case: a hook, "trigger" facts, the court's holding, and the court's reasoning. Sometimes those parts overlap. Together, they will illustrate one principle in the rules you just described.

Example 7.2-B · Parts of a case illustration

Hook ⟶   A person may reasonably believe his liberty has been restrained if a police officer blocks that person's car. *Wenger*, 922 P.2d at 1251. In *Wenger*, the de-

Trigger facts ⟶ fendant was intending to leave a parking lot when uniformed officers parked

Reasoning ⟶ their patrol car and blocked in the defendant's car. *Id.* After noting that a stop occurs when an officer prevents a vehicle from being driven away, the court

Holding ⟶ held that the defendant reasonably believed his liberty had been restrained. *Id.* at 1251-52.

A. The Hook

The hook states the legal principle that the case illustration will clarify and prove to be true. The hook also tells the reader why she should keep reading.

You can create a hook in different ways. One way of creating a hook is to state a legal principle that can be extracted from multiple cases or from a single case, as in Example 7.2-B. In that example, the hook asserts that one legal principle derived from reading the *Wenger* case is that a person may reasonably believe his liberty has been restrained if a police officer blocks that person's car. The rest of the case illustration proves that the asserted principle is accurately stated and illustrates how that principle was applied in a particular case.

If using a legal principle as a hook, think about whether you should state the rule broadly or focus on a particular aspect of the rule. Consider keeping the rules in the rule section more general and using narrower, more specific rules extracted from the case illustration to introduce a case. Using a rule as a hook works especially well when you want to use more than one case to illustrate a legal principle.

A second way to create a hook is to state the court's holding. Using a holding as a rule works well when illustrating a single case. For example, the *Wenger* case illustration could be re-written, as in Example 7.2-C. In that example, the hook is the *Wenger* court's holding that the defendant's "liberty had been restrained." The hook says to the reader, "By reading this case you will learn the circumstances under which one court held that a person's liberty was restrained." When using a holding as a hook, though, focus on the general legal principle in the holding along with any key de-terminative facts. Avoid simply listing all the facts that led to the court's holding without reference to the legal principle. Listing a number of facts will make it more difficult for your reader to see the general legal principle that the case represents. When using a holding as a hook, although you might highlight key determinative facts or the single fact that was most important to the court's decision, as in Example 7.2-C, be sure the reader can also see the relevant rule that the court applied to the facts.

Example 7.2-C · Create a hook by using the court's holding

By contrast, in *Wenger,* the court held that the defendant reasonably be- ◄—— The hook introduces the case
lieved his liberty had been restrained when officers blocked in the defendant's   illustration by explaining the
car. 922 P.2d at 1252. In that case, the defendant was intending to leave a   court's holding.
parking lot when uniformed officers parked their patrol car such that it blocked
in the defendant's car. *Id.* at 1251-52. After noting that a stop occurs when an
officer prevents a vehicle from being driven away, the court held that the defendant reasonably believed his liberty had been restrained. *Id.*

Because the hook explains the relationship between rules and facts
in prior case law while focusing the reader's attention on the legal principle
being illustrated, the hook often distinguishes excellent legal writing and
analysis from serviceable legal writing and analysis.

B. Trigger Facts

Trigger facts are those facts that "triggered" a court's holding in a
prior case. These facts help the reader see *why* the court reached its conclusion. You might think of them as the facts that were "critical" or "key"
to the court's decision.

Many judicial opinions begin with a recitation of facts; however, to
determine the facts that triggered the court's holding, you should first
look at the court's analysis of the issue later in the opinion. What facts
did the court rely on when it reached its holding about the element or
factor you are examining? Those are the trigger facts.

Your case illustration may also need to include a fact because it is
necessary for your reader to understand the trigger facts. These additional,
contextual facts should be limited as much as possible. The more facts
you add, the more difficult it will be for your reader to distinguish the
important from the less important facts.

In the next example, 7.2-D, the trigger facts are shaded.

Example 7.2-D · Trigger facts

A person may reasonably believe his liberty has been restrained if a police officer blocks that person's car. *Wenger,* 922 P.2d at 1251. In *Wenger,* the defendant
was intending to leave a parking lot when uniformed officers parked their patrol ◄—— Trigger facts
car and blocked in the defendant's car. *Id.* After noting that a stop occurs when
an officer prevents a vehicle from being driven away, the court held that the defendant reasonably believed his liberty had been restrained. *Id.* at 1251-52.

C. The Court's Holding

The court's holding is another part of the case illustration. The holding describes the court's answer to one of the legal questions before it.

Remember that a single case may have many holdings. One case, for example, can have holdings about whether a person was "stopped," whether a person's "liberty was restrained," whether the person's belief that his liberty was restrained was "reasonable," and whether a person's car was "blocked." Explain the holding that is relevant to the legal idea you are illustrating. In Example 7.2-E, the court's holding is shaded.

Example 7.2-E · Court's holding

A person may reasonably believe his liberty has been restrained if a police officer blocks a person's car. *Wenger*, 922 P.2d at 1251. In *Wenger*, the defendant was intending to leave a parking lot when uniformed officers parked their patrol car and blocked in the defendant's car. *Id.* After noting that a stop occurs when an officer prevents a vehicle from being driven away, the court held that the de-

Court's holding ————▶ fendant reasonably believed his liberty had been restrained. *Id.* at 1251-52.

When writing your holding, you may sometimes want to consider the procedural posture of the court's decision, as in Example 7.2-F. Because many cases you will cite are appellate cases, you may want to consider whether the court (1) affirmed (in other words, said "Trial court, you got it right."); (2) reversed ("Trial court, you got it wrong."); or (3) reversed and remanded ("Trial court, you are wrong, and we are sending it back to you to fix it.").

Example 7.2-F · Case illustration includes procedural posture

A police officer may request information without restraining a person's liberty. *State v. Gilmore*, 860 P.2d 882, 883 (Or. Ct. App. 1993). In *Gilmore*, an officer requested identification from three people who were sitting in a truck. *Id.* When the defendant opened the glove compartment to retrieve his identification, the officer saw a gun and arrested the defendant for illegal possession of a firearm. *Id.* Although the defendant argued he had been illegally stopped and, therefore, evidence of the gun should be excluded from trial, the trial

Holding includes ————▶ court admitted the gun into evidence. *Id.* In upholding the trial court's deci-
procedural posture sion, the Court of Appeals explained that, even if the defendant felt he was not free to leave, that belief was not objectively reasonable. *Id.* The Court of Appeals explained that, although the officer requested identification, the officer did not require the defendant to alter his course, nor did the officer prevent the defendant from leaving. *Id.*

Including information about what the trial court did in your case illustration may depend on the point you are trying to convey. Although you may not always need this information, sometimes explaining what the higher courts did with a lower court's decision, and why, can be valuable information to your reader.

D. The Court's Reasoning

The court's reasoning is its explanation of how existing law, when applied to the facts, led the court to its conclusion. Sometimes, the court explains its reasoning fully. For example, the court might explain how the legislature's intent is guiding the court's decision.

Other times, a court simply states the relevant facts and the conclusion that results from those facts. In that case, you may have no separate description of the court's reasoning. You may be limited to simply describing the trigger facts and stating the court's holding based on those facts.

If you have a good guess at why the court reached its conclusion but the court has not been explicit, you can explain that as well, but you must indicate that this reasoning is your guess based on information from the case.

In Example 7.2-G, the court's reasoning is shaded.

Example 7.2-G · Court's reasoning

A person may reasonably believe his liberty has been restrained if a police officer blocks that person's car. *Wenger*, 922 P.2d at 1251-52. In *Wenger*, the defendant was intending to leave a parking lot when uniformed officers parked their patrol car and blocked in the defendant's car. *Id.* After noting that a stop occurs when an officer prevents a vehicle from being driven away, the court held that the defendant reasonably believed his liberty had been restrained. *Id.* at 1251.

← Court's reasoning

E. Order of the Parts

Your case illustration will be easiest for the reader to absorb if written in this order: the hook, trigger facts, and then the reasoning and holding.

The hook appears first because it focuses the reader's attention. By telling the reader which legal idea the case will illustrate, the hook tells the reader what to look for in the case illustration and makes it easier for her to absorb the detailed facts that follow.

Although the hook may appear first, it is often written last. Remember, writing clarifies thoughts. As you flesh out your legal argument, you will likely clarify in your own mind the precise legal idea the case illustration represents. Additionally, a well-written hook creates flow between legal concepts. You may craft and re-craft the hook so that your reader can see the connection between a previous legal principle you illustrated and the current legal principle being illustrated. No matter when you actually write the hook, it should appear first in your case illustration.

Next, describe the trigger facts. The reasoning and holding will not make sense until you have described the facts on which both are based.

Finally, finish the illustration with the reasoning and holding. Whether you end with the reasoning or end with holding does not matter. Attorneys write their case illustrations both ways. As you can see in Examples 7.2-H and 7.2-I, both ways can be effective.

Example 7.2-H · Holding is described after reasoning

A person may reasonably believe his liberty has been restrained if a police officer blocks that person's car. *Wenger*, 922 P.2d at 1251-52. In *Wenger*, the defendant was intending to leave a parking lot when uniformed officers parked their patrol car and blocked in the defendant's car. *Id.* After noting that a stop occurs when an officer prevents a vehicle from being driven away, the court held that the defendant reasonably believed his liberty had been restrained. *Id.* at 1251.

Example 7.2-I · Holding is described before reasoning

A person may reasonably believe his liberty has been restrained if a police officer blocks that person's car. *Wenger*, 922 P.2d at 1251. In *State v. Wenger*, the defendant was intending to leave a parking lot when uniformed officers parked their car and blocked in the defendant's car. *Id.* The *Wenger* court held that the defendant reasonably believed his liberty had been restrained. *Id.* at 1251. The court reasoned that a stop occurs, and a person's liberty is restrained, whenever an officer prevents a vehicle from being driven away. *Id.* at 1251-52.

After describing the court's holding, you may realize that you've described the court's holding twice—once as your hook and once to explain how the facts and reasoning led the court to its conclusion. While not required, stating the court's holding twice is fine. A statement of the court's holding at the top and bottom of a case illustration creates effective bookends that reinforce the point of the case illustration.

To avoid sounding repetitious, be sure not to repeat the holding verbatim. Sometimes you can vary the two sentences by adding more specific ideas to the final description of the court's holding, perhaps drawing on the court's reasoning, as in Example 7.2-J.

Example 7.2-J · Holding creates bookends

By contrast, in *Wenger,* the court held that the defendant reasonably believed his liberty had been restrained when officers blocked in the defendant's car. *Wenger,* 922 P.2d at 1251. In that case, the defendant was intending to leave a parking lot when uniformed officers parked their patrol car such that it blocked in the defendant's car. *Id.* at 1251-52. After noting that a stop occurs when an officer prevents a vehicle from being driven away, the court held that the defendant reasonably believed his liberty had been restrained. *Id.*

F. The Length of Case Illustrations

Although all case illustrations typically include the same four components—a hook, the trigger facts, the court's holding, and the court's reasoning—case illustrations vary in length. Some case illustrations, like the ones above, take several sentences to illustrate a legal concept. Others, as in Example 7.2-K, do the job in just one or two sentences. Still others require several paragraphs. The length of a case illustration depends on the legal principle the case is meant to illustrate, the information that needs to be included to illustrate that principle, and your ability to convey that information clearly and concisely.

Example 7.2-K · Case illustrations in a sentence or two

A plaintiff is "closely related" to a victim if the plaintiff resides in the same household as the victim. *Thing v. La Chusa,* 771 P.2d 814, 815 n.10 (Cal. 1989). In one case, a court decided that a cousin who lived with the victim every other weekend and for one month during the summer "resided" with the victim and was, therefore, closely related. *Tonia v. Giers,* 834 P.2d 42, 44 (Cal. Ct. App. 1993).

The first sentence is a rule that acts as the hook for the case illustration. The second sentence includes the trigger facts, the court's reasoning, and the holding.

III. Determining Whether a Case Illustration Is Necessary

Not all explanations of the law require case illustrations. To determine whether a case illustration is necessary, review the purposes for a case illustration and determine whether any of those purposes will be served.

One purpose of a case illustration is to clarify how a rule works. Sometimes, however, a rule is so clear that no further image is necessary. For example, a bystander can recover damages after seeing an injury to someone else if she is "closely related" to the victim. One way a bystander can prove she is "closely related" is to prove that she is the "parent, sibling, child, or grandparent of the victim." If your client is the daughter of the victim, you would not need to provide a case illustration for this rule. In explaining the law, you might state the rule expressed in Example 7.2-L. The rule states that children are "closely related." No case illustration is necessary for the reader to understand that a "daughter" is a "child."

Example 7.2-L · A rule that needs no case illustration

A person is closely related if she is the parent, sibling, child, or grandparent of the victim. *Thing v. La Chusa*, 771 P.2d 814, 829 n.10 (Cal. 1989).

If, however, the rule is more ambiguous, you might need a case illustration. Another way a person can prove she is "closely related" is to prove she "resides in the same household" as the victim. Imagine that your client is the niece of the injured party and that she lives with her aunt when she is home from college. In that case, your argument would rest on whether your client "resides in the same household" as the victim. That language is not so clear. In that case, you would need case law to determine whether living in the victim's home for only a few months a year establishes residency in that household. A case illustration, such as the one in Example 7.2-K, would be the best way to clarify how the rule really works.

A second purpose for a case illustration is to prove the rule is as you have described it. In some instances, a legal citation alone can sufficiently prove the rule is as you have described it. A legal citation tells an attorney the authority for your assertion and how to find that authority if he doubts the assertion. Thus, if no other reason exists for providing a case illustration, consider whether a legal citation will provide all the proof you need that the rule you have asserted is true.

A final purpose for a case illustration is to foreshadow how a court will decide the same legal issue in your client's case. If you have not relied on a case illustration when you apply the law to your client's case, consider whether the case illustration is really necessary to help your reader understand the law that will be relevant to your client's case.

In most instances, however, case illustrations are necessary to show how the rule functions. Omit them only when the rule standing alone is absolutely clear.

IV. Using Case Illustrations

When case illustrations are necessary, you can use them in a variety of ways. For example, case illustrations can establish "parameters of behavior" within which your client's conduct falls. A case illustration can also establish a "threshold of behavior" that your client's conduct must meet to satisfy a standard.

A. Parameters of Behavior

Case illustrations establish "parameters of behavior" by creating a spectrum of behavior within which a client's conduct falls. On one end of the spectrum, one case illustration establishes conduct that did meet the standard. On the other end of the spectrum, another case illustration establishes conduct that did not meet the standard. In most legal issues, your client's conduct will not clearly be on one side of the spectrum or the other. Instead, that conduct will likely fall somewhere in the middle.

For instance, let's say your client wants to sue for the civil tort of false imprisonment. One element of that tort is whether the defendant "confined" a victim. Visually, that spectrum of behavior looks like Figure 7.2-M.

Figure 7.2-M · Spectrum of behavior

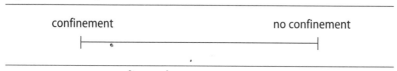

By presenting a case illustration of each parameter, you can effectively convey the scope of the rule to your reader. How has the writer shown the scope of the rule in the following example, 7.2-N?

Example 7.2-N · Case illustrations establish parameters of the rule

In this case, our client was confined. "Confinement" occurs when the victim is significantly deprived of freedom or the victim's personal liberty is obstructed for any length of time. *Garner v. State,* 500 S.W.2d 18, 20 (Tenn. Ct. App. 1997); *Cunningham,* 450 S.W.2d at 727.

[annotation: ◄— **Conclusion** about the element]
[annotation: ◄— **Rules** begin here]

While a defendant need not physically restrain a victim, the objective evidence must indicate that the victim was not free to exit the situation. *Blackmon v. State,* 362 S.W.2d 701, 703 (Tenn. Ct. App. 1997). For example, in *Garner,* the defendant, an accountant, kept his secretary standing in the corner of his office by swinging an antique baseball bat at her when she moved. 500 S.W.2d at 20. Even though she was only five feet from the door, the court held the defendant had "confined" the victim because an objective review of the facts showed she was not able to exit the situation. *Id.*

[annotation: ◄— A rule sets a parameter and acts as a hook for **case illustration 1**.]

On the other hand, a victim is not confined if the objective facts show the victim can freely leave. *Blackmon,* 362 S.W.2d at 703. In *Blackmon,* the defendant locked one of two doors to the warehouse loading area in which he and the victim were located. *Id.* Even though the defendant called the plaintiff his

[annotation: ◄— A second rule sets another parameter and acts as a hook for **case illustration 2**.]

"prisoner" while blocking the front entrance, the victim admitted she could have probably left from the rear door. *Id.* at 703-04. Based on her admission, the court determined she could not have felt her liberty was significantly obstructed and, therefore, ruled she was not confined. *Id.*

By establishing parameters of behavior, you will fully explain to the reader how the rule applied in previous cases, and you will prepare your reader to understand where your client's case falls within that spectrum.

B. Threshold of Behavior

Sometimes courts have not adequately established a spectrum of behavior, perhaps because the issue is relatively new or maybe because the case law itself is sparse. If a spectrum does not exist, examine whether the courts have at least determined the minimum floor of conduct necessary to meet the standard in the rule. Then, you can explain the rule by showing the reader the "threshold of behavior" necessary to satisfy the standard.

For example, imagine your client is sued under the Illinois Animal Control Act, which imposes civil liability on an animal's owner if the animal, without provocation, attacks a victim. Your client's prized cat scratched and injured a guest at the client's home. The guest claims the cat cornered her in the living room. The guest, believing the cat was about to attack, threw a decorative pillow at the cat. The cat then pounced on the guest, biting her arm and requiring the guest to get five stitches.

To recover under the Illinois statute, a plaintiff must prove that any provocation was in self-defense. Only one case in Illinois addresses the self-defense claim under the statute. Thus, although you cannot show a parameter of the rule in your case illustration, you can establish what threshold of behavior would satisfy the self-defense exception.

A diagram of that threshold of behavior may look like Figure 7.2-O. Next look at Example 7.2-P to see how the writer explained the case illustration.

Example 7.2-O · Threshold of behavior

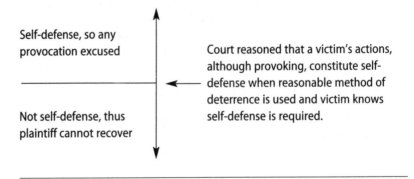

Self-defense, so any provocation excused

Court reasoned that a victim's actions, although provoking, constitute self-defense when reasonable method of deterrence is used and victim knows self-defense is required.

Not self-defense, thus plaintiff cannot recover

Example 7.2-P · Case illustration establishes threshold

Provocation will not be found when the victim acts in self-defense. *Steich-* ◄— Conclusion about the element
man v. Hurst, 275 N.E.2d 679, 681 (Ill. App. 2d Dist. 1996). In *Steichman*, a mail
carrier was attacked on her daily route by a ten-pound dog she knew to be ag-
gressive and that had harassed her on at least twelve occasions. *Id.* at 680. On
the day of the incident, the dog was growling and barking at her, and the mail
carrier sprayed it with an anti-attacking agent twice. *Id.* at 681. As she deliv- — Trigger facts and holding
ered the mail, the dog charged at her, and she again sprayed it. As the dog
tried to bite her leg, the mail carrier fell and was injured. *Id.* The court held that
the victim's actions were not provocation. *Id.* The court characterized the vic- Court establishes why this
tim's actions as self-defense, not provocation, for two reasons: First, the victim ◄— conduct meets self-defense,
knew that self-defense was required because the dog was known to be aggres- *i.e.*, the minimum threshold of
sive, had growled at her many times before, and was acting aggressively by behavior satisfying the self-
growling and barking at her moments before the attack. *Id.* at 681-82. Second, defense rule.
she chose a reasonable method to deter the dog from attack by using a commercial agent that was specifically designed to deter animals, and she used the
agent only after the dog acted aggressively.

The threshold of behavior is essentially one parameter of the rule.
If case law establishes opposite parameters, illustrate both sides; otherwise, frame the illustration as a threshold of behavior so your reader
can see the minimum level of conduct required to satisfy the rule.

As you develop more experience, you will see a variety of ways in which
cases can illustrate rules. Using case illustrations to establish parameters
of behavior or a threshold of behavior are two of the most common ways
to illustrate a rule. Using either of these methods, however, requires you
to choose the best cases to create parameters or establish a threshold.

V. Choosing Prior Cases

While researching an issue, you may find many cases that effectively
illustrate a rule. If you kept a case chart as you researched (*see* Chapter 5,
Organizing Your Legal Authority), you can quickly compare the cases you
found. Still, how do you choose which cases to include in your explanation
of the law? Table 7.2-Q provides guidelines.

Table 7.2-Q · Guidelines for choosing cases to illustrate

- **Choose cases from the governing jurisdiction.**
- **Choose factually analogous cases.**
- **Include both "good" and "bad" cases that are factually analogous.**
- **If two cases illustrate the same point, choose only one to discuss in a case illustration.**

- **Consider the date the case was decided.**
- **Do not include an illustration of a case just because you cited that case when you explained the rules.**

Let's look at each of these guidelines more closely.

Choose cases from the governing jurisdiction. If the rule needs to be illustrated, first look for cases from within the jurisdiction that will be binding. Consider the hierarchy of courts, and prefer cases that are binding on the court that will be reviewing your client's case. Supreme court opinions from the jurisdiction usually carry more weight than appellate or trial court decisions.

Choose factually analogous cases. From the cases that are binding, choose the case or cases that are most factually analogous to your client's case. Be careful when you do this. Determining whether a case is factually analogous requires you to determine which facts were relevant to the prior court's holding and then determine whether similar facts exist in your client's case.

If you cannot find any factually analogous cases in your jurisdiction but you can find a factually analogous case from another jurisdiction, you may consider including that case in your explanation of the law, but you should acknowledge that the case is only persuasive authority. Remember, you should go to an outside jurisdiction only when you have a "gap" in your jurisdiction's law or you are urging a change in the law. You should not jump to another jurisdiction without first addressing the relevant authority in your own jurisdiction.

Include "good" and "bad" cases that are factually analogous. Do not exclude a factually analogous case just because the court reached a holding that is bad for your client. Remember, your goal in writing an objective memo is to inform the attorney with whom you are working about the actual state of the law. Your office must advise your client in light of *all* the relevant law.

If two cases illustrate the same point, choose only one to discuss in a case illustration. The purpose of a case illustration is to show how a rule has been applied in the past and to prove your statement of the rule is accurate. You need to do that only once.

Some novice legal writers want to include all the relevant cases they have found to show that they have done thorough research and have carefully considered each case. Attorneys, however, prefer efficiency and do not want to spend time reading multiple cases that establish the same point. Consider Example 7.2-A, the first example used in this section. Although many cases showed that a plaintiff can establish actual possession by building a fence and planting vegetation, the writer describes only one such case, the *Slak* case. Having once described that a fence and vegetation will establish actual possession, the writer need not make that point again by describing additional cases that make the same point.

(Notice the distinction in using one case to establish a point versus using two cases to establish parameters of the rule. When establishing parameters, the two cases have different holdings based on different fact patterns and, therefore, establish different—although related—points.)

Consider the date the case was decided. Although you will not likely decide to use a case solely because of the date it was decided, sometimes the date may play a part in your case selection. Older cases may be better for illustrating a longstanding rule. Newer cases may be better for illustrating the rule because those cases have not been eroded over time. Even though the factual similarity of a case to your client's case may be more important than the date, you can use the date as a factor in your choice.

Do not include an illustration of a case just because you cited that case when you explained the rules. Rules and case illustrations serve different functions. Rules describe generally how a court decides the presence or absence of an element or factor. When describing the rules, cite the cases that best describe the rules. A case illustration shows how those rules were applied in a factually analogous case. When choosing a case illustration, choose the case that best illustrates the rules, whether or not you cited that case when you described the rules.

VI. Organize Around Legal Principles

At the beginning of this chapter, we pointed out that case illustrations represent legal principles. We have also explained that attorneys introduce case illustrations with a hook, which highlights the legal principle the case illustrates. If you do the same and introduce case illustrations with a hook, you will naturally organize your explanation of the law as an attorney should—around legal principles.

Too often, though, novice legal writers arrange their explanation of the law around cases, not legal principles. We call this arrangement the "case report model." The case report model is ineffective because attorneys are ultimately interested in the legal principle that the case represents. Accordingly, case illustrations should be written and organized to bring out the legal principles.

To see the difference, compare Examples 7.2-R and 7.2-S.

Example 7.2-R · Case illustrations organized around legal principles

In this case, our client was confined. "Confinement" occurs when the victim is significantly deprived of freedom or the victim's personal liberty is obstructed for any length of time. *Garner v. State,* 500 S.W.2d 18, 20 (Tenn. Ct. App. 1997); *Cunningham,* 450 S.W.2d at 727.

The hook identifies the important legal principle. → While a defendant need not physically restrain a victim, the objective evidence must indicate that the victim was not free to exit the situation. *Blackmon v. State,* 362 S.W.2d 701, 703 (Tenn. Ct. App. 1997). For example, in *Garner,* the defendant, an accountant, kept his secretary standing in the corner of his office by swinging an antique baseball bat at her when she moved. *Garner,* 500 S.W.2d at 20. Even though she was only five feet from the door, the court held the defendant had "confined" the victim because an objective review of the facts showed she was not able to exit the situation. *Id.*

The hook identifies the important legal principle. → On the other hand, a victim is not confined if the objective facts show the victim can freely leave. *Blackmon,* 362 S.W.2d at 703. In *Blackmon* the defendant locked one of two doors to the warehouse loading area in which he and the victim were located. *Id.* Even though the defendant called the plaintiff his "prisoner" while blocking the front entrance, the victim admitted she could have probably left from the rear door. *Id.* at 703-04. Based on her admission, the court determined she could not have felt her liberty was significantly obstructed and, therefore, ruled she was not confined. *Id.*

Example 7.2-S · A case report

In this case, our client was confined. "Confinement" occurs when the victim is significantly deprived of freedom or the victim's personal liberty is obstructed for any length of time. *Garner v. State,* 500 S.W.2d 18, 20 (Tenn. Ct. App. 1997); *Cunningham,* 450 S.W.2d at 727.

The hook focuses on the date of the decision. A better hook would focus on a legal principle from *Garner* that will be applicable to the client's case. → In 1997, the Tennessee Court of Appeals decided the *Garner* case. 500 S.W.2d at 20. In that case, *Garner,* the defendant, an accountant, kept his secretary standing in the corner of his office by swinging an antique baseball bat at her when she moved. *Id.* Even though she was only five feet from the door, the court held the defendant had "confined" the victim because an objective review of the facts showed she was not able to exit the situation. *Id.*

Again, the hook focuses on the date. A better hook would focus on a legal principle from *Blackmon* that will be relevant to the client's case. → That same year, the Tennessee Court of Appeals also decided the *Blackmon* case. *Blackmon v. State,* 362 S.W.2d 701, 703 (Tenn. Ct. App. 1997). In *Blackmon* the defendant locked one of two doors to the warehouse loading area in which he and the victim were located. *Id.* Even though the defendant called the plaintiff his "prisoner" while blocking the front entrance, the victim admitted she could have probably left from the rear door. *Id.* at 703-04. Based on her admission, the court determined she could not have felt her liberty was significantly obstructed and, therefore, ruled she was not confined. *Id.*

In Example 7.2-R, the first example above, the cases are organized around the parameters that establish when a person is confined. In other words, those cases are organized to show off the legal principles defining when someone is confined. Notice that in Example 7.2-R each hook announces an important legal principle from the case law.

The next example, Example 7.2-S, is a case report. It simply describes the cases, one after the next, without helping the reader to see the legal principle that each case represents. The case report model is ineffective because it forces the *reader* to do the hard work. It forces the reader to discern how the cases fit together in the body of law and what point each case is supposed to represent. Notice that in Example 7.2-S, each hook simply names the case and date when the case was decided. Neither hook tells the reader why the case is important. As a result, the reader must discern how the cases fit together and work to find the most important information—the legal principle that the case represents.

Of the two, Example 7.2-R, which is organized around legal principles, is more effective.

VII. The Order of Case Illustrations

If you need more than one case to illustrate a rule—for instance, if you are establishing parameters—you will have to decide in what order to describe those cases.

Although two cases might be reasonably similar to your client's case, you may decide that one case is more similar to your client's case, and, as a result, a court would be more likely to follow the reasoning in that case. If so, describe first the case that is most likely to determine the outcome.

Example 7.2-R illustrates this choice. In that example the attorney concludes that the client can prove he was confined. The attorney, therefore, describes first the *Garner* case, a case in which the defendant *had* confined the victim. Doing so indicates that the attorney believes his client's case is more like the *Garner* case than like the *Blackmon* case, which is described second. And it indicates that the attorney believes that, due to the similarity, a court will reach the same outcome in his client's case as in the *Garner* case.

Some novice legal writers think that either chronological order (to show the historical development of the case law) or reverse chronological order (to show the most recently decided case) is a good way to organize. As we discussed above, that is not so. Instead, organize by legal relevance. Organizing by legal relevance gets the reader to the most important cases quickly. To see the difference between ordering by chronology and ordering by legal relevance, go back and review Example 7.2-R and compare it to the explanation in 7.2-S. Which is more effective?

Remember, attorneys want to know the law that will apply to a client's case today. Usually, they do not care about how the law became what it is today. (The historical development of a rule is sometimes relevant to more complex analyses—analyses you are unlikely to see at the beginning of your career.) Instead, base the order of cases on their legal relevance to the point you are trying to prove.

VIII. Writing Case Illustrations

· Crop your case illustrations carefully

The value of a case illustration is that it allows the reader to visualize how a rule or a group of rules was applied to real life facts. The picture is important. Just as a good photograph often focuses on one simple focal point, a good case illustration includes only those facts that are relevant to the court's holding.

In Example 7.2-T, the case illustration is poorly cropped. The reader is forced to wade through details about the date and where the parking lot was located only to learn that those details (shaded) are not at all relevant to the holding. That unnecessary work is frustrating to the reader.

Example 7.2-T · Case illustration cropped poorly

In *Wenger*, on May 24, 1995, the defendant was parked in a parking lot at SE 67th and Foster. 922 P.2d at 1251. The defendant was about to leave the parking lot when officers parked their car in front of the defendant's car blocking in the defendant's car. *Id.* After noting that the Oregon Court of Appeals had previously held that a stop occurs when an officer prevents a vehicle from being driven away, the court held that because the officers blocked the defendant's exit, the defendant had been stopped. *Id.*

If a fact is described, the reader will assume that the fact is important and should be remembered. As a result, including non-critical facts creates problems. You will tax your reader as she struggles to determine whether each fact is actually important, and you will irritate your reader when she realizes that it is not. So, to the extent possible, include only those facts that are critical to a court's holding, as in Example 7.2-U.

Example 7.2-U · Case illustration cropped well

In *Wenger*, the defendant was about to leave a parking lot when officers parked their car in front of the defendant's car blocking the car in the parking spot. *Id.* After noting that a stop occurs when an officer prevents a vehicle from being driven away, the court held that the defendant had been stopped because the officers blocked the defendant's exit. *Id.*

- **Be specific and concrete about trigger facts**

Be detailed about facts that were critical to the court's holding. Details signal to the reader, "Hey! These are the important facts."

Details also allow the reader to visualize how the rule functioned in real life. To create that picture, you must be specific and detailed about the critical facts and the court's reasoning.

Compare Examples 7.2-V and 7.2-W below. Both case illustrations do the job; however, in the first example, 7.2-V, the writer blurs his description of the plaintiff's testimony, a fact critical to the court's holding. Example 7.2-W is better because it allows us to actually hear the testimony that the court heard. In addition, because Example 7.2-W is more specific, we can better gauge how similar or distinct our case might be from the example.

Example 7.2-V · Trigger fact is blurred

In a case where the plaintiff seemed uncertain about the property line, the plaintiff was not able to rely on the pure mistake doctrine to prove her possession of the property was hostile to the owner's claim. *Fisher v. Dean*, 3 P.3d 212, 214 (Or. Ct. App. 2000).

Example 7.2-W · Trigger fact described specifically and concretely

In a case where a plaintiff testified, "I didn't know where the true property line was located," she was not able to rely on the pure mistake doctrine to prove her possession of the property was hostile to the owner's claim. *Fisher v. Dean*, 3 P.3d 212, 214 (Or. Ct. App. 2000).

- **Blur non-critical facts that are necessary to tell the story**

Some non-critical facts, however, should be included because they are necessary to tell the story. For instance, in the case illustration above, (7.2-W), the writer describes the plaintiff's testimony. Notice, though, that the writer does not refer to the plaintiff as Dorothy Engelson. The plaintiff's name was not relevant to the court's holding. So, the writer blurs that detail.

The level of detail about a fact signals its relative importance. If a fact is described very specifically and concretely, the reader will assume that the fact is important and should be remembered. By contrast, if the fact is not critical but needs to be included, generalize the fact so that it will assume less importance.

- **Describe facts in chronological order**

Readers assume that a story will be told in chronological order and naturally read with that expectation. When you describe the trigger facts in your case illustration, you are telling a story about what happened in that case. As your reader reads the facts in your case illustration, she will assume that the story will be told chronologically. If you tell the story non-chronologically, you are apt to confuse your reader and cause her to stumble over your writing.

- **Use the past tense**

Case illustrations describe events in the past and are, therefore, always written in past tense. (By contrast, rules, which describe ongoing, current legal principles, are described in the present tense.)

Practice Points

- Case illustrations should identify a legal principle and allow the reader to visualize how that legal principle was applied to particular facts.

- Case illustrations have four parts: a hook, trigger facts, the court's holding, and the court's reasoning.

- The length and depth of case illustrations will vary.

- In choosing cases, you should consider whether the prior case is factually analogous, whether it illustrates a new idea, and whether it is from the governing jurisdiction.

- Organize your cases around currently applicable legal principles. Do not describe the historical evolution of those principles.

Explaining the Law: Citing and Avoiding Plagiarism

I. Citing

II. Avoiding Plagiarism

I. Citing

A citation is a reference to a legal authority or other source.[1] As you explain the law, you will need to provide a citation for each legal proposition.

A citation is all the proof you need that the legal proposition you have stated is true. So, go ahead. Be bold! Tell the reader what the law is in your own words. Then cite it. If the reader doesn't believe you, the reader can use your citation to find the legal authority and check the law for herself.

Two manuals explain how to cite properly. Those are the *ALWD Citation Manual* and *The Bluebook*.[2] Because both explain proper citation form in detail, we will not do so here. Certain questions do, however, pop up on a regular basis. Here are some frequently asked questions and the answers we give.

- **When I'm explaining the law, do I need to cite every sentence?**

Yes. When explaining the law, a good practice is to cite every sentence. Attorneys care about the law as it is expressed in statutes, case law, regulations, and legislative history, and they want to know where your explanation of the law came from. You will remove any question about the authority for your explanation of the law if you cite every sentence. Although not every individual or organization follows this rule, you can't

---

1. ALWD & Coleen M. Barger, *ALWD Citation Manual: A Professional System of Citation* (6th ed. 2017) (hereinafter *ALWD*).

2. *The Bluebook: A Uniform System of Citation* (Columbia L. Rev. Ass'n et al. eds., 20th ed. 2015) (hereinafter *Bluebook*).

go wrong with citing every sentence in the explanation of the law. *ALWD* Rule 43.2(a); *Bluebook* Intro. at 2.

- **Do any exceptions exist to the cite-every-sentence-in-your-explanation-of-the-law rule?**

Yes. A few exceptions exist. First, you can't cite a negative. At some point, you might need to say, "No court has examined [insert the unexamined issue or fact pattern here]." When no court has examined something, you can't cite to it.

Second, sometimes when you write you may summarize more detailed information that follows. For example, you may write, "Plaintiffs in past cases have shown that they used the disputed land as an owner would in a variety of ways." Then, in the sentences that follow you will explain the several different ways, and those sentences will be cited. Because the sentences that support your summary are cited, you don't need to cite the summary (Example 7.3-A).

Third, if you are following the ALWD Manual, one rule permits writers to omit the citation when all the sentences in one paragraph come from the same page or section in the same source. *See* ALWD Rule 34.2. However, this exception is a narrow one, so use this exception with care.

Example 7.3-A · Summary of law is not cited because supporting sentences are cited

---

Plaintiffs in past cases have shown that they used the disputed land as an owner would in a variety of ways. In one case, the plaintiffs established that they used the disputed property as an owner would by showing that they used the disputed property as they did their adjoining land. *Davis v. Park*, 898 P.2d 804, 806-07 (Or. Ct. App. 1995). In another case, the plaintiffs built a fence and planted vegetation and, in that way, proved actual possession. *Slak v. Porter*, 875 P.2d 515, 518 (Or. Ct. App. 1994).

Please remember that these are very small, narrow exceptions to the cite-every-sentence-in-your-explanation-of-the-law rule. As a general rule, cite every sentence in your explanation of the law.

- **If several different cases state the same principle, do I cite to all of the cases?**

No. When writing an objective memo, if several different cases make the same point, do not cite to all of them. Remember, the purpose of citing is to prove that the legal statement you just made is true. If the same legal principle is repeated over and over again in the case law, the legal principle is not controversial. Since no one is going to contradict a statement that is so often repeated, one citation to a case that states the legal principle will be sufficient to prove that what you have said is true.

If you want to show that the citation represents one of many cases that establish the principle, you can insert the signal "*e.g.*," which means "for example." *ALWD* Rule 35.3, 34.3(b); *Bluebook* Rule 1.2.

Example 7.3-B shows how to use the "*e.g.*" signal.

Example 7.3-B · The signal "*e.g.*"

Circumstantial evidence is admissible to establish a defendant's intent to rob a bank. *E.g., United States v. Buffington*, 815 F.2d 1292, 1302 (9th Cir. 1987).

- **If several different cases state the same legal principle, how do I choose the case to cite?**

Often an attorney will choose to cite the case that established the principle; a recent case or a case from the highest court, to show that the principle is still good law; or some combination. If you choose to cite to more than one authority, you will need to create a "string citation." See below, Example 7.3-C and accompanying text, for a discussion about string cites.

But for an oft-repeated legal principle, it does not matter which case you choose. Just choose one.

- **How do I cite to a synthesized legal principle?**

When you derive a single legal principle from more than one legal source you will need to rely on a string citation. A "string citation" is simply a citation that refers to more than one resource. In a string citation, semi-colons separate the authorities. *ALWD* Rules 36.1, 36.2; *Bluebook* Rule 1.4.

If you go back to Section 7.1, *Rules*, to the discussion about synthesized rules, you will see that each synthesized rule uses a string cite to show the cases that support the synthesized rule. One of those synthesized rules is in Example 7.3-C.

Example 7.3-C · A synthesized rule is supported with a string cite.

A public accusation of socially unacceptable behavior is evidence of extreme and outrageous conduct. *See Woodruff v. Miller*, 307 S.E.2d 176, 178 (N.C. App. Ct. 1983); *West v. King's Dep't Store, Inc.*, 365 S.E.2d 621, 623-25 (N.C. 1988).

- **What's a parenthetical? How do I use it?**

Attorneys include parentheticals to explain the relationship between the individual citation and the legal proposition in the text whenever the citation's relevance might not otherwise be clear to the reader. *See ALWD* 37.1 (discussing explanatory parentheticals); *Bluebook* Rule 1.5. In Example 7.3-D, the explanatory parenthetical is shaded.

Example 7.3-D · Parentheticals explain relevance of citations

---

The court held that the fence gave constructive notice even though the fence was not visible from the owners' land because the plaintiffs and neighbors respected it as the boundary line. *Id.; see also Slak,* 875 P.2d at 518 (holding that a fence gave notice and describing it as the "classic example" of open and notorious use).

Be careful not to overuse parentheticals. Some novice attorneys will attempt to explain an entire case illustration in a parenthetical. To test whether you are using parentheticals well, read your paper with all the explanatory parentheticals removed. If your paper explains your legal argument clearly without the parentheticals, you are using parentheticals appropriately.

- **How do I cite to a sentence that includes two legal principles from two different sources?**

It depends. If you can separate the ideas into two sentences, do that and cite each one. If not, use "citation clauses."

If you can separate the two legal principles into two sentences, you can use "citation sentences," as in Example 7.3-E. A citation sentence indicates that the entire prior sentence is supported by the citation that follows it. *ALWD* Rule 34.1(a); *Bluebook* Rules B2, 1.1(b)(i). The shaded citations in Example 7.3-E are referred to as citation "sentences" because the first letter of the citation is capitalized and the citation ends with a period, just like a sentence.

Example 7.3-E · Citation sentences support two distinct ideas

---

If the encounter is "mere conversation," then evidence acquired during the encounter is admissible against the defendant. *See, e.g., State v. Shelton,* 796 P.2d 390, 392 (Or. Ct. App. 1990). By contrast, if the encounter is a "stop," then any evidence obtained during the encounter is admissible only if the stop is justified by reasonable suspicion. *Spenst,* 662 P.2d at 6.

If you cannot separate the two principles into two separate sentences, you will have to use citation clauses. Citation clauses are used to indicate that only a portion of the previous sentence is supported by the citation. *ALWD* Rule 34.1(b); *Bluebook* Rule 1.1(b)(ii), B2. In Example 7.3-F, each citation clause is shaded. Notice that commas set off citation clauses, just like a clause in an ordinary sentence.

Example 7.3-F · Citation clauses supporting two distinct ideas

---

Citation clauses are set off by commas. Even the last citation has a comma before it, not a period. ⟶

Although evidence acquired during "mere conversation" is not admissible against the defendant, *see, e.g., State v. Shelton,* 796 P.2d 390, 392 (Or. Ct. App. 1990), evidence acquired during a legal stop is, *Spenst,* 662 P.2d at 6.

If you use citation clauses, be sure that you use a comma just before the final citation and not a period. You can see that the final citation in Example 7.3-F, *Spenst*, has a comma before it and not a period. As we explained above, a period before the *Spenst* citation would indicate that the *Spenst* case supported the entire previous sentence. A comma before the *Spenst* cite indicates that the *Spenst* cite is a citation clause and supports only the phrase before it.

Although you may use citation clauses, try to avoid them whenever possible. A citation clause places a citation in the middle of your sentence and will disrupt its flow. Whenever possible, if two distinct legal concepts come from two different sources, separate out the legal concepts so that you can use citation sentences, as in Example 7.3-E.

- **I want to cite a legal idea that I got from a case, but the case I read cites to another earlier case. Do I cite the case I read or the earlier case?**

Cite the case you read. Always. Ethical considerations require you to cite only those cases you have actually read. When you cite to a case, you are suggesting to your reader that you have read that case and you know what that case says. Moreover, it's prudent lawyering to cite only those cases you have read. You don't really know what a case says unless you go and read it. In sum, cite only cases you have read.

Of course, if the case you are reading incorporates an idea from an earlier case, that idea is now a part of the case you are reading, and you can cite to the case you are reading for that proposition.

If, however, the problem is that you simply want to cite the earlier case, the fix is easy: Go read the other case.

- **The case I have read quotes another case. How do I cite to a case that quotes an earlier case?**

This kind of citation is tricky. You can avoid the complicated citing by putting the quote into your own words, which will probably result in better writing.

If you really want to quote a case that is quoting another case, cite to the later case and in a parenthetical include a citation to the earlier case. Use double quotation marks around the words from the later case and single quotation marks around the quote from the earlier case, as in Example 7.3-G. If you want to quote a quotation, be sure to first read *ALWD* Rule 38.4(c) or *Bluebook* Rule 1.6(c).

Example 7.3-G · Quoting a quotation

A victim is confined when the victim is significantly deprived of freedom or "the victim's personal liberty is 'obstructed for any length of time.'" *Garner v. State*, 500 S.W.2d 18, 20 (Tenn. Ct. App. 1997) (quoted in *Cunningham v. Richards*, 450 S.W.2d 724, 727 (Tenn. 1994)).

- **I have stated the case name in a textual sentence. Do I need to repeat the case name in the citation that follows?**

If you provide the case name in the textual sentence, you may omit the case name from a subsequent short citation. *ALWD* Rule 12.16(c); *Bluebook* Rule B4. Example 7.3-H shows a short citation in which the case name is included in the textual sentence but omitted from the citation.

Example 7.3-H · A case name may be omitted in a short cite

Circumstantial evidence is admissible to establish a defendant's intent to rob a bank. *E.g., United States v. Buffington,* 815 F.2d 1292, 1302 (9th Cir. 1987). Testimony from co-conspirators is one type of circumstantial evidence that can establish a defendant's intent. *United States v. Snell,* 627 F.2d 186, 188 (9th Cir. 1984).

In *Buffington,* however, the Ninth Circuit held that the circumstantial evidence was insufficient to establish the defendant's guilt beyond a reasonable doubt. 815 F.2d at 1302.

Most citation manuals require that when a case is mentioned for the first time in a factual sentence, the name must be immediately followed by the citation, as in Example 7.3-I. Many attorneys believe that the embedded citation disrupts the flow of the text. Those attorneys will rewrite the sentence to avoid the embedded citation, as in 7.3-J. *See ALWD* Rule 34.1(c).

Example 7.3-I · *The Bluebook* requires citation to follow case name in a full cite

Circumstantial evidence is admissible to establish a defendant's intent to rob a bank. *E.g., United States v. Snell,* 627 F.2d 186, 188 (9th Cir. 1984). Testimony from co-conspirators is one type of circumstantial evidence that can establish a defendant's intent. *Id.*

In *Buffington v. United States,* 815 F.2d 1292, 1302 (9th Cir. 1987), however, the Ninth Circuit held that the circumstantial evidence was insufficient to establish the defendant's guilt beyond a reasonable doubt.

Example 7.3-J · Attorneys revise to avoid embedded citations

Circumstantial evidence is admissible to establish a defendant's intent to rob a bank. *E.g., United States v. Snell,* 627 F.2d 186, 188 (9th Cir. 1984). Testimony from co-conspirators is one type of circumstantial evidence that can establish a defendant's intent. *Id.*

Circumstantial evidence will not, however, establish guilt in all cases. *Buffington v. United States,* 815 F.2d 1292, 1302 (9th Cir. 1987). In *Buffington,* for example, ...

Ultimately, a citation should allow your reader to quickly identify and, if necessary, retrieve an authority. The formats described above meet those goals. If, however, your law office prefers a particular format, follow the custom of your law office.

II. Avoiding Plagiarism

A person plagiarizes by trying to pass off the words or ideas of another as one's own.

With proper citation, you need not be concerned about plagiarizing ideas from another authority. When you include a citation for every sentence in your explanation of the law, you are giving all the credit you need to for the legal ideas you are relying on.

Sometimes, though, a writer needs both a citation and quotation marks. Quotation marks signal that the writer has borrowed specific words and their unique sequencing. So, if you have appropriated not only a substantive idea, but also the unique sequencing of specific words, use quotation marks around the unique sequencing of specific words and a citation after the sentence.

As you read, you may notice that attorneys appropriate key legal phrases without providing quotation marks. For instance, an attorney might write that a police officer had "reasonable suspicion of criminal activity" without using quotation marks. The language (which is quoted in the previous sentence) is repeated so frequently that the language becomes, essentially, public language. By way of example, a quick search of federal cases showed that over the course of a year twenty-seven federal judicial opinions included that exact phrase, and none used quotation marks.

Pay attention to the cases you read. If a phrase repeats itself in many cases, you can likely use that phrase without quotation marks, but use a citation. The citation is necessary to show the source from which you drew the legal idea.

Chapter 8

Applying the Law

§8.1   Rule-Based Reasoning
§8.2   Analogical Reasoning
§8.3   Counter-Analyses
§8.4   Organizing Your Application of the Law

When you apply the law, you *finally* shift your argument to your client's case.
Up until this point you have explained the law relevant to an element or
factor within the governing rule. In explaining the law, you have chosen
the law that will be relevant to determining whether that element or factor
is present in your client's case. When you explained the law, however, you
focused solely on the legal authority; neither your client nor any of your
client's facts should have been mentioned in your explanation of the law.

Your client enters the picture when you apply the law. Applying the
law requires you to compare and contrast the relevant law with the facts
of your client's case to predict a particular outcome. An effective application
connects the dots between the law you just explained and your conclusion
about the element or factor being examined.

To support your conclusion, your application must examine both the
strengths *and* weaknesses of your argument. By being explicit about how
the law leads to an outcome and examining your argument's strengths
and weaknesses, you will persuade the attorney reading your memo that
your prediction is correct and well-founded in the law.

When you draft your application of the law, you will add no new
legal information. All the law relevant to your client's case should have
been presented first in the explanation of the law. In the application
section, you apply that law to the facts in your client's case to show why
a particular legal outcome is likely.

To effectively draft an application of the law, you will have to
understand the tools attorneys use to connect the law to a predicted
outcome and choose the most appropriate tool to use. Attorneys' tools
include rule-based reasoning and analogical reasoning. Both of these
tools can connect the law to your predicted outcome; however, each is
better suited to some circumstances than to others.

In the sections ahead, we will discuss how to use these tools to apply the law to your client's case and the circumstances in which each tool works most effectively. We will also use these same tools to construct counter-analyses. Finally, we will discuss how to organize the application of the law.

Applying the Law: Rule-Based Reasoning

I. When to Use a Rule-Based Argument

II. Crafting a Rule-Based Argument

The simplest analytical tool an attorney can use to predict an outcome is rule-based reasoning. When using rule-based reasoning to construct an argument, an attorney applies the language of a rule to a client's facts to predict an outcome.

Example 8.1-A illustrates rule-based reasoning by examining one element in a claim for negligent infliction of emotional distress. The short argument in Example 8.1-A addresses whether a boy, Jacob Tulchin, is sufficiently "closely related" to his biological mother, Addie Green, to recover for emotional damages after seeing her injured. The rule explains that a plaintiff is "closely related" if the plaintiff is the "child ... of the victim." The application of the law applies that rule and determines that the plaintiff is a "child" of the victim.

Example 8.1-A • Rule-based argument

Conclusion

Jacob Tulchin is "closely related" to his birth mother, Addie Green. To be closely related, the plaintiff must reside in the same household or be the parent, sibling, **child**, or grandparent of the victim. *Thing v. La Chusa,* 771 P.2d 814, 830 n.10 (Cal. 1989). Although Jacob Tulchin did not grow up in the same household as Addie Green, because he is her biological **child**, he is closely related to her.

Explanation of the law is one sentence: the relevant rule.

The application begins when the client is introduced. Although the explanation and application are in one paragraph, they are distinct sections. The application begins only after the explanation of the law is complete.

The final conclusion — that Jacob Tulchin will be considered closely related — is included in the same sentence that applies the law.

Rule-based reasoning is generally simple and straightforward, but you still need to know when to use this tool and how to use it well.

143

I. When to Use a Rule-Based Argument

When you turn to your client's case, you will have to decide whether to use rule-based reasoning or analogical reasoning to support your legal argument. The difference between the two is that rule-based reasoning relies on the language of a rule or group of rules to predict an outcome. By contrast, analogical reasoning relies on a comparison to prior case law to make a prediction.

Attorneys usually choose rule-based reasoning in two circumstances. First, when a rule is so clear that its application raises no questions, attorneys do not want to waste a reader's time with a lengthy comparison to prior case law. Therefore, they construct a quick and simple rule-based argument.

Second, attorneys choose rule-based reasoning when no analogous case exists. For example, if a new statute has not been interpreted or not frequently applied, relevant case law may not exist. Even in an area with well-developed case law, you may occasionally find that no court has considered a fact pattern like your client's fact pattern. In those circumstances, attorneys will rely on rule-based reasoning to make a prediction.

To help you decide whether to choose rule-based reasoning or analogical reasoning, look back to your explanation of the law. As we explained in Section 7.2, *Case Illustrations*, you do not always need a case illustration in an explanation of the law. If you have decided a rule is so clear that it does not need a case illustration, then you have decided a rule-based argument will be effective. If, however, you have decided a case illustration is necessary to explain the reasoning, then you will typically need to use an analogical argument. Section 8.2 discusses how to craft an analogical argument. The remainder of this section discusses how to craft a rule-based argument.

II. Crafting a Rule-Based Argument

While a rule-based argument is usually straightforward, crafting an effective one takes care. Two techniques will help:

- **Integrate key language from the rule into your analysis of your client's facts**

First, integrate the key language from the rule with your client's facts. Using language from the rule in your application will show how the law supports the outcome you have predicted.

In Example 8.1-A, the word "child" is borrowed from the rule and integrated with the client's facts to show how the rule will likely apply to the client's case. The repetition of the word "child" allows the reader to see how the rule relates to the client's facts.

Example 8.1-B shows an application in which the language of the rule is *not* integrated with the client's facts. When you read Example 8.1-B, you will see a slight gap in the logic that the reader must bridge.

Example 8.1-B · Rule's language is not integrated into application

Jacob Tulchin is "closely related" to his birth mother, Addie Green. To be closely related, the plaintiff must reside in the same household or be the parent, sibling, **child**, or grandparent of the victim. *Thing v. La Chusa*, 771 P.2d 814, 830 n.10 (Cal. 1989). Although Jacob Tulchin did not grow up in the same household as Addie Green, because he is her **biological son**, he is closely related to her.

Although in Example 8.1-B the reader can see the link between the law and the conclusion, the link is less obvious. As the reader begins to consider how the law will apply to the client's facts, the reader must take the word "biological son" and search for the word in the rule to which it connects. Although that search may take only a moment, the reader must stop and do some work. Even a momentary struggle to find a connection will interrupt the flow and force of your argument. By integrating the exact language of the rule with your client's facts, your application will be fluid and easy to follow. Your reader will quickly connect the dots.

• Be detailed about your client's facts

The second technique to creating an effective rule-based application is describing the facts in your client's case concretely and in detail. Specific, concrete facts are your proof that a legal standard is met. As a junior attorney working for a more senior attorney, your job is to inventory all the facts that the senior attorney might rely on to build an argument, should this client's case ever be litigated. Doing so keeps the senior attorney fully informed and will instill confidence in your work product. Look at Examples 8.1-C and 8.1-D. Which will better prepare the senior attorney to represent the client?

Example 8.1-C · Rule-based reasoning with generalized facts

Mr. Ciesick can prove the first element of a workers' compensation claim, ◄— Conclusion
that he subjectively believed his employer expected him to play in the company softball game. An employee can establish that he subjectively believed he ◄— Rule
was expected to engage in an off-duty recreational activity simply by stating, under oath, that that was his belief. *Aetna Cas. & Sur. Co. v. Workers' Compen. Apps. Bd.*, 232 Cal. Rptr. 257, 263 (Cal. App. 5th Dist. 1986).

Application begins when facts
Although he has not yet been asked to do so, Mr. Ciesick would be able to ◄— from client's case are intro-
testify to his belief that his employer expected him to play in the company softball duced.
game. His boss had told him that the softball games help build team spirit, and ◄— Writer sums up the facts. Thus,
the company CEO had asked him why he had missed a game. Based on those ex-   the reader's understanding of
changes, Mr. Ciesick can establish his belief that he was expected to play softball.   the facts supporting the conclu-
                                                                                 sion is less precise.

Example 8.1-D · Rule-based reasoning with specific, concrete facts

Conclusion → Mr. Ciesick can prove the first element of a workers' compensation claim, that he subjectively believed his employer expected him to play in the company

Rule → softball game. An employee can establish that he subjectively believed he was expected to engage in an off-duty recreational activity simply by stating, under oath, that that was his belief. *Aetna Cas. & Sur. Co. v. Workers' Compen. Apps. Bd.*, 232 Cal. Rptr. 257, 263 (Cal. App. 5th Dist. 1986).

Application begins here → when facts from client's case are introduced.

Although Mr. Ciesick has not yet been asked to do so, he would be able to testify to his belief that his employer expected him to play in the company softball game. In our interview with him, Mr. Ciesick stated that when he applied for his

Specific facts keep the senior → attorney fully informed and instill confidence in the novice attorney's work.

current position his future boss, Elizabeth Zimels, asked whether he played softball, and when Mr. Ciesick said that he did, his future boss responded "Good. That's how we build a team around here." When he missed one game, Louise Pearson, the company CEO emailed him to ask why he had missed the game and closed the email by writing, "Don't let us down again." Accordingly, Mr. Ciesick would be able to testify under oath that he believed his employer expected him to play in the company softball game.

Practice Points

- Use rule-based reasoning when the meaning of a rule is so clear that its application will raise no questions or when a comparison to a case illustration would not help explain how the rule applies in the client's case.

- In constructing a rule-based application, integrate key language from the rule with your client's facts so that you can show the reader how the rule supports the outcome you have predicted.

- In constructing a rule-based application, describe the facts from your client's case specifically and concretely to provide proof that the legal standard is met.

Applying the Law: Analogical Reasoning

Analogical reasoning is perhaps the attorney's most valuable analytical tool. When an attorney argues by analogy, she is establishing that the client's case is similar enough to, or different enough from, a previous case that the outcome in the previous case should control the present case.

The frequency with which an attorney reasons by analogy reflects the value our legal system places on stare decisis. If an attorney can establish that a client's case is factually similar to a prior, mandatory case, a court will be bound by the prior decision, and the attorney can predict an outcome. Likewise, if an attorney can establish that a client's case is distinguishable from a prior, mandatory case, a court will not be bound by that decision. So, although certainty in the law is rare, a clear analogy or distinction to a precedential case makes predicting an outcome in your client's case easier.

I. When to Use Analogical Reasoning

As we explained in Section 8.1, *Rule-Based Reasoning,* you will have to decide whether to use rule-based reasoning or analogical reasoning to support your legal argument. Between the two, attorneys most frequently choose to argue by analogy. Because analogical reasoning is powered by stare decisis and because stare decisis *requires* a court to reach a particular outcome, an analogical argument is most compelling to other attorneys. Although attorneys use rule-based reasoning when a rule is so clear its application raises no questions or when no analogous case exists, in most cases, a rule's application is not straightforward and relevant case law does exist. In those cases, argue by analogy.

Again, you can turn to your explanation of the law to help you decide whether to use analogical reasoning. If you need a case illustration to fully explain the law, you will need analogical reasoning to predict an outcome.

II. How to Construct an Effective Analogy

To construct a great analogy, you must remember one basic premise: Show your work. Do not assume that your reader is so knowledgeable or a conclusion is so obvious that you need not explain the steps by which you reached your conclusion. No matter how experienced your reader, you must explain step by step how a similarity to or a distinction from a prior case leads to a particular outcome.

Remember, the way you have applied a prior case to your client's facts may not be the only interpretation, and without *explicitly* walking the reader through your analysis and showing how the precedent supports your conclusion, you cannot assume that your reader will come to the same conclusion. Analytical writing is thus a lot like doing a math problem: If you show each step of your analysis, you get credit. Otherwise, you do not.

Typically, an effective analogical argument has three components, as explained in Table 8.2-A.

Table 8.2-A · Components of an effective analogical argument

1. **A sentence telling the reader the point the analysis will prove.**

2. **A fact comparison establishing a similarity to or distinction from a prior case.**

3. **An explanation of the legal consequence of the similarity or distinction. In other words, explain why the comparison matters.**

You can use the three components whether you are arguing that your client's case is similar to or distinguishable from a prior case. In Example 8.2-B, an attorney uses the three components to argue that a prior case is similar, and therefore a similar outcome is warranted in the client's case. In the next example, Example 8.2-C, an attorney uses those same three components to distinguish a prior case and argue that, therefore, the prior case does not control the outcome. Following the examples, we'll look at each component more closely.

Example 8.2-B · An analogical argument proves a legally significant similarity

The Neros can likely show constructive notice because they built a fence ◄— The point of the analysis.
and planted vegetation. Like the fence in the *Davis* case, the Neros' fence ◄— Fact comparison establishes
marked the purported property line that was respected by the Neros and their factual similarity.
neighbors. In addition, the Neros' fence was always visible from the western
lot, even when they allowed the garden to return to its natural state. Because
the non-visible fence in *Davis* provided constructive notice, the Neros' visible ◄— The legal consequence of the
fence should provide notice, too. similarity is explained.

Example 8.2-C · An analogical argument proves a legally significant distinction

Even though Officer Ephgrave's car did block Mr. Adams's car, a court is ◄— The point of the analysis.
likely to distinguish Mr. Adams's case from the *Wenger* case. In the *Wenger* ◄— Fact comparison shows a
case, the court noted that the defendant was intending to leave at the time his distinction.
car was blocked. By contrast, Mr. Adams told Officer Ephgrave that he was
"going to sit a little while longer," suggesting that he was not intending to
leave. Because he was not intending to leave, a court is less likely to con- ◄— The legal consequence of the
clude that Mr. Adams reasonably felt his liberty was restrained. distinction is explained.

A. State Your Point

The first sentence of an analogical argument should tell your reader the primary point the analogy will prove. Stating the point serves two purposes: First, it quickly establishes the bottom line. Legal reading is not like reading a mystery novel with a surprise ending. Attorneys are busy people. They want to know the outcome *now*. Second, readers absorb more details when they know where an argument is going. By stating the point first, readers will know as they read *why* the details matter.

One way to state the point of an analogy is to state whether the legal standard has been met and identify the prior case and key fact that led to that conclusion, as in Example 8.2-D.

Example 8.2-D · The point of the analogy identifies key fact, prior case law, and standard that is met

The Neros' fence is like the fence in *Davis* and will provide constructive ◄— The first sentence explains that
notice. Like the *Davis* fence, the Neros' fence marked the purported property the point of the analogy is to
line that was respected by the Neros and their neighbors. In addition, the Neros' prove that, because of the
fence was always visible from the western lot, even when they allowed the gar- fences in both cases, the client
den to return to its natural state. Because the non-visible fence in *Davis* pro- can establish the element at
vided constructive notice, the Neros' visible fence should provide notice, too. issue—constructive notice.

As your case comparisons become more complex, however, you may find it difficult to include all the information shown in Example 8.2-D. In that case, you can simply scale back your first sentence.

For instance, you can state the point by concluding whether the standard has been met and identifying just the key fact that leads to that conclusion, as in Example 8.2-E.

Finally, you can simply state whether a particular standard is met, as in Example 8.2-F.

Example 8.2-E · The point of the analogy identifies a key fact and standard that is met

The first sentence explains that the point of the analogy is to prove a particular legal outcome. It also identifies the fact that will trigger the outcome.

➤ **The Neros can show constructive notice because they built a fence.** Like the fence in the *Davis* case, the Neros' fence marked the purported property line that was respected by the Neros and their neighbors. In addition, the Neros' fence was always visible from the western lot, even when they allowed the garden to return to its natural state. Because the non-visible fence in *Davis* provided constructive notice, the Neros' visible fence should provide notice, too.

Example 8.2-F · The point of the analogy identifies the element that is met

The first sentence simply explains that the point of the analogy is to prove a particular legal outcome.

➤ **The Neros can show constructive notice.** Like the fence in the *Davis* case, the Neros' fence marked the purported property line that was respected by the Neros and their neighbors. In addition, the Neros' fence was always visible from the western lot, even when they allowed the garden to return to its natural state. Because the non-visible fence in *Davis* provided constructive notice, the Neros' visible fence should provide notice, too.

All of the examples showing how to state your point are effective. The difference lies in how much information each communicates. Choosing how much information to include is a judgment call. Typically, a reader can easily absorb between twenty and twenty-five words per sentence, so you will have to balance the information you would like to convey against your reader's ability to absorb it and draft accordingly.

B. Construct Your Comparison or Distinction

Establishing that your case is factually similar to or distinguishable from a prior case is the heart of a case comparison; it determines whether stare decisis will apply to control a legal outcome. Constructing an effective factual comparison requires both analytical precision and organized writing.

These five pointers will help you create an effective factual comparison: (1) Determine which facts make your client's case similar to or distinguishable from the prior case; (2) describe the facts from your client's case in concrete detail; (3) determine the depth of detail necessary to describe the facts from the prior case, and describe those; (4) introduce no new information about the prior case; and (5) help your reader see the comparison.

1. Determine which facts make your client's case similar to or different from the prior case

To determine which facts make your client's case similar to or distinguishable from a prior case, you must review the legally significant facts in both the prior case and your client's case. Begin by reviewing your case illustration to see the trigger facts and reasoning that you said led a prior court to its conclusion. Then, review your client's case. Determine which facts in your client's case are similar to or distinguishable from the trigger facts that led the prior court to its conclusion. You will likely find that some of your client's facts are similar to the facts in the prior case and some of your client's facts are distinguishable.

Now, you must decide. On balance, are the facts in your client's case sufficiently similar to the trigger facts in the prior case? Or, are the facts in your client's case, on balance, distinguishable from the trigger facts in the prior case?

If you decide that your client's case is more like than unlike the precedent case, you will rely on those similar facts to make an analogy and argue that a similar outcome should result. Your analogy will focus on only those facts that are similar to the trigger facts in the precedent case. If additional facts in your client's case would also contribute to the same outcome but were not considered by the court in the prior case, incorporate those into your argument, but do so after you have constructed your comparison showing a similarity.

If you decide that your client's case is not like the precedent case, you will rely on the facts that establish a difference to distinguish your client's case from the prior case and argue that the prior case should not be followed. Your comparison will rely on only those facts that suggest the cases are distinguishable.

Whether you decide that your case is similar to or distinct from the prior case, a few facts may weigh in the opposite direction. For the moment, put those facts aside. You will address them in a separate counter-analysis (Section 8.3, *Counter-Analyses*).

Now that you have determined whether your client's case is similar to or distinct from a prior case and identified the facts on which that comparison will be built, you will begin constructing your fact-to-fact comparison.

Sidebar

All cases differ factually in some ways. When analogizing cases, focus on the legally significant facts in the precedential case — those that triggered an outcome in the prior case. Look to see whether your client's case includes facts that are similar to the trigger facts in the precedential case.

2. Describe facts from your client's case in concrete detail

When constructing a case comparison, you should *always* describe facts about your client's case. Your description of your client's facts is your reader's chance to visualize how the law applies to your client. For your reader to clearly see how the law acts upon your client, you must describe the facts of your client's case specifically and concretely.

Compare Examples 8.2-G and 8.2-H. In each, the facts of the prior case are in bold and the facts of the client's case are shaded. Can you see the difference between a comparison that uses concrete details and one that does not?

Example 8.2-G • Client's facts described in a generalized way

---

Point of the analysis. ——————→   Gabrielle Lafille will probably be able to prove she was "then aware" of her

Facts of the prior case are
compared to client's facts ——→
to establish a similarity.
husband's accident. Her situation is similar to the situation in *Krouse*. **In *Krouse*, a husband knew where his wife was standing and heard and felt the impact of the accident come from that location.** Similarly, in our client's

Legal consequence of ——————→
similarity is explained.
case, Ms. Lafille could perceive the accident even though she did not see it. Because the *Krouse* court determined that the plaintiff was then aware, a court should also determine that Ms. Lafille was then aware.

Example 8.2-H • Client's facts described specifically and concretely

---

Gabrielle Lafille will probably be able to prove she was "then aware" of her husband's accident. Her situation is similar to the situation in *Krouse*. **In *Krouse*, a husband knew where his wife was standing and heard and felt the impact of the accident come from that location.** Similarly, in our client's case,

Facts of the prior case are ——→
compared to client's facts
to establish a similarity.
Ms. Lafille knew her husband was just around the bend in the road and heard the sounds of the accident come from that location. Because the *Krouse* court determined that the plaintiff was then aware, a court should also determine that Ms. Lafille was then aware.

---

3. Determine the trigger facts from the prior case that need to be recalled

Although the facts of your client's case *must* be described as specifically and concretely as possible, you will have to judge the appropriate depth of detail with which to describe facts from the prior case.

The facts from the prior case may not need to be described in as much detail because you will have already described those facts in a previous case illustration. Thus, the depth of detail with which you describe facts from the prior case will depend on your assessment of your reader's ability to remember your earlier description.

Whether your reader can remember the details about the prior case will depend on the distance between your case illustration and the point in your application when you apply it. The more space between description and comparison, the less likely your reader is to remember the details and the more important it will be to remind your reader of them so the reader can see the exact comparison that you do.

Examples 8.2-I and 8.2-J show how as the space between the case illustration and your comparison to it increases, so does the depth of detail. If your case comparison directly follows your description of the case illustration, your reader will recall the case illustration, and you can construct your comparison with a less explicit reference to facts from the prior case, as in Example 8.2-I.

Example 8.2-I • Case illustration immediately followed by application: reader can see comparison with few details from prior case

One circumstance under which a person may reasonably believe his liberty has been restrained is if a police officer blocks a person's car. *Wenger*, 922 P. 2d at 97. In *Wenger*, the defendant was about to leave a parking lot when officers parked their car blocking the defendant's car. *Id.* at 96-97. The *Wenger* court held that the defendant had been stopped because the officers blocked the defendant's exit. *Id.* at 97. The court reasoned that a stop occurs whenever an officer prevents a vehicle from being driven away. *Id.*

Explanation of the law provides case illustration of the Wenger *case.*

In this case, Paul Adams could not reasonably believe that his liberty was being restrained because his exit was not blocked. Unlike the defendant in *Wenger*, Mr. Adams was not prevented from leaving when the officers blocked his car. Although Officer Ephgrave blocked Mr. Adams's car, Officer Ephgrave asked Mr. Adams if he was planning to leave. Mr. Adams said he was not. In addition, Officer Ephgrave said that he would move his car if Mr. Adams wanted to leave. Thus, although the court in *Wenger* determined that the defendant reasonably felt his liberty was restrained when the officer blocked his car, Mr. Adams will probably not be able to prove that he felt his liberty was restrained when Officer Ephgrave parked behind his car.

Comparison established without any description of the facts in Wenger.

The writer judges that due to the proximity of the case illustration and the simplicity of the case, the reader can remember the facts from Wenger *that make the cases similar.*

If, however, your explanation of the law is more complex and involves more cases illustrations, your comparison to any one case will necessarily be further from your initial description of it. In that case, you need to refresh your reader's memory so that she can see the same comparison that you do. You can do so by explaining the facts from the prior case in more detail, as in Example 8.2-J.

Example 8.2-J · Application does not immediately follow case illustration: trigger facts from prior case described in more detail

One circumstance under which a person may reasonably believe his liberty has been restrained is if a police officer blocks a person's car. *Wenger*, 922 P. 2d

First case illustration ⟶ at 97. In *Wenger*, the defendant was about to leave a parking lot when officers parked their car blocking the defendant's car. *Id.* at 96-97. The *Wenger* court held that the defendant had been stopped because the officers blocked the defendant's exit. *Id.* at 97. The court reasoned that a stop occurs whenever an officer prevents a vehicle from being driven away. *Id.*

Second case illustration ⟶ In addition, a person may reasonably believe his liberty has been restrained
(drawn from same case) if a police officer alters that person's course of conduct. *Id.* at 97. In *Wenger*, the undercover officer identified himself as an officer and then later placed his hand on the defendant's shoulder and directed the defendant away to question him. *Id.* The court noted that a stop may also occur when an officer requires a defendant to alter his course. *Id.* The court held that the officer's actions of placing his hand on the defendant's shoulder and directing the defendant away also supported the trial court's conclusion that a stop had occurred. *Id.*

In this case, Paul Adams could not reasonably believe that his liberty was being restrained. First, his exit was not blocked. While the defendant in

Facts from prior case ⟶ *Wenger* was prevented from leaving when the officers blocked his car, Officer
described in more detail Ephgrave did not prevent Mr. Adams from leaving, despite blocking Mr.
because writer judges that due Adams's car. Officer Ephgrave asked Mr. Adams if he was planning to leave. Mr.
to the space between the initial Adams said he was not. In addition, Officer Ephgrave said that he would move
description of the facts and the his car if Mr. Adams wanted to leave. Thus, although the court in *Wenger* deter-
comparison, the reader will mined that the defendant reasonably felt his liberty was restrained when the
need a more specific reminder officer blocked his car, Mr. Adams will probably not be able to prove that he felt
to be able to see the similarity his liberty was restrained when Officer Ephgrave parked behind his car.
between the two cases.

If in doubt about how much detail to include, err on the side of caution and add more detail. Analogies that seem obvious to you may not be obvious to your reader. If more detail might clarify the analogy and make less work for your reader, include it.

4. Introduce no new information about the prior case in your analogy

Attorneys expect the explanation of the law to set forth all of the law relevant to analyzing an element or factor. So, in your explanation of the law, you should include all the information about a prior case that you will need to analyze an element or factor. If you do not include all the necessary information in your explanation of the law and your application includes new information, you will surprise and likely confuse your reader. Because all the prior case law should have been cited in the application, you do not usually need to provide citations in the application of the law.

5. Help your reader see the comparison

After you identify the trigger facts in both your client's case and the prior case that you want to compare, you must help your reader see the similarity or distinction that you do. Often, two facts may seem so patently similar that no explanation is necessary. Usually, that is not so. Rarely are the facts of a current case identical to the facts of a prior case. When a difference exists, you need to help your reader see why, despite that difference, the facts are analytically equivalent.

You can do this by using one or more of the following techniques: bringing your facts together, stating explicitly why facts are similar or distinguishable, using parallel structure, and comparing facts only to facts.

One way to help your reader see the analytical equivalence between two sets of facts is to simply write the facts so that the facts are physically close to each other on the piece of paper. Compare Examples 8.2-K and 8.2-L. In both examples, the facts from the prior case are in bold, and the facts from the client's case are in gray. In Example 8.2-K, the facts are far apart. In Example 8.2-L, the facts are brought together. Can you see how the proximity helps the reader see the similarity?

Example 8.2-K • Distance makes comparison more difficult to see

---

The Neros can prove that they had actual possession of their land because they used the disputed property in a manner that an owner would. **The plaintiffs in *Slak* showed actual possession by building a fence and planting vegetation**. Based on those facts, the court determined that the Slaks had established actual possession. In our client's case, the Neros should also be able to show actual possession because they built a fence, kept a garden, and maintained an orchard.

Example 8.2-L • Proximity makes comparison easier to see

The Neros can prove that they had actual possession of their land because they used the disputed property in a manner that an owner would. Like **the plaintiffs in *Slak* who built a fence and planted vegetation**, the Neros built a fence, kept a garden, and maintained an orchard. Therefore, like the plaintiffs in *Slak*, the Neros should be able to prove actual possession.

Although proximity will help, proximity by itself will not always draw out the similarity between facts. In Example 8.2-M, can you see how, despite the proximity of the facts, the similarity is more difficult to see?

Example 8.2-M · Similarity not explained despite proximity

The Neros can prove that they had actual possession of their land because they used the disputed property in a manner that an owner would. **The plaintiffs in *Slak* built a fence and planted vegetation.** The Neros kept a garden, maintained an orchard, and built a fence. Therefore, like the plaintiffs in *Slak*, the Neros should be able to prove actual possession.

- **State explicitly why facts are similar or distinguishable**

Another way to help your reader see a similarity or distinction is to state the similarity or distinction overtly. Read examples 8.2-N and 8.2-O. Does the overt explanation of why the cases are similar help the reader understand the analysis?

Example 8.2-N · Fact comparison without an overt statement of the similarity

Facts of the prior case are compared to client's facts to establish a similarity.

Ms. Gabrielle Lafille will probably be able to prove she was "then aware" of her husband's accident. **In *Krouse*, a husband knew where his wife was standing and heard and felt the impact of the accident come from that location.** Similarly, in our case, Ms. Lafille knew her husband was just around the bend in the road and heard the sounds of the accident come from that location. Since the *Krouse* court determined that the plaintiff was then aware, a court should also determine that Ms. Lafille was then aware.

Example 8.2-O · Fact comparison supported by overt statement of the similarity

Overt statement of similarity →

Facts compared →

Legal consequence of similarity explained →

Ms. Gabrielle Lafille will probably be able to prove she was "then aware" of her husband's accident. Her situation is similar to the situation in *Krouse*. In both cases the family member could perceive the injury to the victim at the time of the accident, even though the family member could not see the accident occur. **In *Krouse*, a husband knew where his wife was standing and heard and felt the impact of the accident come from that location.** Similarly, in our case, Ms. Lafille knew her husband was just around the bend in the road and heard the sounds of the accident come from that location. Since the *Krouse* court determined that the plaintiff was then aware, a court should also determine that Ms. Lafille was then aware.

The overt statement (underlined) is simply a statement that is true about both cases. Similarly, you can overtly state a distinction, as in Example 8.2-P.

Example 8.2-P · Distinction stated overtly

In this case, Paul Adams could not reasonably believe that his liberty was being restrained. <u>First, his exit was not blocked.</u> **While the defendant in *Wenger* was prevented from leaving when the officers blocked his car,** Officer Ephgrave did not prevent Mr. Adams from leaving, despite blocking Mr. Adams's car. Officer Ephgrave asked Mr. Adams if he was planning to leave. Mr. Adams said he was not. In addition, Officer Ephgrave said that he would move his car if Mr. Adams wanted to leave. Thus, although the court in *Wenger* determined that the defendant reasonably felt his liberty was restrained when the officer blocked his car, Mr. Adams will probably not be able to prove that he felt his liberty was restrained when Officer Ephgrave parked behind his car.

Overt statement of distinction that will be proven is underlined.

• **Use parallel structure**

Using a parallel structure can also help your reader see the similarity and distinctions that you do. Sentences are "parallel" when they use the same grammatical structure. Parallelism helps show relatedness of ideas.

In Example 8.2-Q, the comparison uses parallel structure to help the reader see the similarity between two cases. The same ideas labeled 1, 2, and 3 are used to describe both the prior case and the client's case. The writer also sequences the ideas in the same order and uses the same language to further emphasize the similarities between the cases.

Example 8.2-Q · Parallel structure reinforces similarity

The Neros can prove that they had actual possession of their land because they used the disputed property in a manner that an owner would. **[1]** Like the plaintiffs in *Slak* who **[2]** showed actual possession by **[3]** building a fence and planting vegetation, **[1]** the Neros should also be able to **[2]** show actual possession because they **[3]** built a fence, kept a garden, and maintained an orchard.

1. Parties identified
2. Holding explained
3. Facts on which holding is based explained

The repetitive structure subtly reinforces that the two cases are similar. Look what happens in Example 8.2-R when parallel structure is not used: the ideas become difficult to follow.

Example 8.2-R · Ideas more difficult to follow when you don't use a parallel structure to reinforce similarity

The Neros can prove that they had actual possession of their land because they used the disputed property in a manner that an owner would. **[1]** Like the plaintiffs in *Slak* who **[2]** showed actual possession by **[3]** building a fence and planting vegetation, **[1]** the Neros **[3]** built a fence, kept a garden, and maintained an orchard and should, therefore, also **[2]** be able to prove actual possession.

1. Parties identified
2. Holding explained
3. Facts on which holding is based explained

Notice how 2 and 3 are in a different order in the two halves of the comparison.

The beauty of parallel structure is that, typically, your reader is not particularly aware of the parallelism or its influence; however, by using the same language in the same pattern to describe two distinct cases you will subtly lead your reader to the conclusion that the two cases are really the same.

Parallel structure can also be used to emphasize a distinction, as in Example 8.2-S.

Example 8.2-S · Parallel structure used to emphasize distinction

1. Parties identified

2. Similar fact 1

3. Similar fact 2

The description of the holding is not in parallel structure, which is appropriate because the writer is asserting that the holdings differ.

The Neros' claim is distinguishable from the claim in *Hoffman*. Where **[1]** the plaintiffs in *Hoffman* could not prove hostility because **[2]** they had not built the fence and **[3]** the fence did not run along the border of their property, **[1]** the Neros **[2]** built their fence, and **[3]** they built it along the northwest border of their property. Based on these differences, a court should not follow the *Hoffman* case.

A parallel structure can also be used with other techniques. In Example 8.2-T, the writer states the similarity overtly and then uses a parallel structure to draw out the similarity to a prior case. Can you see how the ideas listed below are described for each case in the same order?

Example 8.2-T · Overt statement of similarity, facts in close proximity, and parallel structure establish similarity

Fact comparison begins with an overt statement of the similarity, then facts in close proximity and in parallel structure.

Legal consequence of similarity explained.

Mr. Morgan will probably not be able to prove he was "then aware" of his mother's accident. His situation is similar to the situation in *Fife*. In both cases, the plaintiffs discovered that a family member was injured a few moments after the accident occurred. **[1] In *Fife*, [2] after hearing the sounds of a car crash, [3] the plaintiffs had to climb a fence before they could discover that a family member was injured.** Similarly, **[1]** in our case, **[2]** after hearing the sounds of an accident, **[3]** Mr. Morgan had to run around a bus before he discovered that his mother had been injured. In *Fife*, the seconds delay meant that the plaintiffs were not then aware. Because Mr. Morgan was also delayed in learning that his mother was injured, a court should also hold that Mr. Morgan was not then aware.

• Compare like items

When structuring your comparison, make sure that you are comparing like items. For example, you should compare a case to a case and a fact to a fact. Do not compare a fact to a case name, as in Example 8.2-U.[1]

---

1. The "apples to oranges" analogy in Example 8.2-U is taken from Alan L. Dworsky, *The Little Book on Legal Writing* 62 (Fred B. Rothman & Co. 1992).

Example 8.2-U · Comparing apples to oranges

Like *Pankrantz,* Daniel enticed the spouse by sending her cards and letters.

The writer does not mean that the defendant, Daniel, is like the *Pankrantz* case.[2] Rather, he means to say that the defendant Daniel is like the defendant in the *Pankrantz* case, as in Example 8.2-V. Be precise about the facts you are comparing.

Example 8.2-V · Comparing apples to apples

Like the defendant in *Pankrantz* who frequently plied the wife with phone calls and flowers, Russell enticed the spouse by sending her cards and letters.

C. Explain Why the Comparison Matters

After every comparison you write, your reader will have one question: "So, what?" Your supervising attorney will want to know exactly what the comparison means to the client's case. Thus, after you have helped your reader to see the analogy that you do, you must also concretely and unequivocally explain to the reader why that comparison is important. Giving a great comparison without explaining its legal significance is like stealing the basketball then missing the lay up. In either situation, you score no points for the hard work you have put in.

In Examples 8.2-B, 8.2-C, 8.2-G, 8.2-O, and 8.2-T above, we used arrows to show where the writer explained the significance of the comparison. Go back and look at those examples. Can you see how the writer has, in each instance, explained why the comparisons are significant? In doing so the writer explains "so what" and completes the analogy.

III. Using Analogical and Rule-Based Reasoning Together

Although analogical and rule-based reasoning are two different tools, they can be used within the same argument. Doing so draws on the strengths of each.

The great strength of a rule-based argument is that it is simple. It draws on only the facts of your client's case and the language of the rule.

---

2. The authors would like to thank Professors Laura Graham and Luellen Curry of Wake Forest University School of Law who developed the alienation of affection memo problems and materials from which this example and some examples in Chapter 13, *Questions Presented and Brief Answer,* are based.

Such an argument focuses the reader's attention on the most important aspects of your analysis—your client and the principles of law. Such an argument is simple and straightforward. Analogical reasoning, although more complex than rule-based reasoning, draws on stare decisis and therefore creates a more powerful argument.

You can, however, draw on the strengths of both by using analogical reasoning to support a rule-based argument. You can see this approach in Example 8.2-W. In that example, the writer begins with a rule-based argument. Doing so presents the argument simply and directly. That argument is then supported by analogies to prior case law. Can you see both tools at work in the example?

Example 8.2-W • Rule-based and analogical reasoning used to support argument

Conclusion

> The Neros will very likely be able to prove their hostility to other claims of ownership through the doctrine of "pure mistake." Under the doctrine of pure mistake, they can prove their hostility through evidence that they honestly believed they owned the disputed property. *Hoffman,* 994 P.2d at 110 n.4. A "pure" mistaken belief is one without conscious doubt. *Faulconer,* 964 P.2d at 252. If plaintiffs are aware that they may not own the disputed land, conscious doubt exists, and the plaintiffs cannot prove hostility by "pure mistake." *Id.*

Rules are explained first. Notice how the shaded language is integrated into the rule-based application below.

> In *Davis,* the plaintiffs proved pure mistake by establishing that they had walked the fence line before buying the land, and as a result, they honestly and reasonably believed the fence line to be the property boundary. 898 P.2d at 805, 806. However, in a case where a plaintiff testified that "she was in doubt as to the location of the true [property] line," she was not able to rely on the pure mistake doctrine to prove her possession of the property was hostile to the owner's claim. *Mid-Valley Resources,* 13 P.3d at 122.

Then, two cases—*Davis* and *Mid-Valley*—illustrate the parameters of the rule.

The application of the law begins here. This first part uses **rule-based reasoning**. It applies the language of the rules to the client's facts.

> The Neros will be able to prove that they honestly believed that they owned the disputed property and, therefore, that their use was "hostile." The Neros toured the property before making the purchase and believed from the statements of the realtor that their property line was different from where it actually was. In addition, the Neros did not have any conscious doubts regarding their belief. In explaining her problem, Mrs. Nero exclaimed, "[T]hat's part of our land!" She was convinced that the disputed property belongs to her and her husband and unaware of any alternative claims. Thus, the Neros are like the plaintiffs in *Davis* who toured the property and had an honest and reasonable belief that the fence was the property line and unlike the plaintiffs in *Mid-Valley* who were in doubt as to the location of the property line. Accordingly, the Neros should be able to prove their hostility through pure mistake.

To support the rule-based reasoning, above, the writer does two quick **comparisons**. The comparisons can be quick because the client's facts have already been described in the first part of the application.

The same argument can, however, be presented through analogical reasoning alone, as in Example 8.2-X.

Example 8.2-X · The same argument presented through analogies

---

The Neros will be able to prove that they honestly believed that they owned the disputed property and, therefore, that their use was hostile. The Neros, like the plaintiffs in *Davis*, toured the property before making the purchase and believed from the statements of the realtor that their property line was different from where it actually was. The Neros also did not have any doubts regarding their belief, unlike the plaintiff who testified in *Mid-Valley Resources*. In explaining her problem, Mrs. Nero exclaimed, "[T]hat's part of our land!" She seemed convinced that the disputed property belongs to her and her husband. The Neros made a reasonable and honest mistake regarding the boundary line; therefore, the Neros should be able to prove that, by pure mistake, their possession of the land was hostile.

◄— Analogy 1 (to *Davis*)

◄— Analogy 2 (to *Mid-Valley*)

The argument that relies on both rule-based and analogical reasoning (Example 8.2-W) is not stronger or weaker than the argument that relies on analogical reasoning (Example 8.2-X). Both are strong because both are supported by stare decisis.

Because both present strong arguments, you can decide which format to use based on what will work best in a given context. Consider the legal authorities you are working with, the facts of your client's case, and the preferences of your reader. Then experiment with each form to decide which format will present your argument most effectively.

Practice Points

- An effective analogical argument should contain a point sentence, a fact-to-fact comparison or distinction, and an explanation of the legal consequence.

- When constructing a fact-to-fact comparison, use specific, concrete facts from the prior case and from your client's case.

- To help your reader see the comparisons or distinctions, you can bring the facts from both cases close together, explicitly state the comparison, and use a parallel sentence structure.

- An effective legal analysis may be constructed with rule-based reasoning, analogical reasoning, or a combination of both. You will use analogical reasoning when a direct application of the rule alone would not be clear or no applicable case law exists.

Applying the Law: Counter-Analyses

I. The Role of a Counter-Analysis

To develop a thorough legal argument you must keep an old adage in mind: "Every story has two sides."

When you initially apply the law to your client's facts, you address only one side of the story. That application of the law sets forth the argument you believe a court is most likely to adopt, and you temporarily ignore any alternative perspective that might lead to a different outcome.

The counter-analysis, on the other hand, considers the alternative perspective. It brings to light interpretations of fact and law that might result in an outcome different from the one you predicted.

The purpose of providing a counter-analysis is to explain the best opposing arguments to the attorneys with whom you are working. By understanding the strongest arguments on either side of an issue, attorneys can properly plan their strategy, whether that strategy is to continue litigation or to seek a settlement.

II. Crafting a Counter-Analysis

An effective counter-analysis should do three things: First, a counter-analysis must explain the opposing argument. Then, it must explain why a court is less likely to adopt that analysis. Finally, the counter-analysis must return to your initial conclusion so that the reader has no doubt as to what you believe is the most likely outcome to the argument. The rest of this section explains each of those steps in turn.

A. Explain the Opposing Argument

To explain the opposing argument effectively, you will need to first imagine what the opposing argument might be. Opposing arguments usually develop because people can reasonably differ about how to understand the facts of a case, the law, or how the law applies to the facts. You should consider these possible different interpretations to evaluate whether viable opposing arguments exist.

Once you have identified one or more viable opposing arguments, then you must provide sufficient information for the senior attorney to see why the opposing argument is viable. You will, therefore, need to flesh out the opposing argument in the same way you fleshed out your primary argument. Doing so will allow your reader to see the opposing argument in its full strength.

Example 8.3-A shows how you can use the same skills to present both your primary analysis and your counter-analysis. In Example 8.3-A, the writer considers whether Mr. Bigelow can sue his friend, Mr. Theoroc, after Mr. Bigelow was injured when he was about to board Mr. Theoroc's raft for a weekend rafting trip.

Example 8.3-A • Explaining the opposing argument

A court will likely dismiss Mr. Bigelow's suit against our client, Sam Theoroc. A guest being transported without payment is barred from bringing an action for damages against the owner or operator of a watercraft, unless the accident is caused by gross negligence, reckless disregard, or intoxication. Or. Rev. Stat. §30.115 (2017). The policy behind the statute is to protect a host from liability when offering transportation to another in a spirit of hospitality. *Jewett v. Kosydar*, 512 P.2d 995, 997 (Or. 1973). Mr. Bigelow has not alleged that there was payment or that Mr. Theoroc was grossly negligent, reckless, or intoxicated. Therefore, the only question is whether Mr. Bigelow was being "transported" at the time of the accident.

Beginning of legal argument ➔ about "transportation."

Mr. Theoroc has a strong argument that Mr. Bigelow was being "transported" at the time of his accident. In determining when transportation begins, courts have relied on the underlying policy of the statute, which is to limit actions against a host. *See, e.g., Jewett*, 512 P.2d at 996-97. Thus, "transportation" begins as soon as the gratuitous undertaking has begun, which is when the plaintiff is in the process of entering the vehicle. *Kruse v. Fitzpatrick*, 563 P.2d 680, 682 (Or. 1997).

The plaintiff need not be wholly within the vehicle for the transportation to have begun. *Jewett*, 512 P.2d at 996-97. For example, in *Jewett*, the plaintiff had put one foot into a car when the driver's foot slipped off the brake. *Id.* The car jumped forward, and the plaintiff was injured. *Id.* Although the plaintiff was not wholly within the vehicle at the time of the injury, the court reasoned that because the plaintiff had taken a step into the car, the gratuitous undertaking had begun. *Id.* Because the gratuitous undertaking had begun, the plaintiff was being transported at the time of the injury and was, therefore, barred from making a claim. *Id.* In reaching this conclusion, the court noted that the purpose of the statute was to protect from liability "one who, in a spirit of hospitality, offers transportation to another." *Id.* at 997.

On the other hand, transportation has not begun if a plaintiff has not yet made voluntary contact with the vehicle. In *Kruse*, the plaintiff was walking in front of a car and heading toward the passenger door. *Kruse,* 563 P.2d at 683. The driver's foot slipped off the brake, and the car struck the plaintiff. *Id.* at 682. The court reasoned that because the plaintiff had not made voluntary contact with the car prior to the injury and was still able to change her mind about whether to be transported, she was not in the process of entering the car and the gratuitous undertaking had not begun. *Id.* at 683. She was, therefore, not yet being transported and was not barred from bringing a claim. *Id.*

Mr. Theoroc can establish that Mr. Bigelow was being transported at the time he was injured. **[1]** This case is similar to the *Jewett* case. **[2]** Just as the gratuitous undertaking in *Jewett* had begun when the plaintiff was stepping into the car, here a court is likely to conclude that the gratuitous undertaking had begun because Mr. Bigelow was stepping into the raft. **[3]** If the court concludes that the gratuitous undertaking had begun, Mr. Bigelow, like the plaintiff in *Jewett*, will be barred from bringing a claim against Mr. Theoroc.

[1] Mr. Bigelow will, however, argue that he was injured before he made contact with the raft, and therefore, transportation had not begun. **[2]** Specifically, Mr. Bigelow will point out that he was injured because the raft moved away from the dock. Thus, he never actually entered, or even made contact with, the raft. Based on these facts, Mr. Bigelow will argue that he is like the plaintiff in the *Kruse* case who never actually entered the car but was struck by the car while passing in front of it. In both cases, the plaintiff made no voluntary contact with the vehicle. **[3]** Therefore, Mr. Bigelow will argue, he, like the plaintiff in *Kruse*, should be permitted to bring suit.

Mr. Bigelow's argument has two significant weaknesses. First, his case is factually distinct from *Kruse*. The *Kruse* plaintiff was injured in front of a car, and she could have changed her mind about the transportation before entering the car. Mr. Bigelow, however, was injured while stepping off of the dock; he was not in a position to change his mind about entering the raft. Whether the plaintiff had an opportunity to change her mind was at the crux of the *Kruse* court's decision. Therefore, Mr. Bigelow's inability to change his mind should lead a court to a different conclusion.

In addition, allowing Mr. Bigelow's claim to proceed to trial would run counter to the policy behind the statute. As mentioned above, this state's courts have consistently stated that the purpose of the statute is to protect hosts who have offered hospitality. Relying on that policy, the courts have

Application addressing whether Mr. Bigelow was "transported" begins here.

The application begins with the author's primary analysis—the analysis the writer believes the court will adopt.

After explaining the primary analysis, the writer explains the counter-analysis.

Notice that the primary analysis (the comparison to *Jewett*) and the counter-analysis (the comparison to *Kruse*) use the same structure to flesh out the argument for the senior attorney.

Each argument (1) states the point of the comparison, (2) establishes a factual similarity, and (3) explains the consequence of the similarity.

After explaining both analyses, the writer explains two reasons why the court will ultimately adopt the primary analysis.

construed the statute to limit suits against hosts who have offered hospitality. Thus, if a court must choose between construing the statute to allow Mr. Bigelow's claim to proceed, or to construe the statute to protect a host who has offered hospitality, a court is likely to protect the host and dismiss the suit.

The writer returns to the ultimate conclusion. →

Accordingly, a court is likely to conclude that Mr. Bigelow was being transported at the time of his accident and that, therefore, he cannot bring a claim against Mr. Theoroc.

Notice that in Example 8.3-A the primary analysis and the counter-analysis use the same structure to flesh out the argument. Both analogical arguments (1) state the point of the analysis, (2) establish a similarity, and (3) state the legal consequence. The same structure is used because the counter-analysis should be fleshed out as thoroughly as the primary analysis. Only by fleshing out each argument can the senior attorney truly understand and compare the strength of each argument.

Example 8.3-B provides another example of a counter-analysis. In that example, the issue is whether a falafel stand is a "building" under the terms of the deed restriction. That example presents two possible counter-analyses, one of which relies on a rule-based argument and the other of which relies on an analogical argument. Again, look to see how the same skills that would be used to build a primary analysis are used to build the counter-analysis.

Example 8.3-B · Another explanation of the opposing argument

A court is unlikely to hold that the deed restriction, which prohibits our client, Ms. Izaguirre, from "build[ing] any building on" the property, also prohibits our client's falafel stand. When construing a deed restriction, the language of a restriction is given its "ordinary and common" meaning. *Corley v. Olsson*, 134 S.E.2d 45, 48 (Fla. 2003). However, when in doubt as to the meaning of a restriction, the restriction is narrowly construed such that doubts are resolved "in favor of the free use of the land." *Id.* This state has not interpreted the noun "building" or the verb "to build" in the context of a deed restriction. However, given the common and ordinary meaning of the words and the policy to construe deed restrictions narrowly, a court is likely to permit the falafel stand on the property.

This paragraph is a single legal → *argument that uses rule-based reasoning. The argument does not include a counter-analysis because the writer did not believe there was any worthwhile counter-analysis.*

First, Ms. Izaguirre did not "build" the falafel stand on the property. "To build" means "to construct." *State v. Ahuja*, 56 S.E.2d 142, 144 (Fla. 2d Dist. App. 1988) (relying on *Webster's Third New International Dictionary* 292 (1971)). In this case, Ms. Izaguirre built the falafel stand at her home and towed the stand to its current site. Thus, Ms. Izaguirre did not "build" the falafel stand on the site. For that reason alone, the falafel stand does not violate the deed restriction.

A second legal argument → *begins here.*

In addition, the falafel stand is not a "building." A "building" is "a constructed edifice "designed to stand more or less permanently ... [and] intended for use in one place." *Id.* In this case, the wheels can be added or removed from the falafel stand. To get the falafel stand to its current site, wheels were attached and the falafel stand was towed. At the site, the wheels were removed, but they can be replaced, which would allow the falafel stand to be towed away. Thus, the falafel stand is not "designed to stand more or less permanently" nor is it "intended for use in one place."

The primary analysis uses rule-based reasoning. Note how it re-uses key aspects of the rule to help the reader see how the facts compare to the rule.

The neighbors may make one of two arguments. First, the neighbors may argue that the falafel stand is "designed to stand more or less permanently" and is "intended for use in one place." They will point out that the wheels have, in fact, been removed. In addition, plumbing and electricity now run to the falafel stand. Finally, the falafel stand is now surrounded by a parking curb and two triangular-shaped planting areas. The neighbors will argue that these improvements are permanent and make what might have once been a movable stand a permanent building, which violates the terms of the deed.

The counter-analyses begin here. The writer believes that two counter-analyses may exist.

The first counter-analysis uses rule-based reasoning. Note again how language from the rule is incorporated so that the reader can see how the facts compare to the rule.

The improvements, however, do not make the falafel stand permanent or intended for use in one place. The electricity and plumbing can be quickly disconnected and, once the wheels are re-attached, the cart can be towed across the planted areas to the street and driven away. Based on these facts and because deed restrictions are interpreted in favor of the free use of the land, a court should conclude that the falafel stand is not a building, which would allow the owners to use their land more freely.

Second, the neighbors may attempt to rely on *Charnelton v. Harris* to argue that the falafel stand is a temporary building and, therefore, violates the deed. In *Charnelton*, 52 S.E.2d 27 (Fla. 3d Dist. App. 1984), the court concluded that a porta-potty violated a deed restriction. The deed restriction stated: "No temporary house, and no temporary building, shack, church, mobile or trailer home or tent shall be erected or placed on any lot." *Id.* at 28. The court reasoned that the porta-potty, which could be moved on and off the site, was a temporary storage building and, therefore, violated the deed. *Id.* at 30. The neighbors may argue that just as a movable porta-potty can be a "building," so too can a movable falafel stand be considered a "building." Based on that analogy, the neighbors may argue that the falafel stand is a building and it violates the deed restriction.

The second counter-analysis relies on an analogical argument between this case and the *Charnelton* case. Note that it explains the factual similarity and then the legal consequence of that similarity, just as you would in any other analogical argument.

The *Charnelton* case is not, however, an appropriate precedent for this case. In the *Charnelton* case, the deed restricted "temporary" buildings. The word "temporary" changes the common understanding of the word "building" by doing away with the idea that a "building" stands "more or less permanently." Because the *Charnelton* deed addressed only "temporary buildings" and the deed in this case addresses "buildings" the *Charnelton* case is inapt.

Accordingly, a court should still conclude the falafel stand is not a building and, therefore, does not violate the deed restriction.

The above examples, Examples 8.3-A and 8.3-B, demonstrate how the same skills that you use to explain and flesh out your primary analysis should be used to explain and flesh out your counter-analysis. Explaining the counter-analysis is, however, only the first step.

B. Explain Why a Court is Unlikely to Adopt the Opposing Argument

After explaining the opposing argument, you must then explain why a court is less likely to adopt it, or conversely, why a court is more likely to adopt the primary analysis.

To do so, you cannot merely repeat your primary analysis. (But it was so good! If I repeat it, surely the senior attorney will see why that analysis must win.) Instead of repeating the same analysis, you must step back and consider how a decision about this one legal argument would fit within the broad sweep of the law—just as a judge would.

At the beginning of your legal career, you may find it difficult to step back from your analysis and consider it as a judge would. However, judges routinely ask certain questions when weighing opposing arguments. Considering these questions may help you determine how a judge will decide between two competing, but valid, arguments. Ask yourself these questions:

- Does the counter-analysis rely on the kind of facts that have been persuasive to prior courts?
- Does it rely on mandatory, mainstream authority or does it rely on an outlying statement of the law?
- Is the outcome advocated in the counter-analysis consistent with the policy behind the law?
- Is the outcome advocated in the counter-analysis consistent with the recent trend of decisions?
- Is the outcome advocated in the counter-analysis a just outcome?
- If the counter-analysis were accepted, does it create a workable rule for future cases?
- If the counter-analysis were accepted, does it create a rule that the courts could easily administer?

In Example 8.3-A above (a part of which is repeated here as Example 8.3-C), you can see how asking the above questions can lead to an explanation of why a court is more likely to adopt the primary analysis. In Example 8.3-C, the writer gives two reasons why the court is more likely to adopt the primary analysis. The writer notes, first, that the counter-analysis does not, in fact, rely on the same facts that were important to the *Kruse* court. Second, the writer notes that the counter-analysis advocates an outcome that would run counter to the policy behind the statute and, therefore, be inconsistent with the recent trend of cases. Those explanations address several questions a court is likely to ask as it weighs competing arguments: Which analysis is consistent with prior law? Which analysis relies on the kinds of facts that courts have relied on in the past? Which analysis results in an outcome that is consistent with the policy behind the law?

Example 8.3-C · Explaining why the opposing argument
is unlikely to succeed

Mr. Bigelow's argument has two significant weaknesses. First, his case is factually distinguishable from *Kruse*. The *Kruse* plaintiff was injured in front of a car, and she could have changed her mind about transportation before entering the car. Mr. Bigelow, however, was injured while stepping off of the dock; he was not in a position to change his mind about entering the raft. Whether ⟵ the plaintiff had an opportunity to change her mind was at the crux of the *Kruse* court's decision. Therefore, Mr. Bigelow's inability to change his mind should lead a court to a different conclusion.

Explaining that the opposing argument does not rely on the kinds of facts that were important to the prior court.

In addition, allowing Mr. Bigelow's claim to proceed to trial would run counter to the policy behind the statute. As mentioned above, this state's courts have consistently stated that the purpose of the statute is to protect ⟵ hosts who have offered hospitality. Relying on that policy, the courts have construed the statute to limit suits against hosts who have offered hospitality. Thus, if a court must choose between construing the statute to allow Mr. Bigelow's claim to proceed, or to construe the statute to protect a host who has offered hospitality, a court is likely to protect the host and dismiss the suit.

Explaining that the outcome proposed in the opposing argument would run counter to the policy behind the statute and would be inconsistent with the trend of cases.

Accordingly, a court is likely to conclude that Mr. Bigelow was being transported at the time of his accident and that, therefore, he cannot bring a claim against Mr. Theoroc.

Because stepping back from two opposing arguments and assessing why a judge might favor one argument over another is difficult to do, we recommend that you look at as many examples as possible. For example, if you return to Example 8.3-B (a part of which is reproduced below in Example, 8.3-D), you can see another example of how an attorney explains why the counter-analyses are less likely to succeed. In that example, the attorney explains that the opposing interpretation would be inconsistent with the court's typical policy relating to restrictive deeds. The attorney makes that point because, as mentioned above, one of the questions judges will ask is whether a particular outcome would be consistent with policies behind the law.

Example 8.3-D · Explaining why the opposing argument
is unlikely to succeed

The neighbors may make one of two arguments. First, the neighbors may argue that the falafel stand is "designed to stand more or less permanently" and is "intended for use in one place." They will point out that the wheels have, in fact, been removed. In addition, plumbing and electricity now run to the falafel stand. Finally, the falafel stand is now surrounded by a parking curb and two triangular-shaped planting areas. The neighbors will argue that these improvements are permanent and make what might have once been a movable stand a permanent building, which violates the terms of the deed.

Explaining why the first opposing argument is likely to fail.

The improvements, however, do not make the falafel stand permanent or intended for use in one place. The electricity and plumbing can be quickly disconnected and, once the wheels are re-attached, the cart can be towed across the planted areas to the street and driven away. Based on these facts and because deed restrictions are interpreted in favor of the free use of the land, a court should conclude that the falafel stand is not a building, which would allow the owners to use their land more freely.

Now, try one on your own. Look at the second-to-last paragraph in Example 8.3-B. That paragraph explains why a second opposing argument will fail. In particular, the paragraph identifies a problem that the opposing argument would raise in a judge's mind. What is that problem?

Remember, judges want to reach decisions that are consistent with prior case law, that won't be overturned, and that make sense for future parties. Once you have identified the problem that a counter-analysis would cause for a judge, you can explain why the judge will choose your primary argument over the opposing argument.

C. Return to Your Initial Conclusion

Finally, after you have explained why the counter-analysis is unlikely to succeed, you must return to your ultimate conclusion so that the reader has no doubt as to what you believe is the most likely outcome to the argument. Usually, this return is just one sentence. Often the ultimate conclusion will flow naturally from your explanation about why the counter-analysis is weak and may even be the final sentence in that explanation.

Example 8.3-E highlights the final conclusion of the counter-analysis that you first saw, above, in Example 8.3-A.

Example 8.3-E · Return to your ultimate conclusion

Accordingly, a court is likely to conclude that Mr. Bigelow was being transported at the time of his accident and that, therefore, he cannot bring a claim against Mr. Theoroc.

Example 8.3-F highlights the final conclusion of the counter-analysis that you first saw, above, in Example 8.3-B.

Example 8.3-F · Return to your ultimate conclusion

Accordingly, a court should still conclude the falafel stand is not a building and, therefore, does not violate the deed restriction.

The above discussion describes how to build an effective counter-analysis. You may, however, be wondering whether every legal argument must include a counter-analysis. The answer is "no."

III. When to Include a Counter-Analysis

Although every story has two sides, the strength and credibility of the other side varies. Sometimes the other side of the story is compelling; sometimes, it's just a story. So, too, with counter-analyses.

Although you should *always* consider whether a counter-analysis exists, sometimes no compelling alternative analysis of the law is present. In that situation, your application needs to provide a legal argument to explain why the outcome is clear; however, you will not need to explore any counter-analysis.

Finally, you may at times note a weakness, but that weakness does not warrant a full counter-analysis. For example, sometimes nearly all of the facts point to one legal conclusion, but one or two facts do not support that conclusion. You may want to point out those one or two facts even though those one or two facts do not really support a full counter-analysis. In such a case, consider using a dependent clause rather than a full counter-analysis. Example 8.3-G illustrates how you might dismiss a weakness in a dependent clause.

Example 8.3-G · A dependent clause acknowledges and dismisses a weakness

---

Next, the Neros will be able to prove that their possession of the property was exclusive. To prove exclusivity, plaintiffs need prove only that they used the land as an owner would use the land. *Hoffman,* 994 P.2d at 110. "Actual physical exclusion of all others is not required"; plaintiffs must merely prove "use consistent with ownership." *Slak,* 875 P.2d at 519. The Neros can easily prove that they used the property exclusively. Although the Neros permitted neighbors to harvest and keep some of the garden's vegetables, exercising the right to grant ← neighbors permission to take some of the vegetables shows use characteristic of an owner, which shows exclusive possession. Additionally, as discussed above, the Neros kept a garden, maintained an orchard and built a fence, just as landowners in semi-rural Oregon often do. Accordingly, they can prove they used the property as an owner would and that their use was exclusive.

"Although the Neros permitted neighbors to harvest and keep some of the garden's vegetables," is a dependent clause that acknowledges a factual weakness. The writer includes it at the outset of the application.

When using a dependent clause to dismiss a weakness, be certain that the weakness will be fully understood with just that one clause. The purpose of an objective memo is to allow the reader to fully see the strengths and the weaknesses in an argument. If a dependent clause will not allow a reader to fully understand the implications of a weakness, you will need to develop a full counter-analysis.

Moreover, you should generally use only one dependent clause. If you try to use more than one dependent clause to explain away a series of weaknesses, your analysis will read like a ping-pong match, moving back and forth between strengths and weaknesses.

Example 8.3-H shows you what that ping-pong match might look like. In Example 8.3-H, all the weak facts are shaded.

Example 8.3-H · A ping-pong match between weak and strong facts

The falafel stand is not a building. Although wheels are not currently attached to the stand, wheels can be added or removed. Moreover, although electricity and plumbing are attached to the building, those systems can be easily disconnected. Finally, although there is a curb and plantings, those features also do not inhibit the falafel stand from being moved. Once the wheels are re-attached and the systems disconnected, the cart can be towed across the planted areas to the street and driven away. Thus, the falafel stand is not "designed to stand more or less permanently" nor is it "intended for use in one place." Accordingly, a court should conclude that the falafel stand is not a building, which would allow the owners to use their land more freely.

If you find that you need more than one sentence to address the weaknesses in your prediction, it is probably best to gather those weaknesses together and address them in a full counter-analysis, using the three-part structure described above. You can see how an argument with too many dependent clauses can be improved by comparing the Example 8.3-H, above, with Example 8.3-B.

If ever you are in doubt as to whether an opposing analysis warrants a full counter-analysis, include the full counter-analysis. Your supervising attorney is relying on you to keep her informed about the possible viable alternative arguments. She would rather be over-informed and told about a weak counter-analysis than be under-informed and surprised by an alternative analysis at a later date.

IV. Where to Include a Counter-Analysis

Counter-analyses will always be explained at the end of the application section. Attorneys expect to see your strongest analysis first. So, describe first the analysis that you think will ultimately prevail. Then, explain the counter-analysis and why, ultimately, it will not succeed. Both Examples 8.3-A and 8.3-B show that structure.

If, however, a weakness does not warrant a full counter-analysis, and you believe it can be addressed in a dependent clause, you will likely address the weakness before you dive into your primary argument. Including a dependent clause in the middle of your primary analysis is likely to interrupt the flow your analysis. Putting the dependent clause at the end of your analysis is likely to surprise your reader with a new, uncomfortable fact that will prompt her to go back to your analysis and re-read it with this new fact in mind. For these reasons, if you address a weakness in a dependent clause, you will typically do so at the outset of your analysis, as in Example 8.3-G. *do it at the beginning!*

V. The Counter-Analysis and Your Explanation of the Law

Often times, a counter-analysis will rely on law that your primary analysis does not. For example, in the first Example in this chapter, Example 8.3-A, the primary analysis relied on the *Jewett* case and the opposing analysis relied on the *Kruse* case.

In that situation, when the opposing argument relies on different law, a question arises about where to describe the law that supports the counter-analysis. Two options exist: (1) You can describe the law supporting the opposing argument at the same time you explain all the other law relevant to the element or factor, or (2) you can explain the law relevant to the opposing argument as part of your explanation of the opposing argument.

Usually, the most effective approach is the first approach. That is, explain *all* the law relevant to an element or factor—including the law that supports the opposing argument—in the explanation of the law before you explore either your primary analysis or the opposing analysis. Remember that the idea behind explaining the law is to educate your reader about the relevant law and to provide your reader an appropriate context for understanding your analysis.

You fully educate and prepare your reader for the analysis only by explaining *all* the law and how it fits together. Thus, typically, explain all the law relevant to analyzing an element or factor before exploring either your main argument or the opposing argument. Example 8.3-A shows how all of the law can be explained at the outset, even though some of the law will be relied on only in the opposing analysis.

Only rarely should you wait to explain the law that supports the opposing argument in the counter-analysis section, rather than explaining all the law in the explanation section. An attorney might wait to explain the law that supports the counter-analysis if the attorney thinks that law represents non-mandatory law. In that instance, the attorney is making the judgment that, although opposing counsel might attempt to use that law to support an alternative argument, that law really lies outside the body of relevant law. In Example 8.3-B, the attorney waits to describe the *Charnelton* case because the attorney believes that, although opposing counsel might try to rely on *Charnelton*, that case does not actually address the same issue.

Usually, however, attorneys expect all the relevant law to be explained before a client's case is analyzed. Attorneys do not want to be surprised by new, relevant law in the middle of an analysis. Thus, in most instances, explain all the relevant law before you explain your analysis and counter-analysis.

Practice Points

- An effective counter-analysis should explain the opposing analysis; explain why the opposing analysis will, ultimately, not succeed; and finally, return to your initial conclusion.

- When explaining the opposing analysis, the opposing analysis should be fleshed out in as much detail as you would explain your primary analysis.

- While you should always consider whether a counter-analysis exists, include one only when a viable opposing argument exists. If one does not exist, simply explain why the outcome you predict is clear.

- If your argument includes a counter-analysis, the counter-analysis should appear at the end of your application section. If a weakness can be addressed in a dependent clause, include that dependent clause at the outset of the application, before you dive into the details of your primary analysis.

Applying the Law: Organizing Your Application of the Law

Now that you have applied the law to your client's facts, you will need to check whether you have done so in an organized manner. Checking your organization is rather straightforward and requires comparing your application of the law to your explanation of the law. Those two halves of a legal argument are linked and should reflect each other in content and organization.

In the explanation of the law, you set up a framework by setting forth the rules that guided courts in the past and then illustrating those rules with the facts, holding, and rationale of the case law. In doing so, you followed a deliberate path: You discussed the most important points first; then you presented the "weightiest" authorities before authorities that were less likely to control.

Typically, the application of the law should follow the same organizational path as the explanation did. If your application of the law follows a different path, then you need to stop and consider whether your explanation of the law or your application of the law needs to be re-organized.

Your application should discuss first the argument that a court is most likely to adopt. Do not address the weaker argument first to "get it out of the way." Attorneys expect the strongest argument first.

If you have addressed the strongest argument first, but the rule or case that illustrates that rule is not similarly discussed first in your explanation of the law, you should consider whether you need to re-organize your explanation of the law.

Example 8.4-A shows how to check your application of the law to determine whether it is well-organized.

Example 8.4-A • Checking the organization

The Neros can probably establish constructive notice because they built a fence on the purported boundary and used the land extensively and openly. A plaintiff provides constructive notice of a claim when the plaintiff's use of the property would give the owner knowledge of the use and claim. *E.g., Hoffman,*

Idea 1 explained: Constructive notice when use would give owner knowledge of plaintiff's use. *Davis* case illustrates idea.

994 P.2d at 110. **[1]** The use does not have to be visible from the owner's land to give the owner constructive notice. *Davis,* 898 P.2d at 807. For example, in *Davis,* the plaintiffs built a fence. *Id.* The court held that the fence gave constructive notice even though the fence was not visible from the owner's land because the plaintiffs and neighbors respected it as the boundary line. *Id.; see also Slak,* 875 P.2d at 519 (constructing a fence was the "classic example" of open and notorious use.) **[2]** Intermittent use of the land may also suffice, if that use is sufficient to give notice. *Hoffman,* 994 P.2d at 110. In *Hoffman,* occasional livestock grazing and maintaining a fence were enough activity to establish constructive notice. *Id.* at 111, 112.

Idea 2 explained: Intermittent use may give notice. *Hoffman* case illustrates the idea.

The Neros can likely show constructive notice to Ms. Cramer because **[2]** they used the property in more than an intermittent manner. If, as in *Hoffman,* occasional use and maintaining a fence were sufficient to show constructive notice, then the Neros can show constructive notice because they built a fence and worked the land heavily during the growing season. In addition, **[1]** the Neros' fence marked the purported property line, which the Neros and their neighbors respected. In fact, the Neros' fence was always visible from the western lot, even when they allowed the garden to return to its natural state. Because the non-visible fence in *Davis* provided constructive notice, the Neros' visible fence should provide notice, too.

Idea 2 applied: Discusses intermittent use and applies the *Hoffman* case.

Idea 1 applied: Discusses use that would give notice and applies the *Davis* case.

In Example 8.4-A, the writer applies the law in the reverse order from which it was explained. Applying the law in the reverse order may confuse the reader because the explanation of the law serves as a roadmap for the application; the reader may become disoriented when the application follows a different order. To avoid the confusion, unless there is a strategic reason to do otherwise, the writer of Example 8.4-A should determine which idea is most important and describe that idea first in both the explanation and the application of the law, as in Example 8.4-B.

Example 8.4-B · Order of application section reflects order of explanation section

The Neros can probably establish constructive notice because they built a fence on the purported boundary and used the land extensively and openly. A plaintiff provides constructive notice of a claim when the plaintiff's use of the property would give the owner knowledge of the use and claim. *Hoffman,* 994 P.2d at 110. **[1]** Intermittent use of the land may suffice if that use is sufficient to give notice. *Id.* In *Hoffman,* occasional livestock grazing and maintaining a fence were enough activity to establish constructive notice. *Id.* at 111, 112. **[2]** The use does not have to be visible from the owner's land to give the owner constructive notice. *Davis,* 898 P.2d at 807. For example, in *Davis,* the plaintiffs built a fence. *Id.* The court held that the fence gave constructive notice even though the fence was not visible from the owner's land because the plaintiffs and neighbors respected it as the boundary line. *Id.; see also Slak,* 875 P.2d at 519 (constructing a fence was the "classic example" of open and notorious use).

Idea 1 explained: Intermittent use may give notice. *Hoffman* case illustrates the idea.

Idea 2 explained: Constructive notice when use would give owner knowledge of plaintiff's use. *Davis* case illustrates idea.

The Neros can likely show constructive notice to Ms. Cramer because **[1]** they used the property in more than an intermittent manner. If, as in *Hoffman*, occasional use and maintaining a fence were sufficient to show constructive notice, then the Neros can show constructive notice because they built a fence and worked the land heavily during the growing season. **[2]** In addition, the Neros' fence was always visible from the western lot, even when they allowed the garden to return to its natural state. In fact, the Neros' fence was the property line respected by the Neros and all of their neighbors. Because the non-visible fence in *Davis* provided constructive notice, then the Neros' visible fence should provide notice, too.

Idea 1 applied: Discusses intermittent use and the *Hoffman* case law.

Idea 2 applied: Discusses use that would give notice and applies the *Davis* case.

Although the application of the law should generally follow the same organizational path as the explanation of the law, this advice goes only so far. When your application involves an analogical argument, the order in which you discuss the facts of a prior case in your application may differ from the order in which you discussed those facts in your case illustration. That's because the purpose of a case illustration is to tell a story about what happened in the past and the legal result that followed. As a result, in a case illustration the facts are often explained chronologically. By contrast, in the application, the goal is to show a factual similarity to a prior case. Chronology is no longer important. Although, at times, the facts in a case illustration and the facts in an analogical argument may follow the same order (and that similar order can be helpful to the reader), you should not make it a goal to follow the same chronology in which the facts were originally explained. Rather, when comparing facts to a prior case, your goal should be to establish a factual similarity.

Practice Points

- Compare your application of the law to your explanation of the law to make sure each reflects the other in content and structure.

- Let your application of the law follow the same organizational path that your explanation of the law followed. Address the same points in the same order in both sections.

Chapter 9

Conclusions to One Legal Argument

I.   Using a Conclusion to Begin a Legal Argument
II. Using a Conclusion to End a Legal Argument
III. Using a Conclusion to Introduce Your Application
IV. Drafting Conclusions

Attorneys use conclusions to keep readers focused on the point being made. As a result, attorneys use conclusions to begin a legal argument, to end a legal argument, and sometimes to introduce the application of the law.

I. Using a Conclusion to Begin a Legal Argument

Attorneys state a conclusion at the outset of an argument to identify the element or factor being explored and to tell the reader the direction in which the argument is headed. If a reader knows where an argument is headed, the reader can more easily appreciate the importance of information along the way.

Example 9-A shows a short argument that begins with a conclusion. Notice that the writer ends the paragraph with a conclusion, too.

Example 9-A · Legal arguments begin and end with conclusions

Jacob Tulchin is "closely related" to his birth mother, Addie Green. To be ◄— Conclusion
closely related, the plaintiff must reside in the same household or be the parent, sibling, child, or grandparent of the victim. *Thing v. La Chusa*, 771 P.2d   Explanation followed by
814, 830 n.10 (Cal. 1989). Although Jacob Tulchin did not grow up in the same   application
household as Addie Green, because he is her biological child, he is closely ◄— Conclusion
related to her.

Although attorneys usually begin their arguments with a conclusion, for strategic reasons, you may occasionally begin your argument with a statement of the issue. For example, you may use a statement of the issue if the conclusion is too complex to be easily understood at this point in the memo's text. Or you may use a statement of the issue to focus the reader's attention on the particular legal question being asked. Example 9-B shows you what an issue statement looks like.

Example 9-B · Issue statement begins the legal argument

Issue statement ──────────▶   After proving actual possession, the Neros will have to demonstrate that their possession of the land was open and notorious. To prove that their possession was open and notorious, the plaintiffs must show that the owners had notice that they were asserting title to the disputed property. *Slak*, 875 P.2d at 519. The notice may be actual or constructive. *Id.*

In Example 9-B, the attorney uses an issue statement to introduce an argument because the conclusion is complicated. The conclusion rests on two alternative analyses: whether the landowner had actual or constructive notice. Describing the conclusion for each analysis at the outset would have been difficult for the reader to absorb, so the attorney used an issue statement instead.

II. Using a Conclusion to End a Legal Argument

Attorneys also place a conclusion at the end of a legal argument. The final conclusion reminds the reader of the point that has been established in the legal argument.

Although the final conclusion may seem redundant of your initial conclusion, remember that a legal argument is complex. A legal argument sets out a synthesized explanation of the law—an explanation that often includes many legal authorities—and then applies that synthesized explanation to a detailed description of your client's facts. The conclusion wraps it up for your reader and reinforces your prediction, increasing the likelihood that your reader will retain your point. Example 9-A, above, shows a short argument that both begins and ends with a legal conclusion.

III. Using a Conclusion to Introduce Your Application

In addition to conclusions at the beginning and end of a legal argument, you may also decide to introduce your application of the law with a conclusion. A conclusion at this spot in the analysis helps to focus the reader on the point your analysis will prove. Example 9-C shows a legal argument with three conclusions—one at the beginning, one at the end, and one leading into the application section.

Example 9-C · Using conclusions within a legal argument

Mr. and Mrs. Nero can most likely prove actual possession. Plaintiffs can ◄──── *A conclusion begins the legal argument.*
establish actual possession by showing that they used the land as an owner would use that particular type of land. *Zambrotto v. Superior Lumber Co.,* 4 P.3d 62, 65 (Or. Ct. App. 2000). Courts focus on the type of use for which the land is suited and do not necessarily focus on the amount of activity. *Id.* Plaintiffs in past cases have shown that they used the disputed land as an owner would in a variety of ways. *See Davis v. Park,* 898 P.2d 804, 806-07 (Or. Ct. App. 1995); *Slak v. Porter,* 875 P.2d 515, 518 (Or. Ct. App. 1994). In *Davis,* the plaintiffs established that they used the disputed property as an owner would by showing that they used the disputed property as they did their adjoining land. 898 P.2d at 806-07. In *Slak,* the plaintiffs built a fence and planted vegetation and, in that way, proved actual possession. 875 P.2d at 518.

Mr. and Mrs. Nero should be able to prove that they had actual possession ◄──── *A conclusion introduces the application.*
of their land because they used the disputed property in a manner that an owner would. Like the landowners in *Davis,* the Neros used the disputed land exactly as did their adjacent land: In both parcels of land, they planted and maintained a garden and fruit trees. In addition, like the plaintiffs in *Slak* who showed actual possession by building a fence and planting vegetation, the Neros built a fence and planted vegetation in their garden and orchard. The ◄──── *A conclusion ends the legal argument.*
Neros should, therefore, be able to prove that they actually possessed the disputed land.

IV. Drafting Conclusions

Drafting conclusions is a straightforward process. The goal is simply to convey your bottom-line point as precisely and concisely as possible. The following tips will help you do that.

· Describe the certainty of your prediction

When you state your conclusion, you will have to decide how certain you are about the outcome. As a novice attorney you may think that you are never certain about the outcome. But simply saying that a court could decide one way or a court could decide another way is not helpful to your colleague who has asked you to research a legal question.

You must indicate the outcome that is more likely and how likely that outcome is. To help, Table 9-D contains phrases attorneys commonly use to express their degree of certainty regarding an outcome.

Table 9-D · Degrees of Certainty

- A court **will likely** conclude the plaintiff can (cannot) establish....
- A court **will probably** decide the government did (did not) prove....
- A court **should** determine the employer can (cannot) demonstrate....

- **Focus on the element or factor being explored**

Your conclusion should be about the element or factor being analyzed and not about a larger or smaller legal idea. You can see the difference between a conclusion that focuses on the element at issue and one that does not if you compare Examples 9-E and 9-F. In those examples, the arguments consider whether a falafel stand is a "building." In the first example, Example 9-E, the conclusions (in gray) do not include the word "building," leaving the reader confused about how the conclusion is connected to the argument.

Example 9-E · Conclusions are *not* focused on the element at issue

The deed restriction should not prevent our client from having a falafel stand on the site. Under state law, a "building" is "a constructed edifice designed to stand more or less permanently ... [and] intended for use in one place." *State v. Ahuja*, 56 S.E.2d 142, 144 (Fla. 2d Dist. Ct. App. 1988) (relying on *Webster's Third New International Dictionary* 292 (1971)).

In this case, the falafel stand is not a building because it can be moved. To get the falafel stand to its current site, wheels were attached and the falafel stand was towed. At the site, the wheels were removed, but they can be replaced, which would allow the falafel stand to be towed away. Thus, the falafel stand is not "designed to stand more or less permanently" nor is it "intended for use in one place." Therefore, the deed restriction should not restrict the client's business.

Below, in Example 9-F, the conclusion repeats the word "building," which is the element being explored. By using the language of the element in the conclusion, the writer makes it easy for the reader to see the connection between the conclusion and the argument.

Example 9-F · Conclusions *are* focused on the element being addressed

A court is likely to hold that our client's falafel stand is not a **"building."** Under state law, a "building" is "a constructed edifice designed to stand more or less permanently ... [and] intended for use in one place." *State v. Ahuja*, 56 S.E.2d 142, 144 (Fla. Dist. Ct. App. 1988) (relying on *Webster's Third New International Dictionary* 292 (1971)).

In this case, the falafel stand is not a building because it can be moved. To get the falafel stand to its current site, wheels were attached and the falafel stand was towed. At the site, the wheels were removed, but they can be replaced, which would allow the falafel stand to be towed away. Thus, the falafel stand is not "designed to stand more or less permanently" nor is it "intended for use in one place," and it is not a **building**.

- **The line between your application and your final conclusion may blur**

Often you will not need a final conclusion that is distinct from your application of the law. A complete application explains the legal consequence of the law being applied to facts. As a result, your application often leads directly into a conclusion, as it does in Example 9-G.

Read Example 9-G with and then without the last sentence. As you can see, the application would not be complete without the last sentence. But because the last sentence of the application also states the conclusion, you do not need a separate sentence repeating the conclusion.

Example 9-G · Your application may overlap with your conclusion

---

Jacob Tulchin is closely related to his birth mother, Addie Green. To be closely related, the plaintiff must reside in the same household or be the parent, sibling, child, or grandparent of the victim. *Thing v. La Chusa,* 771 P.2d 814, 830 n.10 (Cal. 1989). Although Jacob Tulchin did not grow up in the same household as Addie Green, because he is her biological child, he is closely related to her.

- **Vary the wording, but not the substance, of your initial and final conclusions**

Although you will assert the same substantive conclusion at the beginning and end of your argument, you do not want to mechanically repeat the same words. In each of the examples in this chapter, you can see that the conclusions at the beginning differ in form from the conclusions at the end (although not in substance).

One way to vary your conclusions is to give more information in the final conclusion than at the beginning. By the time you reach your final conclusion, your reader is more informed about the relevant law and facts. With more knowledge, your reader will be able to absorb more details at the end than at the outset.

Practice Points

- Use a conclusion at the start of an argument to identify the element or factor being explored and to tell the reader the direction in which the argument is headed.

- Use a conclusion at the end of the argument to remind the attorney of the point that has been established in the legal argument.

- Use a conclusion to introduce your application section to help focus the reader as to the nature and scope of your analysis.

Chapter 10

Policy

"Policy" refers to the broader moral, philosophical, or social goals behind a law. Legislatures, for example, enact statutes to address societal problems. The legislature's reason for enacting the statute is the policy behind the statute. Similarly, courts issue judicial decisions that are shaped by policy. When a court interprets statutory language, its decision is often based on the legislature's reason for enacting the statute. In addition, when a court issues a common law decision, policy concerns often motivate its decision. Understanding the policy behind a statute or a judicial decision can strengthen your understanding of the law and can help you to create effective legal arguments.

I. When to Include Policy in a Legal Argument

You may want to use policy in your predictive memorandum to clarify language in a statute or judicial opinion that is vague, ambiguous, or subject to multiple interpretations. Policy can help explain the law's intended meaning and provide the reader with helpful background information to understand your analysis and prediction more fully.

Example 10-A is an excerpt from a memorandum in which the attorney uses policy to clarify the meaning of language in the Americans with Disabilities Act (ADA). The attorney is examining whether an employer must accommodate an employee who has trouble getting along with co-workers. Under the ADA, if an employee's disability limits a major life activity, an employer may not fire the employee because of the disability; rather, the employer must accommodate the employee's disability. The writer predicts the employer will not have to accommodate the employee's inability to get along with others. Her prediction is based in part on the legislative policy that Congress intended the term "major life activity" to be strictly interpreted so as not to unduly burden employers.[1]

Example 10-A • Policy used to clarify law's intended scope

Our client, Maudiere Industries, has a strong argument that Jonathan Kitvan would not qualify as disabled under the Americans With Disabilities Act (ADA). To qualify as disabled, Mr. Kitvan must show: (1) that he has a physical or mental impairment, (2) that the impairment limits a major life activity, and (3) that this limitation is substantial. 42 U.S.C. § 12102(2)(A) (2000); *Toyota Motor Mfg. v. Williams*, 534 U.S. 184, 194-95 (2002). Only the second element, whether the employee's impairment limits a major life activity, is at issue.

Mr. Kitvan will probably not be able to establish that his inability to interact well with others at work is a major life activity. The Supreme Court has defined "major life activity" as an activity of central importance to daily life. *Id.* at 197. Examples of qualifying activities include "caring for oneself, performing manual tasks, walking, seeing, hearing, speaking, breathing, learning, and working." 45 C.F.R. § 84.3(j)(2)(ii) (2005). The federal regulations do not mention interacting with others as a major life activity.

While the regulatory examples are not exhaustive, the Supreme Court explicitly held in *Toyota* that the terms of the ADA "need to be interpreted strictly to create a demanding standard for qualifying as disabled." 534 U.S. at 197; *see also Soileau v. Guilford of Me., Inc.*, 105 F.3d 12, 15 (1st Cir. 1997) (rejecting interacting with others as a major life activity because, the standard is so amorphous, it is difficult for employers to apply effectively to their employees).

In addition, the Court in *Toyota* explained that a "demanding standard for qualifying as disabled" must be adopted so that the ADA does not extend beyond those Congress intended to reach. 534 U.S. at 197. When the term "major life activity" is broadly interpreted to include interacting with others, that standard is significantly lowered and would require employers to accommodate more than Congress intended.

Here, the court is unlikely to adopt a broad definition of major life activity that will circumvent the demanding standard required by the Court in *Toyota*. Because interacting with others is unlikely to be considered a major life activity, we do not anticipate that Mr. Kitvan will need to provide the requested accommodations.

---

1. Example 10-A, referencing an older version of the regulation, is based on a student sample from Whitney Passmore, Wake Forest University School of Law.

II. Identifying Legislative Policy in a Statute

If the law is embodied in a statute, you will look to the statute, legislative history, and case law to find the policy behind the statute.

A. Policy Codified in a Statute

The legislature may explicitly state the policy behind a law and codify the reasons it enacted a statute. As shown in Example 10-B, the Michigan legislature provided the reason it enacted the state's whistleblowers' statute in a preamble to the statute.

Example 10-B · Preamble to Michigan's whistleblowers' statute describes the reason the legislature enacted the statute

AN ACT to provide protection to employees who report a violation or suspected violation of state, local, or federal law; to provide protection to employees who participate in hearings, investigations, legislative inquiries, or court actions; and to prescribe remedies and penalties.

Example 10-C is an excerpt from a California statute in which the legislature explains the purpose for its workers' compensation rules and the effect that purpose should have on the courts.

Example 10-C · Statutory section explains purpose of California's workers' compensation rules

§ 3202. Liberal construction

This division and Division 5 (commencing with Section 6300) shall be liberally construed by the courts with the purpose of extending their benefits for the protection of persons injured in the course of their employment.

B. Policy Recorded in Legislative History

Sometimes the legislature does not specifically explain its reasons for enacting a statute in the statutory text. In this instance, you must research the statute's legislative history to determine whether it contains helpful statements for understanding the statute's purpose. In Chapter 2, *Sources and Systems of the Law*, we explained that the legislature's debate about whether to enact a statute may be recorded. If it is, you may be able to find the reason for the statute there, within the legislative history.

Example 10-D shows how to use a statute's legislative history to explain a court's likely interpretation of statutory language.[2] In this example, the writer examines the legislative history of the Public Safety Officers' Benefits Act to analyze whether a family can recover death benefits on behalf of their son, who died while responding to a fire alarm.

Example 10-D · A policy analysis based on legislative history

We can also use the statute's legislative history and Congress's stated goals when enacting the statute to examine whether Christopher was a "firefighter," entitled to benefits. First, Congress intended the word "firefighter" to be more rather than less inclusive. In the statute's initial draft, the House of Representatives described a firefighter as someone who was "actually and directly engaged in the fighting of a fire." H.R. 365 94th Cong. (1975). The Senate, however, understood "firefighter" as "includ[ing] a person serving as an officially recognized or designated member of a legally organized volunteer fire department." S. 2572, 94th Cong. (1975). When the two houses reconciled the different versions, they explained the final version would follow the Senate's language and "authorize" payment for all line of duty deaths. H.R. Rep. No. 94-1501, at 5-6 (1976).

The broader language incorporated into the statute reflects congressional intent to provide for firefighter death benefits as a matter of equity. *Demutiis v. United States*, 48 Fed. Cl. 81, 85-86 (2000). The Senate explained that "to provide the assurance of a Federal death benefit to his survivors is a very minor recognition of the value our government places on the work of this dedicated group of public servants." S. Rep. No. 94-816, at 3-4 (1976), *reprinted in* 1976 U.S.C.C.A.N. 2504, 2505. In an earlier version, the House Judiciary Committee similarly recognized "society's moral obligation to compensate the families of those individuals who daily risk their lives to preserve peace and to protect our lives and property." H. Rep. No. 94-1032, at 3 (1976).

Based on Congress's goals, the statute has been defined as a remedial statute that "should be construed liberally to avoid frustration of its beneficial legislative purposes." *Demutiis*, 48 Fed. Cl. at 86. When a statute is liberally construed, courts understand "'the statutory rule or principle [to] apply to more things or in more situations than would be the case under a strict construction.'" *Bice v. United States*, 72 Fed. Cl. 432, 441 (2006) (quoting 3 N. Singer, Sutherland Statutory Construction §60.1 (6th ed. 2001)).

Holding that Christopher was a "firefighter" is consistent with Congress's intent. As a junior apprentice firefighter, Christopher's duties were limited. While he was not permitted to actually engage with the fire, he participated

The legislative history is described in two paragraphs.

Previous case law has also researched and interpreted the legislative history.

The writer applies the legislative history explained above to analyze how a court is likely to interpret and apply the statutory language.

---

2. This analysis was constructed from the case *Messick v. United States*, 70 Fed. Cl. 319 (2006), *rev'd*, 483 F.3d 1316 (Fed. Cir. 2007). The analysis shows only a part of what would be a complete analysis.

by bringing out equipment and fire hoses; providing food, drink, and first aid to other firefighters; and cleaning up after fires were under control. Fire Chief Montella asserted that Christopher was "part of the team," explaining that if he was not there, somebody else would have to do his job. In fact, after his death, Christopher was included in the Brookhaven Fire Department's honor roll.

Based on the duties that he did perform, his role within the department, the congressional purpose in recognizing the individuals who risk their life to preserve and protect others, Christopher was arguably "a person serving as an officially recognized or designated member of a legally organized volunteer fire department." Moreover, at each step of our argument, we should remind the court that the statute is to be liberally construed, and thus, any questions about whether benefits should be conferred should be resolved in favor of granting benefits.

C. Legislative Policy Discussed in a Judicial Decision

Sometimes a court has already researched and interpreted the legislative history of a statute. When a court has already researched and used that policy to support its decision, you may need to look no further than the case law for an explanation of the policy. In Example 10-E, a New York court explains why the New York legislature enacted a priest-penitent privilege.

Example 10-E · A judicial opinion explains the policy behind a statute

"It has been recognized, without serious disagreement, that there existed no common-law priest-penitent privilege…. By statute, however, 'a confession or confidence made to [a clergyman] in his professional character as spiritual advisor' shall not be disclosed '[u]nless the person confessing or confiding waives the privilege.' (CPLR 4505.) The Legislature, by enacting CPLR 4505 and its predecessors, responded to the urgent need of people to confide in, without fear of reprisal, those entrusted with the pressing task of offering spiritual guidance so that harmony with one's self and others can be realized."

Keenan v. Gigante, 47 N.Y.2d 160, 166 (1979).

Likewise, in Example 10-F, a federal court examines the legislative history behind the Public Safety Officers' Benefits Act to determine whether the statute should be construed broadly or narrowly. If you look back at Example 10-D, you can see how the federal court's analysis is then incorporated into a memorandum.

**Example 10-F • A judicial opinion examines legislative history to
determine how to interpret the statute**

"In this regard, the Senate Report accompanying the enactment [of the Public
Safety Officers' Benefits Act] explains: ... 'The physical risks to public safety officers are great; the financial and fringe benefits are not usually generous; and
the officers are generally young with growing families and heavy financial com-
mitments.... To provide the assurance of a Federal death benefit to his survivors is a very minor recognition of the value our government places on the
work of this dedicated group of public servants.' S. Rep. No. 94-816, at 3-4
(1976), *reprinted in* 1976 U.S.C.C.A.N. 2504, 2505. *See also Russell v. Law Enforcement Assistance Admin.*, 637 F.2d 1255, 1261 (9th Cir. 1980)...."

"It has long been a 'familiar canon of statutory construction that remedial
legislation should be construed broadly to effectuate its purposes.' *Tcherepnin v.
Knight*, 389 U.S. 332, 336 (1967).... This canon frequently has been applied in
interpreting Federal statutes conferring benefits and rights on employees. *See
Consolidated Rail Corp. v. Gottshall*, 512 U.S. 532, 543 (1994) (Federal Employers'
Liability Act).... The PSOBA is likewise remedial in nature and thus should not
be applied grudgingly, but rather should be construed liberally to avoid frustration of its beneficial legislative purposes."

Demutiis v. United States, 48 Fed. Cl. 81, 85-86 (2000) (footnote omitted).

III. Identifying Judicial Policy in the Common Law

Just as a legislature sometimes explains its social goals in the text or
legislative history of a statute, a court issuing a common law decision may
recognize the social goals it weighed in rendering its decision. Example
10-G contains a portion of the California Supreme Court's decision in
Tarasoff v. Regents of the University of California, 551 P.2d 334 (Cal. 1976),
where the court announced a common law duty to warn when a
psychiatrist's patient poses a serious threat of violence to another individual.

Example 10-G • Court uses policy to adopt a common law duty to warn

"We recognize the public interest in supporting effective treatment of mental
illness and in protecting the rights of patients to privacy,... and the consequent
public importance of safeguarding the confidential character of psychotherapeutic communication. Against this interest, however, we must weigh the public interest in safety from violent assault.... We realize that the open and confidential
character of the psychotherapeutic dialogue encourages patients to express
threats of violence, few of which are ever executed. Certainly a therapist should
not be encouraged routinely to reveal such threats; such disclosures could seri-
ously disrupt the patient's relationship with his therapist and with the persons
threatened. To the contrary, the therapist's obligations to his patient require

that he not disclose a confidence unless such disclosure is necessary to avert danger to others, and even then that he do so discreetly, and in a fashion that would preserve the privacy of his patient to the fullest extent compatible with the prevention of the threatened danger.... We conclude that the public policy favoring protection of the confidential character of patient-psychotherapist communications must yield to the extent to which disclosure is essential to avert danger to others. The protective privilege ends where the public peril begins."

Tarasoff v. Regents of the Univ. of Cal., 551 P.2d 334, 346-47 (Cal. 1976).

IV. Where to Include Policy in Your Legal Argument

You will generally want to set out the relevant policy—whether statutory text, legislative history, or case law—in the explanation of the law section. Because policy is not black-letter law, however, and is not binding on a court, you will generally want to apply it near the end of your legal argument, after your analysis of the other legal authority. The

Table 10-H · Where to include policy in your argument

Conclusion	State your prediction about the element or factor being analyzed.

Explain the Law	Describe
	• Rule(s) relevant to the legal question you are analyzing
	• Case illustrations
	  ○ If a judicial opinion discusses legislative policy or uses policy in its determination of the common law, include the explanation of the policy when describing the case illustration.
	• Legislative history
	  ○ If policy is described in a statute's legislative history, typically describe the policy after you have described any relevant case illustrations.

Apply the Law	First, describe the analysis the court is most likely to adopt. • Use analogical reasoning to apply the case law to the facts of your client's case. • Use rule-based reasoning to apply policy to the facts of your client's case. Second, if a counter-analysis is necessary, describe the analysis that the court is less likely to adopt. • Use analogical reasoning to distinguish the case law from the facts of your client's case. • Use rule-based reasoning to distinguish the policy from the facts of your client's case. Then, explain why a court is less likely to adopt that analysis.
Conclusion	Restate your prediction.

procedure described in Table 10-H provides a starting point for including policy in your application.

Of course, the process described in Table 10-H can be modified according to circumstances. As with all legal writing, you will want to think about policy strategically. For example, when case law is sparse or non-existent, such as in a case of first-impression, or when policy is integral to the analysis, you may want to discuss policy earlier in your explanation and earlier in your analysis. On the other hand, when the body of law is well-established, policy can be used to supplement and reinforce the black letter law. Either way, explaining the policy behind a statute or judicial decision can increase the reader's understanding of the law and how it should be applied. It can also work to the advantage of your client by producing a stronger legal argument.

Practice Points

- Policy is the broader moral, philosophical, or social goals behind a statute or common law judicial decision.

- Policy can help explain the law's intended meaning and provide the reader with helpful background information so that the reader can understand your analysis and prediction more fully.

- If the law is embodied in a statute, you will look to the statutory text, legislative history, and case law to identify relevant policy.

- A court may also use policy to support its decision under common law.

Chapter 11

Statutory Analysis

More and more of our state and federal laws come from statutes. As a result, you must be prepared to carefully read and accurately analyze those statutes for your clients. Chapter 3, *Reading for Comprehension*, explained how to carefully read statutes. This chapter will show you how to interpret and apply statutes to your client's case.

Sometimes after carefully reading a statute, you will discover that language in the statute could be understood in more than one way, and those different interpretations would yield different outcomes in your client's case. When that happens, you must be able to explain the possible interpretations a statute can yield and the interpretation a court is most likely to adopt. This chapter explains how to do that.[1]

I. Statutory Analysis: A Multi-Step Process

Statutory analysis is the process by which attorneys determine whether statutory language is ambiguous and, if so, the interpretation a court is most likely to adopt and apply to the client's case. Statutory analysis is a multi-step process, not a one-stop assessment. Table 11-A summarizes the steps of the process.

---

1. Linda D. Jellum and David Charles Hricik, *Modern Statutory Interpretation: Problems, Theories, and Lawyering Strategies* 17 (2006). Many thanks also go to Professors Steve Johansen and Anne Villella for their guidance and wisdom on statutory interpretation and for reading numerous drafts of the chapter.

Table 11-A • A framework for a basic statutory analysis

1. Read the statute carefully and critically.

2. Interpret the statute.

   A. Find the meaning of the written words. Consider the plain meaning of the statute's text, and then consider the text in the context of the statutory scheme and purpose. Look to intrinsic evidence of the legislature's intent.

   B. If after considering the text and context, the meaning of the statute is still ambiguous, look to extrinsic evidence of the legislature's intent.

3. Apply the analysis to your client's facts and draft an objective analysis.

To understand how to craft your statutory argument, first remember the interplay between the courts and the legislature discussed in Chapter 2, *Sources and Systems of Law*. The legislature creates the statutory rule, but the courts decide what the rule means and how it will apply to your client's facts. When interpreting a statute, the court's primary goal is to implement the statute as the legislature intended.[2]

Discerning the meaning of legislation is difficult, however, for the following reasons: (1) Words are imperfect to communicate intent because words are malleable, ambiguous, and meanings can change over time; (2) legislators cannot foresee all situations in which a statute may apply, so many times words and phrases are drafted without specificity so that the statute will apply to a broader range of circumstances; (3) sometimes legislators must compromise in the language of a statute due to social or political pressures or for purposes of special interests groups; and (4) new technologies and novel legal issues arise that were not contemplated by existing law.

Ambiguity in the law means that a statute (or a particular word or phrase in that statute) is susceptible to more than one meaning and those different meanings can yield different outcomes when applied to a particular set of facts.[3]

Sometimes new attorneys confuse "ambiguity" with "vagueness." "Vagueness," when related to statutes, means that the legislation establishes a requirement, prohibition, or punishment without explaining what

---

2. Scholars typically use one of three following philosophies to guide statutory interpretation: (1) textualism (the statute's ordinary meaning should guide its interpretation), (2) purposivism (courts should interpret a statute in light of the purpose of the legislation), and (3) intentionalism (courts should interpret a statute in light of the intent of the specific legislature that enacted the statute). This chapter does not advocate one philosophy above the other, but tries to set forth information in a balanced manner.

3. Bryan A. Garner, *A Dictionary of Modern Legal Usage* 49-51, 842-43 (3d ed. 2009).

specific conduct is required, prohibited, or will result in a punishment. Such legislation violates due process,[4] and the court can strike down the statute as unconstitutional.

"Ambiguity" and "vagueness" are terms of art. That is, to lawyers, these words have very specific meanings. So, when you use these words in a legal context, keep their precise definitions in mind.

For purposes of statutory interpretation we are primarily concerned with ambiguous text—words and phrases that can yield different plausible meanings and, therefore, different outcomes. This chapter will focus on how a statute with ambiguous terms should be analyzed and applied to your client's facts so that you can correctly advise your client.

II. Reading the Statute

The first step in statutory analysis is to read the statute critically with an eye toward the statute's meaning and its context within the larger statutory scheme. How to read a statute critically is described in Chapter 3, *Reading for Comprehension*. A quick summary of how to read a statute critically is captured in Table 11-B.

Table 11-B · Three steps of critical statutory reading

1. Get context for the statute.	• In what jurisdiction does the statute apply? • Is the statute criminal or civil? • When did the statute go into effect? • Where is your statute located within the statutory scheme? • What does the statutory section govern?
2. Skim the most pertinent statutory sections.	• Does the statute prohibit, require, or simply permit behavior? • To whom does the statute apply? • Does the statute have any limiting language or exceptions? • Does the relevant section cross-reference other sections? • Do any definitions from other sections in the statutory scheme control the words in the section relevant to your client? • Does the statute have elements, factors, or both?
3. Read the text closely and question it.	• Read carefully, slowly, and critically, marking any phrases, words, or punctuation that could affect the meaning of the statute. • Note exactly what the statute prohibits, requires, or permits. • Break down the statute into its components, whether elements, factors, or both. • Highlight every red flag word and understand its function in the text. • Think about how the statute, on its face, applies to your client's question.

---

4. David Mellinkoff, *Dictionary of American Legal Usage* 26, 670 (1992).

The first two steps of the reading process familiarize you with the statute; however the foundational step for competent statutory analysis is the third step, reading the statute closely. In this step, you begin the core work in analyzing a statute by reading the text closely and questioning it. You will read the statute word by word and consider whether any words or phrases might be prone to alternative meanings. Without understanding the statute and how the words of the statute function, you will not be able to effectively analyze and interpret the statute.

To illustrate this point, remember the federal kidnapping statute you read in Chapter 3, *Reading for Comprehension*, which prohibits a person from taking another person, except the parent of a minor child, for ransom, reward, or otherwise. That statute contains language that might be subject to alternative meanings. That statute exempts "parents" from being charged with kidnapping. If your client is a step-parent, the statute is not clear whether your client will be exempt from kidnapping charges. The word "parent" is ambiguous because it is prone to more than one interpretation. The word may be limited to biological and adoptive parents, or the word "parent" might include step-parents.

Because the term is ambiguous, you must discern the ways in which it can be interpreted and determine the definition a court would most likely adopt. To do this, identify the red flag words to see how they operate within the statute by diagramming the statute. Table 11-C summarizes the red flag terms introduced in Chapter 3, and Table 11-D diagrams the statute by breaking down the statute and identifying the red flag words as they are organized within the statute.

Table 11-C · Red flag words

and	or	but
shall	will	may
including	except	not limited to
any	all	some
outweighs	either	

Table 11-D · Finding red flag words and ambiguous terms in a statute

Statutory language	Red flag word	Function
Whoever		
Unlawfully seizes, confines, inveigles, decoys, kidnaps, abducts, *or* carries away	"or"	Disjunctive phrasing means any of these actions of taking will satisfy this element of the statute.
and holds for ransom *or* reward *or* otherwise	"and"	Conjunctive; means that actor must not only take the victim (as described in previous element), but must also hold the person for one of the three reasons listed.
	"or"	As long as a person is taken for one of these three reasons, the element will be satisfied.
	"otherwise"	Here is an **ambiguity**—what does "otherwise" mean? pecuniary gain only? non-pecuniary gain included?
except in the case of a minor by the parent thereof	"except"	**Another ambiguity**—parents cannot be prosecuted for taking their minor children, but the statute does not define the term "parent."

Reading the statute, identifying the red flag words, and diagramming the statute require that you pay close attention to the words of the statute and the context in which those words are presented. These tasks will help you be ready for the next step, interpreting the statute.

III. Interpreting the Statute[5]

Once you have read the statute, you will then have to interpret it. In the practice of law, you will typically find that some of the statutory terminology is ambiguous. You will have to figure out what the legislature intended or more precisely, what the court will think the legislature intended with the language it chose. To unlock statutory analysis, you need two keys: First, you must know the methodology, or steps of analysis, courts in your governing jurisdiction will use to interpret the statute. Second, you must know what evidence the courts rely on at each step of the analysis.

---

5. Many of the examples in this chapter are derived from a handout, *A Basic Guide to Statutory Interpretation*, provided by Debbie Parker, Ruth Morton, and colleagues at Wake Forest University, 2000. The original author and date is unknown. (A copy is on file with the authors.)

Sidebar

Statutory analysis often mentions the terms "interpretation" and "construction." "Interpretation" is the process of determining the legislative intent. Statutory "construction" is the process of giving statutory language a meaning consistent with the legislature's intent. Charles Calleros, *Legal Method and Writing* 32 (Aspen Pub., 5th ed. 2006).

Courts rely on three different types of evidence to ascertain the legislature's intent: intrinsic, extrinsic, and policy.[6] Intrinsic evidence is cues from within the statute itself that illuminate the legislature's intent, such as the words, syntax, grammar, and punctuation of the statutory text. Extrinsic evidence is any source outside the statute that provides persuasive evidence of how the statute should be interpreted, such as legislative history, regulations, some cases, or scholarly commentary. Policy-based sources explain the reasons behind the law and often aid a court's interpretation of what the legislature intended.

This section explains the two dominant methodologies jurisdictions use and takes a closer look at the evidence courts rely on at each step of statutory analysis.

A. Understanding Methodologies

A court's methodology sets out the analytical steps courts of that jurisdiction will use to interpret a statute and the specific evidence a court will use in each step to determine the legislature's intent. Some jurisdictions use a clearly articulated methodology when interpreting a statute; other jurisdictions approach statutory interpretation with more fluidity, following a more general scheme of looking, in turn, to the plain meaning, intrinsic sources, and then extrinsic sources.

For instance, some courts use a clearly articulated two-level approach: The first level uses intrinsic evidence to look at the text—what the written words actually say—within the context of the statutory section and the overall statutory scheme. Then, if the statute is still ambiguous, a court will move to the second level of analysis and review other evidence, usually extrinsic sources—sources outside of the text of the statute—to determine what the legislature intended the language to mean. (See Section B, *Sources of Evidence*, which explains these sources of evidence in more detail.)

On the other hand, other courts use a three-level methodology for statutory interpretation. On the first level, the court will use intrinsic evidence to examine the text and context of the statute.[7] If the meaning of the statute is still ambiguous, the court will move to the second level and look at the legislative history. Finally, if necessary, the court will move to a third level and use extrinsic evidence to determine what the legislature intended the ambiguous statute to mean.[8]

Although as a general rule courts move from intrinsic to extrinsic evidence, courts do vary in the sources allowed on each level. In some jurisdictions, for instance, if the statute as written yields an absurd result,

---

6. *See* Jellum and Hricik, *supra* note 1, at 5-6.

7. *See, e.g., State v. Gaines*, 206 P.3d 1042 (Or. 2009); *P.G.E. v. Bureau of Labor and Indus.*, 859 P.2d 1143, 1145-47 (Or. 1993).

8. *Id.* at 1145-47.

courts may consider extrinsic sources of legislative intent (such as legislative history) as context on a first-level analysis; other jurisdictions may not consider various extrinsic sources as context until a later level of analysis.

Because methodologies can differ greatly among jurisdictions, before you begin to interpret a statute, you must first determine the number of analytical levels in your jurisdiction and the evidence the courts rely on at each level. Your statutory analysis will be persuasive only if you follow the approach that a court in the governing jurisdiction would follow. Further, you will have a much easier time understanding the law that applies to your client's question if you know the methodology a court will use.

Once you understand the nature of the methodology used in your jurisdiction, make sure you understand *which* sources of evidence can be used on each level of analysis. This next section will provide an overview of the sources of evidence commonly used by courts.

B. Sources of Evidence

No matter the methodology, courts typically rely on three different sources of evidence mentioned earlier to ascertain legislative intent: intrinsic, extrinsic, or policy.[9] This chapter will examine the first two sources of evidence, intrinsic and extrinsic evidence. (Chapter 10, *Policy*, examines policy-based evidence.)

1. Intrinsic evidence

In most jurisdictions, the first level of statutory interpretation uses intrinsic sources to review the text in its context. Intrinsic evidence uses cues from within the text of the statute itself that illuminate the legislature's intent. This type of evidence is intrinsic because it looks to the text and the context of the actual statutory language, rather than to outside sources. For example, intrinsic evidence looks at the words, syntax, grammar, and punctuation of the statutory text.[10] Depending on a court's methodology, intrinsic evidence might also include the overall statutory scheme, prior cases interpreting the ambiguous language of the statute, and canons of construction.

(a) Text and the plain meaning rule

Courts start statutory analysis with the text—the exact words of the statute. Courts also start with a presumption that the words mean what they say on their face. Reading the words as written and interpreting them on their face is known as the "plain meaning rule." The plain meaning

---

9. *See* Jellum and Hricik, *supra* note 1, at 5-6.

10. *Id.*

rule dictates that ordinary words are understood to have their primary and ordinary meaning. For instance, in the kidnapping statute, mentioned above, the word "parent" would be understood by its ordinary definition if the statute had not defined it.

When applying the plain meaning rule, however, those critical reading steps you took earlier in the analytical process will help you understand the words of the statute. You will already have noticed the red flag words and how they function at that earlier stage. You will have marked key phrases and noted the number of elements or factors the statute sets out. Now, as you continue to analyze the text, pay attention not only to what the words say but also to how they are arranged. Notice the grammatical structure and punctuation; under the plain meaning rule traditional rules of punctuation apply.

In this level of statutory interpretation, when a word or phrase is ambiguous on its face, courts might look to see if the term is defined elsewhere in the statutory scheme. If the statutory scheme does define the term, the court will use that definition rather than the plain meaning.

In other instances, a court will also go beyond the plain meaning rule if the statute has technical words with specialized meanings. In statutory analysis, technical words are understood to have their technical meaning. For example, in a statute dealing with gas and oil production, the term "denaturing agent" would be defined specifically according to standards of that industry.

(b) Text and context

While courts generally start with a plain meaning analysis of the text, they usually cannot stop there. Because a single word can have many different meanings, courts have to use additional sources of intrinsic evidence to determine the meaning. One source is to look at the text in its context. Because words have little meaning when stripped of their context, text and its context are usually inextricably entwined when interpreting a statute.

A plain meaning rule analysis usually does not end the inquiry because words that seem clear on their face may not be clear when they are applied to a set of facts. For example, the word "possess" may seem clear at first glance. The word usually means to own or control something—one who buys a textbook for class surely "possesses" that book. That word, however, might not be so clear in a different context. If drugs are found in the car of a driver who does not know the drugs were left there by his teenage son's friend, is he in possession of the drugs?

Because words are more easily understood when read in context, to understand the meaning of a statute, courts look at the internal or intrinsic organization of the statutory section, the words within a statutory section that surround the ambiguous text, the statutory scheme as a whole, related statutes, and the evolution of the statute (all prior amendments and revisions of the statute) to analyze the statutory text and context. In addition, courts may also use textual "canons of construction" to support an intrinsic contextual analysis.

(c) Textual canons of construction

Canons of construction are legal maxims that judges sometimes rely on to interpret the law. Numerous canons, too many to mention here, exist. Not all canons are compatible; many canons used by the courts frequently have another canon that says directly the opposite. Canons may be used to understand context, but they are not mandatory rules that must be followed.[11]

Textual canons of construction are intrinsic sources used to determine the meaning of the text in context. Textual canons look to the construction of the statute—the choice and placement of words, the grammar, and the syntax of the words—to discern what the legislature intended. Table 11-E lists some of the more common textual canons of construction and provides an example of how courts may use them. When you use canons to support your analysis of what a statute says, make sure to cite a case that uses that canon.

Table 11-E · Textual canons of construction[12]

1. Canon regarding the plain meaning rule
- "If language is plain and unambiguous it must be given effect."

2. Canons regarding specific words
- "May" means permissive; "shall" means "mandatory."
- "And" means conjunctive; "or" means "disjunctive."
    - Example: "… fruits, seeds, nuts, vegetables, honey, sheep, cattle, pigs, *and* poultry." A person must produce all of these things to come under the statute. Change "and" to "or," and a person would have to produce only one of them.

3. Canons regarding ambiguous modifiers
- "A modifier or exception applies only to the last antecedent in a phrase or list."
    - Example: "Employees shall be paid base wages, environmental hazard pay, and overtime <u>as determined by the lead agency to be consistent with private sector practices.</u>" Under this canon, the underlined phrase modifies only "overtime," the last antecedent; if, however, a comma had followed the word "overtime" the underlined phrase would have modified all three kinds of compensation listed.[13]

---

11. Kent Greenawait, *Legislation, Statutory Interpretation: 20 Questions* 206-09 (1999).

12. These examples of canons have been frequently used over the years. The original source of the examples is unknown.

13. *See Adams v. U.S.*, 979 F.2d 840 (Fed Cir. 1992).

4. Canons regarding lists of things

a. Noscitur a sociis: Interpret an ambiguous word in a list by the company it keeps, that is, in light of the surrounding words.

"... pigs, cattle, sheep, and poultry." Does "poultry" include exotic birds?

b. Ejusdem generis: General, catch-all phrases at the end of a list are construed to mean the same kind or type as the rest of the list.

If "motor vehicle" is defined as a "car, truck, or any other self-propelled vehicle not designed for running on rails," does it include an airplane? A motorized scooter?

c. Expressio unius, exclusio alterius: Enumeration of specific things implies the exclusion of all others. If the word is not in, then it is meant to be out. "rain, sleet, and hail" excludes snow.

5. In pari materia: Statutes with the same subject or purpose should be read together to effectuate that purpose.

For example, a statute setting out the punishment for kidnapping should be read in conjunction with a statute setting out sentencing guidelines for felonies.

(d) Cases

Cases can be intrinsic tools if they directly construe the specific ambiguous language at issue in a statute. If the case interprets the exact language in question, most courts will incorporate that analysis at the textual level. If the case does not actually interpret the relevant statutory language, then it will likely be used as extrinsic evidence.

Whether the case is allowed as intrinsic evidence may also depend on the hierarchical level of the court deciding the case. For instance, if the state supreme court interpreted the statute in a prior case, that interpretation becomes part of the statute as if it were written into the statute at the time of enactment.[14] Decisions by intermediate courts construing the statute may not, however, have the same weight. Understand what weight the courts in your jurisdiction give to precedent in that circumstance.

2. Extrinsic sources

If the meaning of the ambiguous statute is not clear after using the intrinsic sources of evidence, you can look outside the statute to see what other evidence sheds light on legislative intent. Extrinsic evidence derives from sources outside the statute that provide evidence of the legislature's intent. Those sources usually include the following: cases, agency interpretations and regulations, legislative history, non-textual canons of construction, or any other source, such as scholarly interpretations or parallel

---

14. *See, e.g., Holcomb v. Sutherland*, 894 P.2d 457, 459-60 (Or. 1993).

statutes in other jurisdictions, that provides persuasive evidence of how the statute should be interpreted.[15]

(a) Cases

Cases that merely apply statutory language or that deal with issues tangential to the text of the statute in question may be extrinsic evidence a court can consider. Cases from other jurisdictions may also be considered extrinsic evidence. For instance, with the example of the federal kidnapping statute, a federal district court in California would not be bound by the ruling of a federal district court in Tennessee. If, however, the Tennessee court had construed the term "parent," the California federal district court might use that interpretation and construction as extrinsic evidence of what the legislature intended when drafting the statute.

(b) Agency interpretations and regulations

Administrative agencies are charged with the task of implementing or enforcing statutes. To do so, they must first interpret what the statute means. Because the agency implementing the statute often has expertise in the area the statute controls, courts defer to agency interpretations when examining an ambiguous statute.[16]

Agencies may also promulgate regulations to implement the statute. Legislatures may create the statutory rule, but they often cannot create the more specific rules needed to make the statutory scheme work. Thus, legislatures charge agencies with that task. The regulations, or rules, the agency creates to implement the statute are a source of extrinsic evidence.

(c) Legislative history

The legislative history is the record that follows a proposed bill as it makes its way through both houses of the legislature. Remember the legislative process from Chapter 2, *Sources and Systems of Law.* Enacting a statute is a cumbersome business. A bill is proposed in one house, and then must be passed by both houses, before it goes to the president or governor for signature.

While the description is simple, the process is not. Often the bill must stop in various committees in each house where it is tweaked, revised, changed, and tweaked again. The legislative history may be comprehensive or abbreviated, but it will usually contain reports by the committees,

---

15. *See* George A. Costello, *Average Voting Members and Other "Benign Fictions": The Relative Reliability of Committee Reports, Floor Debates, and Other Sources of Legislative History*, 1990 Duke L. J. 41-61 (1990).

16. *See* Jellum and Hricik, *supra* note 1, at 409-13. The United States Supreme Court declared that agency interpretations of a statute were entitled to deference. *Chevron U.S.A. Inc. v. Natural Resources Defense Council, Inc.,* 467 U.S. 837 (1984).

statements made by proponents or foes of the bill, and any research or anecdotal material that the legislators submit with the bill.

A hierarchy exists within the sources of legislative history. Committee reports are typically given more weight than floor debates or legislative hearings on bills.[17] If you use legislative history, understand which source you are using and the weight of authority your jurisdiction gives to that category.

Because a legislative history includes so much information, brought by so many people, legislative history is often a morass of conflicting documents. Thus, a debate exists about the usefulness of relying on legislative history. Some judges want to use legislative history to shed light on the meaning of a statute; they believe that only by reviewing all the committee reports, floor debates, and history surrounding the statute from infancy to enactment, can the legislature's intent be revealed. Other judges revile legislative history as an abyss that does nothing to illuminate the statute's meaning. With the ongoing debate over the appropriateness of using legislative history, be sure to know the statutory methodology your jurisdiction uses and where legislative history falls on that scale.

(d) Non-textual canons of construction

Courts may also rely on non-textual canons of construction, such as those set out below in Table 11-F, to support a particular interpretation.

Table 11-F · Non-textual (substantive) canons of construction[18]

This chart notes a few of the many substantive canons of construction courts use.

1. Statutes in derogation of the common law will be narrowly construed.

2. Statutes are to be read in the light of the common law and a statute affirming a common law rule is to be construed in accordance with the common law.

3. Remedial statutes will be construed broadly.

4. Penal statutes will be construed narrowly.

5. A statutory provision requiring liberal construction does not mean disregard of unequivocal requirements of the statute.

(e) Other sources

Law review articles, scholarly assessments, or even parallel statutes from other jurisdictions may provide extrinsic evidence helpful in inter-

---

17. Costello, *supra* note 15, at 41.

18. Greenawait, *supra* note 11, at 206-09; Jellum & Hricik, *supra* note 1, at 429. Both sources rely on excerpts from Karl N. Llewellyn, *Remarks on the Theory of Appellate Decision and the Rules of Cannon*[sic] *about How Statutes are to be Construed*, 3 Vand. L. Rev. 395, 401-06 (1949).

preting an ambiguous statute. In addition, outside considerations such as historical circumstances may provide extrinsic evidence a court would use to understand the legislature's intent. For example, if a court were considering an ambiguous provision of the Patriot Act, it might consider the historical circumstances of the events on September 11, 2001, which led to the statute's enactment.

Analyzing and interpreting a statute can be challenging, but it will be increasingly necessary as more law becomes codified. Once you have gone through the levels of interpretation and used intrinsic and extrinsic evidence to support your interpretation, you are ready to commit your analysis to paper.

IV. Drafting a Statutory Analysis

Now that you have critically read and interpreted the statute, you are ready to write about it. When writing a discussion about a statute, you will follow the same general framework described in Chapter 12, *The Discussion Section: Introducing and Connecting Legal Arguments*. First, create a roadmap section. That roadmap section will tell the reader your conclusion regarding the most likely way a court will resolve the statutory ambiguity in question. Your roadmap section will likely describe the statutory language at issue and outline the methodology courts in your jurisdiction use to analyze a statute. In doing so, your roadmap section will inform your reader about the major points you will cover and your bottom-line conclusion.

Once you get into the meat of the issue, the structure of the discussion will depend on the methodology your jurisdiction uses and the evidence allowed on each level. Organize your discussion around the evidence the courts will consider. Looking at each kind of evidence, describe the rules relevant to that evidence. That description will be your explanation of the law. Then, consider whether each kind of evidence, on balance, supports the interpretation that is helpful to your client's position. That will be your application of the law. Finally, conclude each individual legal argument.

Example 11-G shows one way a statutory analysis could be drafted in a legal memorandum. Notice how the writer walked through the steps of statutory interpretation. First, the writer sets out the applicable statute and identifies the problem language. Adhering to Arizona's methodology for examining statutes, she then examines the plain language to determine what the statute says on its face. Because the language is ambiguous, she uses intrinsic evidence, looking at the ordinary definition of the word and its statutory context, and then extrinsic evidence in the form of prior cases interpreting the term to answer her client's question.

Example 11-G • A sample statutory analysis in a memorandum

DISCUSSION[19]

Roadmap paragraph sets out statutory issue to be examined and conclusion.

The issue in this case is whether the word "person" in Arizona's anti-human smuggling statute includes human cargo, thus subjecting the human cargo to prosecution for being smuggled. The plain text of Arizona Revised Statutes Annotated § 13-2319 indicates that the Arizona Legislature intended for this statute to prosecute "coyotes," the people in the business of smuggling migrants, not the smuggler's human cargo. Ariz. Rev. Stat. Ann. § 13-2319 (West 2005). Since our clients are not in the business of smuggling migrants, their activity as human cargo falls outside the intended scope of § 13-2319, and they cannot likely be prosecuted.

The writer follows the same basic mechanical structure in statutory analysis that she would have followed when analyzing an issue under case law. She begins with a roadmap, then for each main topic she explains the law by setting out the rules, explaining the rules, and then applying the rules.

In this first roadmap section, the writer explains that under Arizona methodology, she will start first with the text and look to the plain meaning of the statute to ascertain legislative intent. The roadmap section explains that under Arizona's methodology, the court can use extrinsic sources as context on this level of analysis. In looking at the text and context, the writer determines her client cannot be prosecuted under the statute.

Arizona Revised Statute § 13-2319 states

A. It is unlawful for a person to intentionally engage in the smuggling of human beings for profit or commercial purpose.

B. A violation of this section is a class 4 felony....

D. For the purposes of this section 'smuggling of human beings' means the transportation or procurement of transportation by a person or an entity that knows or has reason to know that the person or persons transported or to be transported are not Unites States citizens, permanent resident aliens or persons otherwise lawfully in this state.

Id.

Under Arizona rules of statutory interpretation, the court must begin its statutory analysis with the text of the statute. Plain text is the "best and most reliable" indication of a statute's meaning. *State v. Christian*, 66 P.3d 1241, 1243 (Ariz. 2003). If the court finds the plain text of § 13-2319 ambiguous, the court may next look to the context, historical background, spirit and purpose of the statute. *Blake v. Schwartz*, 42 P.3d 6, 12 (Ariz. Ct. App. 2002). Both the text and context of § 13-2319 indicate that our clients' activity falls outside the intended scope of § 13-2319; accordingly, we can move that the charges be dismissed.

A. The ordinary meaning of the language in Arizona Revised Statute § 13-2319(a) limits the scope of the statute to "persons" in the business of smuggling human beings.

Here, the writer cites a canon of construction previously used by courts in that jurisdiction. The canon is more effective because it has supporting authority with it.

The plain text of § 13-2319(a) limits the meaning of "person" to those in the business of smuggling human beings "for profit or commercial purpose." The purpose of a plain text analysis is to give effect to the legislature's intent. *See Christian*, 66 P.3d at 1243. To do so, Arizona courts must give "each word, phrase, clause and sentence" meaning "its natural, obvious, and ordinary meaning" such that no other part of the statute is rendered "void, inert, redundant or trivial." *Arpaio v. Steinle III*, 35 P.3d 114, 116 (Ariz. App.1 Div. 2001); *Stein*

---

19. This student sample by Alexis Curry, Lewis & Clark School of Law, is based on the 2005 version of the statute.

v. Sonus, USA, Inc., 150 P.3d 773, 776 (Ariz. Ct. App. 2 Div. 2007). When a word is undefined by the statute, Arizona courts turn to any established and widely used dictionary to determine the natural and obvious meaning of a term. *Helvetica Servicing, Inc. v. Pasquan*, 277 P.3d 198, 205 (Ariz. App. 1 Div. 2012).

Section13-2319(a) subjects to criminal prosecution only those "person[s]" who smuggle "for profit or commercial purpose." Under Arizona statute, a "person" includes corporations and a "natural person." Ariz. Rev. Stat. Ann. § 1-215 (West 2002). The statute, however, applies only to those "persons" who smuggle for "profit" or "commercial purpose." "Profit" is "net income . . . from the conduct of business." *Webster's Third New International Dictionary* 1811 (Merriam-Webster 2002). Similarly, the word "commercial" is defined as "having profit as the primary aim." *Id.* at 456. Therefore, a "person" who smuggles for "profit or commercial purpose" is one who seeks a "net income" from the "business" or who has profit as the primary aim of the smuggling operation.

Thus, by choosing the terms "for profit" and "commercial purpose" the Arizona legislature chose to impose criminal sanctions on the smuggler, not the human cargo. In the world of human trafficking, two types of people play two very different roles. One person is the "coyote" or smuggler; the other is the human being who is smuggled by the coyote. Coyotes are in the business of transporting or procuring transportation for migrants. They repeatedly provide this service for monetary gain. In contrast, the human beings transported by the coyotes are not in the business of human smuggling. They pay for a service; they make no "profit" from it, and they have a personal, not commercial motive, in crossing the border.

To read the statute as imposing criminal liability on the human cargo would, effectively, eliminate the requirement that the person prosecuted act "for profit" or for "commercial purpose." Thus, such a reading would render those phrases "void" and "inert" and would ignore the legislative intent expressed through those words.

Accordingly, based on the plain meaning of the text in § 13-2319(a) the court will likely dismiss Count I of the indictment. Our client was not the smuggler. He was merely the human cargo. While the plain meaning of the statutory section demonstrates that the coyotes' activity falls squarely within the intended scope of § 13-2319(a), the plain text also demonstrates that our clients' activity as human cargo does not.

B. The context of § 13-2319(a) demonstrates a legislative intent to make § 13-2319(a) a tool for prosecutors to combat organized crime, not individual migrant activity.

If the court finds the plain meaning of § 13-2319 ambiguous, the court may then look to the context, historical background, spirit and purpose of the statute to determine the legislative intent. *Blake v. Schwartz*, 42 P.3d 6, 12 (Ariz. Ct. App. 2002). As a part of this broadened analysis, the court may consider the headings of the statute to aid the interpretation of the statute and to ascertain legislative intent. *State v. Hauser,* 105 P.3d 1158, 1161 (Ariz. 2005).

The heading of § 13-2319 demonstrates the Arizona State Legislature intended to target members of organized crime. Chapter 23 of the Arizona Crimi-

---

To define the ambiguous term, "person" the writer looks to another statute in which the term has been defined. Notice that the later statute does not appear to be in the same chapters as the smuggling statute at issue here.

The writer uses the plain meaning rule and defines other ambiguous terms (not defined elsewhere in the statutory code or in other cases) by their ordinary definition. To do so, she cites the dictionary.

In this paragraph, the writer applies the law to the facts.

The writer moves on to the context of the statute.

Which of these sources do you think are intrinsic and which are extrinsic?

nal Code is entitled "Organized Crime, Fraud and Terrorism." Ariz. Rev. Stat. Ann. § 12-2301 (West 2005). This heading shows that the Arizona Legislature enacted § 13-2319 to provide a remedy for the problems of organized crime, fraud, or terrorism.

The historical background to § 13-219 also supports the interpretation that the legislature intended to target organized crime, and not human cargo. In 2005, the year § 13-2319 was passed in Arizona, the United States Government Accountability Office reported to Congress that "[p]eople smuggling is a huge and highly profitable business worldwide, involving billions of dollars annually." Colleen DiSanto, *Alien Smuggling Along the Arizona-Mexico Border*, 43 Ariz. Att'y, January 1, 2007, at 29. At that time, the "volume and sophistication" of human smuggling rings had increased dramatically, and Arizona, which shares a border with Mexico, was already feeling the great weight of human smuggling by trafficking organizations. *Id*. Nevertheless, the same year § 13-2319 was enacted, Arizona declared a state of emergency, due to the severe financial burden jailing thousands of illegal immigrants put on local border community economies. *Id*. at 32.

This historical background makes it unlikely that the Arizona Legislature intended individual migrant activity to be treated as a class four felony because it would increase jail time for smuggled migrants. Thus, the Legislature did not likely intend to increase jail time for illegal immigrants. A more natural interpretation of § 13-2319, given this historical background, is that the statute is limited in its scope to coyotes and other members of human smuggling organizations, who smuggle immigrants for profit and are consistently responsible for the burden illegal immigrants put on the state of Arizona.

The spirit and purpose of the statute is also best served by interpreting § 13-2319(a) to limit criminal liability to the coyote and other members of human smuggling organizations. According to a Senate fact sheet, the Arizona legislature created § 13-2319 as a tool to help the state combat these human smuggling and trafficking organizations. Az. Sen. S.F. Sheet, 2005 Reg. Sess. S.B. 1372. Distinguishing the role of the coyote and other members of a smuggling organization from the role of the smuggled migrant serves that purpose. The coyote is a specialist employed by a smuggling organization to smuggle migrants across the border, and he plays an active role in human smuggle organizations. AZCentral, *Terms Used in the Human-Smuggling Business*, http://www.azcentral.com/ specials/special21/articles/ 0720Online-Drophouse-Terms.html (July 23, 2006). On the other hand, a smuggled migrant takes a passive role, that of the commodity and his relationship with the smugglers "ends with the arrival of the migrant at his destination." Ariz. Sen. S.F. Sheet, 2005 Reg. Sess. S.B. 1372. This distinguishable relationship is evidence that an interpretation of § 13-2319 that limits its scope to coyotes properly serves the intended purpose of the statute while the coyotes' human cargo should not be charged under § 13-2319.

Here the writer again begins applying the law to her clients' facts.

Our clients should not be prosecuted under § 13-2319 because they are not members of human smuggling organizations. They are instead the commodities from which these criminal organizations profit. Our clients were nothing more than human cargo whose relationship ended "with the arrival of the migrant at his destination." Our clients did not play an active role in getting across the border; instead, they merely submitted themselves to the smugglers for transport. The statute does not extend to cover our clients' conduct.

The context, historical background, and purpose of § 13-2319 support the interpretation that people in the business of human smuggling, not their human cargo, are the intended target of the statute. As a result, we can make a strong argument that the court should dismiss this charge against our clients.

Here, the writer concludes the issue.

Statutory analysis is a methodical process of reading, interpreting, and constructing a statute. Courts in your jurisdiction will expect you to analyze the statute in accordance with the method they espouse. Know the methodology your jurisdiction uses for statutory construction, and follow the steps of that process when analyzing the statute at issue and drafting a statutory analysis.

Practice Points

- Statutory analysis is a multi-step process requiring you to critically read the statute, assess the ambiguities in the statute, and interpret the statute using intrinsic and extrinsic sources.

- The goal of statutory interpretation is always to construe the statute in the way the legislature intended.

- To properly interpret the statute, you must first know the methodology of statutory interpretation courts in the governing jurisdiction will use, whether that methodology is a fluid process or a clearly articulated two or three-level analysis.

- Evidence of legislative intent typically comes from three types of sources, intrinsic, extrinsic, or policy-based.

- Although courts will start with the plain meaning of a statute, most statutory analyses require a court to investigate additional sources of legislative intent through an analysis of intrinsic evidence, extrinsic evidence and canons of construction.

Chapter 12

The Discussion Section: Introducing and Connecting Legal Arguments

---

I. Introduce Your Legal Argument: The Roadmap Section
   A. State the Conclusion to Your Client's Legal Question
   B. Explain the Governing Rule
   C. Dispose of the Obvious and Uncontroversial (if Necessary)
   D. Map and Assess the Remaining Arguments (if Necessary)
   E. Conclude Again (if Necessary)

II. Create Informative Point Headings
   A. Make Point Headings "Work"
   B. Restate the Conclusion After the Point Heading
   C. Create Professional-Looking Point Headings

III. Use Mini-Roadmaps to Introduce Sub-Arguments

You have now learned how to construct one legal argument: State your conclusion; explain the law on which that conclusion rests; show how that law applies to your client's case; and then restate your conclusion. That one legal argument is the essential building block in answering your client's legal question.

Usually, however, it takes more than one legal argument to address a client's legal question. As we discussed in Chapter 4, *Finding Your Argument*, attorneys address a client's legal question by finding the governing rule and breaking down the governing rule into elements or factors. Each element or factor in the governing rule becomes the source of one or more legal arguments. We say "one or more" because some elements or factors in the governing rule can themselves be broken down into additional elements or factors. In that case, one element or factor in the governing rule may require more than one legal argument.

To answer your client's legal question, you will have to construct the necessary legal arguments and then string those arguments together within one discussion about your client's legal question. That discussion is presented in a section of your memo labeled (not surprisingly) the Discussion section.

To provide coherence to this string of legal arguments, attorneys write an introduction—or roadmap—to the discussion and then, as necessary, insert point headings and mini-roadmaps to guide their reader through. When they are done, their Discussion section might look something like Figure 12-A, below.

Those tools—your introductory roadmap, point headings, and mini-roadmaps—identify the structure of your discussion and explain the relationship among the individual arguments. Allowing your reader to see the structure and how your arguments relate to each other will help your reader move more easily through your discussion. To that end, this chapter discusses how to construct an introduction and how to write effective point headings and mini-roadmaps.

Figure 12-A · The discussion section diagrammed

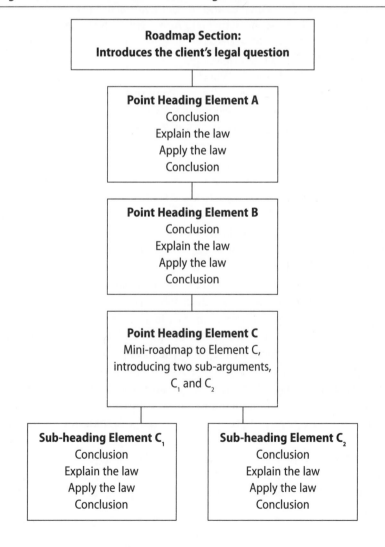

I. Introduce Your Legal Argument: The Roadmap Section

Every discussion about a client's legal question begins with an introduction. In that introduction, you will tell your reader the conclusion you have reached about the client's legal question, explain the governing rule, dispense with arguments that will not be addressed, and then indicate the order in which the remaining legal arguments will appear. The introduction serves as a roadmap to the Discussion section, showing the discussion's starting point, its ending point, and the analytical route between the two. A clear roadmap section will make your discussion more cohesive and understandable for your reader.

A. State Your Conclusion to Your Client's Legal Question

The roadmap section should begin with the ending: State your bottom-line conclusion to the client's legal question. Stating your conclusion reminds the reader of the issue and, simultaneously, tells the reader where your legal analysis is going.

Attorneys write the initial conclusion in a variety of ways. Sometimes you will state your conclusion and include a brief explanation of the critical fact or critical reason that supports the conclusion. Such a conclusion would look like Example 12-B. Other times, you will simply assert your conclusion without further explanation, as in Example 12-C.

Example 12-B · Conclusion with reasoning explained

Mr. Oliver can establish a prima facie case of retaliatory discharge under Michigan's Whistle-blowers' Protection Act since the evidence shows he was fired because he was about to report his employer's illegal use of lead-based paint.

Example 12-C · Conclusion without reasoning explained

Mr. Oliver can establish a prima facie case of retaliatory discharge under Michigan's Whistle-blowers' Protection Act.

Whether you identify a reason for your conclusion, as in Example 12-B, or simply assert your conclusion, as in Example 12-C, often depends on whether it is possible to quickly state a supporting reason. At the beginning of a legal argument, a reader can absorb only so many details. You will have to judge whether you can quickly explain the reason for your conclusion or whether it is better to let that reason develop over the course of your argument.

When the memo addresses a series of dispositive legal issues, your conclusion is more complex. In that case, first state the overall conclusion to your client's question. Then, state your conclusion for each separate legal issue. In Example 12-D, the overall conclusion is that Mr. Jeffers has a viable claim for negligence. The overall conclusion is supported by conclusions to three dispositive legal issues: (1) the liability waiver is unenforceable because it is against public policy, (2) the waiver is also unenforceable because it does not conform to requirements established in state law, and (3) the urgent care facility acted negligently.

Example 12-D · Conclusion for a multi-issue memo with reasoning explained

---

Mr. Jeffers can bring a viable negligence claim against the urgent care facility for its treatment of his cycling injuries. First, a liability waiver is unenforceable when the underlying activity is in the public interest. Because medical care is a regulated service in the public interest, the liability waiver Mr. Jeffers signed is unenforceable. Second, the waiver is also unenforceable because it does not conform to the formatting and language requirement for liability releases under state case law. The language of the release was not clear, and the font size was too small to be read by an average person. Finally, Mr. Jeffers can prove that the urgent care facility acted negligently when it failed to use sterile instruments in his treatment.

No matter how many issues your memo addresses, the introduction should begin by telling the reader the ultimate conclusion you have reached.

B. Explain the Governing Rule

After stating the conclusion, next explain the rule that governs the client's legal question. Doing so indicates the legal basis for your conclusion and the framework for your discussion.

1. State the governing rule

As you now know, the governing rule can be found in a variety of sources. Typically, you will find your governing rule in a statute or a judicial opinion. While your statement of the governing rule should echo the way that rule is set out in the primary source, your statement of the governing rule should also be clear.

When you write the governing rule you do not need to state it word for word as it is written in the statute or explained by the courts. Usually, statutes contain more language than is relevant to your client's question. In addition, statutes are sometimes written awkwardly. Even when the governing rule is rooted in case law, the way in which the courts describe the rule may not work as smoothly in your discussion. For all these reasons, attorneys do not mechanically copy the governing rule into their introduction.

Instead, your description of the governing rule should repeat key phrases, but you may modify language so that the governing rule is clearly explained and flows with the rest of your discussion. The next two examples, 12-E and 12-F, show how you might transform a governing rule that is difficult to read into one that is easier for your reader to absorb.

The first example, Example 12-E, is the text of a Michigan statute that prohibits a public official from coercing public employees to make political contributions. In the example, the parts of the statute that are relevant to the client's case are shaded. Those parts will form the basis for the governing rule that is described in the introduction. The second example, Example 12-F, shows how you might create a governing rule from the relevant parts of the statute.

Example 12-E · Michigan statute prohibiting coerced political contributions

Michigan Compiled Law § 15.405

Sec. 5. A public employer, public employee or an elected or appointed official may not personally, or through an agent, coerce, attempt to coerce, or command another public employee to pay, lend, or contribute anything of value to a party, committee, organization, agency, or person for the benefit of a person seeking or holding elected office, or for the purpose of furthering or defeating a proposed law, ballot question, or other measure that may be submitted to a vote of the electors.

Example 12-F · A governing rule derived from a statute

The state will be able to establish that Councilmember Bennett coerced or attempted to coerce Ms. Larsen to contribute money to an organization established to benefit Councilman Bennett. Under Michigan law, an elected official may not coerce or attempt to coerce a public employee to contribute anything of value to an organization for the benefit of a person holding elected office or for the purpose of furthering or defeating a proposed law. Mich. Comp. Laws § 15.405 (2015).

When you are drafting the governing rule, you will have two competing goals. On the one hand, you want to educate your reader about the language used to discuss the issue. Therefore, you will want to reproduce the language that the statute or courts use. On the other hand, you will want your description to be clear. These goals are often in tension with each other.

You have some options. If the way in which the statute or the courts discuss the governing rule is confusing, you can repeat the rule (with the confusing language) to introduce the language, and then in a sentence or two, clarify the meaning. Alternatively, you can reframe the governing rule in a way that is clearer. If you reframe the rule in a new way, you may want to provide the exact language (either from the statute or that the courts typically use) in a footnote so that your reader can see the origin of your language.

2. Explain how courts interpret or apply the governing rule

When describing the governing rule, you should also describe any rules or policies that affect how courts interpret or apply the governing rule, if that will be relevant to your legal analysis. For example, you might explain the legislative reason behind the statute; the burden of proof, that is how much evidence a party must bring forward; how the courts balance factors in the governing rule; or presumptions the courts apply when interpreting the rule. In Example 12-G, the introduction explains how courts understand the governing rule.

Example 12-G · Governing rule stated, then explained

Conclusion ⟶ Our client has a viable claim for unjust enrichment. In Oregon, the theory of unjust enrichment provides an exception to the state's usual rule that im-

Background information ⟶ provements to rented space typically become the property of the landlord and a tenant may not recover for those improvements. *W.H. Shields v. Or. Dept. of Revenue*, 513 P.2d 784, 789 (Or. 1973); *Gourley v. O'Donnell*, 626 P.2d 367, 371 (Or. Ct. App. 1981). Under the unjust enrichment theory, restitution is available

Governing rule ⟶ when denying such restitution would work an excessively harsh result on the tenant or provide an unreasonable windfall to the owner. *Kerr v. Miller*, 977 P.2d 438, 445 (Or. Ct. App. 1999). Courts determine whether a tenant is entitled to

Explanation of how courts ⟶ restitution based on an assessment of the equities as a whole, in light of the cir-
understand and apply the
governing rule
cumstances of the particular case. *Id.* In this case, our client has a strong claim for unjust enrichment because permitting the landlord to retain nearly $60,000

Conclusion again. The ⟶ in improvements on a $700 per month lease would provide the landlord with
conclusion also maps the
discussion ahead.
an unreasonable windfall.

Be careful, however, to distinguish between those rules and policies that affect the governing rule as a whole and those that affect only one element or factor. The introduction is the place to discuss rules and policies relevant to the *entire* governing rule. If a rule or policy affects only one element or factor, discuss that rule or policy in your legal argument about that one element or factor. Do not muddle your discussion by including information in your introduction that is relevant to only one element or factor.

3. Provide necessary background information

In the introductory roadmap section, you may also need to include background information to provide context for the governing rule and the legal question being addressed. For example, in Example 12-G, above, the introduction explains that the theory of unjust enrichment is an exception to the usual rule that tenants will not be compensated for improvements to a rental property. That information—that the governing rule is an exception—is helpful background information because it explains the relationship between the governing rule and the larger body of law.

C. Dispose of the Obvious and Uncontroversial (if Necessary)

In some arguments, you will address every element in the governing rule. If that is the case, you would not need to dispose of any elements. (If you are working on such an Argument, skip the rest of this section and go to the next section.)

Sometimes, however, an element or factor in the governing rule does not warrant a full legal argument. In that case, you can dispose of that element or factor in the roadmap section.

An element or factor does not warrant a full legal argument if (1) research shows the element is clearly met, *and* (2) your reader can easily see how the element is met.

The roadmap in Example 12-H, which follows, shows how you might quickly dispose of a legal argument in your introduction. The example addresses whether a councilmember has coerced a public employee to act on the councilmember's behalf. It quickly disposes of one element—whether the plaintiff was a "public employee"—by providing the definition of a "public employee" and the facts that show the plaintiff was clearly a public employee. Because the element is clearly met and that conclusion will raise no questions in the reader's mind, no further discussion is necessary.

Example 12-H · Disposing of elements that may not warrant a full legal discussion

---

Ms. Larsen will probably not be able to establish that Councilmember Bennett ◄— Conclusion
coerced Ms. Larsen to contribute something of value to an organization for Councilmember Bennett's benefit. Under Michigan law, an elected official may not coerce or attempt to coerce a public employee to contribute anything of value to an organization for the benefit of a person holding elected office or for the purpose of furthering or defeating a proposed law. Mich. Comp. Laws § 15.405 (2005).

In this case, Ms. Larsen is a public employee. A public employee is defined ◄— Disposing of an element that
as "an employee of the state classified civil service." Mich. Comp. Laws § 15.401. does not warrant a full legal
discussion

Ms. Larsen took her civil service exam in 1973 and is a Grade 14 employee, employed in the Office of the Secretary of State.

The introduction maps the elements that remain and, therefore, the elements that will be discussed in the remainder of the memo.

The remaining portion of the statute raises four issues. First, Ms. Larsen can probably show that she contributed something of value to the organization "Save Our Downtown" because she held the Secretary of State's office open an additional 15 minutes on the evening ballot measures were due. Moreover, that act could likely be construed to be "for the benefit" of Councilmember Bennett because he publicly supported the measure. That act can also be construed as "furthering … a proposed law" because, had she not held the office open, the measure would not have made it on the ballot. However, Ms. Larsen will not be able to prove that Councilmember Bennett coerced Ms. Larsen to act. Thus, she will not be able to establish a claim under the statute.

Your discussion may not address an element or factor in the governing rule for other reasons—perhaps you were asked to address only a subset of the elements or perhaps you do not have access to sufficient information to address one of the elements or factors. No matter what the reason, if an element or factor in the governing rule is not addressed in a full legal argument, your roadmap section should indicate why not so that your reader is not surprised by its absence.

D. Map and Assess the Remaining Arguments (if Necessary)

Your reader will also expect the introduction to tell her the order of the legal arguments that are to come. That map of the arguments to come will be particularly helpful if you assess those arguments: Will there be one element that will be particularly difficult to prove? Is there one factor that is more important than the others? Let's look at some different situations and how you might map and assess the remainder.

If you have not disposed of any elements, then your governing rule might act as the map of the remaining arguments. Remember, the governing rule lists the elements and factors that need to be addressed to resolve a client's question. Your reader—an attorney—knows that and looks for the elements and factors while reading the governing rule. Your reader then assumes that the order of your legal arguments will follow the order of the governing rule.

If the order of your discussion follows the order in which the elements appear in the governing rule, then you need do nothing further to indicate the organization in the remainder of your discussion. The governing rule has already told your reader the order ahead. Sometimes, an attorney will end the introduction here and turn to the first legal argument, as in Example 12-I.

Example 12-I · Governing rule acts as a map of the discussion

The Workers' Compensation Board improperly denied workers' compensation benefits to Mr. Mark Gator, and its decision should be reversed. Under California law, a person injured during an off-duty recreational activity is entitled to workers' compensation if the activity was a reasonable expectancy of employment. Cal. Lab. Code Ann. § 3600(a)(9) (West 2003). An activity is a reasonable expectancy of employment if (1) the employee subjectively believed he was required to participate in the activity, and (2) the employee's belief was objectively reasonable. Meyer v. Workers' Compen. Apps. Bd., 204 Cal. Rptr. 74, 76 (Cal. App. 4th Dist. 1984).

A. Mark Gator Subjectively Believed He was Required to Play Paddleball with His Boss.

The standard for establishing an employee's subjective belief is a "lax standard." Aetna Cas. & Sur. Co. v. Workers' Compen. Apps. Bd., 232 Cal. Rptr. 257, 263 (Cal. App. 5th Dist. 1986).

Sometimes, however, you cannot rely on the governing rule to map the order of the arguments to come. For example, if you dispose of one or more aspects of the governing rule, your reader will want to know what's left. Rather than forcing your reader to return to the governing rule and figure out what's left, do that work for her. The last paragraph of example 12-H, above, shows you one way to map and assess the remaining arguments after disposing of one or more elements in the governing rule.

Other times, you will want to map the remaining arguments because you have decided that one element or factor is so important that it should be discussed first. An element might address an important threshold question, or you might simply decide that it makes sense to address the elements in an order different from the order presented in the governing rule.

Whatever the reason, if the order in which you discuss the elements is different from the order in which the governing rule presents them, be sure to explain your chosen order and *why* you have chosen that order. Remember that your reader expects your discussion to follow the order of the governing rule. If your discussion does not, your reader will become confused and may think that *you* are confused and that your discussion is disorganized.

E. Conclude Again (if Necessary)

Some attorneys state their conclusion again at the bottom of their roadmap section to be more specific about why an argument will succeed or fail. For example, in Example 12-G, the attorney finishes with a more specific conclusion. First, the attorney explained that the plaintiff's claim for unjust enrichment will succeed only if he can prove either that denying restitution would work an excessively harsh result or an unreasonable windfall to the defendant. The conclusion at the end of the introduction specifies that, in that case, denying restitution would be an unreasonable windfall.

You may also want to re-state your conclusion when your roadmap section is long. If you have provided a lot of information to your reader, you may want to remind your reader of your conclusion before moving on to discuss individual legal arguments. As a rough guide, if your introduction is longer than half a page, consider re-stating your conclusion.

Sometimes, however, you will choose to end the roadmap section by simply listing the issues that will be addressed and their order, as in Example 12-H.

No rule tells us when the introduction should end with a conclusion. Rather, you will need to judge whether your reader will be helped by seeing the conclusion restated before moving on.

II. Create Informative Point Headings

After completing the roadmap section, you will likely have a point heading introducing an individual legal argument. Point headings indicate the individual legal arguments, but they also perform other important work for your reader. First, point headings tell the reader the bottom-line conclusion of the upcoming section. Second, point headings visually break up blocks of text and give the reader a "landing spot." At each landing spot, the reader can digest the material she just read and prepare for the next topic.

Finally, point headings function as a table of contents for the reader, giving a sense of the main points and the order in which those points will be presented. Although your reader may read through the whole memo once, when your reader uses the memo—whether to talk to a client or to draft a motion to a court—your reader will jump to different sections in your memo as she needs information from that section. The point headings will allow her to quickly find the argument that she seeks.

A. Make Point Headings "Work"

For point headings to actually perform their work, they should describe two things:

1. **Your conclusion to the section, and**
2. **The primary reason for your conclusion.**

When describing the conclusion and the primary reason for it, you might also include the rule governing the issue, the determinative facts from your client's case, or a combination of rule and facts.

Example 12-J is an effective point heading. It describes the conclusion of the section (that the Neros "actually possessed" the land), the legal support for the conclusion (that they used the land as owners would), and the determinative facts (that they maintained a fence line and harvested crops). With this information, the reader can understand the conclusion to the legal argument, as well as the law and facts that support it.

Example 12-J · Effective point heading

A. The Neros "actually possessed" the land because they used the land as an owner would by maintaining a fence and harvesting fruit trees.

Sometimes, you will not be able to include all the information that you might like to include. If length is an issue, choose clarity over completeness. A reader should be able to glance down at a point heading and quickly pick out the main point. If the reason or facts require too much text, your reader will not be able to pick out your main point, so you will need to scale back your point heading. In that case, you might include your conclusion with just a short statement of the law that supports your conclusion and omit the facts, as in Example 12-K.

Example 12-K · Effective, shorter point heading

A. The Neros "actually possessed" the land because they used the land as an owner would.

Also, you might include your conclusion and the key facts that support that conclusion without the reason, as in Example 12-L. Sometimes, you might simply state your conclusion, as in Example 12-M.

Example 12-L · Another effective, shorter point heading

A. The Neros "actually possessed" the land because they maintained a fence line and harvested the crop of fruit trees.

Example 12-M · Another effective, shorter point heading

A. The Neros "actually possessed" the land.

Determining how much information to put in your point heading is a judgment call. Although ideally you would include your conclusion, the support for your conclusion, and the specific facts that led you to that conclusion, you must consider whether including all that information will still allow your point heading to function effectively. If the reader cannot see the main point quickly, leave out the additional information.

Although you may shorten the information included in your point heading, at a minimum, you must state your conclusion. Some point headings are "lazy." Rather than explaining the conclusion and the reason for it, lazy headings just mention the topic that will be covered in the section. Example 12-N illustrates a lazy point heading.

Example 12-N · A lazy point heading

A. Actual possession.

Although the point heading in Example 12-N notifies the reader of the element about to be discussed, it does not tell the reader the ultimate conclusion of the section, nor does it give any determinative facts or legal reasoning. The heading is a "placeholder," but it does not *work*. Since attorneys value clarity and conciseness, make every word count and make every heading work.

B. Restate the Conclusion after the Point Heading

If you use point headings, you may wonder whether you should state your conclusion in the point heading and then immediately restate that same conclusion in the first sentence of the argument that follows. Often, the answer is yes.

Attorneys frequently state the conclusion to a legal argument three times: once in the point heading, a second time in the first sentence of the legal argument, and a third time at the end of the argument. The attorney may even state the conclusion a fourth time at the beginning of the application section.

Overkill? Not usually. Attorneys want to make sure the reader knows where the discussion is headed, and at the end, attorneys want to make sure they have driven home their point.

Stating the conclusion in a point heading and then in the text may seem overly repetitive; however, readers sometimes skip over point headings, moving from paragraph to paragraph. So, your reader may not see your point heading. On the other hand, you do not want to omit the point headings because your reader will need them when searching for a particular argument within your memo.

To avoid the repetitive feel of stating your conclusion in the point heading and again in your first sentence of your legal argument, simply revise your conclusion slightly so that you are not using the exact same words. Example 12-O shows how you can modify your point heading so that it does not seem overly repetitious.

Example 12-O · Point heading and conclusion

A. The Neros "actually possessed" the land because they used the land as an owner would by maintaining a fence line and harvesting the fruit trees.

The Neros can prove that they actually possessed the land. A person proves actual possession by....

Although we would recommend that you state your conclusion in both the point heading and the first sentence of your legal argument, not all attorneys do so. When you begin your legal career, you might look at samples in your law office to see what the attorneys in your office do. Then, as you read more legal writing, watch what other attorneys do and gauge your own likes and dislikes. As you gain more experience, you'll be able to make a better determination about what will be most helpful to your reader.

C. Create Professional-Looking Point Headings

Your memo makes an impression by the way it looks, and the point headings will contribute to that impression. Creating professional-looking point headings takes only a few steps.

First, start with a traditional outline format. Example 12-P illustrates a traditional outline format.

Example 12-P · A traditional outline

I. POINT HEADINGS ASSERT A CONCLUSION THAT THE WRITER BELIEVES THE COURT WILL ADOPT.

    A. Roman numerals are used for dispositive point headings, while capital letters are used to identify individual legal arguments.

        a. <u>Underlining is used for sub-issues within one legal argument.</u>

        b. <u>Notice how point headings convey, graphically, the hierarchy of an argument.</u>

    B. Each point heading should be one sentence that is not too long to be absorbed.

II. POINT HEADINGS SHOULD PROVIDE A SKELETAL OUTLINE OF YOUR ARGUMENTS.

In legal writing, Roman numerals designate dispositive legal issues. If your discussion addresses only one legal issue, your outline may begin with the capital letter A.

Each point heading should be in a legible font and set out so that it stands out from your main text. If the formatting requirements of your office do not require it, do not use all caps in point headings for memoranda or internal documents. As you can see in Example 12-Q, all caps are difficult to read.

Example 12-Q • All caps are difficult to read

A. THE NEROS "ACTUALLY POSSESSED" THE LAND BECAUSE THEY USED THE LAND AS AN OWNER WOULD BY MAINTAINING A FENCE LINE AND HARVESTING THE CROP OF FRUIT TREES.

Finally, use a "hanging indent." That is, the first word of the second line should align with the first word in the first line, not with the signpost letter or numeral. Example 12-Q, although difficult to read because of the all caps, uses a hanging indent. Example 12-R does not.

Example 12-R • Point heading without a hanging indent

If a hanging indent were used, the text would align along the vertical line.

A. The Neros "actually possessed" the land because they used the land as an owner would by maintaining a fence line and harvesting the crop of fruit trees.

III. Use Mini-Roadmaps to Introduce Sub-Arguments

Typically, one element or factor in a governing rule will be explored with one legal argument. Sometimes, however, an element or factor in the governing rule requires more than one argument. When it does, you will need a mini-roadmap to alert your reader to the upcoming structure and to give your reader context for the issues being explored.

A mini-roadmap does for one element or factor what the roadmap section does for your discussion as a whole: It sets out the governing rule for one element or factor, lets the reader know which elements or factors within that rule will be discussed (or disposed of), states the order in which the remaining elements or factors will be discussed, and gives your bottom-line conclusion on the issue.

Take, for example, the fourth element in a claim for adverse possession: hostility. A plaintiff can prove hostility in one of two ways. A plaintiff can establish a "pure mistake" or a "subjective intent" to take possession of the land. Because the element "hostility" can be proven in two ways, the attorney needs to explore whether both those avenues are open to his client and explain why or why not. As a result, explaining the one element of hostility will require two legal arguments.

A mini-roadmap in Example 12-S alerts the reader that the discussion about hostility will require two legal arguments, rather than just one, as is ordinarily the case.

Example 12-S · Mini-roadmap alerts reader to upcoming structure

Fourth, the Neros must establish that their use of the disputed property was hostile. To prove hostility, the plaintiffs must have used the disputed land intending to occupy the land as its true owners and not in subordination to the true owner. *Faulconer v. Williams*, 964 P.2d 246, 252 (Or. 1998). Plaintiffs can prove hostility in two ways. *Hoffman*, 994 P.2d at 110. Plaintiffs can establish that "possession was under an honest but mistaken belief of ownership." *Id.* at 110 n. 4. This rule is the "pure mistake" doctrine. *Id.* Alternatively, plaintiffs can establish that, subjectively, they intended to deprive the owners of ownership. *Faulconer*, 964 P.2d at 251.

    ◄— A mini-roadmap alerts the reader to two upcoming arguments.

The Neros will very likely be able to prove "pure mistake"....

In the alternative, if Ms. Welch and Mr. Bruce find a neighbor to testify to any doubt by the Neros during the 12-year period, then the Neros would have to prove hostility through their subjective intent to own the land....

    ◄— Each argument is then explored in the order in which they were presented in the mini-roadmap.

In Example 12-T, which omits the mini-roadmap, the reader will not understand how the two arguments that follow relate to any of the prior arguments. A mini-roadmap spares the reader from confusion by clarifying both the law that applies to the element and the structure of the arguments that follow.

Example 12-T · No mini-roadmap to alert reader to the upcoming structure

Fourth, the Neros must establish that their use of the disputed property was hostile. To prove hostility, the plaintiffs must have used the disputed land intending to occupy the land as its true owners and not in subordination to the true owner. *Faulconer v. Williams*, 964 P.2d 246, 252 (Or. 1998).

The Neros will very likely be able to prove "pure mistake".... Plaintiffs can establish a pure mistake when the "possession was under an honest but mistaken belief of ownership." *Hoffman*, 994 P.2d at 110....

In the alternative, if Ms. Welch and Mr. Bruce find a neighbor to testify to any doubt by the Neros during the 12-year period, then the Neros would have to prove hostility through their subjective intent to own the land....

    ◄— Without a roadmap, the reader will be surprised by this alternative argument.

As in your introductory roadmap section, you can also use a mini-roadmap if an element requires two arguments and you dispose of one. Example 12-U does just that.

Example 12-U · Mini-roadmap identifies two arguments and then disposes of one of them

A mini-roadmap identifies two ways to prove possession is "open and notorious," disposes of one (actual notice), and identifies the remaining argument (constructive notice).

After proving actual possession, the Neros will have to demonstrate that their possession of the land was open and notorious. To prove that their possession was open and notorious, the plaintiffs must prove that the owners had notice that they were asserting title to the disputed property. *E.g.*, *Slak*, 875 P.2d at 519. The notice may be actual or constructive. *Id.* Owners have actual notice when they are aware that their claim of the land is being challenged. *See id.* Because Ms. Cramer was unaware that the Neros were asserting a claim to the disputed land, she did not have actual notice. Instead, the Neros must prove that they gave constructive notice of their possession.

The Neros can probably establish constructive notice because they built a fence on the purported boundary and used the land extensively and openly.

The Discussion section in your memorandum will require you to bring together a series of legal arguments. To effectively present those arguments, you will have to help your reader clearly see your organizational structure. You can do that through an introductory roadmap section, point headings, and mini-roadmaps along the way.

The primary goal in a memorandum is to communicate your legal analysis clearly and succinctly. The more legal arguments you present in one document, the clearer you must be about your organizational structure and the relationship among your arguments.

Practice Points

- Give the reader a roadmap to your memorandum with an introductory section that establishes your conclusion to the issue, explains the governing rule, dispenses with arguments that will not be addressed, and indicates the order in which the remaining arguments will appear.

- Restate your conclusion at the beginning and, if you think it is necessary, again at the end of the roadmap section.

- A working point heading reflects your legal conclusion and the reasons for that conclusion. Together, point headings should reflect the main points of your argument and how those points fit together.

- Well-formatted point headings will reinforce the professionalism of your work product.

- A mini-roadmap at the beginning of an individual legal argument will help orient your reader when an element or factor needs to be addressed with more than one legal argument. A mini-roadmap performs the same functions as your introductory roadmap, but it does so for a sub-section of your discussion.

Chapter 13

Question Presented and Brief Answer

Busy people like quick answers. As a result, your memorandum should begin by stating the legal issue your memo will address and your ultimate conclusion, respectively, in a Question Presented and Brief Answer. The Question Presented sets forth the precise legal question your client needs answered. The Brief Answer then provides the bottom-line answer to that question and a few of the critical reasons that support your conclusion. Together, the Question Presented and Brief Answer will describe the analytical crux of your argument.

Both the Question Presented and the Brief Answer must convey a great amount of information concisely and precisely. Because you are distilling much information into a short statement, both the Question Presented and the Brief Answer can be challenging to write. These sections contain valuable information, however, and are the first part of your memo the supervising attorney will read, so you must learn to draft these sections well.

I. The Role of a Question Presented and Brief Answer

The Question Presented and Brief Answer serve three purposes. First, the Question Presented and Brief Answer are time-management devices. They allow your supervising attorney to quickly determine the question addressed in the memo, the answer to it, and the basis for that answer, even if she does not have time to read your entire analysis at just that moment.

Second, the Question Presented and Brief Answer make your detailed analysis easier to absorb. Every reader is subconsciously asking, "Why should I bother reading this material?" The reader wants to know why the details matter and how the details relate to the larger picture. The Question Presented and Brief Answer tell the reader why the material should be read. Once the reader knows the legal question addressed and the final answer, the reader can understand *why* those details in the memorandum matter and *how* those details relate to the client's question.

Finally, these sections are an aid to future colleagues. Law offices often catalog memos so that future attorneys do not have to re-create work that has already been created. When a similar issue subsequently arises, an attorney can simply pull the old memorandum and look at the Question Presented and Brief Answer to see whether it examines the same legal issue. The old memorandum will probably not answer the new question completely, and the research will certainly have to be updated; however, the old memorandum will give a good starting point for the attorney's research and analysis of the new problem, saving the attorney time and the client money.

II. The Form of a Question Presented and Brief Answer

Questions Presented and Brief Answers take many forms from workplace to workplace. They may have different names, such as Issue Presented and Conclusion, and the style in which each part is presented may differ as well. So, when you begin working in a new law office or if you begin working with a new senior attorney in that office, you should ask for a sample memo and follow whatever form your office or the senior attorney prefers.

You can see two typical formats for a Question Presented and Brief Answer in Examples 13-A and 13-B. Although named and structured differently, both describe the precise legal question the memo will address and state a conclusion to that question. They accomplish the same goal.

Example 13-A · A typical Question Presented and Brief Answer

QUESTION PRESENTED

The Question Presented describes the legal question and the critical facts from the client's case on which the question will turn.

Under Oregon law, which allows a defendant's statement into evidence if the statement was made during "mere conversation," will Mr. Adams's statement be admissible when he made the statement after the undercover officer parked an unmarked police car behind Mr. Adams's car and Mr. Adams told the officer he was not yet planning to leave?

BRIEF ANSWER

Yes. The statement will be admissible against Mr. Adams. Evidence is admissible against a defendant if it is gathered during "mere conversation" rather than during a "stop." An officer stops another individual only if that individual could reasonably believe that his liberty was being restrained. Mr. Adams could not reasonably believe that his liberty was being restrained. Therefore, Mr. Adams's statement will likely be admissible.

The Brief Answer provides an answer to the question and states the key rule on which the answer is based.

Example 13-B • A typical Question Presented and Brief Answer with different labels

ISSUE STATEMENT

Our client, Paul Adams, made a statement to an undercover officer that implicates him in a local robbery. He made the statement after the undercover officer parked his unmarked police car behind his car. When the officer asked if he was planning to leave, Mr. Adams said "no." Under Oregon law, which allows such evidence to be admitted if the encounter is "mere conversation," will Mr. Adams's statement be admissible?

The Issue Statement (the Question Presented) describes the critical facts from the client's case and the legal question.

CONCLUSION

Yes. The statement will likely be admissible. Oregon law says that evidence gathered during "mere conversation" as opposed to a "stop" is admissible. A person is stopped only if he could reasonably believe that his liberty was being restrained. Mr. Adams could not reasonably believe that his liberty was being restrained. Therefore, his statement likely will be admissible against him.

The Conclusion (the Brief Answer) provides an answer to the question and explains the key reasons for that conclusion.

No matter how the Question Presented and Brief Answer are named or styled, they should convey the vital information an attorney expects.

III. Writing a Question Presented

A proper Question Presented has three parts: a description of the specific governing law and its jurisdiction, the precise legal question, and the most determinative facts giving rise to the question. Together, these parts ask, "What legal question is presented by these facts?" While the language and format in which you present these parts can vary, make sure that your Question Presented has all three parts.

Because the Question Presented is the first section your reader encounters, the focus of the question must be clear and all essential information must be included.

A. Structuring the Question Presented

The easiest way to structure your Question Presented is in one of two formats: the under/does/when[1] format or the statements-and-question format.[2] Look at how each format works.

1. Structuring a Question Presented with under/does/when

The under/does/when format presents the three vital parts of a Question Presented in one sentence. This format works this way:

Under   [this controlling law—give jurisdiction, the law, and what the law allows or prohibits]

Does/Is/Can [this legal consequence occur]

When   [these determinative facts are present]?

In this format, you will move from the controlling law to listing determinative facts. Notice each of the parts in Example 13-C.[3]

Example 13-C · Under/does/when format

QUESTION PRESENTED

Under South Dakota statutory law, which prohibits a third party from seducing another man's spouse, is the third party liable for alienating the spouse's affections when the third party sent her flowers, texted her daily, and invited her out on dates when she was contemplating a marital separation from her husband?

Each component of the under/does/when format gives the reader valuable information. The reader needs all three parts to fully understand the question you are posing.

(a) "Under" the controlling law

In the "under" section, you tell the reader the controlling jurisdiction and the law that governs the client's question. When describing the law that governs the client's question, be careful to provide enough information

---

1. We believe the originators of this format are Laurel Currie Oates, Anne Enquist, & Kelly Kunsch, *The Legal Writing Handbook: Analysis, Research, and Writing* (1st ed. 1993).

2. Although we do not know who originated this format, Bryan Garner describes it in *Legal Writing in Plain English* 73, 78 (2d ed. 2013) (explaining how attorneys should "spill the beans" on the first page).

3. The authors thank Professors Laura Graham and Luellen Curry of Wake Forest University School of Law for materials used to create Example 13-C, 13-E through 13-I, and 13-Q. See Section 8.2, *Applying the Law: Analogical Reasoning*, note 2.

so that the reader can quickly understand the purpose of the law. For example, in Example 13-D, the reader does not have enough information to understand what law controls the client's question because only the statutory number is given.

Example 13-D · "Under" part of Question Presented not developed

---

QUESTION PRESENTED

Under § 20-9-7 (2015), can a husband bring a claim against his wife's alleged paramour for sending the wife flowers, texting her daily, and inviting her out on dates, when the wife was already contemplating a marital separation?

Having read Example 13-D, answer these questions: Does the question address a federal or state law? If the latter, which state? And, what exactly does § 20-9-7 prohibit or require? Without additional information, the reader may not understand what jurisdiction controls the analysis, or even worse, the reader may not immediately understand the exact law being evaluated.

In Example 13-D, the reader may eventually figure out that the statutory section cited gives a cause of action for alienation of affections; however, the *reader* should not have to work to figure out this information. If you reference an authority, immediately explain what that authority provides.

Now look at Example 13-E to see a question presented with the "under" part more developed.

Example 13-E · "Under" part of Question Presented is well developed

---

QUESTION PRESENTED

Under South Dakota's § 20-9-7 (2015), which prohibits the seduction of a wife from her husband by a third party, can a husband bring a claim against the third party for sending the wife flowers, texting her daily, and inviting her out on dates, when the wife was already contemplating a marital separation?

After reading the Question Presented in Example 13-E, the reader has valuable information. He knows what jurisdiction controls, and he knows what law governs the client's question.

You will have to use your own good judgment in deciding the level of specificity needed in the "under" section. For example, although you will often want to include a statutory section, you may decide to describe the statute that controls, and leave the citation to the statutory section for later, as in Example 13-C, above. Similarly, when the Question

Presented involves a common law claim, you will simply name the common law claim. Usually, the name itself describes the law that controls, as in Example 13-F.

Example 13-F • "Under" part of Question Presented is well developed

---

QUESTION PRESENTED

Under North Carolina's common law, which prohibits intentional infliction of emotional distress, can a businessman recover for emotional distress when a former relative posts to the Internet accusations of sexual and financial misconduct, causing the businessman to lose an important client and seek psychiatric treatment?

(b) "Does/Is/Can" this question or legal consequence occur

The "does" part of the Question Presented is straightforward. This part, illustrated in Example 13-G, explains what precise legal question is being asked. Be as specific and precise as possible in stating the legal question.

Example 13-G • Examples of "does" part of the Question Presented

---

"... does a police officer violate § 1983 when...."

"... is a third party liable for alienating the affections of another man's wife when...."

"... can a husband establish a claim for alienation of affections when...."

(c) "When" these legally significant facts occurred

In addition to describing the legal question, you will need to explain the facts that will determine the outcome in your client's case. Those facts are the legally significant facts. You will not, however, be able to include all of the legally significant facts.

Your Question Presented has to remain brief so that it is a quick and understandable summary. Generally, two or three legally significant facts will be all you can use without sacrificing clarity.

When the desire to include facts conflicts with the need to keep the summary short, you will simply have some hard choices to make: Of the many facts that will have an influence on the court, which will be *most* legally significant? List the most important facts on which the court will base its decision. Choose only those two or three facts most determinative to the issue. Compare Example 13-H with Example 13-I to see how too many facts convolute the question.

Example 13-H • Too many facts included in Question Presented

QUESTION PRESENTED

Under South Dakota statutory law, which prohibits a third party from seducing another man's spouse, is a paramour liable for alienating the wife's affections **when** he sent her flowers on three occasions, wrote her amorous notes, took her out on several dates, and called her daily for three months, when she and her husband were already having problems and thinking about separating, but were still cohabitating and seeing a marriage counselor?

Example 13-I • Only the determinative facts included

QUESTION PRESENTED

Under South Dakota statutory law, which prohibits a third party from seducing another man's spouse, is the third party liable for alienating the wife's affections **when** he sent her flowers, notes, and invited her out on dates while she was contemplating a marital separation from her husband?

(d) Vary the order of the three parts if it makes the Question Presented clearer

Although presenting the three parts in the under/does/when order may be easiest, you can alter the order if doing so makes the question easier for your reader to understand. Example 13-J shows how.

Example 13-J • Under/does/when re-ordered

QUESTION PRESENTED

When a married couple is separated and a third party sends flowers, asks the wife out on dates, and writes her notes, is the third party liable for alienation of affections under South Dakota law, which prohibits the seduction of a wife away from her husband?

2. Structuring a Question Presented with statements and a question

Many attorneys present their Question Presented in one sentence. Some attorneys, however, use several sentences to describe the Question Presented. In this alternative format, the attorney will describe the determinative facts and then pose the legal question under the controlling law.

This format is less confining than the previous under/does/when format because you can use several sentences to convey the Question Presented. Although you are not confined to writing one sentence with this format, you should not write too many sentences. Two or three sentences, then the legal question, should suffice. Clarity and conciseness are still the goals in this format.

Even though you have more structural freedom, you must still tell the reader the three vital parts of the question—the exact controlling law, the precise legal question, and the determinative facts on which the question will turn. You can see each of these parts in Example 13-K.

Example 13-K · A Question Presented structured with statements and a question

---

QUESTION PRESENTED

Our client, Paul Adams, made a statement to an undercover officer that implicates him in a local robbery. He made the statement after the undercover officer parked his unmarked police car behind Mr. Adams's car. When the officer asked if he was planning to leave, Mr. Adams said "no." Under Oregon law, which allows such evidence to be admitted if the encounter was "mere conversation," will Mr. Adams's statement be admissible at trial?

The **determinative facts** are described in the first three sentences.

The **controlling law** and the **legal question** are identified in the final sentence.

(a) Describe the determinative facts in chronological order

If you use a statement-and-question format, you should begin by presenting the determinative facts. Again, select the most important facts a court would use to decide the legal question.

When presenting the determinative facts, present them chronologically. Readers assume that facts will be presented chronologically. When facts are not presented chronologically, readers often stumble and become confused as they try to sort out the chronology of events. Read Example 13-L to see how a random factual chronology can be confusing to the reader.

Example 13-L · Facts presented in random order are difficult to absorb

---

QUESTION PRESENTED

Mr. Adams made a statement to an undercover officer that implicated him in a local bank robbery. Beforehand, Mr. Adams told Officer Ephgrave he was not planning to leave after Officer Ephgrave parked his unmarked car behind Mr. Adams's car. Under Oregon law, which allows statements into evidence if made during "mere conversation," will Mr. Adams's statement be admissible?

Avoid the confusion. State the facts chronologically.

(b) Describe the controlling law and pose the legal question

You can describe the controlling law and the question being asked in one of two ways. After describing the facts in one or more sentences, you can combine the controlling law with the precise legal question in the last sentence of the Question Presented (see Example 13-M). Alternatively, you can divide these two parts and state the controlling law in the first sentence of your question presented and the legal question being asked in the last (see Example 13-N). Use your judgment in deciding which position will be clearer for the reader.

Example 13-M · Controlling law is combined with the legal question

QUESTION PRESENTED

Paul Adams made a statement to an undercover officer that implicates him in a local robbery. He made the statement after the undercover officer parked his unmarked police car behind Mr. Adams's car. When the officer asked if he was planning to leave, Mr. Adams said "no." Under Oregon law, which allows statements into evidence if the encounter is "mere conversation," will Mr. Adams's statement be admissible against him at trial?

Example 13-N · Controlling law begins the statements-and-question format

QUESTION PRESENTED

Oregon law allows a defendant's statements into evidence if it occurs during "mere conversation." Our client, Paul Adams made a statement after an undercover officer parked his unmarked police car behind Mr. Adams's car and after Mr. Adams said he was not planning to leave. Will Mr. Adams's statement be admissible against him at trial?

Whether you are using the under/does/when format or the statements-and-question format, make sure that your Question Presented contains the vital information the attorney reading it will be seeking: the exact controlling law, the precise legal question being asked, and the determinative facts on which the question will turn.

B. Tools for Drafting an Effective Question Presented

1. Create one Question Presented for each main issue in the memorandum

Each dispositive legal issue in the memorandum gets its own Question Presented (and Brief Answer). If your client's question is whether she has a valid claim for adverse possession, which is one issue, your memo would have one Question Presented (and one Brief Answer). But if your client has additional, dispositive legal issues (such as whether she can bring a claim for trespass or whether the statute of limitations has expired on her claim), then you would need to include a Question Presented (and Brief Answer) for each dispositive legal issue.

The order in which you present a series of Questions Presented should follow the order in which the legal issues are addressed in the body of the memo.

2. Describe the facts that will be determinative to the court

In your Question Presented, the facts are important because a court's decision is fact-specific. If the facts were to change, the court's conclusion might change. Thus, a well-drafted Question Presented must describe the facts that would be determinative to the court's conclusion.

For example, the legal issue in the Adams case in Examples 13-A and 13-B is not just whether Officer Ephgrave stopped Paul Adams. More precisely, the issue is whether Officer Ephgrave stopped Paul Adams *when* Officer Ephgrave parked his car behind Mr. Adams and told Mr. Adams he would move his car if Mr. Adams wanted to leave. Include enough factual detail so that the reader can see the facts most determinative to the court.

Detailed facts are excluded from the Question Presented in only two circumstances. First, detailed facts are not necessary if the issue the memo addresses is a pure question of law. For example, if the issue is how to interpret the language of a statute, then detailed facts may not be relevant.

The second occasion when you might not include detailed facts to describe the issue is when omitting them is the practice in your law office. Some law offices do not include detailed facts in the Question Presented. Often, those law offices structure their memo so that the Statement of Facts appears first, and the Question Presented follows. The Question Presented assumes that the reader has read and remembered the Statement of Facts. If the custom in your law office is to state the Question Presented after the Statement of Facts and exclude facts from your question presented, by all means, do that.

If, however, you have a choice, state the Question Presented first and include detailed facts in it. The Question Presented and Brief Answer are most helpful if they are at the top of your memo. That is where they are easy to see and can most effectively serve their purpose: to give a quick, easy to read summary. Buried in your memo after the Statement of Facts, the Question Presented and the answer to it will be more difficult to find.

3. Describe determinative facts in concrete detail

When describing your client's determinative facts, describe them in concrete, specific detail. Your reader should see a fact with the same degree of specificity that a court would. Compare Examples 13-O and 13-P to see the difference between a description that allows the reader to clearly visualize the facts and one that does not.

Example 13-O · Facts described in concrete, specific detail

QUESTION PRESENTED

Officer Ephgrave, who was working undercover, parked his unmarked car behind Mr. Adams's car. He told Mr. Adams that he would move his car when Mr. Adams wanted to leave. Mr. Adams said, "Oh, okay. No problem." During the conversation that followed, Mr. Adams made a statement that implicated him in a local robbery. Under Oregon law, will that statement be admissible at Mr. Adams's trial?

Example 13-P · Facts are generalized

QUESTION PRESENTED

Officer Ephgrave blocked Mr. Adams's car. Mr. Adams said it wasn't a problem. During the conversation that followed, Mr. Adams implicated himself in a local robbery. Under Oregon law, will that statement be admissible at trial?

The first example, Example 13-O, describes the facts in concrete, specific terms. The specificity allows the reader to visualize the issue. The second example, Example 13-P, generalizes the facts. Instead of describing how Officer Ephgrave blocked Mr. Adams's car, the second example simply asserts that the car was blocked. Similarly, instead of explaining Mr. Adams's exact statement to the officer, the second example paraphrases his response. In the second example, the issue remains fuzzy because the facts are fuzzy.

When drafting a Question Presented, you will have to balance the competing needs of factual specificity with concise sentences. When using the under/does/when format, your Question Presented will appear in a single sentence. Therefore, you will need to be especially careful to draft your facts to get optimum specificity without too much length. Although the Question Presented should be as complete as possible, it still needs to be clear, readable, and understandable.

4. Avoid legally significant phrases that assume the answer

In stating the Question Presented, you must avoid assuming the legal conclusion. You will assume the legal conclusion by describing a legal conclusion as a fact.

For instance, in Example 13-Q the writer was asked to determine whether a person's conduct alienated the affections of another man's wife.

The example assumes a legal conclusion because it asserts that "the paramour alienated the wife's affection for her husband" (shaded). Thus, rather than just giving the determinative facts of what happened, the writer assumed the answer to the ultimate question the memorandum was designed to answer.

Example 13-Q · Avoid legally significant phrases

QUESTION PRESENTED

Under South Dakota statutory law, which prohibits a third party from seducing another man's spouse, is the third party liable for alienating the wife's affections when the third party alienated the wife's affection for her husband by sending her flowers, notes, and expensive gifts?

5. Avoid "whether" when introducing your Question Presented

Traditionally, attorneys would begin a Question Presented with "whether," as in Example 13-R.

Example 13-R · Avoid "whether" at the beginning of your Question Presented

QUESTION PRESENTED

Whether an individual is stopped when an officer blocks an individual's car but tells the individual he will move the car when the individual wishes to leave.

"Whether" is stiff and makes for convoluted writing. Additionally, this format does not yield a complete sentence with a subject and a verb. Unless your office format or local custom requires it, avoid "whether" when introducing your Question Presented. Try instead to write a sentence that is grammatically correct and easier for your reader to understand.

6. State the question concisely

Remember that the Question Presented is a *summary* of the legal question being addressed. An entire memo follows and will flesh out those details you want to include. As a guide, try to keep each Question Presented to 75 words or fewer.[4]

---

4. Garner, *supra* note 2, at 73.

IV. Writing a Brief Answer

Every Question Presented in the memorandum should be partnered with a corresponding Brief Answer. The Brief Answer gives the reader two things: the ultimate answer to each issue in the client's legal question and the most important reasons for that answer.

The Brief Answer should be a single, concise paragraph. The first sentence of the paragraph should answer the question posed in the Question Presented, without elaboration. In the rest of the paragraph give the most important reasons that support your answer. Keep this paragraph short—include only the fundamental reasons for your answer, as in Example 13-S. Remember, your reader will get a full explanation of your prediction in the Discussion section.

Example 13-S · Example of a Brief Answer

BRIEF ANSWER

Yes. Our client can likely bring a successful claim for contractual misrepresentation. Misrepresentations are material when they are likely to affect the conduct of a reasonable person in the transaction. A representation is likely to affect a person's conduct when that person is peculiarly disposed to attach importance to that particular representation. Therefore, the representation that the house was haunted can be material because it was ultimately what affected our client's decision to buy the house.

Unlike the Question Presented, the Brief Answer does not come in alternate forms. Even though the Brief Answer is straightforward, a few tools can help you write a more effective Brief Answer.

- **State the answer concisely and visibly**

Because the Brief Answer should give a quick and easy-to-absorb answer, keep your initial answer short, and place it at the top of the paragraph. Short sentences are easier to absorb, and sentences at the beginning of a paragraph are easier for the eye to pick out. A simple "Yes," "No," "Most likely, yes," or "Mr. Adams was probably not stopped" are good short answers. The rest of your answer can explain why. All together, if you want your answer to be quick and easy to absorb, it should not exceed 75 words.[5]

- **State the specific rule on which your answer turns**

Your answer should include the underlying legal rule that will guide the court to its conclusion. Sometimes you will have several different

---

5. *See id.* at 61.

rules to choose from. For instance, in explaining why Mr. Adams's statement will be admissible against him, you could choose from among the following rules:

- A person is stopped if his liberty is restrained.

- To be stopped, a person must "reasonably believe that his liberty was restrained."

- A defendant is stopped if an officer blocks the defendant's car and the defendant was intending to leave.

If you have several rules to choose from, you will want to focus on the rule that best explains the principle on which the court's decision will hinge. In Mr. Adams's case, you might choose to focus on the second rule, which says "to be stopped, a person must 'reasonably believe that his liberty was restrained.'" That rule clearly articulates the principle on which the court will decide the case. Although the other two rules also communicate important concepts, the first rule is broad, and the third rule may seem curious to a reader who has not yet learned why a blocked car or an altered course is relevant.

• State your degree of certainty

Your goal in writing a memo is to give advice. As a result, you must take a position. That said, your memo has to be honest. It must reflect the degree of certainty that your analysis of the relevant law permits. Sometimes an outcome is certain. Often, however, you cannot say with absolute certainty that a jury will *not* find your client guilty. Or you may not be able to say that your client *will* be able to acquire title through adverse possession. You can, however, take your best guess at the likeliest outcome given the relevant law and the facts of your client's case as you know them to be. Table 13-T suggests language you can use depending on your degree of certainty.

Table 13-T · Degrees of certainty

- Yes. Our client will be able to prove/establish ...

- Our client will likely be able to prove/establish ...

- Our client will probably not be able to prove/establish ...

- No. The company cannot prove/establish ...

• Link your answer to your Question Presented

Your reader should be able to see the connection between your Question Presented and your answer. You can create that connection by repeating language from your Question Presented in your Brief Answer.

Consider the two examples below. In the first example, 13-U, the answer is not linked to the issue. By contrast, in the next example, 13-V, the word "stop" links the answer to the issue.

Example 13-U • Question Presented and Brief Answer are not linked

---

QUESTION PRESENTED

Our client, Paul Adams, made a statement to an undercover officer that implicates him in a local robbery. He made the statement after the undercover officer parked his unmarked police car behind his car. When the officer asked if he was planning to leave, Mr. Adams said "no." Under Oregon law, did Officer Ephgrave stop Mr. Adams?

BRIEF ANSWER

No. Mr. Adams's liberty was not restrained. For an individual's liberty to be restrained, the individual must reasonably believe that his liberty was being restrained. Mr. Adams could not reasonably believe that his liberty was being restrained.

Example 13-V • Question Presented and Brief Answer are linked

---

ISSUE PRESENTED

Our client, Paul Adams, made a statement to an undercover officer that implicates him in a local robbery. He made the statement after the undercover officer parked his unmarked police car behind his car. When the officer asked if he was planning to leave, Mr. Adams said "no." Under Oregon law, did Officer Ephgrave **stop** Mr. Adams?

SHORT ANSWER

No. Officer Ephgrave did not **stop** Mr. Adams in either circumstance. An officer stops another individual if that individual could reasonably believe that his liberty was being restrained. In neither case, could Mr. Adams reasonably believe that his liberty was being restrained.

- **Answer the question asked**

Your Brief Answer should address the question asked. Sometimes, after researching a question, your extensive research and thinking about the issue can lead you down a path other than the one you were pointed to. Writing the Question Presented and Brief Answer gives you a moment to check and see whether you have, in fact, answered the question you were asked to address.

A Question Presented and Brief Answer give your reader a quick summary of the issue your memo addresses and the answer to it. Writing an effective Question Presented and Brief Answer can be challenging. Because this section will be the first part of your memo presented to the reader, spend time to draft these well.

Practice Points

- The Question Presented and Brief Answer open your memo. They should give the reader an immediate understanding of the legal question and your prediction of how a court will treat the issue.

- Questions Presented and Brief Answers can be styled and labeled in various forms. Choose the format your supervising attorney prefers.

- The Question Presented needs three vital parts: the controlling law and jurisdiction, the precise legal question, and the determinative facts on which the legal question will turn.

- When using the under/does/when format, draft the question in a single sentence.

- In the statements-and-question format, include two or three statements before the legal question.

- In either Question Presented format, balance clarity with completeness. Include as much of the vital information as possible, but if the section becomes too long or unwieldy, revise to make the section understandable and readable.

- Begin your Brief Answer with a short, one or two word statement that answers the question. Predict the answer with as much certainty as your analysis will allow.

- Be concise in your Brief Answer. Choose the fundamental reasons that support your prediction. You can fully explain your prediction in the Discussion section.

Chapter 14

Statement of Facts

The Statement of Facts in a legal memorandum tells your client's story as it relates to the legal question your memo addresses.[1] As it tells your client's story, the Statement of Facts has many jobs if your memo is to be effective. This chapter discusses the role of the Statement of Facts, the types of facts to include, how to organize your Statement of Facts, and how to review it for thoroughness.

I. The Role of the Statement of Facts

Of the many jobs the Statement of Facts performs, its most important is to explain the factual foundation for your analysis of your client's legal question. The resolution of most legal questions—certainly the legal questions your clients will be asking—ultimately turn on the facts. Therefore, a clear explanation of the relevant facts is essential to supporting your analysis.

The Statement of Facts, however, performs other jobs. For example, it synthesizes the relevant facts. As an attorney, you will have to investigate and gather the facts relevant to your client's question. That investigation will include interviewing your client and reviewing relevant documents. It may also include interviewing others who are knowledgeable about the events and researching public records. Because you will be pulling

---

1. The authors would like to thank Professor Laura Graham of Wake Forest University School of Law for providing materials helpful in drafting this chapter.

facts from many different sources, the Statement of Facts provides one place to lay out the relevant, known facts in an easy-to-read manner.

The Statement of Facts also tells your reader the facts on which you based your legal analysis. It provides the reader with an opportunity to correct any factual misunderstandings or omissions that could affect the legal analysis. If additional facts come to light later, the Statement of Facts allows the reader to consider the facts that were known as of the date the memo was drafted and how the analysis might change based on the new facts. Finally, if a new attorney begins to work on the matter, the Statement of Facts provides that attorney with an overview of the facts giving rise to your prediction.

II. Types of Facts to Include

Three kinds of facts appear in the stories lawyers tell. Those are the facts that are legally significant to your client's case, background facts, and emotional facts. But not all facts are created equally. Legally significant facts are most important to the story you tell. Background facts are necessary, but should be kept to a minimum. And emotional facts, although important to advocacy writing, are not frequently included in predictive writing.

The legally significant facts are those facts in your client's case that will affect a court's analysis. (Legally significant facts were described in Chapter 13, *Question Presented and Brief Answer.*) Typically, legally significant facts are those that affect your prediction of the outcome. These facts are sometimes called "determinative," "key," or "critical" facts. You can think of these facts as the trigger facts in your client's case. Your Statement of Facts should be crafted so that your reader can focus on these legally significant facts.

Background facts are facts that provide context for understanding your client's situation. Although your client's story would be difficult to understand without any background facts, be careful about how many background facts you include. The more non-legally significant facts included, the more difficult it will be for your reader to determine which facts will actually affect the outcome.

Emotional facts are facts that are not necessary to resolve the legal issues but that help the reader understand what motivated the parties to act or react in a particular way. Many times, emotional facts cause the reader to feel sympathy for one party or distaste for another party. Emotional facts are appropriate in a predictive memo only if they affect your analysis or are likely to affect a court's analysis of your client's case.

In a Statement of Facts for a predictive memo, you should include every legally significant fact as well as enough background facts for your reader to understand the story you are telling. To include all the legally significant facts and sufficient background facts, you should do the following:

- **Include negative facts**

Legally significant facts include facts that are favorable to your client as well as facts that are unfavorable to your client. The primary purpose of your memo is to predict the likely resolution of the legal issues, so your reader can proceed accordingly. Only a balanced view of the facts will enable you and your reader to correctly analyze the issues and accurately predict an outcome.

- **Include unknown legally significant facts**

If, in writing your Discussion section, you determine that a fact may exist, but it is uncertain or unknown, you should indicate in your Statement of Facts that that fact is unknown. Although you should include relevant unknown facts, do not create wild conjectures about facts that could possibly exist. Generally, legally significant unknown facts are included at the end of your fact statement.

- **Include the procedural posture of the case**

"Procedural posture" refers to the steps in the litigation process. Are you trying to determine what claims or defenses to assert on behalf of a client? Have pleadings already been filed? Or are you simply trying to determine whether you should agree to represent a potential client? Explaining the point at which you are analyzing your client's claims will help your reader understand the information that was at your disposal and the purpose for your analysis. Often a sentence or two at either the beginning or end of the fact statement will provide this context.

- **Stick to the facts**

In a predictive memo, the Statement of Facts is not the place to slant the facts in favor of your client. In a predictive memo, your goal is to allow the attorneys you are working with to see the facts, warts and all.

The Statement of Facts is also not a time to draw legal conclusions or cite authority. To avoid drawing legal conclusions, avoid language that appears in your explanation of the law. For example, most of us would think that whether an establishment is a "building" is a fact that could be included in the Statement of Facts. If, however, the effect of a deed restriction turns on whether an establishment is a "building," that word becomes charged with legal meaning and should not be included in your Statement of Facts.

III. Organizing Your Statement of Facts

Begin your Statement of Facts by providing context for your reader. "Providing context" means introducing your client (your reader will want to know whose side you are on), introducing the other parties or key players, and explaining the crux of their conflict.

When introducing the parties, it is helpful to state the parties' names and designate their relationship. You might explain that one party is "our client," and you might use the word "employer," "landlord," "neighbor," "wife," or "husband" to explain the relationship to the other key players.

When you state the crux of the conflict, consider describing the conflict in human rather than legal terms. For example, in a memo about adverse possession, you might begin your statement of facts by providing the context, as in Example 14-A.

Example 14-A • Begin your statement of facts by providing context

STATEMENT OF FACTS

Clients introduced ⟶   Our clients, Linda and Tom Nero, purchased property in semi-rural Oregon
Crux of the conflict is ⟶ in 1978. The Neros recently learned that a garden and apple orchard they had
explained, and the other party always believed to be theirs, in fact, belongs to their neighbors, Ms. Welch and
is introduced. Mr. Bruce. The Neros would like to claim the garden and apple orchard as their own.

Notice that in Example 14-A, the conflict is described in human terms: It is a dispute about property. Although the memo later analyzes the dispute as a claim for adverse possession, the Statement of Facts avoids the legal terminology. Doing so keeps the Statement of Facts focused on the facts—and your client's real problem.

After introducing the main actors and the conflict, you will then need to decide how to organize your story. Attorneys use three different strategies to organize their facts.

A **chronological organization** describes facts in the order in which the events occurred. Readers expect facts to be told in sequence, so a chronological organization will be easy for your reader to absorb.

A **topical organization** groups facts by issue or category. For example, you might organize your Statement of Facts around the components of a transaction. Or, you might describe first the specific conflict now at issue between the parties and then go back and describe their history. When using a topical organization, short objective headings may help your reader see your organizational plan.

A **perceptual organization** presents facts from the various participants' vantage points. It is used primarily when the key players would tell different stories about the events at issue.

Often, attorneys use a combination of the above strategies. For example, if an attorney uses either a topical or perceptual organization, within each topic or perspective the facts will be described chronologically. Then, when the attorney moves on to the next topic or perspective, the attorney will start a new chronology.

At the end of your fact section—after setting out the relevant legal and background facts—remember to include any facts that are unknown but possibly relevant. In addition, some attorneys will describe the relief their client seeks, the specific question they have been asked to examine, or the procedural posture of their client's case. This final paragraph then functions as a transition paragraph linking the facts to the Discussion section.

IV. Reviewing for Thoroughness

You must review your Statement of Facts after you have drafted your Discussion section. You cannot know exactly which facts will be legally significant until you have worked through the analysis of your client's question. Once you have a good working draft of your Discussion, go back, and make a list of every fact mentioned in the Discussion. Be sure to include each fact on that list in your Statement of the Facts. Your reader should never encounter a fact for the first time in your Discussion.

After you have incorporated into your Statement of Facts every fact relied on in your Discussion, you should return once more to your client's records. Search for any facts inadvertently omitted from your Discussion. After drafting your legal analysis, you will be more attuned to facts that might make a difference. Facts that initially seemed insignificant may take on new meaning. Any missing facts should be incorporated into your Statement of Facts and, of course, into your Discussion.

V. Writing the Statement of Facts

Attorneys draft their Statements of Facts at different times. Some attorneys draft their Statement of Facts first to get a grasp of the facts before beginning their analysis or because drafting the Statement of Facts seems easier and it gets the writing juices flowing. Other attorneys draft their Statement of Facts after they have written their Discussion because writing the Discussion helps them know which facts will be relevant.

No matter when you first draft your Statement of Facts, your first draft will not be your last. As discussed above, your Statement of Facts will evolve as your analysis deepens. Below, we have provided some writing suggestions for the final revisions of your Statement of Facts.

- **Describe your client's legally significant facts in concrete detail**

As we discussed in Section 7.2, *Case Illustrations*, details signal to the reader that a fact is important. So, be specific and concrete about the facts in your client's case that will affect the outcome, and be less detailed about background facts.

- **A Statement of Facts is a story, not a list. Make it flow.**

When a Statement of Facts is viewed as a simple list of facts, it becomes difficult to follow. At one extreme, the statement will fall prey to run-on sentences in which too much information is listed at one time. At the other extreme, short, choppy sentences will mechanically deliver a list of facts.

To avoid either extreme, read your Statement of Facts out loud. Doing so will help you determine whether your Statement of Facts has succumbed to either extreme.

- **Use paragraphs to divide the facts into manageable units**

Just as you naturally pause periodically to catch your breath when you tell a story out loud, allow your reader to catch a breath by using paragraphs in your Statement of Facts.

Sometimes when writing a Statement of Facts, it can be difficult to identify where the natural breaks should go. After all, if you are describing facts chronologically, one fact occurs right after the next. Nevertheless, most chronologies describe a series of events. Consider dividing your Statement of Facts between events.

If you are still in doubt as to where the paragraph breaks should go, read your Statement of the Facts out loud. Insert a paragraph break at the spots where you find yourself naturally pausing.

- **Use status designations**

Using status designations in addition to proper names can help your reader remember the relationships among all the players in the Statement of Facts. "Employer," "employee," "husband," "wife," "landlord," and "tenant" are all status designations. Status designations will particularly help your reader remember the roles of minor players whose names may not be repeated frequently enough to be remembered.

- **Use the past tense**

Most of the time, you will be explaining events that have already occurred; therefore, use the past tense in relating your story. An exception exists if your prediction is contingent on events that have not occurred, in which case you may need to use a future or conditional tense for those particular facts.

VI. Examples

The two examples below, Examples 14-B and 14-C, allow you to compare a more effective Statement of Facts and a less effective Statement of Facts. The issue addressed in the memo is whether the defendant was "stopped." If the defendant was stopped, then any evidence gathered during the stop will be admissible only if the stop was justified by reasonable suspicion. Under Oregon law, an officer "stops" an individual if the officer blocks the individual's car. In light of the applicable legal rule and principles of good writing, what makes one version more effective than the other?

Example 14-B · An effective Statement of Facts

STATEMENT OF FACTS

On August 15, 2018, Police Officer Ephgrave spoke with Paul Adams, a suspect in a local bank robbery. During that conversation, Paul Adams revealed information that implicated him in the bank robbery.

Earlier that day, Officer Ephgrave saw a white Ford Probe pull into a parking lot. The car looked similar to the car involved in the Davinsk Mutual Bank robbery, and Officer Ephgrave decided to investigate. At the time, Officer Ephgrave was working undercover and was wearing ordinary street clothes and driving an unmarked car.

Officer Ephgrave pulled into the parking lot and parked behind the Ford Probe. As he got out of the car, Mr. Adams yelled at the officer to move his car. Officer Ephgrave walked over to the bench where Mr. Adams was sitting and asked if he was planning to leave. According to the officer, Mr. Adams said, "no, I'm going to sit a little longer." Officer Ephgrave pointed out that there was nowhere else to park because all the other spaces were full and told Mr. Adams he would move his car before Mr. Adams had to leave. According to Officer Ephgrave, Mr. Adams said, "Oh, okay. No problem."

Officer Ephgrave and Mr. Adams began chatting. Officer Ephgrave steered the conversation to the recent bank robbery. As they spoke, Officer Ephgrave remarked that the bank teller had said that the robber was very polite. Mr. Adams added, "Yeah, I heard he even gave a strawberry lollipop to a kid in the bank." Officer Ephgrave knew that the media had reported that the bank robber had given a child a lollipop, but not its flavor. Officer Ephgrave then arrested Paul Adams.

Mr. Adams was arraigned on August 20, 2018. He pleaded not guilty to the charges. He is now awaiting trial.

The first paragraph provides context. It introduces the main characters and the crux of the problem.

Background facts help the reader to make sense of the story.

Legally significant facts — that the officer was undercover, where the Officer parked, and Mr. Adams's reaction — are described in as much detail as possible.

Client's admission — a very important background fact — is described precisely.

Procedural facts are included.

Example 14-C · Less effective Statement of Facts

STATEMENT OF FACTS

On August 15, 2018, Officer Ephgrave saw a car pull into a parking lot. The car was similar to the car involved in a robbery. Officer Ephgrave pulled into the parking lot. **He blocked the car.** Mr. Adams complained. Officer Ephgrave walked over to the bench where Mr. Adams was sitting, asked if he was planning to leave, and even though Mr. Adams said he was not, Officer Ephgrave told Mr. Adams he would move his car before Mr. Adams had to leave. Mr. Adams acquiesced. They talked about the bank robbery. Officer Ephgrave recalled that the bank teller had said that the robber was very polite. Mr. Adams then made a statement about the bank robber giving a child a strawberry lollipop. Officer Ephgrave knew that the media had reported that the bank robber had given a child a lollipop, but not its flavor. Officer Ephgrave then arrested Paul Adams.

Choppy sentence syndrome

Run-on sentence syndrome

Compare the description of the client's admission here and above. Which description would be more helpful to the senior attorney?

When you read the two Statements of Facts, you may have noticed some or all of the similarities and differences described below.

- The effective Statement of Facts, Example 14-B, begins with a paragraph that gives context to the facts that follow, while the ineffective version, Example 14-C, jumps into the middle of the facts.

- Both versions are organized chronologically, but the effective Statement of Facts contains background facts that provide context without overwhelming the reader with unnecessary detail. The effective Statement of Facts, therefore, does a better job of telling the story.

- The effective Statement of Facts excludes legally significant phrases. By contrast, the ineffective version includes a legally significant phrase (in bold). An officer "stops" a citizen if the officer "blocks" that citizen's car. By using the phrases "blocked the car" the memo states a legal conclusion.

- In the effective Statement of Facts, legally significant facts are described in precise detail. By contrast, the ineffective Statement of Facts merely alludes to legally significant facts. For instance, the ineffective Statement of Facts says that "Mr. Adams acquiesced," when what Mr. Adams said was important.

- The effective Statement of Facts consists of several shorter paragraphs that break the story into manageable segments. The ineffective version is one long paragraph.

- The effective Statement of Facts uses short and long sentences to keep the reading interesting. The ineffective version is either very choppy or falls into run-on sentences.

- The effective Statement of Facts concludes with a few sentences describing the procedural context of the memo. The ineffective version omits this information.

On balance, the first example, Example 14-B, is better. Although longer, it clearly and objectively presents all the facts necessary to analyze the client's legal question. That example also uses effective sentence structure, paragraphs, and background facts to tell the story well.

Practice Points

- The Statement of Facts can include three types of facts: legally significant facts, background facts, and emotional facts.

- When drafting the Statement of Facts, concentrate on the legally significant facts. Add only those background facts necessary for your reader to understand your client's story.

- Begin the Statement of Facts by providing the reader with the context of your client's story. End the Statement of Facts with a transition sentence that flows into your Discussion section.

- Organize the Statement of Facts using a chronological, topical, or perceptual organization.

Chapter 15

Conclusion to the Memorandum

After you have addressed each element or factor with a full legal argument, your discussion is complete. After your Discussion section, a memo should have a new section, the Conclusion section. The Conclusion section concretely articulates your ultimate conclusion to the client's question and, if applicable, gives practical advice about what to do next.

A Conclusion section should begin by stating your bottom-line answer to your client's question. Since attorneys want to be able to find your answer quickly, state your answer to the client's question in the first line, as shown in Example 15-A. Do not bury it in the middle or make your reader wait until the end of the section, as in Example 15-B.

Example 15-A • Stronger Conclusion section states the conclusion at the outset

CONCLUSION

Mr. Richards has a viable claim for unjust enrichment under two different theories. First, permitting his landlord, Mr. Henry, to retain nearly $60,000 in improvements on a $700-per month lease would provide the landlord with an unreasonable windfall. Second, when a tenant makes improvements believing he has the right to purchase the property and is then denied that opportunity, those improvements will support a viable claim for unjust enrichment. Accordingly, Mr. Richards could file a claim seeking relief under both theories.

← Attorney states bottom line to client's question at the beginning.

Example 15-B • Weaker Conclusion section states the bottom line at the end

CONCLUSION

Mr. Richards can assert two theories. First, permitting his landlord, Mr. Henry, to retain nearly $60,000 in improvements on a $700-per month lease would provide him with an unreasonable windfall. Moreover, in this state, a tenant may recover for improvements he makes under the reasonable belief that he has the right to purchase the property if that opportunity is then denied to him. Under both those theories, Mr. Richards has a viable claim for unjust enrichment.

← Attorney waits to state bottom line to client's question.

The Conclusion section does not function like the conclusion to an academic paper. It does not re-cap the arguments presented in the paper. Rather, this section sets out only the bottom-line conclusion to your client's overarching question.

That bottom-line conclusion will be the same conclusion that you stated at the beginning of your discussion, although the words may vary. While it may include the most critical reason for your conclusion, avoid long explanations about your reasoning. If your reasoning was explained well in the Discussion section, you will not need a lengthy explanation here.

After stating your conclusion to the client's question, and perhaps the critical reason behind it, connect your conclusion to the real world: Provide the attorney reading your memo, and your client, with any practical advice you might have about any contingencies and what needs to be done next.

Remember that your client has a problem that needs to be solved. Thus, your legal analysis should always return to that real-world problem and consider how the client's problem should be managed in light of your legal analysis. Given your conclusion, what steps should the client take next? Do any other issues need to be researched? Do any more facts need to be gathered? In Example 15-C, the attorney advises the client that despite a viable legal claim a mediated settlement may be preferable to litigation.

Example 15-C · A Conclusion section that also provides practical advice

---

CONCLUSION

Attorney states bottom-line → conclusion to client's question.

Attorney gives practical → advice about how the client should proceed in light of the legal analysis.

The Neros have a strong claim that, under Oregon common law, they gained title to the disputed land by adverse possession. Though the Neros will likely win if they file suit, they may want to consider alternatives to filing suit, since litigation is always a gamble and usually time-consuming. Ms. Welch and Mr. Bruce may be eager to sell the disputed property at below market value rather than face litigation since a claim against the property could stall their pending construction loan. As lawyers, Ms. Welch and Mr. Bruce are likely to recognize the strength of the Neros' claim to the land. If they refuse the Neros' offer to buy the land, the Neros should first suggest mediation before filing suit.

Practice Points

- The Conclusion section should give your bottom-line answer to your client's legal question and any practical advice about what to do next.

- Do not use this final conclusion to re-cap your entire discussion.

- The Conclusion section should be succinct—typically, no more than a paragraph or two at the most.

Chapter 16

Editing and Polishing

Editing and polishing. Although they sound like tedious tasks, completing these tasks can make or break your analysis. They allow you to clarify, refine, and rework the parts of your arguments so that your intricate legal analysis is easy to understand and retain. Ultimately, effective editing and polishing distinguish the professional from the unprofessional.

Editing and polishing are separate and distinct tasks. When you edit, you check whether each argument is complete and whether the arguments are arranged logically. When you polish, you look for any snags over which your reader might trip or mistakes that might distract your reader from your words. With effective editing and polishing, the intricate patterns of your legal analysis will be woven into a tapestry that is pleasing to both the mind and the eye.

Not surprisingly, editing and polishing require time. In fact, effective writers spend more than half their time editing and polishing.[1] These tasks take time because they happen in rounds. You cannot re-read your argument once and call it quits. Rather, you must be aware of the kinds of problems that typically arise in a legal analysis and do a separate check for each kind of problem. In addition, fixing a problem in one area might affect other areas of your analysis. So after checking for problems separately, you must still review your document as an integrated whole.

---

1. Anne M. Enquist, *Unlocking the Secrets of Highly Successful Legal Writing Students,* 82 St. John's L. Rev. 609, 633-34 (2008).

As a novice legal writer, you may not know the kinds of problems that are common in a legal analysis. The point of this chapter is to provide you with the tools to identify those problems and then to correct them in your own writing. At the end of the chapter, we provide a checklist you can use to edit your own work.

I. Edit Your Memorandum

Editing—the process of reviewing the content and structure of your analysis—requires three steps. First, you must check the content of each legal argument. For each legal argument in your Discussion section you must ask yourself, "Do I have everything I need but no more?"

Second, check the organization of each legal argument. In this second step, assess whether the content of each argument is logically ordered.

Finally, edit for context and flow. Here, ask whether your reader will be able to transition easily from one legal argument to the next.

A. Edit the Content of Each Legal Argument

Perhaps the most difficult decision for both novice and experienced legal writers is deciding what to include and what to exclude from each legal argument. To decide, an effective writer thinks about the information the reader needs to know. As someone new to the law, it may be difficult to imagine exactly what your reader will need to know.

New legal writers sometimes include too much information when the law is complex and they feel unsure about their analysis. Including a lot of information feels safe. They hope that if they include a lot of information, the supervising attorney can just figure out the unclear pieces.

On the other hand, new writers sometimes include too little information. They believe the law and the legal conclusions to be drawn from the law are obvious, and thus they do not need to explain the authority or the logic of how that law applies to their case. Many times, novice writers think that a longer explanation appears redundant or is tantamount to "talking down" to a more experienced, supervising attorney. So, they leave out pieces of their analysis.

Because every legal argument is different, we cannot provide you with a content checklist, but we can provide you with a way to check each argument for signs of excess and omissions. To check the content of one legal argument, (1) separate the explanation of the law from the application and then (2) compare the explanation of the law to the application for omissions and excess.

1. Separate the explanation of the law from the application

To separate the explanation of the law from the application and compare their content, you must first identify every legal argument within your discussion. Remember that a Discussion section is typically made up of one or more legal arguments. One legal argument generally includes a conclusion or issue statement at the beginning, an explanation of the law (including rules and case illustrations), an application of the law to your client's facts, and a conclusion at the end.

To catch every argument, print out a copy of your paper. Then, use three different-colored highlighters to identify the parts of each argument. For each argument, do the following:

- In one color, highlight the conclusion or issue statement at the top and the conclusion at the bottom.
- In a second color, highlight the explanation of the law.
- In a third color, highlight the application of the law to your client's facts.

Each section should be a distinct color.[2] If you cannot see three distinct sections, you need to revise.

Next, double-check to make sure that the explanation of the law has really been kept separate from your application. To do that, draw a line across your page between your explanation of the law and your application. Then, ask yourself these questions:

- Do any facts from my client's case appear above the line? If so, review and revise.
- Do any citations appear below the line? If you are explaining new law, review and revise.

Your explanation of the law should have no facts about your client's case. The only above-the-line reference to your client should be in the conclusion or issue statement that begins your argument. Remember, attorneys prefer that their first look at the relevant law be stripped of any mention of a particular client. For that reason, your explanation of the law should not mention your client.

Your application usually does not need citations because your explanation of the law should cite to everything your application relies on. If you have citations below the line, ask yourself why. Some attorneys use a citation when they directly quote language from a case in their application. However, the instances when you want to cite new law in your application are limited. One instance is in a counter-analysis. As we explained in Section 8.3, *Counter-Analyses*, occasionally attorneys will

---

2. The idea to use colored highlighters to separate and see different sections of a draft is from Mary Beth Beazley. *See Mary Beth Beazley, A Practical Guide to Appellate Advocacy* 92-96 (2002). The suggestions here are a variation on that idea.

cite to new law when explaining the law that supports a counter-analysis. Frequently, though, if you have citations to new law or new details about a precedential case in the application, you need to revise your explanation of the law to include those details.

After you have separated your initial explanation of the law from its application, then you can check for omissions and excess.

2. Compare the explanation to the application and check for omissions and excess

The points you make in your explanation of the law should be mirrored in your application. Remember, your explanation of the law sets forth the law that is *relevant* to analyzing the client's legal question. So, if an idea is explained in your explanation of the law, that idea should be explicitly relied on or reflected in your application. Conversely, if an idea is explained in your explanation of the law but is *not* relied on or reflected in your application, then either your explanation of the law has an excess idea or your application has omitted a relevant idea.

(a) Verify that ideas explained are applied

For each idea in the explanation of the law, look in the application for language that matches, reflects, or furthers that idea. Put a check mark over each set of matching ideas. By the end, nearly all the ideas on either side of the line should have a check mark over them. If an idea is explained but not later relied on in the application, ask yourself these questions:

- Have I explained an aspect of the law that is not relevant to my client's question?
- Have I failed to address a relevant concept in my application?

If you have explained an aspect of the law that is not relevant to your client's legal question, usually it should be omitted. Alternatively, if you have explained relevant law but not addressed it in your application, then you will need to revise your application to address that idea.

In a few, rare instances you will explain an aspect of the law but not apply it. If the law provides necessary background information, provides context, or answers a question that is likely to be on your reader's mind, you may want to include an explanation of that aspect of the law, even though you do not directly rely on it in your application. Remember, however, that attorneys do not like to waste time. You should not include an idea just because it is "interesting." Therefore, you should rarely include an idea in your explanation of the law that is not relied on in your application.

You can see how this system works below in Example 16-A. Example 16-A is a small legal argument examining whether a client can prove actual possession, one of the elements of adverse possession. You will notice that some of the ideas explained are not addressed in the application.

Example 16-A · Compare the explanation to the application

Mr. and Mrs. Nero can most likely prove actual possession. ←

"Actual possession" does not have a check mark over it because that language is not used in the application.

⇓ **Explanation of the Law** ⇓

?

Plaintiffs must establish actual possession by showing that they used the land

✓

as an owner would use that particular type of land. *E.g., Zambrotto v. Superior*

Lumber Co., 4 P.3d 62, 65 (Or. Ct. App. 2000). Courts focus on the type of use ←

?

for which the land is suited, not necessarily focus on the amount of activity. *Id.*

"Type of use for which the land is suited" and "in a variety of ways" do not have check marks. The language is not used in the application, and the author has to ask whether the language is excess.

Plaintiffs in past cases have shown that they used the disputed land as an owner

?

would in a variety of ways. *See, e.g., Davis v. Park*, 898 P.2d 804, 806-07 (Or. Ct. ←

App. 1995); *Slak v. Porter*, 875 P.2d 515, 518 (Or. Ct. App. 1994). In *Davis*, the

plaintiffs established they used the disputed property as an owner would by

✓

using the disputed property as they did the adjoining land. 898 P.2d at 806-07.

✓   ✓

In *Slak*, the plaintiffs built a fence and planted vegetation. 875 P.2d at 518.

?   ?   ?

Even the limited use of land for hiking and hunting rattlesnakes has been ←

enough evidence to prove actual possession. *Id.*

These ideas do not have check marks over them because the language is not used and the ideas do not seem represented in the application below.

⇓ **Application of the Law** ⇓

✓

The Neros can prove they used the disputed property in a manner that an

owner would. Like the landowners in *Davis*, the Neros used the disputed land

✓

exactly as they did their adjacent land: Both contained part of the garden and

apple trees. In addition, like the plaintiffs in *Slak* who built a fence and

✓

planted vegetation, the Neros will be able to show they built a fence, kept a

garden, and maintained an orchard. The Neros should, therefore, be able to

✓

prove that they used the land as an owner would.

After comparing the ideas that are explained to the ideas that are applied to your client's facts, you can see that several ideas were explained but not then used. For instance, the explanation of the law begins with the main idea, "actual possession." The check reveals that the writer has never mentioned "actual possession" in the application. If the writer were to ask herself whether she failed to address a key concept in her application, she should immediately answer, "Yes!" The writer inadvertently forgot to prove her main point, that the Neros can establish actual possession.

Sometimes an idea will seem interesting and applicable when you begin thinking about a client's problem, but it will not later when you apply the law. For example, the check reveals that "limited use," "hunting," and "rattlesnakes" were not relied on in the application. The author would have to ask herself, "Why?" If it no longer seems relevant to the client's problem, that idea should be omitted from the explanation.

Ideas that are subtly relied on in the application should be kept in the explanation. For example, the author explains that courts focus on "the type of use for which the land is suited." That idea is not explicitly referenced in the application. The author may, however, decide that "the type of use for which the land is suited" is reflected in the case comparisons she relies on to support her argument. In that case, the author would keep the "type of use" reference in the explanation because it is relied on, albeit subtly, in the application.

Finally, Example 16-A includes one of those rare instances when an idea is explained but not applied. The example states that plaintiffs have demonstrated their type of use "in a variety of ways," but the phrase "variety of ways" never appears in the application. Here, she might decide that the "variety of ways" language is a helpful transition from one idea in her explanation to the next, and so although not explicitly relied on in the application, it is necessary to explaining the law cohesively. Accordingly, that idea should remain in the explanation of the law even though it is not explicitly relied on in the application.

After comparing your explanation of the law to your application, you should revise so that the two reflect each other. In Example 16-B, you can see how the author might revise the text. She has revised the application to *include* "actual possession," which is an important concept that she had initially failed to address in the application, and she has revised the explanation of the law to *exclude* the references to "limited use," "hunting," and "rattlesnakes" since those ideas were not relied on in the application.

Example 16-B · Revised explanation and application

Mr. and Mrs. Nero can most likely prove actual possession.

⇓ Explanation of the Law ⇓

Plaintiffs can establish ✓ actual possession by showing that they used the land ✓ as an owner would use that particular type of land. *E.g., Zambrotto v. Superior Lumber Co.,* 4 P.3d 62, 65 (Or. Ct. App. 2000). Courts focus on the ✓ type of use for which the land is suited and do not necessarily focus on the amount of activity. *Id.* Plaintiffs in past cases have shown that they used the disputed land as an owner would ✓ in a variety of ways. *See, e.g., Davis v. Park,* 898 P.2d 804, 806-07 (Or. Ct. App. 1995); *Slak v. Porter,* 875 P.2d 515, 518 (Or. Ct. App. 1994). In *Davis,* the plaintiffs established they used the disputed property as an owner would by using the ✓ disputed property as they did the adjoining land. 898 P.2d at 806-07. In *Slak,* the plaintiffs ✓ built a fence and ✓ planted vegetation and, in that way, proved actual possession. 875 P.2d at 518.

"Actual possession" is now referenced in the topic sentence and final conclusion of the application.

The author decides that although "type of use" and "in a variety of ways" are not explicitly referenced in the application, their absence below is justified.

The "limited use," "hunting," and "rattlesnake" ideas have been removed from the explanation of the law because they were not relied on in the application and there was no other justification for keeping them in the explanation.

⇓ Application of the Law ⇓

The Neros can prove they had ✓ actual possession of their land because they ✓ used the land as an owner would. Like the landowners in *Davis,* the Neros ✓ used the disputed land exactly as they did their adjacent land: Both contained part of the garden and apple trees. In addition, like the plaintiffs in *Slak* who showed actual possession by ✓ building a fence and ✓ planting vegetation, the Neros should also be able to show actual possession because they built a fence, kept a garden, and maintained an orchard. The Neros should, therefore, be able to prove they ✓ actually possessed the land.

(b) Remove elegant variation

After checking that the ideas expressed in the explanation of the law are relied on in the application, you should make sure that your reader can easily see that your explanation of the law supports your application. You can do that by echoing the language of your explanation in your application.

In many forms of writing, authors are discouraged from using the same phrase over and over again. When writing about the law, however, such repetition is usually welcomed. Legal phrases are terms of art. Each has a very specific meaning. If the same idea is expressed differently, an attorney will assume you are discussing a new idea.

You can use the matching exercise shown above in Example 16-A to consider variations in words. Look for changes in language, and ask yourself whether that change will make an attorney think you are discussing a new idea. If so, change the "elegant variation" and, instead, make the terms for like ideas consistent.

Creating consistency still permits some variation. For example, an attorney will understand that "actually possessed" represents the same idea as "actual possession." But, in Example 16-B, had the author concluded that the Neros had merely "possessed" the land, the attorney would be momentarily confused and wonder whether the writer was actually referring to the same idea. Although she might ultimately decide that the writer had intended to refer to the same idea, you do not want your reader to have to pause and wonder what you mean.

(c) Check the completeness of your case illustration

The above check—comparing your explanation of the law to your application of the law—may be sufficient to ensure that you have included everything you need to, but no more. Before moving on, however, you may want to do a second, individual check of your case illustrations and their applications.

Determining whether a case illustration has enough but not too much detail is often particularly challenging for new legal writers, so a special check is often warranted. One way to check whether you have provided sufficient, but not too much, detail is to compare the facts, reasoning, and holding provided in the case illustration with the information relied on in the application.

Remember, the explanation and application should mirror each other. For example, if a fact is relied on in the application, that exact fact should be described in the explanation of the law. The same is true for the reasoning and the holding. (Of course, some facts, such as those that give context, will be explained but not relied on. Those facts, however, should be kept to a minimum so they do not distract from the more critical facts.)

Similarly, if a precedential case is heavily relied on for several points in your application, your explanation of the law will need to thoroughly cover each of those points. Conversely, if you rely on a case briefly to elucidate one minor point in your application, your case illustration can be shorter in your explanation.

By comparing your explanation of the law to your application and, in particular, by carefully comparing how you described a prior case with how you used that prior case in your application, you can assess whether an argument has everything it needs, but no more.

B. Edit the Organization of Each Legal Argument

Once you have determined that an argument is complete, yet without extraneous ideas, you should then check to see whether the ideas are well organized.

An argument is well organized if its ideas are ordered logically. The catch is that your ideas must be ordered logically for the typical attorney, which may or may not be how you would instinctively order your ideas. For instance, the order in which you think through the ideas may not be the most logical order in which to present them.

You can check whether your argument is logically ordered by, again, comparing the explanation of the law to the application. Your reader assumes that your explanation of the law explains a logical way to step through a legal argument and, therefore, assumes that your explanation and application will follow the same steps in the same order.

For example, if you were to outline the argument in Example 16-B, you would see that the explanation and application of the law are ordered, generally, in the same way:

- *Actual possession*
- *As an owner would*
- *Courts focus on type of use, not amount of use*
    Land used as the adjoining property is used (Davis)
    Fence and vegetation (Slak)

To avoid confusing your reader, check the order of your ideas in your explanation against the order of your ideas in your application. Jot down a quick outline of the ideas in your explanation of the law. Then, compare that outline to the order of ideas in your application. If the ideas in your explanation are not in the same order as in your application of the law, you will have to consider whether you need to change the order and, if so, which ordering is more effective. For recommendations about how to effectively order your explanation and application, return to Section 8.4, *Organizing Your Application*.

Once you have checked one legal argument for its content and organization, you have to repeat those checks for all the legal arguments in your memorandum.

C. Edit the Discussion Section for Context and Flow

In a well-written legal memorandum, the reader glides through complex legal concepts. For your reader to glide through your analysis, you will need to create "context" for each new idea and "flow" between legal ideas.

"Context" refers to the ideas that your reader brings to a given passage that throw light onto its meaning.[3] "Flow" refers to the smooth transition from one idea to the next. Together, context and flow explain why a passage is worth reading and how ideas are connected.

To create context and flow you can use three tools: (1) roadmaps and signposts, (2) topic sentences, and (3) transitions from argument to argument. Doing so will keep your reader oriented to each point you are presenting.

1. Insert roadmaps and signposts

Your reader will transition more easily from one idea to the next if she knows what to expect ahead. To help a reader see what is ahead, writers provide roadmaps and signposts.

A roadmap is any passage that indicates the organization ahead. We first discussed roadmaps and mini-roadmaps in Chapter 12, *The Discussion Section: Introducing and Connecting Legal Arguments*. In that chapter, we explained that mini-roadmaps should be used when one legal idea within your discussion is broken down into more than one argument.

Example 16-C shows a mini-roadmap used in the middle of a discussion to alert the reader that a single legal idea will be addressed with more than one legal argument. That idea—whether an employee's belief is "objectively reasonable"—will be examined in three distinct legal arguments, each of which are labeled "(1)," "(2)," and "(3)." (For more examples of mini-roadmaps, see Chapter 12, Examples 12-R and 12-T.)

Once you have provided a roadmap, signposts will help. A "signpost" is a transition between arguments. It also reminds the reader where she is within the structure of the whole analysis. Example 16-C also includes signposts. After the roadmap identifies three factors, the "First" at the beginning of the second paragraph is a signpost that reminds the reader of where she is within that structure. Later in the memo the author will follow with signposts "Second" and "Third," which will introduce each of those factors and, again, remind the reader where she is.

---

3. *See Webster's Ninth New Collegiate Dictionary* 243 (1986).

Example 16-C • A mini-roadmap and signpost orient the reader to the structure ahead

In addition to proving he subjectively believed he was required to ◄——— participate in the company softball game, Mr. Ciesick will be able to prove that ◄— his belief that his employer expected him to play was objectively reasonable. To determine whether an employee's belief that she was expected to engage in an off-duty activity is objectively reasonable, courts usually look for the presence of three factors: (1) the employer's involvement in the off-duty activity, ◄—— (2) the benefit to the employer from the employee's participation in the off-duty activity, and (3) job related pressure to participate. *Meyer*, 157 Cal. App. 3d at 1041. In this case, each factor weighs in favor of proving that Mr. Ciesick's belief was objectively reasonable.

First, Mr. Ciesick's employer, Zoe Foods, was involved in the softball game. ◄— To determine an employer's involvement....

Substantive transition from last legal argument.

Conclusion to and beginning of the next legal argument.

Roadmap identifies 3 sub-arguments.

"First" is a signpost indicating that the writer is beginning the first of the three arguments.

2. Check topic sentences

Topic sentences also guide your reader because they tell the reader what to expect from each paragraph. In an excellent legal argument, a reader should be able to read only the topic sentences and generally understand the argument's organizational structure and main points.

Example 16-D lists all the topic sentences in the memo about whether Paul Adams was stopped (taken from the memo provided in Chapter 1, *How Attorneys Communicate*). Read through the example. Do the topic sentences allow you to see the argument's development?

Example 16-D • Good topic sentences show an argument's development

1. Paul Adams's statement about the flavor of the lollipop will be admissible because the statement was "mere conversation" and not made during a stop.

2. Mr. Adams's statement was mere conversation rather than a stop because Mr. Adams could not reasonably believe his liberty was restrained during his encounter with Officer Ephgrave.

3. A police officer may request information without restraining a person's liberty.

4. By contrast, a person may reasonably believe his liberty has been restrained if a police officer blocks that person's car.

5. In this case, Mr. Adams's encounter with Officer Ephgrave was mere conversation rather than a stop because he could not reasonably believe his liberty was being restrained.

6. However, seeking information does not convert their conversation to a stop.

7. In fact, a court is likely to conclude that Mr. Adams's encounter with the officer to be even less restrictive than the encounter in *Gilmore*.

8. Even though Officer Ephgrave's car did block Mr. Adams's car, a court is likely to distinguish Mr. Adams's case from the *Wenger* case.

By contrast, the following example, Example 16-E, shows topic sentences that do not help the reader see the argument's development.

Example 16-E · Problematic topic sentences

1. Under Oregon law, citizens can have different kinds of encounters with police officers.

2. A person's liberty may be restrained "if an individual believes that his liberty has been restrained and that belief is objectively reasonable."

3. In *Gilmore*, an officer requested identification from three people who were sitting in a truck.

4. In *Wenger*, the defendant was intending to leave a parking lot when officers parked their car blocking the defendant's car in.

5. In this case, the encounter was mere conversation.

6. In the same *Wenger* case, the undercover officer identified himself as an officer and then later placed his hand on the defendant's shoulder and directed the defendant away to question him.

7. Because Mr. Adams was not blocked from exiting the park and because his course was not altered in such a way that he could reasonably believe his liberty was restrained, a court should find that, under the totality of the circumstances, Mr. Adams was not stopped.

For example, the first topic sentence in Example 16-E does not indicate the overall point of the argument. Additionally, the third and fourth topic sentences do not clearly establish the point each paragraph is trying to convey. Rather, the third and fourth topic sentences jump into the details of a case, and the reader cannot see the idea that those details will prove. As a result, the topic sentences in Example 16-E do less to help the reader move through the argument than the topic sentences in Example 16-D.

To determine whether you have written effective topic sentences, highlight every topic sentence in your Discussion section. Then read just your topic sentences asking yourself whether they allow your reader to see the structure and main point of your argument. If not, for each paragraph, ask yourself what is the point you want to convey in that paragraph and revise accordingly.

3. Check paragraph cohesion

Once you are satisfied that your argument is logically developed through your topic sentences, you need to compare the topic sentence with the paragraph's content. For each paragraph, ask yourself whether each sentence in the paragraph supports the point asserted in the topic sentence.

Sometimes you will discover just one sentence that does not support the main point of the paragraph. Other times, you will discover several sentences in the paragraph that do not support the topic sentence. If several sentences do not support the topic sentence, ask yourself what point you *really* want that paragraph to make. You may find that you really want to make a different point, and the topic sentence should be revised.

4. Check transitions between arguments

You will need to help your reader make the leap from one developed idea to the next, so make sure that you have good transitions. The point in your writing where you will most frequently need to create a transition is between legal arguments.

Transitions come in many forms. A "transition" is any word or phrase that indicates to the reader the relationship between two ideas. By explaining the relationship between two ideas, transitions create a bridge from one idea to the next. (Above, we discussed signposts, which are transitions keyed to an earlier roadmap.)

Transitions include the words and phrases in Table 16-F. After looking at the transitions in that table, notice the effect of using transitions in Table 16-G. Table 16-G also illustrates "substantive" transitions, which create a transition by identifying the key point in one idea and using that as a lead-in to the next idea.

Table 16-F · Transitions*

Introduce		Restate		Add	
First	Initially	That is	In other words	Again	Moreover
To begin	The first reason	More simply	As noted	Additionally	Similarly
Primarily	In general	**Exemplify**		Also	Likewise
Alternatively	A further reason	For example	For instance	Further	
Sequence		To illustrate	In particular	**Connect**	
First, second,	Initially	Namely	Specifically	Because	Thus
third	Then	**Contrast**		As a result	Thereby
Finally	Before	However	Although	Therefore	Hence
Next	Last	But	Yet	**Conclude**	
Emphasize		Unlike	In contrast	Finally	As a result
Certainly	Above all	Nevertheless	Nonetheless	Thus	Therefore
Indeed	Especially	Rather	Despite	In short	Consequently
Accordingly	Since	Instead	Still		
Not only ... but also		On the other hand			

* Excerpted from L. Oates, A. Enquist & K. Kunsch, *The Legal Writing Handbook: Analysis, Research and Writing*, 613-22 (3d ed. 2002), and supplemented by Bryan A. Garner, *Legal Writing in Plain English: A Text with Exercises* 68 (Univ. Chi. Press 2001).

Table 16-G · Transitions guide the reader

Transition	Transition's Effect
Next, the Neros will be able to prove that their possession of the property was exclusive.	"Next" establishes a sequential relationship between the prior section and the current section.
Fourth, the Neros must establish that their use of the disputed property was hostile.	"Fourth" also establishes a sequential relationship and may help key the reader to a roadmap.
In addition to proving he subjectively believed he was required to participate in the company softball game, Mr. Ciesick will be able to prove that his belief was objectively reasonable.	"In addition" with the accompanying introductory phrase creates a substantive transition, telling your reader to expect an outcome similar to the outcome in the prior section.
Mr. Ciesick can **also** prove that his belief was objectively reasonable.	Even the word "also" can create a substantive transition. It tells your reader to expect an outcome similar to the prior outcome.
Although our client can prove he subjectively believed his employer required him to play in the softball game, he cannot prove that that belief was objectively reasonable.	"Although" with the accompanying introductory phrase creates another substantive transition. This transition, however, tells your reader to expect an outcome that will be different from the outcome in the prior section.

As you can see, a transition helps your reader by telling her how the parts of your argument relate to each other.

To determine whether you have created effective transitions, find the conclusion (or issue statement) at the top of each legal argument and the conclusion at the end of each legal argument. Wherever two legal arguments abut, ask yourself, "How do these arguments relate?" Then, check whether you have provided a transition that indicates that relationship.

The steps described above will help ensure that each legal argument has everything it needs, but no more; that the content of each argument is logically organized; and that your reader can see and understand the organization among those arguments. Having done that, you are ready to begin the next phase of writing: polishing your work.

II. Polish Your Memorandum

Polishing is the final step in the writing process. When you polish, you will make sure the sentences you have written are as clear and concise as possible. Polishing includes "wordsmithing"—that is, checking to make sure each word works hard, is clear, and is accurate. Polishing also includes proofreading, checking citations, and ensuring the document is the clearest, most professional work you can give the supervising attorney.

You can think of polishing as removing the spinach from between your teeth. Although you can speak eloquently with spinach between your teeth, your audience will listen better if you remove the spinach.

A. Strengthen Sentences

When you polish, begin by looking at each sentence. As an attorney, you are dealing with complicated ideas. Do not add to the difficulty by putting your ideas into sentences that are difficult to read.

Determining whether a sentence is difficult to read is itself difficult. After all, you wrote it. You understand what it means, and you may be too close to the sentence to recognize any problems it poses to a reader. So, instead of asking whether the sentence makes sense, look for common problems and try to eliminate those. Common problems include sentences that are overly long and sentences without clear subjects and verbs.

1. Find and revise overly long sentences

Long sentences are often difficult to read. Although not all long sentences need to be revised, a long sentence is suspect. After 25 words, a reader will usually stop absorbing. Read Example 16-H. At some point, you will likely stumble as you read because the ideas are too many to absorb. At what point do you stumble?

Example 16-H · 50 words, unreadable

Summary judgment is appropriate if there is no genuine issue as to any material fact and the moving party is entitled to judgment as a matter of law when the court examines the factual record and makes reasonable inferences in the light most favorable to the party opposing summary judgment.

Did you stumble near the word "when"? At that point, your brain has already absorbed 28 words.

Exceptions do exist. A well-constructed sentence can exceed 25 words and still be absorbable. For instance, in Example 16-I, items in a list are written in parallel form, making the sentence easy to absorb. Thus the sentence in Example 16-I is readable, despite being 52 words long. Conversely, problems can exist in relatively short sentences, that is, sentences under 25 words. So, use the techniques discussed below to address overly long sentences, but also use them to examine your shorter sentences.

Example 16-I · 52 words, yet readable

To determine whether an employee's belief that he was expected to engage in an off-duty activity is objectively reasonable, courts usually look for the presence of three factors: (1) the employer's involvement in the off-duty activity, (2) the benefit to the employer from the employee's participation in the off-duty activity, and (3) job-related pressure to participate.

Writers use different techniques to identify suspiciously long sentences. You can choose one that works for you. One method is to highlight sentences in alternating colors. Alternating colors will allow you to distinguish one sentence from the next. If you see any blocks of color that exceed three lines, that sentence is suspect. Another method is to read your sentences aloud. Here is what will happen: You'll be reading along slowly, and then, suddenly, you'll start to stumble. You've become confused about the point of the sentence or its meaning. If you cannot read a sentence without stumbling, that sentence is suspect.

When you find a suspiciously long sentence, you should look for two typical problems. Does the sentence have too many ideas (idea-overload)? Does it use too many words to express a single idea (wordiness)? Finding and fixing those problems will help you create shorter sentences that are easier for your reader to absorb.

(a) Revise sentences with too many ideas

Generally, one sentence should have one main idea. If a sentence has too many ideas, the sentence will become too complicated for the reader to absorb. In that case, you will need to break the sentence into separate pieces so each idea can be more easily absorbed.

Often, novice writers use commas or prepositions to attach additional ideas to a sentence. So, looking for commas and prepositions will help you identify independent ideas that might be better in their own sentence. In Example 16-J, the writer has used commas to embed multiple independent ideas into one sentence. Doing so, though, creates idea-overload.

Example 16-J · Commas embed multiple ideas and create idea overload

The Neros, having built a fence and planted vegetation, can show constructive notice to Ms. Cramer because, having marked the purported property line with the fence and vegetation, they, like the plaintiffs in *Davis*, indicated a property line that was respected by the Neros and their neighbors.

Although some may count them differently, the sentence in Example 16-J conveys about 5 different ideas:

1. The Neros built a fence and planted vegetation.
2. The fence and vegetation marked a property line.
3. The Neros and neighbors treated that line as the property line.
4. These facts make the Neros' case like the *Davis* case.
5. Therefore, the Neros can prove constructive notice.

To address the problem, consider which of the embedded ideas can be addressed in an independent sentence. Then, test it. Put the idea into its own sentence, and re-read the sentences to see whether the two ideas are more clearly explained. It might take re-ordering the sentences or creating new transitions. In Example 16-K, you can see that it took two sentences and some re-ordering to create more digestible sentences.

Example 16-K · Embedded ideas given independent sentences

The Neros can show constructive notice to Ms. Cramer because they built a fence and planted vegetation. Like the fence in the *Davis* case, the Neros' fence marked the purported property line that was respected by the Neros and their neighbors.

As you are testing new sentences, if you are not sure which way is better, err towards placing each idea in its own sentence. It will chunk the ideas into smaller units and make the ideas easier for your reader to absorb.

Looking for prepositions can also help you find sentences with too many ideas.[4] Prepositions are simply words that express a relationship between a subject and another thing. For example, a man stood *on* the train platform. "On" is the preposition. Other common prepositions are "of," "by," "for," "to," and "with."

Prepositions are necessary in your writing; however, if you have too many prepositions, you will have too many relationships for your reader to track. For that reason, you can simplify your writing by searching for prepositions and eliminating as many as possible.

Example 16-L (which you saw above as Example 16-H) has four different prepositions or prepositional phrases (and several conjunctions), all of which connect ideas.

Example 16-L · Prepositions signal new ideas being attached

Summary judgment is appropriate if there is no genuine issue as to any material fact and the moving party is entitled to judgment as a matter of law when the court examines the factual record and makes reasonable inferences in the light most favorable to the party opposing summary judgment.

---

4. *See* Bryan A. Garner, *Legal Writing in Plain English: A Text with Exercises* 50-51 (2d ed. 2013) (recommending writers remove "of" to avoid bloat).

As we noted above, when you read the sentence in Example 16-H, you likely stumble near the word "when." At that point, you have already absorbed 28 words, but "when" indicates you need to add another idea. In a rewrite, you might see if you can eliminate the preposition "when" and thereby separate out different ideas. Is Example 16-M easier to read?

Example 16-M · Preposition omitted

Summary judgment is appropriate if there is no genuine issue as to any material fact and the moving party is entitled to judgment as a matter of law. The court will examine the factual record and make reasonable inferences in the light most favorable to the party opposing summary judgment.

(b) Revise wordy sentences

You should also examine each sentence for wordiness. Removing surplus words will make your sentences simpler in structure and easier to comprehend.

Every sentence contains both working words and glue words.[5] A working word carries meaning in a sentence. A glue word holds the working words together to form a sentence. While every sentence must have both, problems arise when the proportion of glue words is too high.

To determine the proportion of glue words to working words, simply highlight all the words in the sentence that carry meaning, as in Example 16-N. Then, try to omit as many of the glue words as possible, as in Example 16-O.

Example 16-N · Glue words create bloat

There was sufficient evidence found with respect to whether the plaintiff was "about to report" for the request for summary judgment to be denied by the court. (27 words)

Example 16-O · Omit glue words to make sentence easier to read

The court found sufficient evidence showing the plaintiff was "about to report" and, therefore, denied the request for summary judgment. (20 words)

2. Create clear subject-verb pairs

Finally, your sentences will be more readable if you create clear subject-verb pairs. In every sentence, readers search (consciously or not) for who is doing what. As a result, sentences are easier to absorb if your

---

5. Richard Wydick, *Plain English for Lawyers* 7 (5th ed. 2005).

reader can quickly identify the subject and action. Moreover, creating clear subjects paired with active verbs will make your writing jump off the page. Although the concepts you are discussing may be dry, your writing does not have to be.

(a) Bring subject and verb close together

The first step to creating a clear subject and action is to bring them close together. Compare Example 16-P with Example 16-Q. Which is easier to read?

Example 16-P · Subject and verb far apart

The Neros, like the plaintiffs in *Davis* who built a fence, can establish constructive notice.

Example 16-Q · Subject and verb brought together

The Neros can establish constructive notice. Like the plaintiffs in *Davis* who built a fence,....

Example 16-Q was probably easier to read because the subject (the Neros) was close to the action it was performing (establishing constructive notice).

(b) Minimize passive voice

Minimizing passive voice will also help your reader find the subject and action in your sentence. Passive voice is a difficult concept for many. "Passive voice" refers to whether a sentence clearly states *who* is doing the action in the sentence. In a sentence with passive voice, the main actor is no longer the subject of the sentence. As a result, the reader has difficulty determining who did what. The sentence in Example 16-R illustrates passive voice. In that sentence, you are left to wonder who did the action: Who made mistakes? "Passive voice" is different from "past tense." "Past tense" refers to *when* certain actions took place—now or in the past. "Passive voice" refers to whether the reader knows *who* did the action.

Example 16-R · Passive voice

Mistakes were made.

Example 16-S identifies who made the mistake and is easier to read.

Example 16-S · Passive voice is eliminated when the actor is identified

John made the mistakes.

Sometimes you will want to use passive voice. Passive voice will hide an actor if you do not want to ascribe blame. Sometimes you will choose to use passive voice because you want to focus on the object rather than the subject of the sentence.

In Example 16-T, the writer properly uses passive voice if he wants to focus on summary judgment, rather than on the court or judge that issued the decision.

Example 16-T · Writers sometimes prefer the passive voice

Summary judgment was improperly granted.

Typically, however, you do not need or want to hide the actor. As you read each sentence, ask yourself who is doing each action. Then, ask yourself whether your sentence will be clearer if the actor is made the subject of the sentence. You can see this process in the revisions to Examples 16-U and 16-V. (You saw these examples above as Examples 16-N and 16-O.)

Read the sentence in Example 16-U and ask yourself who "found" sufficient evidence? And who "denied" the motion for summary judgment? Asking yourself those questions might lead you to the revision in Example 16-U.

Example 16-U · Actor is hidden

There was sufficient evidence found with respect to whether she was "about to report" and, therefore, the request for summary judgment was denied by the court.

Example 16-V · Actor is identified and sentence is clarified

The court found sufficient evidence showing she was "about to report" and, therefore, denied the request for summary judgment.

Notice that the sentence that hides the actor, Example 16-U, includes the phrase "by the court." The preposition "by" is often a signal that the actor has been made the object of the sentence. You can clarify the sentence by making the actor the subject of the sentence, as in Example 16-V.

(c) Minimize nominalizations

Another way to create clear subjects and actions is to minimize nominalizations. A nominalization is a noun that could be expressed as a verb. For example, "supervision" is a nominalization of the verb "supervise." Because nominalizations embed verbs within a noun, nominalizations make it difficult for your reader to find the action. Removing nominalizations will often make your sentences more active and clear.

So, if a sentence is difficult to read, scan the sentence for any words that can be converted from a noun to a verb. Look particularly for words that end in "ion" and "ment," which are frequently nominalizations. Then, convert the noun to a verb and see whether your sentence becomes stronger using the verb. Table 16-W shows how to convert a noun to a verb.

Table 16-W · Converting nouns to verbs

Nominalization	Verbs preferred
The hearing officer was subject to the supervision, direction, and control of the Attorney General.	This hearing officer was supervised, directed, and controlled by the Attorney General.
The Neros can prove constructive notice through the establishment of property boundaries.	The Neros can prove constructive notice because they established property boundaries.
We find that there was adequate probable cause to support the trial court's issuance of the Search Warrant.	We find there was adequate probable cause for the trial court to issue the Search Warrant.

Polishing your sentence structure will tighten your writing and make it more enjoyable for your supervising attorney to read. At its best, your reader will float through the document.

B. Proofread Your Work

Polishing also requires you to carefully re-read what you have written. You probably know that just using a computer's spell check function will not catch all proofreading errors. For example, spell check will not notice whether you have erroneously written "trail" instead of "trial" or used "statue" instead of "statute." While the spell check and grammar functions are good starting points for this task, they are no substitute for carefully re-reading what you have written.

At this point, though, you have read your paper so many times that you may find it difficult to see errors. Your mind will read what it thinks is on the page rather than what is actually there.

To help you track what is actually on the page, consider using one of the techniques attorneys often use. You can use a colored piece of paper to move line by line down through your paper. The piece of paper will cover up the words below the line you are reading and will prevent you from skipping lines. The color will provide a helpful contrast to your page.

You can also read your paper aloud. Reading your paper aloud will cause you to read more slowly and to actually look at what is written on your paper.

C. Check Your Citations

Finally, check your citations. Citations inform your reader where to find the authorities on which you based your argument. In addition, citations indicate to the reader your level of attention to detail. If you want your reader to believe that you are an attorney who pays attention to details, then you should do a separate citation check.

Creating consistent, professional citations depends on a separate set of guidelines explained in *The Bluebook* and the *ALWD Citation Manual*. We will not repeat those rules here. We will however, give a few tips for checking your citations.

Before you begin to check your citations, your sentences must be in their final order. For that reason, checking cites is the last thing you should do.

So that you can focus on only your citations, print out a clean copy of your memorandum and highlight each citation. And, like the other processes that we discussed in this chapter, you may want to check your citations in rounds, so that you can concentrate on one task at a time.

You will want to check four things in your citations: First, make sure you are following the preferred citation format for your jurisdiction and your law office.

Then, identify the first time you cited an authority and make sure that you used a full cite. Make sure that each subsequent cite to that authority is a short cite.

Next, check that the substance of each citation is correct. Cite by cite, use *The Bluebook* or the *ALWD Citation Manual* to check whether each citation is in a proper citation form. For example, for a case, that would mean verifying the case name, volume, reporter, initial page number, and parenthetical information.

Finally, *every* citation needs a pinpoint cite unless you actually want the reader to read the entire case, article, or authority. Check that each citation has a pinpoint cite or is an *id.* Then, check each pinpoint cite to verify that it references the correct page, and check each *id.* to determine that it actually refers to the same authority and page as the citation before it.

III. Customize Your Editing Checklist

The table (Table 16-X) below gives you a sample checklist for editing and polishing your memorandum. Use it as a starting point to ensure your work product is complete, understandable, and professional.

Ultimately, however, you must create your own checklist. Every writer struggles with different aspects of writing. Examine your writing to determine the particular problems you routinely face and create a personalized checklist.

Table 16-X · Checklist for editing and polishing

I. Edit Your Memorandum

    A. Edit the content of each legal argument:
    In this legal argument, do I have everything I need but no more?

        1. Separate the explanation of the law from the application.

            ❏ Print out a copy of your paper.

            ❏ Use three highlighters in different colors to highlight:

                ° The conclusion (or issue statement) at the top and the conclusion at the bottom of each argument.

                ° The explanation of the law.

                ° The application of the law.

            ❏ Draw a line across the page to separate your explanation of the law from your application.

            ❏ Ensure your explanation is distinct from your application.

                ° Do any facts from your client's case appear above the line? If so, revise.

                ° Do any citations appear below the line? If you are explaining new law, revise.

            ❏ Label the top half "Explanation" and the bottom half "Application."

        2. Compare the explanation to the application to ensure each section matches in content and coverage.

            ❏ For each idea in the explanation of the law, look in the application for language that matches, reflects, or furthers that idea.

            ❏ Put a check mark over each set of matching ideas.

            ❏ For ideas without check marks, ask yourself these questions:

                ° Have I explained an aspect of the law that is not relevant to my client's question? If so, omit.

                ° Have I failed to address a relevant idea in my application? If so, revise the application by applying the relevant idea.

                ° Be very careful about ideas that are explained but not applied. Only rarely are ideas explained but not applied.

            ❏ Check for elegant variation. Review "matches" to determine whether language is consistent.

        3. Check case illustrations.

            ❏ Apply step 2, above, to case illustrations.

B. Edit the organization of each legal argument:
In this legal argument, is the content logically ordered?

❑ Compare the order of ideas in your explanation of the law to the order of ideas in your application.

○ On a separate piece of paper, jot down a quick outline of the ideas in your explanation of the law.

○ Compare that outline to the order of ideas in your application.

○ If ordering is inconsistent, review and revise.

Repeat. The above edits—Step A for content and Step B for organization—will check one legal argument. Be sure to repeat those edits for each legal argument in your discussion.

C. Edit the Discussion section for context and flow:
Is my logical order apparent to my reader?

1. Insert roadmaps and signposts.

❑ If a legal idea is composed of two or more arguments, consider providing a mini-roadmap.

❑ For each mini-roadmap, include signposts in the discussion that follows.

2. Check topic sentences.

❑ Highlight every topic sentence in your Discussion section.

❑ Read only the topic sentences.

❑ Ask whether they allow the reader to see the structure and main points of your argument.

❑ If not, revise.

3. Check paragraph cohesion.

❑ Compare each topic sentence to the sentences within the paragraph.

❑ Does each sentence in the paragraph support the point asserted in the topic sentence?

❑ If not, revise.

4. Check transitions between arguments.

❑ Mark the beginning and end of each legal argument.

❑ Wherever two legal arguments abut

○ Ask yourself, "How do these arguments relate?"

○ Check whether you have provided a transition that indicates that relationship.

○ If not, revise.

II. Polish Your Memorandum

    A. Strengthen your sentences.

        1. Find and revise long sentences.

            ❑ Eyeball sentence length.

                ◦ Using alternating colors, highlight each sentence.

                ◦ Note any sentences longer than 3 lines.

            ❑ Read your paper aloud.

                ◦ Note any sentences that cause you to stumble.

            ❑ Revise sentences with too many ideas.

                ◦ Scan for commas. If a comma embeds an idea that can be put into its own sentence, revise.

                ◦ Scan for prepositions. If a preposition can be omitted to simplify the sentence, revise.

            ❑ Revise wordy sentences.

                ◦ Highlight every working word in a sentence.

                ◦ Squeeze out as many glue words as possible.

        2. Create clear subject-verb pairs.

            ❑ Bring subject and verb close together.

            ❑ Minimize passive voice.

            ❑ Minimize nominalizations.

    B. Proofread your work.

        ❑ Use a colored piece of paper to read line-by-line.

        ❑ Read your paper aloud.

    C. Check your citations.

        ❑ Print out a clean copy of your paper.

        ❑ Highlight each citation.

        ❑ Verify the appropriate format for your jurisdiction and law office.

        ❑ Check for a full cite for each legal authority the first time it is relied on.

        ❑ Use a citation manual to check citation content.

        ❑ Check pinpoint cites.

            ◦ Check that each citation has a pinpoint cite.

            ◦ Check that each pinpoint cite references the correct page.

            ◦ Check each "*Id.*" to ensure it correctly refers to the same authority and page referenced in the cite immediately before it.

Chapter 17

Client Letters

After examining a client's legal problem and sharing your analysis with colleagues, you will need to communicate that analysis to your client. Sometimes you will meet with your client to communicate your analysis, and sometimes you may simply send an email. Often, however, you will convey your analysis in a letter. This chapter first reviews the types of letters that attorneys frequently write. The chapter then focuses on client letters—the form of correspondence in which you will often convey an objective legal analysis. In particular, this chapter addresses how to transform the objective legal analysis you produced in memo form into an analysis appropriate for a letter to a client.

I. The Types of Letters Lawyers Write

Attorneys write many kinds of letters. As you see in Table 17-A, such letters include client letters, opinion letters, demand letters, status letters, or engagement, disengagement, or non-engagement letters. You will likely write a variety of these letters in your legal career.

Table 17-A · Common types of letters lawyers write

Client	A letter that examines a particular issue of law and the claims or legal options available to the client.
Opinion	A formal letter that examines a particular area of law or a legal transaction and provides a specialized opinion on the legal question.
Demand	A letter that demands action, or cessation of action, or the satisfaction of a legal or monetary obligation.
Status	A letter or report typically sent on a regularly agreed upon basis to update the client about what is happening in the litigation or transaction and what will likely happen next. This kind of letter may request input from the client on strategic choices that need to be made.
Engagement	A letter that establishes a working relationship and defines the scope of services, the fees, timelines, and any other details between the attorney and client.
Non-Engagement	A letter that declines representation of the client or handling of a legal matter after investigation or research.
Disengagement	A letter that terminates the working relationship between the attorney and client and provides details about how remaining work and fees should be settled.

Each of the letters listed in Table 17-A has its own purpose. For instance, if a client has consulted you about a neighbor's unauthorized storage of trailers on the client's property, a client letter would inform the client of the legal rules that apply and her options in resolving the situation. By contrast, if you are writing to the neighbor on behalf of your client, your goal would be to both inform the neighbor of the legal restrictions and to persuade the neighbor to act consistently with your client's wishes. In that case, you would be writing a demand letter. When you begin drafting a letter, you should first consider the purpose of the letter. Doing so will affect the content and tone of your correspondence. As we stated earlier, for this chapter we focus on writing client letters because that is the form of correspondence in which you will often convey an objective legal analysis.

II. The Basic Parts of a Letter

A client letter has several distinct parts: (a) the date, (b) the return address, (c) the recipient's address, (d) the subject line, (e) the salutation, (f) the opening paragraph, (g) the body of the letter, and (h) the closing. You can see each of these parts in Example 17-B.

Example 17-B · Sample client letter

KOENIG MCCLELLAN AND TRENDOR, LLC
1400 SW FIFTH AVENUE, SUITE 5550
PORTLAND, OREGON 97201

← Return address

PERSONAL & CONFIDENTIAL
ATTORNEY-CLIENT COMMUNICATION

← Confidentiality warning

October 12, 2018

← The date that the letter was sent

Tom and Linda Nero
8762 Barlow Road
Boring, Oregon 97287

← Recipient's address

RE: Potential Land Dispute Claim—Client No. 097562

Dear Mr. and Mrs. Nero:

The **opening paragraph** concisely sets out the context—describing legal research conducted after a consultation; the purpose of the letter—whether the client will be successful in gaining legal title to disputed land; and the bottom-line conclusion—the client will likely gain legal title.

    Thank you for consulting with me about your disputed land claim. I enjoyed meeting both of you and hearing about your property. I am pleased to tell you, based on the facts you described in our meeting, I believe you can successfully gain legal title to the land you have been farming since 1978.

    I base my opinion on the following facts. If I have omitted a fact or have described a fact incorrectly, please let me know immediately.

← Background facts

Notice how the discussion concisely establishes the facts as the attorney understands them and asks the reader to correct any errors or misconceptions.

- You purchased property outside of Boring, Oregon, in 1978. That property abutted a vacant lot. You believed that the western boundary of your property included an apple orchard and a strip of area where your garden now stands.

- In 1979, you began pruning the apple trees on the property and clearing a 60 x 100 square foot area along its northwest corner. There, you planted a vegetable garden and built a two-foot-high fence. Although it no longer exists, a fence existed for many years.

- You maintained the orchard and openly had a garden most years since 1979, except in 1986 and the span between 1990 through 1993. Neighbors, their children, and their grandchildren often helped you bring in the harvests in both the garden and the orchard.

- The owner of the property, Dot Cramer, has lived in Wisconsin for the past thirty years and has not visited the property. She recently sold the property to another couple, Jennifer Welch and James Bruce.

- When the new owners recently surveyed the property, the survey established that the orchard and garden belonged to Ms. Welch and Mr. Bruce.

Based on these facts, I believe you have a strong likelihood of gaining legal title to the property. As we discussed in our meeting, your claim falls under an area of property law called "adverse possession." I understand you thought the term "adverse possession" carried a negative image of "squatters" who unfairly made land claims against legitimate property owners. Let me alleviate your concerns. Most adverse possession claims involve boundary disputes in which an owner is genuinely mistaken about a property line. In Oregon, adverse possession claimants *must* believe that the property in dispute actually belongs to them. Because you believed the land was yours for the last thirty years, and for the reasons explained below, you have a strong likelihood of gaining legal title to the land.

Oregon law allows adverse possession claimants who mistakenly believe they own land that actually belongs to someone else to gain title if they use the land for ten consecutive years. To acquire property in this way, claimants must prove by clear and convincing evidence that their possession of the land was actual, open and notorious, exclusive, hostile, and continuous during that ten-year period.

Under the facts you have described, your use of the land meets those requirements. First, you can prove "actual" possession because you have planted a garden and maintained the orchard. You have also used the land "exclusively" since the original owner has not visited in three decades.

"Continuous" use of the land includes seasonal use, like your agricultural uses of the land during growing and harvest seasons; thus, you can prove that you have used the land "continuously." The ten-year requirement is also satisfied since you have used the land as if it were yours since 1979.

The most challenging element will be whether your use of the land was "open and notorious." To prove this element, we must show that the owners had notice or constructive notice of your use. Constructive notice means that the owner is legally presumed to have notice even if she does not have actual notice. In deciding whether use is open and notorious, courts often consider whether the claimant has fenced the land, which you did for many years. Also you allowed neighbors and friends to help you tend the garden and orchard. By the way you openly farmed and maintained the land, we can most likely show that the owner had constructive notice you were using the land.

Options ⟶
Here, the lawyer describes the viable courses of action available to the client.

You have three options about how to handle this property dispute with Ms. Welch and Mr. Bruce. First, you could abandon any claim you have and abide by the survey results. This option will cost you nothing, but you will be losing a piece of property that is economically and emotionally important to you. Second, you could offer to buy the portion of land from the legal owners. This option may be cost-effective. The owners may be amenable to giving you the land for a reasonable price to avoid the time and expense of defending a legal claim. This route may also contribute to a better relationship with your new neighbors. Third, you can bring a claim of adverse possession and seek title to the land. You have a good chance of succeeding on this claim, but you should also consider the costs of litigation when evaluating this option. I suggest we meet within the next two weeks to discuss which option may serve you best. If you choose to file a claim, we should not delay because most claims have a particular time limit in which they can be filed.

In the meantime, I would like for you to gather any evidence that we can use in your claim. You mentioned that you have numerous photographs and videotapes of the land taken through the years. Please bring those to our next meeting along with any letters, journals, or other documents describing your activities on the disputed property.

Next steps

This section sets out what action the client needs to take in order to determine what option may be the best course of action.

Once again, I appreciate the opportunity to help you with this matter, and I look forward to hearing from you soon.

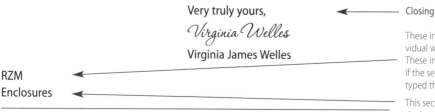

Very truly yours,

Virginia Welles

Virginia James Welles

Closing

These initials belong to the individual who typed the letter. These initials are usually omitted if the sender of the letter also typed the letter.

RZM

Enclosures

This section tells the reader that the letter will be accompanied by additional documents. Mentioning any enclosures in the body of the letter is also helpful.

Let's begin by breaking down the letter into separate parts and discussing the purpose each part serves.

A. Date

Always date your letter and try to send it on that day. Not only does the date help maintain a paper trail of who did what and when, but the date also establishes a time frame for action (for example, "contact me within two weeks").

B. Return Address

Your office letterhead will contain your return address and contact information. Accordingly, you do not need to provide your return address and contact information again.

C. Recipient Address

Get names and addresses correct. Spelling or addressing errors detract from the power of the letter and from your credibility. Who likes to get a letter with their name spelled wrong? No one.

D. Subject Line

The subject or "Re:" line should be a specific, one-phrase statement of the letter's purpose or subject (for example, "Viability of Adverse Possession Claim"). You may also include the client number and matter number your office has assigned to the case.

E. Salutation

Traditional, formal greetings are most appropriate. The greeting to the recipient of a letter will be more formal than you might send in an email. For example, most times you would address a letter using the recipient's title, as in "Dear Ms. Nero." If writing to someone you know personally, you could use the person's first name only (e.g., "Dear Linda"), but you would not simply write "Linda" for the salutation as you could in an email.

F. The Body of the Letter

The body of your letter is the critical section. The body describes the background facts upon which you relied, your analysis, the potential options you have discovered, and the next recommended steps for yourself and your client. However, before drafting any part of your analysis, you must remember to whom you are writing the letter.

A "client letter" is (obviously) going to a client; however, you must think about the particular client to whom you are sending the letter and what that client needs from the letter. Unlike an objective memo, which will be written for another attorney, your letter will be written for a client who may be a sophisticated, legally-trained general counsel of a Fortune 500 Company, an indigent client who never had the social or economic means to obtain a meaningful education, or someone in between. The more sophisticated your client, the more detailed your analysis may be. However, even the most sophisticated clients sometimes do not want detail; rather, even some very sophisticated clients simply want a bottom line so that they can move on and make decisions in their lives and businesses. Because of the wide variety of clients and their legal problems, there is no "one size fits all" approach with respect to client letters. The goal, as explained above, is to educate the client in a straightforward and understandable way about the legal issue, the client's options, and the next steps that you and the client should take.

That said, all letters, regardless of the client's sophistication, benefit from using plain English and a simple organization. Unfortunately, too many letters are lengthy, overly complicated, or too formal for common understanding; too many letters are, in a word, ineffective. Avoid creating a confused and disgruntled client by avoiding legal terms and stuffy phrasing. Keep the information provided succinct and to the point.

1. Opening paragraph

The first paragraph of the letter should establish the purpose of the letter (the legal problem or why you are writing), give any necessary context, identify any attachments to the letter, and state your bottom-line conclusion, as in Example 17-C.

Example 17-C · Example of opening paragraph

Dear Mr. and Mrs. Maclean:

I appreciate the opportunity to advise you regarding your claim. While the outcome of any litigation is uncertain, I believe you have a strong claim to recover the medical fees and property damage caused by your neighbor's dog. To ensure a complete understanding between us, below, I set out my understanding of the facts you provided to me. Following those facts, I explain the law that will govern your claim and analyze the strength of the arguments we could present on your behalf. Following that analysis, I consider various options we have to resolve the disputed dog bite.

---

2. Background facts

Always explain the background information or facts as you understand them and specifically identify any assumptions you have made. Because even a slight change of fact can change the answer to a legal question, always describe the facts upon which you base your opinions or conclusions. Include a warning that any change in facts or background could alter your opinions, and ask your client to correct any factual mistakes or erroneous assumptions.

3. Analysis

After explaining the relevant facts upon which your analysis is based, you will then explain your analysis. The analysis in a letter is analogous to the Discussion section in a memo; however, to accommodate your client, who is typically not a lawyer, you will make a few adjustments to your analysis to make it more accessible.

First, as in a discussion section in a memo, you will need to begin your analysis with a roadmap. Chapter 12, *The Discussion Section: Introducing and Connecting Legal Arguments*, explains the typical parts of a roadmap in a memo: a conclusion, a description of the governing rule, disposal of aspects that don't require a legal argument, a roadmap and assessment of the remaining elements, a conclusion again (if necessary).

In a letter, you will likely include all of those parts except, at times, the initial conclusion. The conclusion at the beginning of the analysis may be omitted for two reasons. First, you will have already stated your conclusion in the opening paragraph. Second, because the analysis is not set off by a new section heading, re-stating your conclusion may seem a bit abrupt and interrupt the flow of the letter.

In addition, you will want to think carefully about the background information you give about the governing rule. In an objective memo, the roadmap paragraph provides a senior attorney with information about the governing rule and how the courts interpret or apply the governing rule. This information provides the senior attorney with the context necessary to understand your legal analysis. For client letters, on the other hand, a more detailed description of the legal claim should be provided to educate your client about the language you will be using to discuss the options.

Compare Example 17-D, the roadmap section of a memo, with Example 17-E, the roadmap section of a client letter. As you can see from Example 17-E, particularly where your client is not a lawyer, you may sometimes need to provide additional information to help educate the client or explain certain terms. Other times, you may need to limit the background information you give so that you don't overwhelm your client with detail.

Example 17-D · Roadmap section of a memo

Start with a conclusion. →

Set out the governing rule and break down the elements, factors, or steps in the governing rule. →

The memo provides the legal reader with background information about a related statute that, ultimately, does not apply to the client's case. That information would be important to a senior attorney; however, because the information about the related statute is technical in nature, and ultimately does not apply to the client's situation, that information is omitted from the client letter in Example 17-E. →

The Neros will very likely be able to gain ownership of the disputed property, including the apple orchard and vegetable garden, through adverse possession. To acquire property by adverse possession plaintiffs must prove by clear and convincing evidence that their possession of the land was actual, open and notorious, exclusive, hostile, and continuous for a ten-year period. *Hoffman v. Freeman Land and Timber, LLC.*, 994 P.2d 106, 109 (Or. 1999). Oregon Revised Statute § 105.620 (2017), prescribes these same elements of adverse possession, but also requires that the land be possessed through an honest belief that the plaintiffs owned the land. The statute applies only to claims that vested and are filed after January 1, 1990. *Mid-Valley Resources, Inc. v. Engelson*, 13 P.3d 118, 121 n.2 (Or. Ct. App. 2000). The Neros should be able to prove that their claim vested by the late spring of 1989; consequently, their claim is not subject to Oregon Revised Statute § 105.620, and a review of their potential claim should analyze only those activities on the disputed land that occurred from 1979 through 1989. The element that will be most difficult for the Neros to prove is that their possession was open and notorious; however, they should be able to prove that element and the other common law elements of adverse possession and, therefore, gain ownership of the disputed property.

Example 17-E · Analogous roadmap for a letter

This roadmap begins with an issue statement rather than a conclusion because the writer already stated her conclusion in the opening paragraph. →

As we discussed in our meeting, your claim falls under an area of property law called "adverse possession." I understand you thought the term "adverse possession" carried a negative image of "squatters" who unfairly made land claims against legitimate property owners. Let me alleviate your concerns. Most adverse possession claims involve boundary disputes in which an owner is gen-

uinely mistaken about a property line. In Oregon, adverse possession claim- ← Rather than listing the elements
ants *must* believe that the property in dispute actually belongs to them.   first, the writer provides different
Because you believed the land was yours for the last thirty years, you have a   background information to
strong likelihood of gaining legal title to the land.   educate the client about the
                                                                                legal claim.

Oregon law allows adverse possession claimants, who mistakenly believe they ← Governing rule provided here.
own land that actually belongs to someone else, to gain title if they use the land
for ten consecutive years. To acquire property in this way, claimants must prove by
clear and convincing evidence that their possession of the land was actual, open
and notorious, exclusive, hostile, and continuous during that ten-year period.

Under the facts you have told me, your use of the land meets these
requirements. First, you can prove …   ← Note that no elements are
                                                                                disposed of in this roadmap.

If one of the elements, factors, or steps in the roadmap to an objective
memorandum is uncontroversial and therefore does not warrant a full
discussion, you can dispose of the element, factor, or step and then map
out and explain those that remain as the writer did in Example 17-F. As
you may notice in Example 17-G, in a client letter, unlike a memorandum,
you will not include as much detail about the legal basis for disposing of
that element, factor, or step.

Example 17-F · A roadmap that disposes of an element in a memorandum

Ms. Larsen will probably not be able to establish that Councilmember Bennett coerced Ms. Larsen to contribute something of value to an organization for
Councilmember Bennett's benefit. Under Michigan Law, an elected official may
not coerce or attempt to coerce a public employee to contribute anything of
value to an organization for the benefit of the person holding elected office or
for the purpose of furthering or defeating a proposed law. Mich. Comp. Laws
§ 15.405 (2015).

In this case, Ms. Larsen is a public employee. A public employee is an "employee of the state classified civil service." Mich. Comp. Laws § 15.401. Ms.
Larsen took her civil service exam in 1973 and is a Grade 14 employee, em- ← Disposing of an element that
ployed in the Office of the Secretary of State.   does not warrant a full legal
                                                                                discussion.
To determine whether Ms. Larsen was improperly coerced, this memo will
consider whether (1) Ms. Larsen contributed something of value to the organization …

Example 17-G · A roadmap that disposes of an element in a client letter

Based on the facts as I understand them, establishing a claim against
Councilmember Bennett for coercion will be quite difficult. In our meeting, we ← Conclusion. Remember, you
discussed that Michigan law prohibits an elected official from coercing a public   have an ethical obligation to
employee to contribute anything of value to an organization for the benefit of   deliver "bad news" when your
the elected official. We further discussed your concern that Councilmember   legal research shows that your
Bennett improperly coerced you into holding the Secretary of State's office   client does not have a viable
open an additional 15 minutes on the evening ballot measures were due and   legal claim.

that this was a contribution of value to the organization "Save Our Downtown," as well as a contribution for the benefit of Councilmember Bennett.

Unfortunately, my research into the matter shows that these actions are unlikely to establish that Councilmember Bennett violated Michigan Law. You are unquestionably considered a public employee since you are a Grade 14 employee in the Office of the Secretary of State. As explained below, however, it will be quite difficult for us to establish that holding the Secretary of State's office open for an additional 15 minutes was something of value or that this act was for the benefit of Councilmember Bennett.

Disposing of an element that does not warrant a full legal discussion. In a client letter, particularly to a non-lawyer, you will focus primarily on the client's facts rather than providing a technical description of background law that is not in controversy.

Following a roadmap section, you will want to address each remaining element of the governing rule, just as you would in a memo. What is likely to change is the level of detail in your analysis. In a memo, you tend to rely on analogical reasoning over rule-based reasoning; by contrast, in a letter, you are likely to prefer rule-based reasoning.

As we have discussed previously in Chapter 8.2, *Applying the Law: Analogical Reasoning*, attorneys usually prefer to argue by analogy when possible. They prefer analogical arguments because *stare decisis* is central to our legal system. *Stare decisis*, of course, requires the same outcome for cases that have the same legal issue and the same facts. Thus, if an attorney can find a case with the same facts, the same legal issue, and the desired outcome, an attorney will always argue by analogy because *stare decisis* makes the court's decision predictable.

When talking with a client, however, the factual detail required for an analogical argument may bog down your reader. Thus, you may prefer to rely more heavily on rule-based arguments. In the event that the factual similarities to a prior case are crucial to your analysis, you may still rely on an analogical argument. However, take extra care to hone the case to its essentials so that the reader is not overwhelmed by detail.

Finally, you may decide to make one other adjustment to your analysis. In a traditional memo, within a single legal argument (which examines one element, factor, or step), you always explain all the relevant law before applying the law to the client's case. That's because attorneys like to have a cohesive understanding of the law before they consider how it will apply to a client's case.

By contrast, a client simply wants to understand the likely outcome and the reasons for that outcome. Having a cohesive understanding of the legal support for the application of the governing rules to your client's facts is less important to a client. (That's why your client hired you.) You should, instead, select an organization that focuses primarily on your prediction and on applying the facts in the client's case relevant to your prediction.

Throughout, avoid citations wherever possible. In the examples above, all citations are omitted. Most readers, particularly readers who are not lawyers, do not need citations to cases or statutes. They are unlikely to look up a pinpoint cite or assess the weight of the authority you are citing.

Citations often make the work look cluttered and can be distracting. If writing to a client or non-lawyer, keep citations to a minimum and focus more on rule-based reasoning and general principles.

If, however, you feel your reader needs or wants the reference, put the citation in a footnote or use an abbreviated citation. "Under the 2011 Oregon Supreme Court case of *Abraham v. T. Henry Construction,...*"

Table 17-H, summarizes adjustments you might make to convert your discussion section from your memo to an analysis in a letter.

Example 17-H · Converting your discussion section to an analysis in a client letter

	Discussion Section in a Memo	Analysis in a Client Letter
Roadmap	Begin with an introductory roadmap section, as described in Section II.F.iii., *Analysis.*	Same, but because you have stated your conclusion in the opening paragraph, you may decide to omit an initial conclusion at the beginning of the roadmap paragraph and, instead, identify the issue.
		Consider, also, what background information about the legal issue will be helpful to your client. Adjust accordingly.
Organization of discussion or analysis	Organize around elements, factors, or steps.	Same.
Analogical v. Rule-Based Reasoning	Prefer analogical arguments because of their predictive force in a legal system based on *stare decisis*.	Prefer rule-based arguments because they are less detailed and easier to absorb. When relying on analogical arguments, case illustrations should be honed to their essentials.
Organization of a single legal argument	For each element, factor, or step, explain all the relevant law (rules, case illustrations, and policy); then, apply that law to the facts of your client's case. Do not introduce the client when explaining the law.	For each element, factor, or step, explain the law in a manner that educates your client about the relevant rules and, to the extent necessary, explain the case illustrations that will support the strongest argument. Then apply.
Citations	Include after every legal proposition.	Generally omit, but if needed, use in footnotes or abbreviate the citations in the text.

To see the effect of these adjustments, review the analysis below in Example 17-I. That example shows a portion of a letter to a client discussing whether the client can sue for intentional infliction of emotional distress. The excerpt below focuses on the first element of the claim, whether the client can prove extreme and outrageous conduct. After reading Example 17-I, below, go to Appendix B, and review the same analysis as it would be written in a memo.

Example 17-I · Legal analysis in a client letter

CONFIDENTIAL ATTORNEY-CLIENT COMMUNICATION
DO NOT COPY OR DISCLOSE TO ANYONE ELSE

January 5, 2018

Mr. Joseph McLaughlin
101 South Elm Street
Greensboro, North Carolina 27109

Re: McLaughlin v. Dixon — claim for Intentional Infliction of Emotional Distress (client no. 065001)

Dear Joe:

[*Opening paragraph and background facts omitted.*]

As we discussed in our meeting, I believe you have a strong claim for intentional infliction of emotional distress based on Ms. Dixon's alleged harassment. Intentional infliction of emotional distress is a claim that is designed to compensate a victim who is severely emotionally abused by another person. If we are successful in proving this claim, you may be able to recover costs associated with your medical bills, lost wages, and any pain and suffering you have experienced. To prove this claim, however, we would have to show (1) that Ms. Dixon engaged in "extreme and outrageous conduct," (2) that her conduct caused you severe emotional distress, and (3) that she intended to cause you severe emotional distress.

Ultimately, I believe we will be able to prove each of these elements; however, the first element — that Ms. Dixon engaged in "extreme and outrageous conduct" — will be more difficult to prove. I will thus begin by explaining that element.

To prove that Ms. Dixon engaged in extreme and outrageous conduct, we must show that her behavior was "beyond the bounds of decency" or "atrocious and utterly intolerable in a civilized society." We must show that the conduct was much more than simply insulting, bothersome, or offensive. While these standards are somewhat nebulous, past cases have shown that conduct is extreme and outrageous if it is public, persistent, and derogatory, with no purpose for the conduct other than spite.

In this case, Ms. Dixon's harassing postings were public because they were posted on the Internet. They were also persistent because they went on for several months and continued even after you asked her to take them down. In addition, we can show that they were derogatory because she repeatedly accused you of illicit sexual misconduct, adultery, failure to pay child support, and being a "mentally unstable monster." Although Ms. Dixon may argue that her postings did have a purpose (such as protecting the public), the facts as you have described them likely show that her assertions were meritless. Thus, we will likely be able to prove that she posted her statements for no reason other than spite.

The two remaining elements will be easier to prove. To prove severe emotional distress, North Carolina law requires you to show that a medical professional diagnosed you as having a severe and disabling emotional or mental condition. Here, because your medical records from Dr. Smith show that as a result of the harassment you are now suffering from severe, chronic depression and anxieties, we can establish this element.

* * *

Best regards,

Carla Izaguirre

Carla Izaguirre

---

4. Options

After explaining the analysis, discuss the available options under the law and the facts. In addition to explaining the available options, your client will likely appreciate your assessment of which options provide the best course of action.

Throughout the body of your letter, but particularly when discussing options, you will sometimes be required to deliver bad news. Beware of trying to soften bad news with a too optimistic promise or an imprudent guarantee. If you predict the options are bleak, then say so. Your client needs a wise assessment devoid of false hope. If chances are slim, but possible, be clear about the odds and the likelihood of success.

5. Next steps

Concretely state the next steps that need to be taken and clearly establish who should take those steps. Be direct and specific.

Example 17-J · Example of options and next steps paragraphs

You have two options. Since litigation is costly, we can first try to resolve the dog bite dispute directly with your neighbor. Since you have had an amicable relationship in the past, she may be amenable to reimbursing you for the medical fees and property damage her dog caused. If your neighbor does not respond favorably, we can file a claim seeking reimbursement for your damages. Please be aware that our state imposes a one-year statute of limitations on dog bite cases, meaning that your claim must be filed within one year from the date the bite occurred.

I will call you later this week to discuss these two options and how you would like to proceed. In the meantime, please send me the final hospital bill you received last month. If you have any questions or concerns, please call or email me. I am hopeful that we can resolve this matter quickly and with minimal additional expense.

G. Closing

Include a closing such as "Very truly yours," or "Sincerely," and close by typing your full business name, as in Example 17-K. You can vary the closing according to your relationship with the recipient (just as you did in the salutation), but keep a professional tone. If you are particularly close to the recipient or have a long-standing relationship, you may sign the letter with just your first name, as in Example 17-L.

Example 17-K • Example of a traditional closing for a professional letter

Very truly yours,

Virginia James Welles

Virginia James Welles

Example 17-L • Example of a closing for a professional letter when you have a more personal relationship with the recipient

Very truly yours,

Virginia

Virginia James Welles

Always sign the letter, and use an electronic signature only when you cannot physically sign the letter.

H. Confidentiality Warning

Letters sometimes reach the wrong person, or an unwitting client might violate attorney-client privilege by sharing a letter that contains sensitive or privileged information. One of your ethical duties as a lawyer requires you to protect client confidences and to help your client protect those confidences. So, you should make it a practice to include a confidentiality warning on every letter that you send. If you have any worries that the client may inadvertently share the letter, put a specific warning in a header or footer so that it appears on every page, as in examples 17-M and 17-N. Otherwise, a general statement of confidentiality at the end of the letter should suffice. Typically, this warning would be in the form of a footer on the last page.

Example 17-M • Example of a confidentiality warning

This letter is a confidential attorney-client communication. Please do not copy, distribute, or disclose to any other person.

Example 17-N · Example of a confidentiality warning

PERSONAL & CONFIDENTIAL
ATTORNEY-CLIENT COMMUNICATION
ATTORNEY WORK PRODUCT

As with all other forms of legal writing, drafting the body of the letter is only the first step. Next, you must edit and polish.

III. Editing and Polishing Your Letter

Editing and polishing take on heightened importance when sending a letter to a client. All readers make assumptions about your competency based on your writing. Your reader may see typographical errors and assume you are less careful and competent. Your reader may hear a condescending tone and become less accepting of your analysis.

A client is no different from other readers except for one thing: Your client has *paid* you to be competent. Thus, those errors which signal a lack of care or competence are especially frustrating to a client. Those errors communicate that the client's money has not been well spent, and those errors may undermine your client's confidence in your advice.

Thus, edit and polish your letters vigilantly. You can do that by conducting several rounds of review. In particular, review your letter's tone to ensure that it is professional and respectful. Then, edit to eliminate all errors and as much legalese as possible. Finally, review the letter's format to ensure that it appears in a traditional, reader-friendly format.

A. Create a Conversational, yet Professional Tone

Every piece of correspondence conveys a tone, that is, a general mood or feeling. Your tone communicates your attitude toward your work and toward your client, and your client will perceive that attitude. Tone is conveyed through word choice and sentence construction. Thus, after writing the substance of your letter, check that the tone is conversational, yet professional.

A conversational tone is one that is not too formal. Avoid complex sentences and unusual vocabulary words. In other words, keep it simple. By choosing commonly used words and simple sentence phrasing (subject before action verb, for example), your letter will be understandable and approachable.

Taking care to edit and polish your letter will convey your authority and professionalism and, at the same time, allow you to avoid the embarrassment of sending a letter like the one in Example in 17-O.

Example 17-O · Less effective client letter with a too colloquial tone

Dear Mr. and Mrs. Nero,

The opening paragraph does not explain the law very well. What tone do you perceive in the letter?

    I hope this letter finds you in good health. Having reviewed your notes, I am happy to inform you that you stand a good chance at keeping the land under Oregon laws. We will have to file a claim for adverse possession of the property. Adverse possession allows title of the property to be granted to people who have made extensive and prolonged use of the land.

The contractions and slang give this letter a flighty air. The claim and its elements are not explained well. Notice that the attorney did not recite the facts as she understood them. Accordingly, the facts that support the elements are not clear, and mistakes in the attorney's understanding of the facts cannot be identified.

    To successfully make such a claim, we need to prove openness, actual possession, exclusive possession, hostility, and continuous possession. Openness requires that the occupation of the land was publicly open — you have your "flag flying" so to speak. The fence you put up meets this part of the requirement. Actual possession means actually using the land in dispute, which has obviously been done, between the gardening, the planting, and all of the other uses you have made from the land. Hostility may sound confusing, but in layman's terms, it's the matter of intent — whether the person making the claim intended to or believed that the property was rightfully theirs. Exclusive possession is just that — and from the sounds of it, you and your family were the only people using the land. Finally, the element of continuous possession requires for the claimant to have used the land for ten or more years continuously.

This paragraph yields ambiguity. These sentences suggest that the opposition has a good claim too. How would you interpret this paragraph?

The attorney has not assessed any options or clearly indicated what next steps should be taken. The client will likely be confused as to what will happen next.

    The two owners may be able to take this case to court. Although you have a pretty strong case for claiming the land, there is the possibility that the title owners will dispute the claim and move for summary judgment. Thus the question arises as to how much in the way of resources you are willing to expend to keep this part of the land. I cannot guarantee that your claim will win without a trial happening, but from the evidence I have, you will be able to win this case and keep the land.

This last paragraph is vague and does not explain what next steps either the attorney or the client will take. The open-ended time frame will likely result in the passage of time without any action on the case.

    We will continue to be in touch and preparing for this case. Feel free to call us if you have any questions.

> Sincerely,
> Janie
> Jane Malscrit, Esq.

Review and use the techniques discussed in Chapter 16, *Editing and Polishing*, to help ensure your letter will be as professional and as error-free as possible.

    If the content of the letter prevents you from tempering its formal tone, tell your reader you recognize that formality (as in Example 17-P). No matter the complexity of the subject, you can always use more conversational phrasing at the beginning or end of the letter to establish a more personal connection.

Example 17-P · Conversational connection in a formal letter

Dear Ms. Stone,

On behalf of Trendor McClellan Law Firm, I want to thank you for letting us assist you with the formation of your limited liability corporation. I enjoyed meeting you yesterday and getting to know more about you and your new business. I apologize for the formal tone of this letter, but I wanted to outline our understanding of the scope of representation and our firm's billing policy. Federal law requires us to provide a copy of our privacy policy, and you will find that document enclosed. As we discussed, I do not directly handle tax ◄— preparation, but I will be happy to refer you to other specialists if you need further assistance. If you have any questions about the terms of this letter, please call or email me.

> Listing enclosures at the beginning of a letter will not only help your administrative assistant but will also help your client in making sure they received the documents.

When using a conversational tone, however, beware of crossing into colloquial slang. Slang is the informal use of vocabulary. Slang can transform a letter from conversational to flippant. See how contractions, clichés, and too many prepositional phrases in Example 17-Q result in a colloquial, non-professional client letter.

Example 17-Q · Less effective letter that uses slang, contractions, clichés, and too many prepositional phrases

You have two options. Because litigation costs a small fortune and takes a long time, we can first try to resolve the dog bite dispute directly with your neighbor. However, since your neighbor has been a "jerk" to you over and over throughout this situation, she probably won't give you the money for your medical bills or for the property damage caused by her dog. We'll probably end up needing to file a lawsuit to seek money for your damages from this incident. Be warned, though, that our state imposes a one-year statute of limitations on dog bite cases, meaning that we need to get moving on any claim.

Although too much slang can result in an overly-colloquial tone, too much jargon can create an overly-formal tone. Jargon is the technical, specialized language of a profession or group. Using too much jargon can create a barrier with the reader who may not understand the terms. For instance, you may have a case that involves specialized scientific, medical, business, or technological terms. Unless your client is a sophisticated reader who is familiar with the industry's jargon, explain any specialized terms.

Finally, be respectful. We do not always get to choose our clients, and a time may come when you have a client who you do not like very much. When writing to such a client, never be condescending, and never express irritation or frustration in writing. Although there may be a time when you will need to have a direct conversation with a client about your working relationship, have that conversation in person or, at the very least, over the phone. Do not let those emotions slip sideways into a letter.

B. Omit Legalese. Explain Legal Terms as Necessary.

Next, review your letter for legalese. Legalese, like other kinds of jargon, can create a barrier with your reader. Omit as much legal jargon as possible. Look at how the legalese in Example 17-R muddles the content and directions in the letter.

Example 17-R · Letter legalese

Dear Chaplain Cleveland,

   Enclosed please find the documents relating to the formation and estab-lishment of the Circle of Friends Foundation. Time is of the essence, so please **provide your signature** on the documents and return them to my office as soon as your schedule will allow. **Pursuant to** the bylaws of your diocese, we must provide a copy of the documents to Bishop John Peters within thirty days of the foundation's official formation. I have **appended** a copy of the proposed letter to Bishop Peters **herein**. Please review the letter and return it along with the **aforementioned** documents. I am **cognizant of the fact that** you want to get the foundation running at **utmost haste**, and I am **at the present moment** finishing the remaining paperwork. I will alert you when the loose ends are tied.

Example 17-R shows legalese in the extreme. Example 17-S illustrates how a letter without legalese increases reader understanding and retention of the material.

Example 17-S · Letter without legalese

Dear Chaplain Cleveland,

   I have attached the documents relating to the formation and establishment of the Circle of Friends Foundation. Please sign the enclosed documents and re-turn them to my office by Friday, October 12. The bylaws of your diocese re-quire us to provide a copy of the documents to Bishop John Peters within thirty days of the foundation's official formation. I have attached a copy of the pro-posed letter to Bishop Peters. Please review the letter and return it with the other documents. I know you are eager to get the foundation running, and I am finishing the remaining paperwork. I will call within the next two days when the final round of paperwork is finished.

Although you should keep legal jargon to a minimum, you need not eliminate every legal term in your writing. If your client needs to understand a legal term such as "statute of limitations" or "constructive notice," then explain the term with common words.

Essentially, get rid of the stuffiest legalese and just say things simply.

C. Eliminate Errors

After checking the tone of your letter, review it again to be sure that the letter is error-free. Because of the inherent formality of a letter, mistakes or disorganization stand out. Always use the grammar and spell check functions on your computer, but remember that these aides are no substitute for careful reading. Spell check will not correct improper word choice (like "their" instead of "there" or "do reply" instead of "do not reply"). Thus, you must proofread. As discussed in Chapter 16, *Editing and Polishing*, after spending time writing your letter, you may find it difficult to step back and see the errors. To force yourself to take a fresh look, consider one of these techniques: You can use a colored piece of paper to move line by line through your letter, you can read your letter aloud, or you can use the text-to-speech function on your computer to listen to your letter. Choose one of these techniques and read everything. An error in your client's name or address or in the "RE" line is just as embarrassing as an error in the body of your letter.

Finally, keep track of the kinds of errors you make, such as substituting "their" for "there," "it's" for "its," or "council" for "counsel" and search for those issues using the "find" function in your computer's toolbar.

D. Choose a Traditional, Reader-Friendly Format

After reviewing your letter's tone, ensuring that it is written in a direct and easy-to-understand way, and eliminating all errors, you are ready to put your letter in its final format. Your firm or employer likely has a template for letters. If so, use that template. If you are not using a template, you can choose one of two traditional formats.

Within the body of the letter, paragraphs can be indented five spaces, and the date, salutation, and signature lines are indented to the center of the page. A block style, in which all text starts at the left margin without indentations, is also popular. If you use the block style, be sure to leave a blank line between each paragraph.

When formatting, try not to crowd the information at the top of the page.

IV. Letters vs. Emails: Which to Send When?

More and more, attorneys communicate with their clients through email. That fact raises the question of which mode of communication to use when.[1] Unfortunately, no hard and fast rule governs when to send an email versus when to send a letter. To decide whether to send an email or a letter, take a moment to consider some differences between letters and email.

First, letters are usually considered a more formal mode of communication than email. They arrive on thick bond paper, and we tend to assume that a letter takes more time and effort to prepare. Thus, letters convey a sense of importance that email does not.

Second, remember that emails are easy to forward. As a result, when you send an email, you run a greater risk that the email will be forwarded to an unintended recipient.

Finally, people receive relatively few letters, but are inundated by email. Thus, a letter stands out in a client's mind and is less likely to get lost in the clutter of an inbox.

These different characteristics lead to a few recommendations:

1. If you want to signal to your client that the information is important or you wish to formalize your opinion for your client, put it in a letter.[2]
2. If you would like the communication to become a part of your client's permanent file, send a letter.
3. If the communication contains highly sensitive or highly confidential material, and you are concerned the communication could be improperly shared, send a letter. A letter is less likely to be inadvertently forwarded.
4. If the recipient is from an older generation or less technologically sophisticated, send a letter—at least initially. You can then discuss with your client the preferred mode of communication.
5. If ever you are unsure whether to send an email or letter, err on the side of formality and send a letter.

---

1. Thank you to attorneys Margaret Kushner, Karen O'Connor, and Thom Brown for their input on using letters and emails in law practice.
2. Comments from attorney Karen O'Connor.

Practice Points

- Consider what your client needs from your letter before you draft it. Is your client sophisticated or unsophisticated? Does your client simply want the bottom line or is your client interested in more detail? Draft accordingly.

- Always provide the background facts that have been communicated to you so that your client can correct any misunderstanding of the facts.

- Although the level of detail you provide in a client letter will vary depending on the client, as a general rule, prefer simpler rule-based analyses over more detailed analogical analyses.

- Always provide your client with the options that are available, advice about which options you think are preferable, and specific instructions about who should do what next and when.

- Strive for a conversational, yet professional tone.

- Use a confidentiality warning.

- Make it error-free.

- Think carefully about whether the information you want to convey is best conveyed by letter or by email.

Chapter 18

Professional Emails

Using email is critical to practicing law effectively. Email allows users to communicate ideas quickly, easily, efficiently, and without regard to schedule or geography. Thus, you will likely communicate often with your clients, other attorneys, and the courts electronically. Although other forms of electronic communication exist, like text messaging, email remains the dominant form of communication in legal practice. In fact, as much as eighty percent of your business correspondence may occur via email.

Because electronic correspondence will be part of your daily routine, you should know how to compose a professional email. No matter whether the email is to quickly confirm an appointment or to convey a legal analysis, a professional email should be easy for your reader to absorb and should maintain the appropriate formality for a business setting. This chapter provides guidelines to achieve those goals.

I. Correspond Professionally

Even with many kinds of communication options available today, email is a preferred mode of communication among professionals, and lawyers use it daily. Thus, an email's form and content should always reflect professional standards—that is, it should be clear, accurate, concise, free from errors, and have a degree of formality appropriate for the workplace. With personal correspondence to friends or family, a casual style is often acceptable, and the reader will easily forgive the occasional typographical error, misspelled word, or improper punctuation. In a law practice, however, those errors may take on negative significance.

As an attorney, your credibility will be constantly evaluated with every piece of work you complete, whether that work is a complex memorandum or a three-line email. In other words, your work makes a loud statement about your credibility. Sending an email to a colleague or client that is too casual is like wearing a swimsuit to the office. It reflects poor judgment. In addition, your correspondence tells people how you view *them*. Correspondence that is too casual can send a message to the reader that you do not value or respect them. Most importantly, your work reflects on your employer and your client. As you draft any piece of correspondence, make sure it reflects well on you, your law office, and your client.

For each professional email, take the same care as you would in a paper letter sent out with your signature. Read each email before you send it. For very important emails, print them and read them just as you would a draft of a letter. Remember that emails can quickly and easily be seen by millions of people around the world.

II. Decide Whether Email Is the Best Mode of Communication

Before constructing an email, take a moment to consider whether email is the best medium in which to communicate.

To make that decision, consider the purpose of your email. Do you need to address a simple administrative matter? Do you need to convey information that may be unsettling or upsetting to the recipient? Do you need to convey your legal analysis? Your answer to these questions will help you decide whether to send an email.

A. Administrative Matters

Administrative matters include scheduling meetings; providing updates, whether to a senior attorney, colleague, or client; and giving directions to others who are working with you. These matters include all the day-to-day communications that allow you to manage your workflow.

Administrative matters can often be handled with a short email. However, if resolving the administrative matter will require several emails back-and-forth, it may be more efficient to either pick up a phone or walk down the hall and actually speak to the person. Following these communications, you may want to send an email to confirm the conversations and relevant details.

B. Difficult Conversations

As a lawyer, you may need to deliver bad news or convey information that will be upsetting to hear. You may need to tell a client that, despite a terrible injury, she has no legal claim or that a case was lost on appeal. You may disagree with a colleague's analysis. You may need to explain to a colleague that a work product was not good enough and needs to be reworked. Or you may be angry about an email you received, and you want to respond immediately. In all of these cases, email may not be the best form of communication.

Before you send any email, take a moment to consider how it will be received. In the end, you may decide to send your message by email, perhaps because you want a permanent record of the message, because email is the quickest way to reach someone, or because you believe you can convey a difficult message with more finesse if you write it out. On the other hand, you may decide that you can more effectively convey the message (or soften its emotional impact) if you reach out by phone or talk in person. Particularly when facing a difficult conversation, take a moment to consider an email's impact and whether you should adjust your mode of communication.

C. Legal Analyses

Lawyers also use email to convey their analyses. Those emails might analyze the law and how it applies to a client's problem, or they might address a strategy for pursuing a client's claim or negotiating a settlement. Deciding whether to convey your legal analysis in an email or in a traditional memorandum requires you to consider the preferences of your recipient as well as the length and complexity of the analysis. Part IV of this chapter, *Sending a Legal Analysis in an Email,* addresses that choice and how to modify a legal analysis if you choose to convey your legal analysis in an email.

III. Crafting a Professional Email

To craft a professional email, you must first be familiar with the basic components of a professional email. Then, you must craft those component parts, keeping an eye on a variety of concerns. You will want your text to be structured so that an online reader can easily absorb your point. You will want to convey the required degree of formality in a professional email. Finally, you will want to ensure that sensitive information remains confidential.

A. The Basic Components of an Email

An email has up to eight parts: the recipients' addresses, the subject line, the salutation, the body of the email, the closing, the name and signature block, the confidentiality warning, and any attachments.

1. The recipients' addresses

Addressing an email is simple and, therefore, fraught with danger. Because emails can be so easily disseminated to vast numbers of people, you will want to take special care to protect private or sensitive information and any privileges that attach to that information. As a legal professional, pay attention to the information in the email and to whom that information will be sent. First, be aware of the difference between listing a recipient in the "To," "CC," or "BCC" line. The "To" line indicates the recipient to whom the sender is speaking. "CC" stands for "carbon copy." It's a phrase that comes from the days when secretaries used typewriters and put a sheet of carbon paper between two blank pieces of paper to create copies as they typed. Today you may hear the phrase referred to as a "courtesy copy." A sender will "CC" other recipients if the sender wants the CC'd recipients to be aware of the email message. Recipients in the "To" line and in the "CC" line can see that the email has been sent to each other.

"BCC" stands for blind carbon copy (or blind courtesy copy). A sender puts a recipient in the BCC line if the sender wants the recipient to be aware of the email but does not want others to know that the email has been sent to that person. Recipients in the "To" and "CC" lines will not know that the email has been sent to someone who is in the BCC line.

You have to be particularly careful with those you list in the BCC line. You have to be confident that someone who is sent a blind copy will not acknowledge the email by, for example, sending a reply to others on the email. A communication becomes awkward when people suddenly realize others—about whom they were unaware—were privy to the conversation all along. (Similarly, if you are a BCC recipient, others will not know that you have received that email, and so if you reply, you should reply only to the sender, and you should probably not refer to the email publicly since the email was sent to you confidentially.)

The ease with which we can populate email addresses can cause problems. Most email systems automatically populate an email address after you have typed in a few letters of a person's email address. If you do not carefully review the final email addresses, you may be sending the email to jlewis@nytimes.com rather than to John Lewis with whom you work.[1] Alternatively, you can press "reply all," when, in fact, you intended for your reply to go only to the sender. Thus, always review the "To," "CC," and "BCC" lines not only when you receive the email, but also before you send an email to verify that all of the recipients are intended recipients.

As an attorney, you will be expected to adhere to the highest standards of discretion and confidentiality when working, and you certainly do not want to send an email with confidential matters to unintended recipients. Even if an email does not contain confidential information, when it is inadvertently sent to the wrong recipients, a misfired email may undermine the recipient's faith in your ability to be discreet and keep a confidence. Be safe: Review the "To," "CC," and "BCC" lines before pressing send.

2. Subject line

When conveying information about legal matters in a business setting, an accurate and specific subject line is essential. The subject line provides context and pinpoints the purpose of the email. Lawyers and most clients receive many emails every day. They must make decisions about how to prioritize emails. Further, if recipients cannot look at your email right away, they need to be able to retrieve it easily. A vague—or worse, an inaccurate—subject line makes it more difficult both to assess whether an email needs immediate attention and to retrieve that email later. Thus, be specific. "Research re: Court's duty to determine jurisdiction" is specific. "Research" is not. Also, be accurate. Do not re-use the same subject line simply because pressing "reply" seems easier than editing the subject line or starting a new email.

3. Salutation

Each new email exchange should begin with a salutation: "Carla," "Professor Miller," or "Dear Dr. Lenehan." A salutation is not necessary, however, once you have exchanged several emails about the same topic. An email exchange is like a conversation, and in a conversation you would not say hello each time it is your turn to speak.

When including a salutation, make sure you have spelled the recipient's name correctly, and address a person by first name only if you know that person well enough to do so.

Titles or honorifics (terms of respect like Mr., Mrs., Ms., or Mx.) are still customarily used in professional correspondence, especially if you

---

1. *See, e.g.,* Judith Newman, *The Perils of Email Auto-Fill*, N.Y. Times, Aug. 28, 2015, *http://www.nytimes.com/2015/08/30/fashion/the-perils-of-email-auto-fill.html?_r=0.*

have not met the recipient. When using gendered honorifics, be careful. Never assume that gender is obvious. If you are not sure how a recipient identifies or prefers to be addressed, use a neutral salutation without the name. For example, you might use a simple, stand-alone salutation like, "Hello" or "Good morning."

4. Body

The body of the email conveys your message. Part I.B, *Creating an Effective Email Through Content, Tone, and Style*, below, describes how to craft the body of a professional email. If you are including a legal analysis in your email, Part IV, *Sending a Legal Analysis in an Email*, will explain how to do that.

5. Closing

The closing, whether a paragraph or sentence, should set out any next steps that you or the recipient will complete as well as any parting words you want to share. If a timely completion of those next steps is important, the closing should specify any deadlines or timelines for either party.

In addition, as a junior attorney, you should always close by offering further assistance if it is needed. Some typical closings include the following: "Please let me know if you have any questions"; "If you need any additional research, please let me know"; and "Please let me know if you'd like me to [take the next logical step, such as draft a formal letter to the client, draft a motion, or conduct additional necessary research]."

Finally, depending on the custom of your office and the person to whom your message is sent, you may want to include a complimentary closing following the last paragraph. "Sincerely," "Best regards," and "Regards" are examples of a complimentary closing. A complimentary closing is most often used when sending an email to a client or another recipient who you do not know well. At the end of an interoffice or other email to a colleague, however, you may want to exclude these kinds of closing phrases and just sign your name. Above all, avoid ending an email with any kind of cute or sarcastic phrase, even if you are good friends with the recipient: "Besties," "Working toward Friday," or similar comments are never appropriate for a professional email.

6. Name and signature block

You will always include your name after the closing, and you should also include a "signature block." A signature block is a block of text automatically included at the end of an email. It should include your contact information such as your email address and phone number. Often a colleague or client will want to follow up with you after reading your email; including your email address and phone number on every email makes that follow-up easier.

7. Confidentiality warning

Confidential or sensitive information about a client's case is too often distributed either to the wrong people or distributed when it should not be distributed at all. Make sure that privileged information, whether attorney-client privilege or your attorney work product, is protected. Include a confidentiality warning, like the ones below (and illustrated in Examples 18-A and 18-B), on each email you send just in case it is erroneously distributed to the wrong recipients. You can set up your mail to automatically include this statement along with the signature block. The best advice, though, is to stop and think before you send an email, making sure its information can be communicated and that you are distributing it to the correct recipients.

The content and format of confidentiality warnings can vary depending on the jurisdiction and your employer's preference. For example, notice how the coverage and content of these confidentiality warnings differ:

- **A shorter warning**

Notice: This email may contain material that is confidential, privileged, and attorney work product for the sole use of the intended recipient. Any review, reliance, or distribution by others or forwarding without express permission is strictly prohibited. If you are not the intended recipient, please delete the email and any attachments and notify us immediately.

- **A longer warning that also disclaims technological problems stemming from the email**

EMAIL CONFIDENTIALITY NOTICE: The contents of this email message and any attachments are intended solely for the intended recipient(s) and may contain confidential and legally privileged information. If you are not the intended recipient of this message or if this message has been addressed to you in error, please immediately alert the sender by reply email and then delete this message and any attachments. If you are not the intended recipient, you are notified that any use, dissemination, distribution, copying, or storage of this message or any attachment is strictly prohibited. Although this email and any attachments are believed to be free of any virus or other defect that might affect any computer system into which it is received, it is the responsibility of the recipient to ensure it is virus-free. No responsibility is accepted by the sender or Zal Associates for loss or damage arising from any such virus or defect.

8. Attachments

For important attachments, indicate to the reader what attachments are included. Because your reader may need to download and save attachments, use relevant and descriptive names that clearly identify each attached document. You will make the reader's work easier if you name the document in a way that is easy to save and find again later. For example, "Hernandez Affidavit.docx" is a better name than "Affidavit.docx."

B. Creating an Effective Email Through Content, Tone, and Style

No matter what type of email you are sending, every piece of correspondence has three components: the substantive content you want to convey, the tone (or the voice your reader will hear when reading the correspondence), and the style (the way the correspondence looks and reads). Because each component can either add to or detract from the reader's perception of your credibility and competency, draft your email with each component in mind.

1. Keep the content short, clear, and readable

Your first priority in sending an email is to convey information. To convey that content effectively, it should be short, clear, and readable.

The optimal length for an email is one screen. When a reader has to scroll through multiple screens, the information becomes more difficult to absorb. Unlike a page that ends and needs to be turned, a scrolling screen has no landmarks that allow the eye to rest or register the end of a unit. As a result, online readers tend to simply scan text rather than absorb and fully comprehend the text,[2] and a lengthy email can quickly become an overwhelming mass of information in which your message is lost.

A short email may look like Example 18-A.

Example 18-A • A short email answering a legal question

From: Anna Blake [ablake@zalassociates.com]
Sent: Friday, October 24, 2018
To: John MacLean [jmaclean@zalassociates.com]
Subject: Research re: Court's duty to determine jurisdiction

Attachments: Steel v. Citizens.docx

John:

You asked me to find a case stating that a federal court must determine that it has jurisdiction over a case even if neither party raises the issue.

---

2. Ruth Ann McKinney, *Reading Like a Lawyer* 265 (2d ed. 2012).

The U.S. Supreme Court in *Steel Co. v. Citizens for a Better Environment*, 523 U.S. 83, 94 (1998), addresses the issue and states that "the first and fundamental question is that of jurisdiction.... This question the court is bound to ask and answer for itself, even when not otherwise suggested, and without respect to the relation of the parties to it."

A copy of the case is attached, and the relevant portion is highlighted. Please let me know if you need further research regarding this issue.

Anna

Notice: This email is sent by a law firm and may contain information that is privileged or confidential. If you are not the intended recipient, please delete the email and any attachments and notify us immediately.

Realize, though, that while one screen is ideal, the topic of the email or the need to send ample information expeditiously may mean that your email is longer than one screen.

If your email must extend beyond one screen, you can make information easy for your reader to absorb by using the techniques listed below and used in Example 18-B that follows. These techniques are appropriate for either short or long emails; however, the longer your email becomes, the more important it will be to employ all the techniques listed below.

- **State your bottom line up front**

Everyone with whom you will be working—from paralegals, to clients, to other attorneys—will be busy, and they will want to know the bottom-line quickly. As a result, at the outset of your email, include a quick summary of the issue that the email is addressing and state your conclusion to that issue, as in Example 18-A, above, or 18-B, below. Then provide any additional explanation necessary to support your conclusion.

If you want the recipient of the email to take some action after receiving the email, put that request up front right after the bottom-line. Often, people skim emails, and they may not see your request if it is not on the first screen of your email. Thus, especially if your email extends past one screen length, note your question or request in the introduction.

- **Use thesis sentences**

Each paragraph should begin with a sentence that asserts the point of that paragraph. Because we often use emails for informal communication, it's easy to drift away from the paragraph's main point. Check the first sentence of each paragraph; then, make sure that the sentences that follow support that assertion.

- **Keep paragraphs short**

Big blocks of text are difficult to read on the printed page. They are even more difficult to read on the screen. So, keep your paragraphs in an email short. A paragraph of two to three sentences will likely be manageable. Paragraphs that are more than five sentences long are likely to tax your reader.

- **Insert a line of white space between each paragraph**

Insert a line of white space between each paragraph. Doing so allows your reader's eyes to rest. Moreover, it prevents your email from becoming that overwhelming mass of information that encourages a reader to merely skim or skip altogether.

- **Use bolded text or point headings to make the structure visible**

You can help your reader see the structure of your analysis by using point headings or bolded text, as in Example 18-B.

Example 18-B · Techniques to keep email content short, clear, and readable

---

From: Lance Carl <lcarl@zalassociates.com>
Sent: Thursday, April 17, 2017
To: Mike Cohen <mcohen@westernshoredevelopment.com>
Subject: Cannon Beach land-use dispute

Mike:

The first paragraph sets out the legal question being analyzed and puts the bottom-line answer up front. →

You asked that I research whether any land use restrictions would prevent your company from converting an historic home in Cannon Beach, Oregon, into a fast food restaurant. The answer depends on where the historic home is located.

Fast food restaurants are prohibited in Cannon Beach's downtown. The city's zoning code prohibits fast food restaurants in its downtown:

> Commercial uses that detract from the unique character of downtown or are detrimental to the small town atmosphere of Cannon Beach shall be prohibited. These uses include formula food restaurants....

Line spaces between paragraphs and bolded headings break up the information, clarify the structure, and emphasize the thesis for main paragraphs.

Short paragraphs keep the reader focused on the most important points and make those points easier to absorb.

Cannon Beach Mun. Code (Or.) §84-8 (2017). A "formula food" restaurant is any business that is required to "offer standardized menus, ingredients, food preparation, interior or exterior design, or uniforms." *Id.*

Outside the downtown, the company has two options. The city's zoning code controls changes to a historic designation or renovation of a historical landmark. Both options require a public hearing and approval by a majority of the members of the City's Zoning Board. *Id.* at §§ 33.846.040, -.050.

> **Removal of historic designation.** A request to remove a historical designation "will be approved" if the board finds that "[t]he benefits to the public and the property owner of retaining the historic designation

no longer outweigh the benefits of removing the designation" and the owner consents. *Id.* at § 33.846.040.

Renovation. Approval to renovate an historic home requires "consistency with neighborhood plans; no significant lessening of residential appearance or function of the area; physical compatibility; no significant livability impacts (e.g. noise, late night operations, privacy); and adequacy of services. *Id.* at §§ 33.445.610, 33.846.050.

The most significant hurdle would be the requirement that the renovation create "no significant lessening of residential ... function." If the building is currently being used as a home, its conversion to a fast food restaurant would necessarily lessen the residential function. However, if the home is a single-family home, then the lessening may not be deemed "significant."

If the company decides to move forward and identifies a particular home of interest, I can re-evaluate which path would be most efficient in terms of time and money. In the meantime, please let me know if you would like additional information about either non-downtown option.

Best regards,

Lance Carl
Partner
Zal Associates, LLP | 800 SW Fifth Avenue, Suite 200 | Portland, OR 97204
Direct: 503-222-5555 | Fax: 502-222-5550
lcarl@zalassociates.com | www.zalassociates.com | Bio | vCard | LinkedIn

Notice: This email may contain material that is confidential, privileged, and attorney work product for the sole use of the intended recipient. Any review, reliance, or distribution by others or forwarding without express permission is strictly prohibited.

---

2. Keep the tone polite and professional

Every piece of writing, particularly correspondence, conveys a certain tone—that is, a general mood or feeling. Your correspondence not only tells readers about your attitudes and credibility, but it also tells readers what you think about them. Your tone may convey as much information as the substance of the email, so always think about the tone you would like to convey and the tone the email is actually sending.

Tone is particularly tricky because readers can perceive it so differently. For instance, a sentence intended to be funny may be perceived by the reader as sarcastic or offensive. Be particularly aware of tone when you receive an emotionally charged email or when you are tempted to send one. Your interpretation of the tone might not be the sender's intended tone.

Tone is most often conveyed through word choice and sentence construction. Make deliberate choices about the words you choose and about how you phrase your sentences. Your goal is to convey the substance politely and professionally.

- **Review every email to consider how it will be received by the reader**

Email communications can be easily misinterpreted even if they are neutral because of the lack of nonverbal expressions in the message. When you communicate in person, you rely on facial expressions, body language, and tone of voice to express your intent. Even on the telephone, the pace and tone of voice in a phone conversation provides context. Emails are devoid of those cues. Consider the email exchange between two associates in Example 18-C.

Example 18-C · Consider an email's tone

From: Abigail Manzanita [amanzan@zalassociates.com]
Sent: Friday, September 5, 2018
To: Adam Donaldson [adonaldson@zalassociates.com]
Subject: Re: Help with Smith Discovery

Sorry. Can't.

On 9/5/18, Adam Donaldson wrote:

Abby –

I need some help making my way through the *Smith* discovery documents. Would you have some time to help me out?

Adam

In writing the email, Abby may have assumed that Adam knows how busy she is, and she just wanted to send a reply quickly. Adam, however, may be offended that Abby gave his request such short shrift. Before you send any email, take a moment to consider how it will be received. A little more time and explanation may smooth some rough edges.

- **Do not send email while emotional**

If neutral emails are easily misinterpreted, you can imagine how much harm can occur when you vent anger or frustration in an email. Never send an email when you are angry, upset, or frustrated—even if you were the target of an emotionally charged email. When you are tempted to send an emotional reply, ask yourself these questions:

- Would I say this to the person's face?
- How would I feel if I received this email message?
- How would I feel if this email became an exhibit in court or appeared on the front page of the *New York Times* with my name attached to it?

Usually, after considering the above questions you will be calm enough to write your message differently and more professionally. If not, wait until you are calm enough to reply in a professional manner. Consider the difference between the email messages in Table 18-D.

Example18-D · Send emotionally appropriate emails

Emotionally inappropriate message:

> If you don't get this memo done, I will report you to the managing partner TOMORROW!!!! I am tired of your incompetence.

Emotionally appropriate message:

> I am growing increasingly concerned about the timing of this memo. Can we set up a time to talk about this more?

While it is tempting to fire off a quick and equally nasty response to a rude email, do not let someone else's unprofessional behavior pull you down to that level. When it appears that an electronic dialogue has turned into a conflict, it is best to suggest a time to speak or meet in person. Remember that emails can be forwarded to multiple recipients virtually instantaneously. Only if you would feel comfortable with your email being seen by the rest of the world should you go ahead and press send.

3. Keep the style formal

Although emails are more casual in nature, writing in a law practice setting should be more formal. In a professional email, use the same grammar, syntax, punctuation, writing style and, if possible, formatting that you would use in a memorandum, paper letter, or other professional document. Avoid defaulting to the casual style that you might use with personal emails or on social media.

- **Do not type in ALL CAPS**

Writing in ALL CAPS is perceived as yelling.

- **Use proper capitalization, punctuation, and grammar**

You are not e.e. cummings. Failing to adhere to traditional writing norms will come across as flippant and unprofessional—even to members of your own office or people who know you well.

- **Edit and spell check**

Miss steaks can detract from your professional image, especially if their pervasive. Use spell check, but also read the email carefully.

- **Do not use internet acronyms**

Although you and most of your friends may know what IMHO[3] or FWIW[4] means, a more senior colleague may not. Do not risk confusing and frustrating that colleague as she tries to figure it out.

---

3. In my humble opinion.
4. For what it's worth.

- **Do not use emoticons or emojis**

Emoticons and emojis include images like smiley faces, icons, and graphics created from type. They are typically used to convey tone; however, since you would not draw a smiley face in a client letter or office memorandum, do not do it in a professional email. If the email text by itself does not convey the tone you are seeking, re-draft. In many cases, you should simply omit the questionable text.

IV. Sending a Legal Analysis via Email

You may often transmit a substantive legal analysis via email. When doing so, you must first choose whether to include your analysis in the body of the email or whether to draft a memorandum and attach the memorandum to the email. If you decide to include your analysis in the body of the email, you will need to condense your analysis so that it can be more easily absorbed by an online reader. Condensing your analysis will require you to make choices about what should stay and what should go. This section leads you through those decisions.

A. Using an Attached Memorandum vs. the Body of the Email

Determining whether to attach a memorandum or incorporate your analysis into the body of an email requires you to consider the preferences of your recipient, the formality you wish to convey, and the length of the analysis.

1. Consider your recipient's needs and preferences

When choosing whether to send a legal analysis in the body of an email or as an attached memorandum, first consider the preferences of the recipient. If a lawyer or a client you are working with has a stated preference for how information should be conveyed, then follow that preference.

You might also consider the recipient's needs for speed and brevity. If the recipient (whether a client or other attorney) needs to see the information quickly, then email will be preferable. Drafting a formal memo often takes longer than drafting your analysis in the body of an email. Likewise, if the analysis is straightforward and can be communicated succinctly, then, as discussed below, your analysis can be appropriately conveyed within the body of the email.

2. Consider the formality you wish to convey

Emails are considered a less formal mode of communication than letters or, for that matter, memoranda. We tend to assume that letters and memoranda take more time and effort to prepare. Moreover, people receive relatively few letters and memoranda during a day, but may receive dozens of emails each day. Thus, letters and memoranda convey a sense of importance that an email does not. For those reasons, if you want to signal that information is important, you may want to provide your legal opinion in a letter or a formal memorandum.

3. Consider the length of your analysis

The length of the analysis is a primary consideration when choosing how to send a legal analysis. As explained earlier in this chapter, the optimal length for an email is one screen. A short legal analysis conveyed in the body of an email might look like Example 18-E.

Example 18-E · A short legal analysis in an email

From: Gail Mosse [gmosse@zalassociates.com]
Sent: Friday, September 5, 2018
To: Dina Wong [dwong@zalassociates.com]
Subject: Enforceability of Oursine Living Will

Dina –

You asked whether Tom and Kitty Oursine's living will would be enforceable in Oregon. The answer is that it will not be enforceable.

The Oursines drafted their living will on their computer and signed it themselves without any witnesses. Under Oregon Revised Statutes § 127.531 living wills "must be the same as the form set forth in this section to be valid." That section also requires that two witnesses sign the form. *Id.*

As a result, the Oursines will need to re-draft their living will. The Oursines can access the correct form at http://egov.oregon.gov/DCBS/SHIBAadvanced_ directives.shtml.

Please let me know if you have any further questions.

Gail

The longer an email, the harder it will be for a reader to absorb your analysis within the body of an email, and the more likely it is that you should send your analysis in an attached memorandum. Although an analysis in an attached document requires extra keystrokes to reach, an attached analysis can be saved more easily in document files and can take advantage of the formatting features of a word processing program. Formatting, such as indented and bolded headings, paragraph breaks, and pagination all help the reader organize the information on the page. Importantly, those formatting features will be retained even when an attached document is forwarded to another person.

If you decide to explain your legal analysis in an attached memorandum, you should still summarize your analysis in a short email. Your summary should identify the issue and state your bottom-line conclusion, as in Example 18-F.

Example 18-F · An email attaching the legal analysis in a separate memorandum

---

From: Gail Mosse [gmosse@zalassociates.com]
Sent: Friday, September 5, 2018
To: Dina Wong [dwong@zalassociates.com]
Subject: Bar Application Question re: Expunged Convictions

Attachments: Expunged Convictions Memo.docx

Dina,

You asked that I research whether it's permissible for our state bar to ask an applicant for information regarding convictions that were set aside or expunged under state law.

The answer is that such a question appears to be permissible. I have attached a memo discussing the relevant law and considering how an applicant might respond to the question.

If you have any additional questions, please let me know.

Gail

Alternatively, you can condense the analysis as much as possible and keep your analysis in the body of the email. With a carefully crafted introduction, focused thesis sentences, and effective formatting, you can make a lengthy email more manageable. The next section will show you ways to craft that analysis succinctly.

B. Crafting a Condensed Email Analysis

An email containing a legal analysis has the same parts as other emails, such as the salutation, body, and closing, and the same guidelines for drafting an ordinary business email apply.

The challenge comes in condensing a full or lengthy analysis into a succinct email that your reader can absorb and understand. A legal analysis conveyed in the body of an email is like a legal analysis conveyed in a memorandum in some ways, but different in others. Both will convey the major points of the legal analysis, and the general structure of that analysis will likely be the same.

In emails, unlike in an office memo, lawyers usually omit sections like the question presented, brief answer, and the statement of facts. The question presented and brief answer are replaced with an introduction. The facts section is omitted because lawyers usually assume that the recipient knows the relevant facts, and they will simply rely on the relevant facts as necessary without having previously explained them.

1. The introduction

As discussed previously, you should begin any professional email by stating your bottom-line up front. The same is true when that email explains your legal analysis. That introduction should include a short statement about the issue that the email addresses and your conclusion or proposed resolution, as in Example 18-G. Just as in any other professional email, stating the bottom-line up front allows the reader to know where the analysis is going, thereby making it easier for the reader to absorb the more detailed analysis that follows.

The introduction of your legal analysis will thus function much like the roadmap section in a memo; that is, the introduction helps orient your reader, tells the reason for the email, and allows the reader to see the bottom-line up front.

As with other professional emails, if you would like the reader to take some action, you might alert the reader to the need for action in the introduction where the reader is most likely to see it.

Example 18-G · An introduction to an email states the issue and the bottom-line conclusion

---

From: Barry Chin [bchin@zalassociates.com]
Sent: Wednesday, January 18, 2018
To: Carla Izaguirre [cizaguirre@zalassociates.com]
Subject: McLaughlin IIED claim

Carla:

You asked that I research whether Ethan McLaughlin has a claim for intentional infliction of emotional distress against Ms. Dixon. The answer is that he likely does....

---

2. The legal analysis

Providing your legal analysis in email form requires you to significantly shrink your work. As mentioned above, reading text on a screen is more draining than reading the same text on paper. Accordingly, a person reading information on a screen is more likely to scan and scroll through the text than to read it slowly and carefully. Making your analysis more concise and focused will make it easier for your reader to absorb. Thus, you will need to determine the essential points in your analysis and focus on those points. Keep the following guidelines in mind:

- **Think about what the recipient needs to know**

After explaining your bottom-line in the introduction to your email, focus on the most important reasoning that supports your conclusions, citing the most relevant authority. Any sub-points should similarly be addressed with a clear conclusion at the outset and supported by the most important reasons for that conclusion. Do not spend time demonstrating how much research you have done or explaining every authority or every reason that supports your conclusion.

- **Focus on the elements that will be in dispute**

In a formal memorandum of law, a writer typically provides the governing rule and explains why certain elements are not in dispute. *See* Chapter 12, *The Discussion Section: Introducing and Connecting Legal Arguments.* By contrast, in an email, after explaining the governing rule, simply state which elements are in dispute and focus on those elements in the remainder of the email.

- **Focus on rules rather than case illustrations**

In explaining the law relevant to an element, explain the relevant rules, but whenever possible, omit case illustrations. Detailed case illustrations often make an emailed analysis unmanageably long. If you need to include information from the underlying case, try to keep that illustration short—maybe one or two sentences. You could also consider putting the information in an explanatory parenthetical after a citation.

You can include the information you would usually provide in case illustrations by attaching cases to the email. To make your product as user-friendly as possible, attach each factually comparable case with its key points highlighted so that the points are easy to find.

- **Rely on rule-based reasoning**

Because your analysis will focus on the rules, your application will have to rely on rule-based reasoning. You may want to reinforce your rule-based argument by comparing your conclusion to the conclusion a court reached in a prior case.

To make that comparison as succinctly as possible, consider using a signal, like *see* or *cf.* before the citation to the comparable case. The signal indicates the weight of authority your reader should give the case.[5] For example, "*cf.*" means "compare," and by using that signal you will be asking the reader to compare your assertion about what the conclusion in your client's case should be to the facts or conclusion reached in the cited case. You may also add an explanatory parenthetical with a succinct summary of the proposition for which you are citing the case. The parenthetical will give the reader a quick look at the most salient facts in the prior case that would be compared to your case.

---

5. *See ALWD* Rule 35.3 (rules regarding *cf.*) and Rule 37 (parentheticals); *Bluebook* Rules B.1.2, B.1.3.

- **Quickly explain any opposing arguments**

Again, when explaining the opposing arguments, focus on the rules supporting that argument rather than on the details of specific cases.

- **Provide citations, but less frequently**

When your analysis is condensed for an email, an attorney may have questions and want to check the authority, so include citations for important authority. But, you may cite less frequently than you would in a formal memo. Use good judgment. You may always attach the key cases with the relevant portions highlighted.

You can see these techniques at work in Example 18-H. The email in Example 18-H is based on the memorandum in Appendix B. You can compare the memo in Appendix B to the email below to see how an eight-page memorandum can be condensed to seven paragraphs.

Even though the email in 18-H is longer than the optimal one screen, the main points of the analysis are explained succinctly in as few screens as possible. Thus, if your office communicates by email, the attorney you work with prefers an email instead of a memo, or you just don't have time for a full memo, the example below illustrates what a shortened analysis in the body of an email looks like.

Example 18-H · A lengthy legal analysis condensed for an email

From: Eli Chin [echin@zalassociates.com]
Sent: Wednesday, January 10, 2018
To: Carla Izaguirre [cizaguirre@zalassociates.com]
Subject: McLaughlin IIED claim

Attachments: Woodruff.docx
Briggs.docx
West.docx

Carla:

You asked that I research whether Ethan McLaughlin has a claim for intentional infliction of emotional distress against Ms. Dixon. The answer is that he likely does.

> The first paragraph serves as an introduction, setting out the legal question being analyzed and the bottom-line answer.

To prove a claim for intentional infliction of emotional distress, a plaintiff must prove that (1) the defendant's conduct was extreme and outrageous; (2) the defendant intended to cause harm; and (3) the plaintiff suffered severe emotional distress. *Woodruff v. Miller*, 307 S.E.2d 176, 178 (N.C. Ct. App. 1983).

1. Dixon's conduct qualifies as extreme and outrageous conduct.

A defendant's conduct is extreme and outrageous when the defendant persistently distributes derogatory, misleading information. Here, Dixon's accusations of sexual misdeeds, tax evasion, failure to pay child support, violence, and mental instability are derogatory statements. Her attacks were

> Notice the choice of rules in the explanation of the law. The writer does not explain all the rules that were explained in the memo. Rather, the writer focuses on the rules that are most important to the analysis.

Notice also the use of rule-based reasoning. The writer states a rule, and then key ideas from the rule are repeated in the application.

To draft succinct comparisons, the writer simply cites to a prior case and explains the comparison in a parenthetical.

Notice also that the cases are first explained through the comparison. In a formal memo, the prior cases would first be explained in a case illustration before being relied on in the application. To keep the email short, the case is described only in the application.

"persistently distributed" because they appeared on the internet, and she refused to remove them. *Cf. Woodruff v. Miller*, 307 S.E.2d 176, 178 (N.C. Ct. App. 1983) (finding conduct extreme and outrageous when defendant posted "Wanted" poster based on plaintiff's 30-year old arrest arising from a college prank).

Dixon will likely argue that her postings were a sincere attempt to warn the public. However, her postings are not factually true, and are therefore unlikely to be viewed as a sincere attempt to warn the public. *Cf. Briggs v. Rosenthal*, 327 S.E.2d 308, 311 (N.C. Ct. App. 1985) (holding newspaper article chronicling alcoholism and anti-social behavior of recently deceased child was not extreme and outrageous because the article was 'honest, sincere, and sensitive.'")

Thus, we have a strong argument that her conduct was extreme and outrageous.

2. The evidence is sufficient to show Dixon intended to cause harm.

The same evidence establishes that she intended to cause harm. Mr. McLaughlin told Dixon that the assertions on her website were false and damaging to him, but she continued to maintain the web pages. *Cf. West v. King's Dept. Store, Inc.*, 365 S.E.2d 621, 626 (N.C. 1988) (explaining that evidence of defendant's unrelenting attack established both intent and extreme and outrageous conduct because defendant knew that plaintiff was likely to suffer).

3. Mr. McLaughlin suffered severe emotional distress.

Finally, Mr. McLaughlin suffered severe emotional distress. Although claims of severe emotional distress can be challenged when the plaintiff lacks sufficient documentation, *see Waddle v. Sparks*, 414 S.E.2d 22, 27 (N.C. 1992), here Mr. McLaughlin has documented distress. He is, among other things, receiving *daily* therapy and taking anti-depressants prescribed by his doctor. Moreover, Mr. McLaughlin can prove causation because his emotional distress began within a few days of the postings.

The closing again gives the bottom-line answer for the legal question being discussed and an invitation to the recipient to provide next steps.

Thus, Mr. McLaughlin has a strong claim against Ms. Dixon for intentional infliction of emotional distress. Please let me know if you have any questions or if you need additional research.

Best regards,

Eli

Eli Chin
Zal Associates, LLP | 800 SW Fifth Avenue, Suite 200 | Portland, OR 97204
Direct: 503-222-5556 | Fax: 502-222-5550
echin@zalassociates.com | www.zalassociates.com | Bio | vCard | LinkedIn

3. The closing

The closing, much like a conclusion section of a memo, again answers the legal question. Like the closing in any other professional email, it should also set out any next steps you or the recipient should take, offer further assistance, and if appropriate in your office, include a complimentary sign-off such as "Sincerely" or "Best Regards." Example 18-H shows a concise closing.

V. Stop and Think Before You Press Send

Before you press send, take a moment to review your email. First, check your subject line again to make sure that it still corresponds to the content of your email.

Similarly, check your introduction. Although you may have begun an email thinking you would address just one issue, sometimes you find that, in the end, the email addresses two or three issues. Perhaps you began the email thinking you would make a particular recommendation, but after typing your thoughts, you realize you have a more nuanced recommendation to make. Because writing often refines or changes one's thinking, always re-check your introduction to make sure that it accurately reflects the end product.

Next, check your formatting. Have you used bolded text, short paragraphs, and white space to make your email easy to read?

Then, assess the tone of your email. Does the text connote a positive and professional tone? Could a reader construe any phrases or sentences to have a disdainful, condescending, or rude tone? If so, change them. Do you have any misspelled words or grammatical goofs? Fix them.

The last thing you should do is double- (or triple-) check the addresses of the people to whom the email will be sent. Once you have completed the above steps and ensured that the email is going to the right people, you are ready to press "send."

Completing a final edit is time well spent. For each email, take the same care that you would with any other professional document distributed over your signature. Doing so will enhance your reputation while simultaneously protecting the interests of your clients and employer.

Practice Points

- Email communications allow attorneys to communicate information quickly, easily, and efficiently. Because the medium is fast-paced, take extra care to maintain a proper level of formality and professionalism.

- Determine whether email is the appropriate mode of communication by considering the content of the email, the length of the email, and the recipient's content.

- Every email should have a polite and professional tone. Use a formal style that follows traditional rules of grammar, syntax, and punctuation.

- If you are sending an email with your legal analysis, condense your analysis to make it easier to absorb.

- Use the same confidentiality warning on emails that you would use on any legal document.

- Because every email has the potential to be seen by the entire world, stop, think about it, and review the email before you send.

Chapter 19

The Transition from Objective to Persuasive Writing

Up to this point, this book has focused on writing an objective analysis that will review the legal arguments and options that exist on both sides of a dispute. After considering the options, your client may seek to avoid litigation by, for example, settling the matter out of court; other times, your client may decide that the best option is to go to trial. If so, your objective analysis may be transformed into a persuasive argument for a court. This chapter will explain how to transform that objective analysis into a persuasive one.

I. Objective vs. Persuasive Writing

Persuasive writing is not so very different from objective writing. To be effective, writing—whether objective or persuasive—must be supported by the law and facts, well organized, clearly written, and free from grammatical, typographical, and other errors. Thus, all the skills you have learned so far will be applied to writing a persuasive argument.

That said, you should be aware of the following differences as you transform your objective analysis into a persuasive analysis. First, your perspective will shift. Second, your audience is different. Third, the format in which you present your argument will change. And, finally, you may spend more time developing an underlying theme for your brief—that is, a simple argument that both unifies the factual and the procedural aspects of your case and that explains why your client should win.

A. A New Perspective: The Advocate

The most significant difference between an objective analysis and a persuasive analysis is the perspective from which the analysis is presented. In writing an objective analysis, your goal is to present a neutral assessment of how a court will likely interpret and apply the law to your client's facts. You highlight the strengths and weaknesses of arguments on either side. In reaching a conclusion, you predict the most likely outcome, even if that outcome is not what your client may want.

By contrast, when writing a persuasive analysis, you become an advocate for your client's desired outcome. No longer does the analysis merely predict the likely outcome of the issue. The analysis now urges the judicial reader to accept the advocate's assertion as the most legally sound and just path to follow.

This shift in perspective does not mean that you ignore weaknesses in your client's case. Rather, you approach those weaknesses differently. Instead of highlighting them so that your client can fully appreciate those weaknesses, as an advocate you will explain why, despite those weaknesses, your client's desired outcome should still prevail. Acknowledging weaknesses, yet explaining why they do not undermine your client's desired outcome, is perhaps the most difficult aspect of writing a persuasive argument.

B. A New Audience: The Judge

In addition to taking on a new perspective, you will also be taking on a new audience. When writing as an advocate, your most important audience will be the court, which includes the judge and any staff attorneys or law clerks working on your client's case. Your goal is to convince the court to take the action that your client desires. You will be more likely to convince the court if your writing accounts for the wants and needs of this new audience. For example, when writing to a judicial audience, remember that judges want to do the right thing. Your job as an advocate is to make it easy for them to do that. Thus, you want to explain why your client's desired outcome is correct and just. Providing credible, clear arguments that are well researched and supported by the law will help you to achieve those goals. Ideally, you will write your brief in such a logical and reasonable way that a judge (if he or she wanted to) could copy and paste your argument right into a final opinion.

Finally, remember that judges and their staff are busy, overworked people. Federal appellate court judges, for example, read around 13,000 pages[1] in motions and briefs each year—and that staggering number does not include the pages of records, trial transcripts, and background materials for each case. Because your reader is so busy, you must make your brief concise. Include only the most important arguments and avoid presenting every possible argument.

C. A New Format: The Brief

Writing to a court[2] also requires a new format. That format is usually dictated, at least in part, by court rules and the conventions of the jurisdiction in which the document will be filed. Court rules may prescribe, among other things, the brief's length, font, margins, citation style, and sections to be included. The rules will vary from court to court and jurisdiction to jurisdiction, and the rules may change over time. Thus, before beginning to write a document that is to be submitted to a court, check that specific court's rules. Court rules are almost always available on a court's website. Failure to follow the rules—even just failing to use the required font—could result in the case being dismissed.

However, as you will see, the basic components of a memo and brief are not so very different. In fact, each part of an objective memo has an analogous counterpart in a trial brief, as explained in Table 19-A.

---

1. The Honorable Mark P. Painter, *Appellate Practice—Including Legal Writing from a Judge's Perspective*, 2 (originally printed in *Ohio Trial*, Aug. 1996), and revised May 1, 2000.

2. You may write persuasive documents for other entities such as an administrative law judge, arbitrator or arbitration boards, or a mediator. For ease of discussion, however, this chapter focuses on writing generally to a court and, in particular, to trial courts.

Table 19-A · Parts of an objective memo compared to analogous parts of a trial brief

Sections in an Objective Memo	Sections in a Trial Brief	Purpose
Caption	Caption	Identifies the document
Question Presented & Brief Answer	Introduction	Provides context and focuses the reader on the issues to be addressed
Statement of Facts	Statement of Facts	Describes all the facts relevant to the analysis
Discussion	Argument	Analyzes the legal questions
Conclusion	Conclusion	Concludes the legal analysis

D. A New Focus: The Theme

When writing objectively, you explore possible arguments and weigh their strengths and weaknesses given the facts of your client's case. As you transition to persuasive writing, you will want to consider developing a theme—a unifying idea that explains why you win. One very famous theme comes from the O.J. Simpson trial: "If the glove does not fit, you must acquit." That single, catchy sentence explained the crux of O.J. Simpson's argument. Simpson was accused of killing his estranged wife and a local restaurant server at his wife's home. Part of the evidence against him included a bloody glove found on Simpson's estate and a matching glove found at the crime scene. In a surprising move, prosecutors had Simpson try on the exhibit during trial, but the glove did not fit. From that event, the defense latched on to a winning theme of the case, and Simpson was later acquitted of murder.

Having a theme is helpful because it counter-balances a problem that can arise when trying to tell a compelling legal story. A compelling legal story must account for all the relevant facts and law. A compelling legal story is, therefore, detailed and often lengthy. A theme can help the judge organize and make sense of the details within your story by providing a bottom line to which all those details connect.

Although a memorable theme can be very helpful, themes are often not as "catchy" as the one used in the O.J. Simpson trial. When you are writing to a court, the judge and court staff are trained to examine the legal issue within its procedural posture or legal standard. Because the judge and staff focus on whether the legal standard is met, a persuasive theme often emerges from (1) the procedural posture of the case, (2) a favorable substantive legal standard or favorable facts, or (3) a policy argument.

For example, if you are opposing a motion for summary judgment, you will likely build a theme around the standard for denying a motion for summary judgment, as in Example 19-B.

Example 19-B · Using the procedural standard to develop the theme

The case	You want to argue that summary judgment should not be granted.
Legal standard	Summary judgment may be granted only if "there is no genuine dispute as to any material fact and the movant is entitled to judgment as a matter of law."*
Theme	There *is* a "material issue of fact" and, therefore, summary judgment is inappropriate.
Technique	As frequently as possible (1) state that a genuine disputed issue of fact exists and that the fact is material, and (2) prove the dispute by pointing to contradictory factual assertions and prove that the factual dispute is material by explaining the relationship between the fact and the legal standard. Thus, the summary judgment standard becomes the touchstone to which you will return because it governs how the court will decide the issue.

* Fed. R. Civ. P. 56(a) (2016).

In addition to considering where you are in the litigation process, you may also want to consider substantive legal or policy arguments. Consider for example, the case of *Oregon v. Ashcroft*.[3] In that case, the State of Oregon had passed a statute that permitted physician-assisted suicide. The U.S. Attorney General then issued an interpretive regulation that would revoke the license of any physician who dispensed a controlled substance sufficient for a person to commit suicide under the state statute. Plaintiffs, including the State of Oregon, sought to enjoin the U.S. Attorney General from enforcing his interpretive regulation. Example 19-C shows how the U.S. Attorney General might approach the argument for a motion to dismiss based on the substantive law. Example 19-D shows how the State of Oregon might approach its brief using a policy-based approach.[4]

---

3. 192 F. Supp. 2d 1077 (D. Or. 2002), *aff'd*, 368 F.3d 118 (9th Cir. 2004), *aff'd*, *Gonzales v. Oregon*, 543 U.S. 1145 (2005).

4. Examples 19-B and 19-C are based on Brief for Appellants and Appellee's Brief of the State of Oregon (respectively) in *Oregon v. Ashcroft*, 368 F.3d 118 (9th Cir. 2004).

Example 19-C · Using a legal doctrine to develop your theme

The case	The State of Oregon passed a statute that permitted physician-assisted suicide. Under the Controlled Substances Act, the U.S. Attorney General issued an interpretive regulation that would revoke the licenses of physicians who prescribed drugs sufficient for an individual to commit suicide under the state statute. Among other things, the interpretive regulation stated that, "assisting suicide is not a 'legitimate medical purpose' within the meaning of [the Controlled Substances Act and its regulations]."* A group filed a complaint that sought to enjoin the Attorney General from enforcing that interpretive regulation. You are a U.S. Assistant Attorney General seeking to dismiss that complaint.
Legal standard	Under the Controlled Substances Act, "[a] prescription for a controlled substance … must be issued for a legitimate medical purpose."** The Attorney General has the authority to promulgate "rules and regulations … relating to the registration and … distribution and dispensing of controlled substances."***
Theme	The Controlled Substances Act permits the distribution of controlled substances only for "legitimate medical purpose" and assisted suicide is not a "legitimate medical purpose."
Technique	In the brief, emphasize that "legitimate medical purpose" has historically been understood to entail "healing." Moreover, Congress delegated to the U.S. Attorney General authority to regulate controlled substances. In this case, the U.S. Attorney General properly used that authority.

 * 66 Fed. Reg. 56,607, 56,608 (Nov. 9 2001).
 ** 21 C.F.R. § 1306.04 (2005).
*** *Id.* at § 801.

In Example 19-D, the State of Oregon's policy-based argument emphasizes that the State should have the primary authority to regulate the practice of medicine, rather than the Federal Government.

Example 19-D · Using a policy-based argument to create a theme

The case	Same scenario as above, but you are an Assistant Attorney General for the State of Oregon, and you are arguing against the motion to dismiss and in favor of an injunction.
Legal standard	The clear statement doctrine: When "Congress intends to alter the 'usual constitutional balance between the States

	and Federal Government,' it must make its intention to do so 'unmistakably clear in the language of the statute.'"*
Theme	The U.S. Attorney General's interpretive regulation is an unwarranted federal intrusion into the sovereign interests of Oregon, the medical practice of its physicians, and end-of-life decisions.
Technique	In the motion, emphasize states' historical right to regulate medical practice and that, in enacting the Controlled Substances Act, Congress meant to regulate drug trafficking, not medical practice. Thus, the U.S. Attorney General's overreached his authority under the Controlled Substances Act.

---

* *Will v. Michigan Dept. of State Police*, 491 U.S. 58, 65 (1989) (quoting *Atascadero State Hospital v. Scanlon*, 473 U.S. 234, 242 (1985)).

Like many aspects of the writing process, developing a theme is a recursive process that tends to evolve. While you may not see a distinct theme early on, it may emerge after you have started researching more about the procedural posture of the case, organizing your arguments, or developing the legal and factual strengths and weaknesses of your case. Once a theme has emerged, you can go back and integrate that theme

---

Motion vs. Brief

A "motion" is a request to a court to do something. A "trial brief," sometimes called a "trial memorandum" or a "memorandum of law," is a legal analysis that explains why the court should grant (or deny) the motion.

Not all motions require an accompanying trial brief. For example, a motion asking the court to reschedule a hearing would simply explain the conflict and request the change. There would be no need to provide the court with a legal analysis justifying a scheduling change.

Other motions must be submitted with an accompanying trial brief that explains the legal justification for granting the motion. A motion to dismiss, a motion for summary judgment, a motion to exclude evidence, and a motion to overturn a jury verdict are all motions that would need to be accompanied with a supporting trial brief.

When a motion needs to be supported by a legal analysis, the moving party will often submit two separate documents—a motion and an accompanying trial brief in support of that motion. In some jurisdictions, however, these two functions are merged into one document.

If the responding party opposes the motion, and that opposition requires legal analysis, the responding party would submit a trial memorandum in opposition to the motion.

into your structure and argument. The bottom line is, in persuasive writing, work to craft a focus or theme that is consistent with the law, facts, or policy relevant to the argument, along with applicable procedural standards based on where you are in the litigation process.

II. The Parts of a Trial Brief: An Overview

To transition from an objective to a persuasive analysis, it helps to have a more specific overview of what a persuasive analysis will look like once it is presented to a court. To that end, Example 19-E reminds you of a typical objective memo that addresses whether a statement a defendant made to an undercover police officer was "mere conversation" and thus admissible at trial or whether the statement was made during the course of a stop and therefore inadmissible at trial. Example 19-F shows you how a prosecutor might transform that memo into a persuasive argument in a trial brief.

As you read through the memo and brief, notice the similarities between an objective memo and a persuasive trial brief. Perhaps most importantly, notice that individual legal arguments are presented in the same way. That is, the writer asserts a conclusion, explains the law that supports that conclusion, applies the law to the client's problem, and then concludes. In other words, all the basic parts explained first in Chapter 6, *One Legal Argument*, and then more thoroughly in Chapter 7, *Explaining the Law*; Chapter 8, *Applying the Law*; and Chapter 9, *Conclusions to One Legal Argument*, are present in a persuasive analysis.

Example 19-E • A sample objective memorandum

MEMORANDUM

TO: Rita Zal
FROM: Theo Thomas
DATE: September 9, 2017
RE: Paul Adams — Admissibility of evidence

QUESTION PRESENTED

In a persuasive trial brief, the **Question Presented** and **Brief Answer** are converted into the **Introduction**, which provides relevant procedural history and identifies the issues that will be argued.

Under Oregon law, which allows a defendant's statement into evidence if the statement was made during "mere conversation" with an officer, will Mr. Adams's statement be admissible when it was made after the undercover officer parked an unmarked police car behind Mr. Adams's car and Mr. Adams told the officer he was not yet planning to leave?

BRIEF ANSWER

Yes. The statement will be admissible against Mr. Adams. Evidence is admissible against a defendant if it is gathered during "mere conversation" rather than during a stop. An officer stops another individual only if that individual could reasonably believe that his liberty was being restrained. Mr.

Adams could not reasonably believe that his liberty was being restrained. Therefore, Mr. Adams's statement likely will be admissible.

STATEMENT OF FACTS

On August 15, 2018, police officer Ephgrave spoke with Paul Adams, a suspect in a local bank robbery. During that conversation, Paul Adams revealed information that implicated him in the bank robbery.

Earlier that day, Officer Ephgrave saw a white Ford Probe pull into a parking lot. The car looked similar to the car involved in the Davinsk Mutual Bank robbery, and Officer Ephgrave decided to investigate. At the time, Officer Ephgrave was working undercover and was wearing ordinary street clothes and driving an unmarked car.

Officer Ephgrave pulled into the parking lot and parked behind the Ford Probe. As he got out of the car, Mr. Adams yelled at the officer to move his car. Officer Ephgrave walked over to the bench where Mr. Adams was sitting and asked if he was planning to leave. According to the officer, Mr. Adams said, "No, I'm going to sit a little longer." Officer Ephgrave pointed out that there was nowhere else to park because all the other spaces were full and told Mr. Adams he would move his car before Mr. Adams had to leave. According to Officer Ephgrave, Mr. Adams said, "Oh, okay. No problem."

Officer Ephgrave and Mr. Adams began chatting. Officer Ephgrave steered the conversation to the recent bank robbery. As they spoke, Officer Ephgrave remarked that the bank teller had said that the robber was very polite. Mr. Adams added, "Yeah, I heard he even gave a strawberry lollipop to a kid in the bank." Officer Ephgrave knew that the media had reported that the bank robber had given a child a lollipop, but not its flavor. Officer Ephgrave then arrested Paul Adams.

Mr. Adams was arraigned on August 20, 2018. He pleaded not guilty to the charges. He is now awaiting trial.

DISCUSSION

Paul Adams's incriminating statement about the flavor of the lollipop will be admissible. Whether a defendant's statement to a police officer is admissible depends upon the circumstances under which the statement was made. Oregon courts distinguish between statements that were "mere conversation" and statements that followed a "stop." *State v. Warner*, 585 P.2d 681, 689 (Or.1991). Statements that were made during mere conversation with a police officer are admissible. *State v. Shelton*, 796 P.2d 390, 392 (Or. Ct. App. 1990); *State v. Spenst*, 662 P.2d 5, 6 (Or. Ct. App. 1983). By contrast, statements made by a person during a stop are admissible only if the stop was justified by reasonable suspicion. *Spenst*, 662 P.2d at 6. As explained below, Mr. Adams made his incriminating statement during "mere conversation," and not during a stop. Accordingly, his statement will be admissible without any further justification by the officer.

Mr. Adams's statement was mere conversation because Mr. Adams could not reasonably believe his liberty was restrained during his encounter with Officer Ephgrave. Whether an encounter with a police officer is "mere conversation" or a "stop" depends upon the extent to which the person's liberty

---

The **Statement of Facts** tells your client's story. In a persuasive brief, however, the writer will emphasize the positive facts and attempt to neutralize bad facts by providing a positive context.

In a persuasive brief, the **Discussion** section is converted to the **Argument**, which sets forth the law and analysis to convince the court to rule in a manner that favors the client.

In both objective memos and persuasive briefs, the Discussion (or Argument) begins with an introductory **roadmap**. In a persuasive brief, the writer frames the roadmap in a way that emphasizes the outcome the client seeks.

is restrained. If a person's liberty has not been restrained, then the encounter is "mere conversation." *See, e.g., State v. Smith*, 698 P.2d 973, 975 (Or. Ct. App. 1985). By contrast, a "stop" occurs if a person's liberty is restrained by a police officer lawfully present in any place. Or. Rev. Stat. § 131.605(6) (2017); *State v. Warner*, 901 P.2d 940, 942 (Or. Ct. App. 1995). A person's liberty may be restrained if that person believes that his liberty has been restrained and that belief is objectively reasonable. *Warner*, 901 P.2d at 942. To determine whether a person reasonably believes his liberty has been restrained, a court will consider the totality of the circumstances. *State v. Wenger*, 922 P.2d 1248, 1251 (Or. Ct. App. 1996).

A police officer may request information without restraining a person's liberty. *State v. Gilmore*, 860 P.2d 882, 883 (Or. Ct. App. 1993). In *Gilmore*, an officer requested identification from three people who were sitting in a truck. *Id.* When the defendant opened the glove compartment to retrieve his identification, the officer saw a gun and arrested the defendant for illegal possession of a firearm. *Id.* Although the defendant argued he had been illegally stopped and, therefore, evidence of the gun should be excluded from trial, the trial court admitted the gun into evidence. *Id.* In upholding the trial court's decision, the Court of Appeals explained that, even if the defendant felt he was not free to leave, that belief was not objectively reasonable. *Id.* The Court of Appeals explained that, although the officer requested identification, the officer did not require the defendant to alter his course, nor did the officer prevent the defendant from leaving. *Id.*

By contrast, a person may reasonably believe his liberty has been restrained if a police officer blocks that person's car. *Wenger*, 922 P.2d at 1251-52. In *Wenger*, the defendant was intending to leave a parking lot when uniformed officers parked their patrol car and blocked in the defendant's car. *Id.* After noting that a stop occurs when an officer prevents a vehicle from being driven away, the court held that the defendant reasonably believed his liberty had been restrained. *Id.* at 1251-52. In this case, Mr. Adams's encounter with Officer Ephgrave was mere conversation rather than a stop because he could not reasonably believe his liberty was being restrained.

Mr. Adams's encounter is similar to the encounter in *Gilmore*. In both cases, an officer approached the defendant seeking information. In *Gilmore*, the officer asked for identification, and in Mr. Adams's case, the officer wanted to learn whether the defendant was involved in the bank robbery.

However, seeking information is not enough to convert their conversation to a stop. In Mr. Adams's case, as in the *Gilmore* case, the officer did not alter the defendant's course or prevent him from leaving. Officer Ephgrave asked Mr. Adams whether he was planning to leave. Mr. Adams said he was not. In addition, Officer Ephgrave said that he would move his car before Mr. Adams had to leave. According to Officer Ephgrave, Mr. Adams agreed, saying "Oh, okay. No problem." Therefore, Officer Ephgrave did not prevent Mr. Adams from leaving nor did the officer alter Mr. Adams's course. Thus, a court should follow the reasoning in Gilmore and conclude that Mr. Adams could not reasonably believe his liberty was restrained.

(Margin notes:)

In both objective and persuasive writing, the attorney **explains the law** after stating the conclusion. Here, the writer provides *State v. Gilmore* and *State v. Wenger* as case illustrations. In a persuasive brief, the writer may use the same cases, but should apply persuasive techniques to minimize any difficulties posed by the prior cases.

Notice that the explanation of the law does not mention the client. Omitting the client gives your reader an opportunity to absorb the relevant law before she has to understand how the law will apply to the client's case. The same rule applies in persuasive writing.

The application of the law begins here.

In fact, a court is likely to conclude that Mr. Adams's encounter with the officer was even less restrictive than the encounter in *Gilmore*. In addition to not altering Mr. Adams's course and not preventing him from leaving, Officer Ephgrave was not in uniform. Because Mr. Adams believed he was talking to a civilian, Mr. Adams should have felt even more free to leave than did the defendant in *Gilmore*, who knew he was talking to a uniformed officer. Thus, a court is likely to hold that Mr. Adams's encounter with the officer was mere conversation and that the evidence is admissible.

Even though Officer Ephgrave's car did block Mr. Adams's car, a court is likely to distinguish Mr. Adams's case from the Wenger case. In the *Wenger* case, the court noted that the defendant was intending to leave at the time his car was blocked. By contrast, Mr. Adams told Officer Ephgrave that he was "going to sit a little while longer," suggesting that he was not intending to leave. Because he was not intending to leave, a court is less likely to conclude that Mr. Adams reasonably felt his liberty was restrained. Accordingly, a court will likely determine that Mr. Adams was not stopped and that his statement about the lollipop is admissible.

CONCLUSION

Because the evidence against Mr. Adams is likely to be admissible, we should discuss with Mr. Adams the risks associated with going to trial, the costs and benefits of pleading guilty, and plea bargains he might be willing to make.

In an objective memo, the **Conclusion** is typically a sentence or two that sums up the entire legal question and recommends any next steps.

Example 19-F · A sample persuasive trial brief

IN THE STATE OF OREGON FOR
LANE COUNTY CIRCUIT COURT

| State of Oregon,
Plaintiff,

v.

Paul R. Adams,
Defendant. | No. 18-285 CR

RESPONSE TO
DEFENDANT'S MOTION
TO EXCLUDE EVIDENCE
FROM TRIAL |

The **Caption** states the court in which the case is being heard, lists the parties, provides the docket number, and states the title of the document.

INTRODUCTION

Defendant Paul Adams's statement to an undercover police officer should be admitted into evidence at his trial for bank robbery. The State of Oregon filed charges against Adams for an alleged bank robbery on August 15, 2018. Adams was arraigned on August 20, 2018. He has pleaded not guilty, and the trial is set for September 16, 2018. Shortly after the robbery, Adams spoke to an undercover police officer. That statement implicated him in the robbery. Defendant Adams now moves to suppress that statement. Oregon law, however, allows a defendant's statement to be admitted into evidence where, as here, the statement was made during "mere conversation" with a police officer. Because Adams's statement was made during a conversation and not during a police stop, his statement should be admitted into evidence.

The **Introduction** provides the relevant procedural history leading up to the motion before the court and identifies the legal issue to be addressed in the trial brief supporting that motion.

Depending on the jurisdiction this preliminary section may include other information or be called by a different name, such as "Preliminary Statement," "Summary" or "Statement of the Nature of the Matter Before the Court." Be sure to check your local rules and confer with colleagues about the customs in your jurisdiction.

The **Statement of Facts** tells your client's story as it relates to the motion before the court. Like an objective Statement of Facts it provides all the relevant facts — both positive and negative. In a persuasive brief, however, the writer will emphasize the positive facts and attempt to neutralize bad facts by providing a positive context.

STATEMENT OF FACTS

On August 15, 2018, Police Officer Ephgrave spoke with Adams. During their conversation, Adams revealed incriminating evidence that implicated him in a bank robbery, and Adams now wants that evidence to be suppressed.

Earlier that day, Officer Ephgrave saw a white Ford Probe pull into a parking lot. The car looked similar to the car involved in a bank robbery at Davis Mutual Bank earlier that day, and Officer Ephgrave decided to investigate. At the time, Officer Ephgrave was working undercover. He was therefore wearing ordinary street clothes and driving an unmarked car.

Officer Ephgrave pulled into the parking lot and parked behind the Ford. As the officer got out of the car, Adams yelled at Officer Ephgrave to move his car. He walked over to the bench where Adams was seated and asked if he planned to leave. According to Officer Ephgrave, Adams said, "No, I'm going to sit a little longer." Officer Ephgrave pointed out that there was nowhere else in the lot to park his car because every other space was full and offered to move his car when Adams was ready to leave. According to the officer, Adams said, "Oh, okay. No problem."

Adams and Officer Ephgrave began chatting. Officer Ephgrave steered the conversation to the bank robbery earlier that day, and remarked that the bank teller had said the robber was very polite. Adams added, "Yeah, I heard he even gave a strawberry lollipop to a kid in the bank." Officer Ephgrave knew that the media had reported the bank robber having given a child a lollipop, but had not reported its flavor. As a result, Officer Ephgrave arrested Adams.

Point headings in a trial brief function much like they do in an objective memo: They signify the beginning and end of a section and they assert the conclusion to the analysis in that section. In a trial brief, point headings should also reflect what you are asking the court to do.

ARGUMENT

I. THE DEFENDANT'S STATEMENT IS ADMISSIBLE EVIDENCE BECAUSE THE STATEMENT WAS "MERE CONVERSATION."

This short trial brief has just one legal argument. Notice that this one legal argument has the same structure as an objective argument — in other words, the writer states the conclusion to his analysis, then **explains the law,** then **applies the law,** and finally restates his conclusion.

The defendant's motion to exclude evidence of his statement should be denied because his statement is admissible as "mere conversation." Under Oregon law, citizens can have differing encounters with police officers. *State v. Warner*, 585 P.2d 681, 689 (Or. 1991). Where an encounter is "mere conversation," evidence acquired by an officer during the encounter is admissible against the defendant. *State v. Shelton*, 796 P.2d 390, 302 (Or. Ct. App. 1990). *But see State v. Spenst*, 662 P.2d 5, 6 (Or. Ct. App. 1983) (explaining that even where the encounter is a "stop," evidence is admissible against the defendant if the stop was justified by reasonable suspicion).

As in an objective memo, the **explanation of the law** begins immediately after the conclusion.

In a persuasive argument, however, an attorney is likely to frame the explanation of the law so that it most effectively supports the outcome the client seeks. Here, the writer emphasizes the idea of an encounter being a "mere conversation" by describing that idea first.

An encounter is "mere conversation" if, under the totality of the circumstances, a person could not reasonably believe his liberty was restrained. *See, e.g., State v. Smith*, 698 P.2d 973, 975 (Or. Ct. App. 1985). By contrast, a "stop" occurs if a person's liberty is restrained by physical force or a show of authority by a police officer lawfully present in any place. Or. Rev. Stat. § 131.605(6) (2017); *State v. Warner*, 901 P.2d 940, 942 (Or. Ct. App. 1995). To determine whether a person reasonably believes his liberty has been restrained, a court will consider the totality of the circumstances. *State v. Wenger*, 922 P.2d 1248, 1251 (Or. Ct. App. 1996).

Police officers are allowed to request information without restraining a person's liberty. *State v. Gilmore*, 860 P.2d 882, 883 (Or. Ct. App. 1993). In

Gilmore, an officer requested identification from three people sitting in a truck. *Id.* When the defendant opened the glove compartment to retrieve his identification, the officer saw a gun and arrested the defendant for illegal possession of a firearm. *Id.* Although the defendant argued that he had been illegally stopped and that the evidence should be excluded from trial as a result, the trial court admitted the gun into evidence. *Id.* The Court of Appeals upheld that decision and explained that even if the defendant felt he was not free to leave, such a belief was not objectively reasonable. *Id.* Although the officer requested identification, he did not require the defendant to alter his course or prevent him from leaving. *Id. But cf. Wenger*, 922 P.2d at 1251-52 (holding that stop did occur where uniformed officer prevented the vehicle from being driven away, and defendant believed his liberty was restrained).

Here, the statement made by Adams was mere conversation, and not a stop, because Adams could not reasonably believe his liberty was ever restrained at any point during his encounter with Officer Ephgrave. Like the officer who asked for identification in *Gilmore*, here Officer Ephgrave wanted to learn if Adams was involved in the bank robbery. In addition, as in *Gilmore*, Officer Ephgrave did not alter Adams's course or prevent him from leaving. Officer Ephgrave asked Adams if he was planning to leave, to which he responded that he was not. Further, Officer Ephgrave said he would move his car whenever Adams needed to leave. According to Officer Ephgrave, Adams said, "Oh, okay. No problem." Therefore, Officer Ephgrave did not prevent Adams from leaving nor did he alter Adams's course. Adams could not reasonably believe that his liberty was restrained in this case and the statement was mere conversation.

In fact, Adams's encounter with Officer Ephgrave was even less restrictive that the encounter in *Gilmore*. Unlike the officers in *Gilmore* or *Wenger*, Officer Ephgrave was working undercover and was therefore not wearing a uniform. Adams believed he was talking to a civilian and should have felt even freer to leave than did the defendants in *Gilmore* or *Wenger* who were talking to uniformed officers.

In addition, even though Officer Ephgrave blocked Adams's car, Adams intended to "sit a little while longer," and Office Ephgrave informed Adams he would move whenever Adams needed him to do so. Because Adams could not have believed his liberty was restrained, especially because Officer Ephgrave was not in uniform, he was not "stopped." His statement "Yeah, I heard he even gave a strawberry lollipop to a kid in the bank" should therefore be admissible at trial under the mere conversation exception. The encounter between Adams and Officer Ephgrave was mere conversation and is therefore admissible evidence against Adams.

CONCLUSION

For the reasons stated in the brief, the State requests that this Court deny Defendant's motion to exclude.

The sections below examine the components of a trial brief in more detail and provide you with advice in drafting those components.

After explaining the law, the writer applies the law to the case.

In persuasive writing, attorneys use the same tools to make their arguments as a writer does in an objective argument. Here, the attorney is using an analogy to make his argument. Just as in an objective analysis, analogies are much more effective when the writer compares specific facts from the prior case with the specific facts from the client's case.

The most difficult aspect of writing persuasively is often addressing a weakness in your client's case. When addressing a weakness, you must explain why, despite that weakness, the outcome your client seeks is justified. In this paragraph, the prosecutor addresses a weak fact—that Officer Ephgrave blocked Adams's car.

The **Conclusion** requests the relief the prosecutor seeks from the court. This section is very short and formulaic, often consisting of only a sentence or two in which you respectfully request that the court render a decision in your client's favor.

III. The Caption

The Caption, as illustrated in Example 19-G, provides procedural details about the case. It includes the name and division of the court in which the case is proceeding, the parties, and the file number. The Caption should appear at the top of the brief or document, such as a motion. The Caption also includes the title of the brief or document. Usually, the title will be in all capital letters.

Your firm or organization will likely have a template for the Caption that meets the local court rules. Even so, take time to make sure the names and numbers in the Caption are correct and that the Caption is neat in appearance.

Example 19-G • Example of a caption

The **Caption** states the court in which the case is being heard, lists the parties, provides the docket number, and states the title of the document.

IN THE STATE OF OREGON FOR LANE COUNTY CIRCUIT COURT	
State of Oregon, Plaintiff,	No. 14-285 CR
v.	RESPONSE TO DEFENDANT'S MOTION TO EXCLUDE EVIDENCE FROM TRIAL
Paul R. Adams, Defendant.	

IV. The Introduction

Most trial briefs begin with an Introduction that provides an overview of and context for the arguments that are to follow. The name of the Introduction varies from jurisdiction to jurisdiction. It might be called an "Introduction," a "Preliminary Statement," a "Summary," the "Statement of the Nature and Matter Before the Court," or something else entirely.[5]

Whatever it's called, the introductory material usually establishes the procedural posture of the case, the nature of the litigation, the kind of motion before the court, and the specific legal questions the court is being asked to decide. In some jurisdictions, the Introduction has a more objective tone, such as in 19-H. In other jurisdictions, where the introductory

---

5. Check your jurisdiction's local rules or talk with colleagues to determine the local custom.

material also presents a quick preview of the arguments, your Introduction may take a more persuasive tone, such as in Example 19-I.

Example 19-H • An Introduction describing the procedural posture, nature of the case, and motion before the court

INTRODUCTION

On November 29, 2017, Plaintiff Julie Stark was dismissed from her employment with Defendant Michigan Power & Electric Company (MPE). Immediately after her dismissal, Ms. Stark filed a complaint alleging that Michigan's Whistleblowers' Protection Act protected her from discharge. This motion for summary judgment seeks to dismiss her Whistleblowers' claim because no material issues of fact exist, and as a matter of law, Ms. Stark cannot prove that she was engaged in an activity protected by Michigan's Whistleblowers' Protection Act.

Example 19-I • An Introduction that also previews the argument

INTRODUCTION

Defendant Paul Adams's statement to an undercover police officer should be admitted into evidence at his trial for bank robbery. The State of Oregon filed charges against Adams for an alleged bank robbery on August 15, 2018. Adams was arraigned on August 20, 2018. He has pleaded not guilty, and the trial is set for September 16, 2018. Shortly after the robbery, Adams spoke to an undercover police officer. That statement implicated him in the robbery. Adams now moves to suppress that statement. Oregon law, however, allows a defendant's statement to be admitted into evidence where, as here, the statement was made during "mere conversation" with a police officer. Because Adams's statement was made during a conversation and not during a police stop, his statement should be admitted into evidence.

Especially in those jurisdictions that preview the arguments to come, the Introduction plays a vital persuasive role. It sets forth your vision of the precise legal question and the most important facts the judge should consider while reading your brief. And, importantly, the Introduction is the first part of the trial brief that the judge will read.

Although the Introduction should play a persuasive role, the tone should still be reasonable. Introductions framed too passionately can trigger a defensive attitude or heightened skepticism in the reader. By presenting yourself as a reasonable advocate from the outset of the brief, the judge will be more likely to trust the path you are encouraging the court to take.

V. The Statement of Facts

The Statement of Facts typically follows the Introduction.[6] As with an objective Statement of Facts, a persuasive Statement of Facts provides the factual foundation for your legal analysis. Thus, in both an objective and a persuasive Statement of Facts, you must provide *all* the facts relevant to the analysis, whether those facts will help or hurt your client. Also, as you would with an objective Statement of Facts, you must consider how to organize those facts in a way that will make them easy for your reader, in this case, the court, to absorb.

At the same time, in a persuasive trial brief, the Statement of Facts should tell your client's story and provide the foundation for your theory of the case. In other words, the Statement of Facts is a place where you can highlight the facts that will help your client and minimize the facts that might hurt your client (or at least present those facts in context).

Example 19-J shows how a Statement of Facts in an objective memo might be transformed for purposes of a persuasive trial brief. Both examples are written from the perspective of the employer. The objective Statement of Facts is written at the time the employer is considering firing the employee, while the persuasive Statement of Facts is written at a time when the employer has to defend that decision.

Example 19-J • Transforming an objective Statement of Facts to a persuasive Statement of Facts

Facts in an objective memo addressing whether an employee can be fired	Facts in a brief defending the decision to fire the employee
STATEMENT OF FACTS	**STATEMENT OF FACTS**
MPE intends to discharge Julie Stark, an employee in its customer service department. Stark is a known supporter of environmental causes. On occasion, she participates in environmental rallies, which causes her absence from work. In the past, Stark received positive job performance reviews.	Plaintiff Julie Stark was an MPE employee who, on October 6, 2017, received a negative employment review. (Dep. Julie Stark 10:1-2, Dec. 30, 2017.) On November 29, Ms. Stark was dismissed from MPE. (*Id.* at 10:21-22.) Four days after she was dismissed, Ms. Stark filed a complaint with the state attorney general alleging that MPE had violated the federal Clean Air Act. (*Id.* at 11:1-4.) Ms. Stark contends that she should be protected from dismissal because she was about to report her allegations when she was dismissed. (Pl.'s Compl. ¶ 15, Dec. 6, 2017.)
Following the departure of MPE's chief executive nearly a year ago, Stark began to cause problems for MPE. About three months ago, Stark attempted to unionize MPE's operators. More recently, Stark objected to what she alleged were violations of the Clean Air Act by MPE. MPE's management responded by giving Stark an unfavorable job performance review. Upon receipt of the performance	Ms. Stark was not about to report her allegations at the time of her dismissal. Sometime

---

6. Again, the order of the sections may be determined by the rules of your jurisdiction or the customs of your office.

review, Stark approached her supervisor and made personal attacks towards both her supervisor and MPE's president. In addition, Stark threatened to tell "everyone" including the media that MPE's practices allegedly violate the Clean Air Act.

A few days later, MPE's president was walking through the office late at night and found on Stark's desk a complaint to the Attorney General's office. The complaint, which was drafted by Stark and dated approximately a month ago, listed the provisions of the Clean Air Act that Stark alleged MPE violated.

Stark currently is on vacation and will return to work on November 26. MPE intends to discharge Julie Stark when she returns which, due to Stark's vacation, will be three business days after MPE became aware of Stark's complaint to the Attorney General's office.

during the first few days of October, Ms. Stark downloaded a complaint form from the state attorney general's office, filled it out with allegations against MPE, and saved it to her computer. (Dep. Julie Stark 11:6-11:18; *id.* at Ex. 1.) She never submitted the complaint—not that month, nor the following month. (*Id.* at 11:22-12:1.)

During that time, what she did do was express her anger at receiving a negative job review. (Dep. Eric Block 22:3-23:12.) On October 6, Ms. Stark and her supervisor, Eric Block, reviewed her job performance. (*Id.* at 18:6-8.) Her evaluation stated, among other things, that she "fails to follow directions" and that she "lacks the degree of teamwork and cooperation that MPE seeks in its employees." (*Id.* at Ex. 1.) Ms. Stark responded by yelling at her supervisor that MPE was a bunch of "mega-polluters" and "criminals," that they would "live to regret it," and that she would "tell everyone." (*Id.* at 24:2-25:15.) It was not clear to her supervisor, Eric Block, what Ms. Stark was referring to. (*Id.* at 26:4-8.)

Two months followed Ms. Stark's exchange with her supervisor. Still, she did not submit any complaint to the state Attorney General's office or to any other public official. (Dep. Julie Stark 11:22-12:15.) In fact, it was not until Monday, December 3, 2017, four days after she was dismissed from MPE, that Ms. Stark submitted her complaint. (*Id.* at 10:21-11:4, 11:19-12:2.) Thus, until she was discharged, Ms. Stark allowed her complaint to languish for months.

The persuasive Statement of Facts in Example 19-J uses several techniques, discussed below, to present the facts in a way that supports the employer's theory of the case. As we review those techniques, we will return to this example.

A. Organizing the Statement of Facts

You should always start the facts in a way that will grab the reader's attention and provide necessary context for you to tell your client's version of the story. As we discuss in further detail below, the facts are usually organized chronologically, topically, or perceptually, depending on the type of issues you are presenting and the complexity of the story.

In telling your client's story, use the same strategies previously discussed for a memorandum in Chapter 14, *Statement of Facts*. The first paragraph or two should always provide context for your reader by explaining who the parties are, their status in the story, and the crux of the conflict. Giving even minimal context is more effective than jumping into the details of the story. In addition, when constructing a persuasive Statement of Facts, try to choose facts that not only provide context but also grab the reader's attention and generate sympathy or positive emotions toward your client.

Example 19-K provides context and begins to generate sympathy for the employer, Michigan Electric & Power, who has fired the employee, Julie Stark. The employer's perspective is that Julie Stark is suing the company because she is a disgruntled employee who has been fired. Thus, the employer's Statement of Facts opens with the fact that she received a negative job review and was fired. A Statement of Facts in that same case, but written from the employee's perspective, would open in a different way, as in Example 19-L.

Example 19-K • **The opening paragraph in a persuasive Statement of Facts (defendant's perspective)**

STATEMENT OF FACTS

On November 29, 2017, Plaintiff Julie Stark was dismissed from her employment with Defendant Michigan Power & Electric, Company (MPE). Immediately after her dismissal Ms. Stark filed a complaint alleging that Michigan's Whistleblowers' Protection Act protected her from discharge. This motion seeks to dismiss her Whistleblowers' claim because no material issues of fact exist, and, as a matter of law, Ms. Stark cannot prove that she was engaged in any activity protected by Michigan's Whistleblowers' Protection Act.

Example 19-L • **The opening paragraph in a persuasive Statement of Facts (plaintiff's perspective)**

STATEMENT OF FACTS

Plaintiff Julie Stark, a long-time employee of defendant Michigan Power & Electric, has also been a long-time advocate for a healthy planet. Thus, in October 2017, when Julie Stark discovered that MPE might be ignoring environmental regulations, she spoke out. As a result, MPE fired her.

After providing an opening that introduces the parties and the problem from your client's perspective, you must decide on an organizational structure for all the facts that follow. Like the objective memo, you may want to consider organizing your Statement of Facts in one of the following ways:

- Chronologically: presenting facts in the order in which the events occurred

- Topically: presenting facts by topics like issues or categories
- Perceptually: presenting facts from the various participants' viewpoints

Facts are usually set forth in chronological order. Because readers expect facts to be told in sequence, chronological order is easiest to absorb. Other organizations may be more effective in some situations. For instance, if your case concerns a business transaction in three states, a topical organization divided by locale might be easiest to understand. If you have a case in which the various witnesses have different versions of the events, presenting the facts from the various participants' vantage points may be most effective. As with an objective memo, you may use a combination of these three strategies. You may have a topical organization, but then tell the facts chronologically within each topic.

The last paragraph is also important. The last paragraph should provide a smooth transition to whatever section is next in the brief. You may reiterate the procedural posture of the case or what your client is seeking now. No matter how you end, use the last sentence as a bridge to the next brief section.

B. Choosing Which Facts to Include

Whether you call them "determinative facts," "key facts," or "critical facts," you should include every fact that will affect the analysis of your argument. Because readers—especially judges—do not like to be surprised, make sure every fact used in the Argument section is first mentioned in the fact section.

Never omit facts just because they are bad for your case. If you omit a negative fact, you lose the opportunity to present that fact in context and minimize its impact. Moreover, your work will be more credible and trustworthy if the judge sees that you have forthrightly presented *all* the facts. Finally, the judge will see the negative facts anyway when reading the opposing party's brief and examining the record or supporting documents. Instead of ignoring negative facts, take advantage of the opportunity to frame the negative facts in a way that supports your theory of the case. The next section provides techniques for doing just that.

In addition to including all the facts that will affect the court's analysis, you should carefully consider which emotional facts you will include. In a persuasive document, you usually have more opportunity to include emotional facts that are not necessary to resolve the issue, but that may shed light on the parties' actions or cause a reader to feel sympathy for one party or distaste for another. Be selective in which emotional facts you choose. Throwing in every sympathetic fact for your client may backfire. Courts are not often swayed by emotion, and the court may be skeptical of the brief's credibility if the Statement of Facts contains too many emotional or self-serving facts. Examine Example 19-M to see how the writer, the attorney for plaintiff Karen Garrett, incorporated both background facts and emotional facts to tell her client's story.

Example 19-M • Using background fact and emotional facts

On February 15, 2017, Ms. Karen Garrett, an experienced employee of Ramsey, Inc., with a black-belt in karate and a master's degree in counseling, was denied a promotion to the position of first-shift Boys Group Leader because of her sex. (Dewey Dep. 30:4-18, September 17, 2017.) Leading up to this denial, Ms. Garrett had worked for the company in its operation of Lincoln Juvenile Detention Center in Macon County, Georgia for three years. (Priddy Dep. 27:3-9, October 22, 2017.)

During Ms. Garrett's employment, she advanced from a third-shift Girls' Group Leader to a second-shift Girls' Group Leader and acquired a more comprehensive range of job duties. (Garrett Aff. 6, August 28, 2017.) Ms. Garrett consistently performed her duties to her supervisor's satisfaction and received superior ratings in all categories in her annual performance reviews. (Dewey Dep. 30:17-10.) When she learned that a first-shift Boys Group Leader was opening, Ms. Garrett applied assuming that she was the ideal candidate given her superior performance ratings, her seniority, and Ramsey's preference to promote from within. (Garrett Aff. 7.) In fact, Ginger Dewey, Ramsey's Director of Human Resources, explicitly told Ms. Garrett she was qualified for the job in all respects except that she was not male. (Dewey Dep. 30:20-21.) However, company policy requires that Boy's Group Leaders be male for safety.

> **Emotional facts** are facts not necessary to resolve the legal issues but that help the reader understand what motivated the parties to act in a certain way or to feel sympathy toward one party or distaste for another party. Here, the emotional facts showing that Ms. Garrett had a black-belt in karate, a master's degree in counseling and had superior job performance ratings in all categories leads the reader to believe that she was qualified for the job, and that only her sex stood in her way. In other words, those facts generate sympathy for the plaintiff.

> **Background facts** are facts that provide context for understanding your client's situation. Here, background facts about Ms. Garrett's employment history help the reader make sense of the story and why she brought the lawsuit.

C. Refining the Statement of Facts

As with memoranda, attorneys draft their Statement of Facts for briefs at different times—some draft before the argument section of the brief is started, some draft after the Argument section is finished, and some write both sections simultaneously. No matter when you initially draft the Statement of Facts, you will want to spend time revising the facts after the Argument section of the brief is finished to ensure the Statement of Facts is accurate, complete, succinct, and effectively supports the analysis. The following tips will help you draft a more persuasive Statement of Facts.

Facts should be written in a way that subtly evokes empathy for your position, without sounding overly emotional or passionate. Consider using the following seven strategies to help create a tone that suggests objectivity while presenting the facts in a way that supports your theory of the case: (1) place favorable facts strategically; (2) describe favorable facts in detail; (3) pair favorable facts with unfavorable facts; (4) avoid overstating or misrepresenting facts; (5) avoid characterizing the facts, (6) identify people by their roles in the story; and (7) cite the facts.

1. Place favorable facts strategically

One way to highlight favorable facts is to put them in "positions of emphasis"[7] within the brief. Positions of emphasis include the beginning and end of the fact section, the first and last sentences of any paragraph, or in any point heading within the section (if using point headings to divide facts).[8] Review Examples 19-K and 19-L, above, to compare the facts that the plaintiff and defendant in the Stark case chose to highlight in the position of emphasis directly after the Statement of Facts heading.

2. Describe favorable facts in detail

Another way to highlight favorable facts is to describe those facts in more detail and to give those facts more "air time." Review example 19-N and examine how less favorable facts are described with less detail and addressed more quickly, and the favorable facts are described in more detail.

Example 19-N · Using details to emphasize favorable facts

STATEMENT OF FACTS

Plaintiff Julie Stark was an MPE employee who, on October 6, 2017, received a negative employment review. (Dep. Julie Stark 10:1-2, Dec. 30, 2017.) On November 29, Ms. Stark was dismissed from MPE. (*Id.* at 10:21-22.) Four days after she was dismissed, Ms. Stark filed a complaint with the state attorney general alleging that MPE had violated the federal Clean Air Act. (*Id.* at 11:1-4.) Ms. Stark contends that she should be protected from dismissal because she was about to report her allegations when she was dismissed. (Pl.'s Compl. ¶ 15, Dec. 6, 2017.)

Ms. Stark was not on the cusp of reporting her allegations at the time of her dismissal. Sometime during the first few days of October, Ms. Stark downloaded a complaint form from the state attorney general's office, filled it out with allegations against MPE, and saved it to her computer. (Dep. Julie Stark 11:6-11:18; *id.* at Ex. 1.) She never submitted the complaint—not that month, nor the following month. (*Id.* at 11:22-12:1.)

During that time, what she did do was express her anger at receiving a negative job review. (Dep. Eric Block 22:3-23:12.) On October 6, Ms. Stark and her supervisor, Eric Block, reviewed her job performance. (*Id.* at 18:6-8.) Her evaluation stated, among other things, that she "fails to follow directions" and that she "lacks the degree of teamwork and cooperation that MPE seeks in its employees." (*Id.* at Ex. 1.)

Did you notice the "air time" given to the idea that Ms. Stark was not taking any action with respect to her complaint? This lack of action helps

---

7. Mary Beth Beazley, *A Practical Guide to Appellate Advocacy* 122 (3d ed. 2010).
8. *Id.* at 122-23.

prove that Ms. Stark was not "about to report" at the time she was fired, an important point for the employer. Thus, the employer's Statement of Facts states "she was not on the cusp of reporting the allegations." The writer then adds detail: "She never submitted the complaint—not that month, nor the following month," and "[t]wo months followed ... [s]till, she did not submit any complaint." By repeating that important fact in detail, the employer emphasizes the employee's lack of action.

3. Pair favorable facts with unfavorable facts

Placing unfavorable facts in a dependent clause at the beginning of a sentence, paired with favorable facts, minimizes the impact of the negative facts. Be careful in overusing this technique, however; too many dependent clauses in a row can be distracting to the reader. Example 19-O minimizes the impact of an unfavorable fact by putting it in a dependent clause (where it gets less attention) and by pairing it with a positive fact.

In an argument about whether a client had "exclusive possession" of land, the fact that others were allowed to harvest vegetables is a negative fact. Thus, in the Statement of Facts, that negative fact is paired with a more positive fact that shows "exclusive possession."

Example 19-O · Example of using a dependent clause to pair a negative fact with a positive one

---

Although neighbors harvested and kept some of the vegetables, the Nero's granted explicit permission for them to do so.

That same technique—coupling a bad fact with good facts—is used in Examples 19-J and 19-N. In those examples, it's bad for the employer that Ms. Stark threatened to tell people about the employer's possible environmental misdeeds. That fact can help the employee establish that she was "about to report." Thus, the employer provides context for that fact—namely that her threat occurred because the employee was angry. That fact suggests that the threat was simply a heated statement, not one the employee actually intended to act on.

4. Avoid overstating or misrepresenting the facts

Although you want to present the facts from your client's perspective, never overstate or misrepresent a fact. Overstating or misrepresenting a fact not only triggers ethical questions about your practice, but doing so can alienate your reader, especially if the reader is a judge. Your facts will not always be good. Some facts will probably be quite detrimental to your case. While you can highlight good facts, never promise what you cannot deliver. In the zeal to be good advocates, it is easy to stretch the facts to serve a client, particularly when you know your client has been wronged. In telling your client's story, however, make sure to protect your credibility by always telling the truth and never exaggerating or lying.

5. Avoid characterizing the facts

Although using adjectives and adverbs can contribute to an interesting and compelling story, avoid using them to characterize facts.[9] Both adjectives and adverbs can often appear to be argument rather than description. For example, saying that "the defendant brutally attacked Ms. Jimenez," is a characterization of the facts that could be off-putting to a judge. Rather than telling the judge that the attack was brutal, simply describe the facts without the characterization: "The defendant struck Ms. Jimenez fourteen times with the wine bottle, leaving a span of bruises across her face, torso, and back."

Another way to characterize is to implicitly assume the answer to events at issue in the case. For instance, look at the following sentence in a case alleging sexual harassment: "Ms. Li was sexually harassed on three occasions." That statement assumes the answer to the claim in question and, thus, is a characterization. Instead, directly give the facts without characterization: "Ms. Li's supervisor showed her pornography on four separate occasions while other co-workers looked on." The second example avoids characterizing the facts, while giving the reader a clearer description of the events. Simply describing facts without characterization tells a more vivid story, while letting the judge come to his or her own conclusion about the events.

6. Identify individuals by their roles

Refer to the primary parties in the story by their role in the story or procedural designation. Often referring to someone by a role, such as "the landowner" or "the buyer," is easiest for your reader. You may sometimes use the procedural designation (such as plaintiff or defendant), particularly when prosecuting or defending a criminal law case, but understand that procedural labels are impersonal and can put distance between the reader and the people in the story. Moreover, procedural labels can be confusing in civil cases—the buyer could be the plaintiff in one case and the defendant in another. Finally, in some jurisdictions, court rules may discourage or disallow the use of such designations.

Introduce minor characters in the story by name and role, but you may refer to them by their roles in the remainder of the fact sections. For example, after introducing a minor player like "Investigating Detective Jerry Briscoe" or "Director of Operations, Erin Nalle," in the facts, you can then just refer to the party by the designations of "the investigating officer" or "Director of Operations" in the facts and argument sections. Keeping track of too many minor players' names becomes tiresome and distracting for the judge.

---

9. We would like to thank Federal Magistrate John Acosta for his comments and insights on the effective use of facts in documents prepared for the court.

7. Cite the facts

Cite the source of your facts. If the facts came from witness statements, interrogatories, depositions, police reports, or so forth, tell the judge where the fact can be found.[10] As in Example 19-P, peppering your Statement of Facts with citations to the record shows that your description of the events is grounded in reality. In addition, citations make it easier for the judge to find the fact you are describing. Thus, when writing your facts, you should cite nearly every sentence. The only sentences that you might not cite are those that summarize other facts. The underlying facts, the ones that support the summary statement, should be cited.

Example 19-P · Adding citations in your Statement of Facts

Defendant Jennifer Soto received a telephone call from her neighbor, Allison Moore, at approximately 6:00 p.m. on Aug. 31, 2017. (Def.'s Resp. to Pl.'s Interrog. No. 5.) Moore explained she was planning a party for about ten people at nearby Cascade Park, and wanted Soto's assistance obtaining a twelve-pack of beer. (Moore Dep. 26:9, March 7, 2018.) The party was in honor of Soto's younger brother who had been chosen for the Grimsley varsity soccer team. (Moore Dep. 26:10.) Defendant agreed to assist and provided the twelve-pack to Moore at her house around 6:30 p.m. (Moore Dep. 26:11.)

One question that sometimes arises is whether the Statement of Facts can include inferences drawn from the facts. The answer is a cautious "yes." When writing a persuasive document, courts will usually allow *reasonable* inferences drawn from the facts. You must, however, take care not to extrapolate facts beyond what is reasonable. Assuming facts in dispute is not a reasonable inference.

VI. The Argument

The argument section is the heart of your trial brief. It's where you present your analysis and where you will convince the court that the solution you offer is the correct one. Although the Argument section in your brief will largely resemble the Discussion section in your memo, you may need to rethink how you present your arguments to maximize your opportunities to persuade the court.

---

10. The format for citations to the record may vary according to your jurisdiction. Both the *ALWD Manual* and the *Bluebook* describe how to cite to applicable court documents, transcripts, and the record.

A. Organizing the Argument

When writing to a court, you will need to consider how to organize multiple legal claims, as well as any individual legal arguments within each claim.

1. Multiple claims

When involved in litigation, attorneys usually think of legal issues in terms of the "claims" that those issues present. A "claim" is an assertion of a right that, if proved, entitles a party to relief. Usually, litigation will involve multiple claims arising from a single event. That's because, if a party fails to raise all the claims arising from a single event, that party can be barred from raising a claim in later litigation if that claim could have been raised in the earlier litigation.[11] Thus, most litigation will include multiple claims.

If a trial brief you are working on addresses multiple claims, you need to consider carefully the order in which to present those claims. Whenever possible, present your strongest claim or defense first. Leave weaker arguments for later.

Although that's the general rule, you may not always be able to present your strongest substantive claim first. Procedural issues—such as the court's jurisdiction or a statute of limitations—must be presented before the substantive claims because the court cannot proceed to the substantive issues until the procedural issue is resolved. In that situation, the procedural issue should be presented first, even if the procedural issue is not your strongest argument.

If your argument involves multiple claims, remember to start your argument section with a roadmap (discussed in Chapter 12, *The Discussion Section*), as in Example 19-Q.

Example 19-Q · A roadmap to an argument section that addresses two claims

---

ARGUMENT

Defendants John Ashcroft, in his official capacity as United States Attorney General, and Asa Hutchinson, in his official capacity as Administrator of the Drug Enforcement Agency, hereby oppose plaintiff's motion for a preliminary injunction. That injunction would prohibit the Attorney General from enforcing the Controlled Substances Act, 21 U.S.C. §§ 801-971, against doctors who prescribe federally controlled substances to help patients commit suicide. As explained below, the State of Oregon, the principal plaintiff in this case, lacks standing to seek an injunction against the enforcement of federal law against

---

11. The doctrine that bars parties from raising a new claim in future litigation if that claim could have been raised in earlier litigation is called *res judicata*. *See generally* 47 Am. Jur. 2d *Judgments* § 463-72 (2013).

private parties and should therefore be dismissed from the case. In addition, plaintiffs cannot sustain their burden of showing both a likelihood of success on the merits and irreparable injury absent a preliminary injunction.

Remember to review the number of claims or defenses you are presenting and consider whether you should omit any weaker claims or defenses. Judges and their staff are busy, so it may be most persuasive to present two strong claims that will satisfy your client's needs rather than to present ten claims, which may bog down the court and weaken the strength of your client's case.

2. Multiple legal arguments

Each legal claim is, in turn, made up of multiple legal arguments. In mapping your individual arguments consider which order would be most advantageous, remembering that most judges expect arguments to track the order of elements or factors in the over-arching rule governing the claim. If, strategically, you choose to deviate from the governing rule's expected order, use the roadmap section to briefly discuss the reason why the order of arguments was changed. You need to have a good reason to deviate from the traditional approach when doing so might confuse the court or make the court wonder whether you are putting off an argument because you lack confidence in it. After providing a roadmap section, you will present the arguments about each element or factor within the claim in the order you indicated in the roadmap section.

B. Developing Persuasive Rules

Sidebar

As explained in Section 7.1, *Explaining the Law,* courts sometimes set out a rule explicitly. Other times, however, courts do not state explicitly the standard they used to conclude whether an element or factor is present. In those cases, patterns of judicial or legislative thinking are called "implicit rules" before they are expressly articulated. To make such implicit rule explicit, you need to (1) synthesize or identify a pattern in the cases that seems to explain why courts reach their results, and then (2) craft a rule from the pattern that encompasses both the prior cases and your client's case.

When presenting legal arguments in an objective memo, you craft rules and case illustrations to explain the law upon which your prediction rests. Similarly, in a persuasive argument, you craft rules and case illustrations to explain the law upon which your conclusion rests. In a persuasive argument, however, you will craft your explanation of the law so that it emphasizes those aspects of the law that are most important to your argument. Accordingly, you begin persuading as soon as you begin explaining using a two-step process: Step one is to determine whether your rule is explicitly stated or whether you have an implicit rule from which you can create an explicit rule. Step two is to craft the rule strategically to emphasize the parts of the rule that are most helpful to your client by stating the rule either positively or negatively, or stating the rule more broadly or narrowly.

1. Step one: Determine your rule

As stated above, step one is determining whether your rule is explicit or implicit. If your rule is already explicitly stated, go directly to step two to determine how to draft the rule consistently with the outcome your client seeks. If your rule is implicit, however, you will need to create a rule that advances your client's position. Example 19-R shows you how you might do that.

Recall the California client, discussed in Chapter 7, *Explaining the Law: Rules*, who was out bicycling with her husband, saw him round a curve, then heard a crash and a scream. After rounding the corner, she realized her husband had been hit by a car. She came to you to see whether she can sue the driver for the emotional damages she suffered after seeing her injured husband.

You researched the issue and learned that in California, a person who witnesses an accident to a family member can sue for emotional damages only if she was "then aware" of the injury to the family member. You uncovered the two cases listed in Example 19-R. Those cases discuss what it means to be "then aware" of the injury, but the cases do not explain why the courts reached different conclusions when looking at similar facts. By looking for the reasoned distinction that explains the different outcomes, you might extract the rule proposed in Example 19-R from the cases.

After determining your rule, you would then move on to step two to craft your rule strategically.

Example 19-R · Synthesizing a series of prior cases to create a rule that advances your client's cause

Case	Facts	Holding
Krouse v. Graham, 137 Cal. Rptr. 863 (Cal. 1977).	Husband knew his wife was standing by the trunk of his car. In his rear view mirror he saw a car approach. He then felt his car being hit by the other car. The plaintiff admitted that he did not actually see the other car strike his wife.	Yes. The husband was "then aware" of the injury to his wife.
Fife v. Astenius, 284 Cal. Rptr. 16 (Cal. App. 4th Dist. 1991).	A father heard a crash and saw debris fly over a wall. The father rushed out to the street and within seconds discovered his daughter was in the car accident.	No. The father was not "then aware."
Possible synthesized rule:	A plaintiff is "then aware" of a family member's injury if she is aware of the accident's location and knows the family member was in that location as the accident occurred.	

2. Step two: Craft your rule strategically

Crafting the rule for a persuasive argument, however, may require you to refine the rule by stating it positively or negatively or broadly or narrowly, depending on the outcome your client is seeking.

You may first want to consider whether you can state the rule positively or negatively. If you are arguing that a standard is met, then you should frame the rule in a positive manner to emphasize that the required standard is met. By contrast, if you are arguing that a standard is not met, then frame the rule so that it emphasizes when the required standard is not met. For example, if you are representing a client that is alleging gender discrimination, you will want to describe the rule so that it focuses on when discrimination takes place. If you are defending against a charge of discrimination, explain when a party complies with the law, as in Example 19-S.

Example 19-S · Drafting the rule positively or negatively

The rule as written	A recipient which operates or sponsors interscholastic … athletics shall provide equal athletic opportunity for members of both sexes. In determining whether equal opportunities are available the Director will consider, among other factors: (1) Whether the selection of sports and levels of competition effectively accommodate the interests and abilities of members of both sexes.*
Plaintiff (drafted negatively)	A university discriminates against its female students if it fails to effectively accommodate the interests and abilities of its female students.**
Defendant (drafted positively)	A university complies with Title IX if it effectively accommodates the interests and abilities of its female students.***

  *   34 C.F.R. § 106.41.
 **   Id.
***   Id.

Similarly, depending on the outcome your client is seeking, you may want to state a rule broadly or narrowly. For example, compare the explanations of the standard for granting summary judgment in Example 19-T. Notice how the use of the word "only" in the third part of Example 19-T suggests that summary judgment should be granted in very limited circumstances.

Example 19-T · Drafting the rule broadly or narrowly

The rule as written	The court shall grant summary judgment if the movant shows that there is no genuine dispute as to any material fact and the movant is entitled to judgment as a matter of law.*
The moving party (drafted broadly)	Summary judgment **must** be granted if there is no issue of material fact and the moving party is entitled to judgment as a matter of law.**
The non-moving party (drafted narrowly)	Summary judgment may be granted **only** if there is no issue of material fact and the moving party is entitled to judgment as a matter of law.***

  *   Fed. R. Civ. P. 56(a).
 **   Id.
***   Id.

Let's look at step one and two together now. Example 19-U re-examines the synthesized rule set forth in Example 19-R and illustrates how the plaintiff's attorney and the defense's attorney may want to craft the rule. As you can see, the plaintiff may be happy to frame the rule just as it was synthesized in the objective analysis because that framing is favorable to her. The defense, however, would want to revise the rule and present a narrower version of the "then aware" rule to make it more favorable to the outcome sought.

Example 19-U · Crafting a persuasive rule strategically

Synthesized Rule	A plaintiff is then aware of a family member's injury if she is aware of the accident's location and knows the family member was in that location as the accident occurred.
Rule as crafted by plaintiff's attorney (positively and broadly)	A plaintiff is then aware if she is aware of the accident's location and knows the family member was in that location when the accident occurred.
Rule as crafted by defense attorney (narrowly)	A plaintiff can establish she was then aware only by showing she knew the precise location of the accident and that the family member was in that precise location at the time of the accident.

C. Developing Persuasive Case Illustrations

In addition to presenting rules in the most persuasive way, you will also want to present case illustrations of those rules in the most persuasive way.[12] With respect to cases, you will usually be making one of two arguments: (1) that your client's case is like the prior case and the same outcome is warranted, or (2) your client's case is distinguishable from the prior case and, therefore, a different outcome is warranted for the current case.

The process is quite similar to that of an objective memo except that you will strategically craft the case illustration to persuasively explain why the case is analogous to or distinguishable from your case. Consider the Stark whistleblowing case described in the Statement of Facts section of this chapter. After you conduct your research, you find the case of *Richards v. Sandusky Community Schools*, 102 F. Supp. 2d 753 (E.D. Mich. 2000), which addresses the circumstances in which an employee should be protected by the state's whistleblowers' statute. According to *Richards*, to be protected, the employee must prove (among other things) she was

---

12. Note that some legal arguments, like pure rule-based arguments or statutory construction arguments, may have no case illustrations. *See* Chapters 8.1, *Applying the Law: Rule-Based Reasoning,* and Chapter 11, *Statutory Analysis.*

"about to report" a violation of law. In the client's case, the plaintiff had received paperwork and filled out the paperwork to report a violation, but she never sent the paperwork in. The issue you are briefing is whether the plaintiff was "about to report." Examine Example 19-V, which illustrates how an attorney might draft a case illustration of *Richards* in an objective memo and how attorneys on either side might draft that case illustration for a persuasive brief.

Example 19-V · Converting a case illustration from an objective memo to a persuasive brief

Objective memo	In *Richards v. Sandusky Community Schools*, the court concluded that the plaintiff was not "about to report" a violation. 102 F. Supp. 2d 753, 755, 763 n.14 (E.D. Mich. 2000). In that case, the plaintiff contacted OSHA and received the appropriate paperwork to file a complaint. *Id.* at 763 n.14. The plaintiff never completed the paperwork. *Id.* at 763. The *Richards* court held that the only relevant evidence was that the plaintiff received the appropriate paperwork to file a report; this evidence, the court held, fell "drastically short of the clear and convincing proof required." *Id.*
Plaintiff's brief	Receiving paperwork necessary to report a violation is evidence that a plaintiff was "about to report." *Richards v. Sandusky Community Schs.*, 102 F. Supp. 2d 753, 755, 763 n.14 (E.D. Mich. 2000). In *Richards*, the plaintiff contacted OSHA and received the appropriate paperwork to file a complaint. *Id.* at 763 n.14. Because the plaintiff did not take any steps beyond receiving the paperwork, the court held that the plaintiff in *Richards* was not about to report a violation. *Id.* The court did, however, note that plaintiff's receipt of the appropriate paperwork was evidence that "would support a contention that she was about to report." *Id.*
Defendant's brief	Merely receiving paperwork from a public agency falls "drastically short" of the clear and convincing evidence needed to prove that an employee was "about to report" a suspected violation. *Richards v. Sandusky Community Schs.*, 102 F. Supp. 753, 763 (E.D. Mich. 2000). In *Richards v. Sandusky Community Schools*, the employee received Occupational Safety and Health Act paperwork that would have enabled the employee to report alleged health and safety violations to this federal agency; however, the employee never filled out the forms and never sent the forms in. *Id.* at 763. The district court held that merely receiving paperwork from a public agency "falls drastically short of the clear and convincing proof required under the WPA." *Id.*

When you reviewed Example 19-V, did you note the transformation the case illustration took between the objective version and the two persuasive versions? In the objective form of the case illustration, the "hook" was an objective statement of the court's holding. In contrast, the plaintiff's attorney used a rule as a hook, then crafted the case illustration to mitigate any possible damage from *Richards* by emphasizing that her receipt of paperwork is evidence that she was "about to report" the violation, even if that evidence by itself is not sufficient. On the other hand, the defendant focused on the part of the *Richards* case that supports how "merely receiving paperwork" falls "drastically short" of what is necessary to provide the plaintiff was "about to report."

D. Developing Counter-Analyses: Addressing Weaknesses from Your Client's Perspective

The aspect of persuasive writing that is most different from objective writing is addressing weaknesses in your argument. To be an effective advocate, you must be able to identify weaknesses in your argument and explain why, despite those weaknesses, your client's desired outcome is the most appropriate outcome. In other words, you must address the weaknesses from your client's perspective and not from your opponent's perspective.

Attorneys commonly minimize weaknesses in their client's case by showing that an opposing party's argument is based on one or more of the following:

- An incorrect or incomplete view of the facts
- An incorrect or incomplete view of the law
- Case law that is distinguishable
- A misapplication of a rule to the facts
- Faulty rationale, reasoning, or policy arguments

When considering how to address weaknesses in an argument, consider whether you can rely on any arguments listed above. You may be able to rely on one or more of these arguments, or the list may give you a starting point for developing other persuasive arguments to minimize weaknesses from your client's perspective.

Avoid the natural impulse (and indeed the technique in objective writing) to first explain the weakness from an opponent's perspective and then explain why that perspective is incorrect. Why is that technique ineffective in persuasive writing? By first explaining your opponent's argument, you highlight, rather than minimize, your opponent's argument. Look at Example 19-U, in which the writer presents the opposing argument first and then explains why that argument would not ultimately be successful.

Example 19-W • Less effective approach: Highlighting your opponent's argument

Plaintiff addresses a weakness by first explaining that weakness.

Defendant's attempt to carve out an exception for four-year olds who are supervised by an adult is unsupported by the weight of authority. Defendant has pointed to three cases, *Ehrlich, Trent,* and *Romanchuk*. In those cases, the courts have held that, as a matter of law, the four year old could not be held liable for negligence. In each of those cases, the parent was present when the alleged negligent act took place. Defendant, therefore, contends that if a parent is present a child may not, as a matter of law, be held liable for negligence.

After explaining the weakness, plaintiff turns to its counter-argument.

Defendant's contention is, however, wrong. The majority of courts that have considered whether to follow the rule espoused in *Ehrlich* have declined to do so. *See e.g., Sun Jeong Koo v. St. Bernard*, 392 N.Y.S.2d 815, 816 (N.Y. App. Div. 1977) (considering *Ehrlich* but rejecting a bright-line rule in negligence case against a child of 4 years and 10 months); *Searles v. Dardani*, 347 N.Y.S.2d 662, 665 (N.Y. App. Div. 1973) (considering *Ehrlich*, but concluding that jury should decide whether a child of four and a half years was negligent). No court has followed *Trent* or *Ehrlich*. Thus, *Ehrlich, Trent,* and *Romanchuk* represent a minority view, and those cases should not be followed.

The danger in explaining your opponent's perspective first is that the judge may decide that your opponent's argument sounds correct before even reading your argument. You should not help your opponent in that way.

The fix, however, is easy. To the extent possible, avoid the first step. Do not explain the weakness from your opponent's perspective. Instead, skip right to the second step: Explain the weakness from your perspective. That is, explain *how* and *why*, despite that weakness, your client's position is ultimately the correct or just conclusion. Example 19-X shows you how.

Example 19-X • More effective: Present the argument from your client's perspective

Here, plaintiff's counsel has removed his explanation of opponent's argument.

The weight of authority does not support carving out an exception for four-year-olds who are supervised by an adult. Although *Ehrlich, Trent,* and *Romanchuk* assert a novel rule, the majority of courts that have considered whether to follow the rule in *Ehrlich* have declined to do so. Moreover, no court has followed either *Trent* or *Romanchuk*. *See e.g., Sun Jeong Koo v. St. Bernard*, 392 N.Y.S.2d 815, 816 (N.Y. App. Div. 1977) (considering *Ehrlich* but rejecting a bright-line rule in negligence case against a child of 4 years and 10 months); *Searles v. Dardani*, 347 N.Y.S.2d 662, 665 (N.Y. App. Div. 1973) (considering *Ehrlich*, but concluding that jury should decide whether a child of four and a half years was negligent).

When initially drafting an argument, you may find it easier to first draft your opponent's argument and then respond to it, as in Example 19-V. Doing so may help you clarify your opponent's argument and write a more effective response. But that version is your *draft*. In the final product, eliminate as much of your opponent's argument as possible and construct the argument so that the court reads about the issue from your client's perspective.

When deciding where to address a weakness, you have two good options: You can fully present your argument and then, after presenting your argument, address the weakness, or if the weakness doesn't merit a significant discussion, you can use a dependent clause to acknowledge and then dispose of the weakness. These two possible locations may sound familiar. As you may recall from § 8.3, *Applying the Law: Counter-analysis*, these locations are the same two locations in which you would address possible counter-arguments in an objective memo.

E. Other Ways to Shape Your Argument

To help the court see a case from a client's perspective, attorneys use a variety of techniques to emphasize why the outcome a client seeks is a correct and preferable outcome to the one opposing counsel seeks.

Although this chapter discusses many techniques attorneys use to present their arguments persuasively, these techniques do not work magic. Courts are populated with smart people. If the law and facts are not on your side, no amount of impressive prose will change the law or facts, and you are unlikely to prevail. That said, when you have an argument that might win, you can make it easier for the court to see why it should win. The techniques described below will help you do that.

1. Use location strategically

One of the best ways to emphasize your main points is to put them where a judge is most likely to see them. The eyes of most readers—including judges—tend to fall and rest upon a few positions of emphasis. Many of the techniques described below flow from this simple idea: Put information where a judge is most likely to see it, rest upon it, and absorb it. In particular, review your point headings, the first sentence of each paragraph, and the last sentence of each paragraph to ensure that you have used those locations effectively. By contrast, disclose information that is less helpful to you in the middle of a paragraph and in the middle of sentences. In those locations, the information will receive less emphasis.

2. Use assertive point headings

One of the prime locations where your reader's eyes will rest will be on your point headings. Thus, in addition to using point headings to guide your reader through the organization of an argument, you will want to construct point headings that emphasize the main points of your argument that you want the court to accept.

To create persuasive point headings in your argument, follow the same advice we gave in Chapter 12, *The Discussion Section: Introducing and Connecting Arguments*. First, make your point headings work. Each point heading should assert the conclusion you want the judge to reach when reading that section. Second, the point headings should work together so that they provide an outline of your argument. Finally, make your point headings look professional by using traditional formatting. Review Chapter 12, *The Discussion Section: Introducing and Connecting Arguments*, where these points are discussed in more detail.

Let's focus on the few ways in which you will want to tweak your point headings to make them most effective in your trial brief. Point headings may have two parts:

1. **The action you want the court to take or the conclusion you want the court to adopt, and**
2. **The primary reason the court should take that action or adopt that conclusion.**

Of the point headings you will craft, you will need to think most carefully about the main point headings designated by Roman numerals. Those point headings designate a new claim. They should, therefore, assert the procedural action that you want the court to take with respect to that claim. Compare Example 19-Y and 19-Z. Example 19-Y is a more effective opening point heading because it tells the court the procedural action it should take.

Example 19-Y • A point heading that asserts the procedural action the court should take

---

I.   PLAINTIFFS' COMPLAINT SHOULD BE DISMISSED BECAUSE THE ADEA DOES NOT PERMIT DISPARATE IMPACT CLAIMS.

Example 19-Z • A point heading that does not assert the procedural action the court should take

---

I.   THE ADEA DOES NOT PERMIT DISPARATE IMPACT CLAIMS.

Because more than one element or factor will be argued within each claim, attorneys use sub-headings to alert the reader to each new element, factor, or part of the argument. These sub-headings provide the reader with an overview of the legal and factual support for the heading's conclusion. Therefore, an effective sub-heading often includes more specific facts or assertions than the point headings for dispositive issues.

As you can see in Example 19-aa, the sub-headings should support the conclusion in the initial point heading and work together to present an outline of the argument.

Example 19-aa · Example of an initial point heading and supporting sub-headings[13]

I. **PLAINTIFFS' COMPLAINT SHOULD BE DISMISSED BECAUSE THE ADEA DOES NOT PERMIT DISPARATE IMPACT CLAIMS.**

　　A. **The text of the ADEA precludes disparate impact claims.**

　　　　1. **Section 4(a) of the ADEA, which prohibits discrimination "because of age," prohibits only intentional discrimination.**

　　　　2. **Section 4(f) of the ADEA, which permits employers to consider "reasonable factors other than age," precludes a discrimination claim based on the impact of an employment decision.**

　　B. **The legislative history confirms that disparate impact claims are not cognizable under the ADEA.**

You will notice that in Example 19-aa not all the point headings state the conclusion counsel wants the court to adopt *and* the reason the court should adopt that conclusion. That's because the longer a point heading becomes the more difficult it is to absorb what the point heading is saying. If a point heading is becoming too long for the reader to absorb its meaning, you might consider stating the conclusion you want the court to reach in one point heading and the reason for that conclusion in sub-headings.

Different practitioners have different ideas about when a point heading becomes too long and the importance of including both your conclusion *and* the primary reason the court should adopt that conclusion. So, if you are working with a more senior attorney, follow the senior attorney's preference.

Generally, most judges and attorneys prefer short point headings. We recommend aiming for one to two lines. Your goal is to keep the point headings short, but choose words that convey as much substance as possible.

3. Create paragraph-level persuasion

The techniques for persuading at the paragraph level are straightforward. Although simple, these techniques are powerful. Their appropriate use will provide organization and direction to your reader and will be critical to the effective explanation of your argument.

---

13. The format and font requirements for point headings may vary according to your jurisdiction or the customs of your office.

a. Thesis sentences

A "thesis" is a proposition put forward for consideration—one that the speaker intends to prove. Thus, no surprises here, a thesis sentence is a sentence in which that proposition is stated. By contrast, a "topic sentence" is a sentence in which the topic of a paragraph is described, but the sentence makes no assertion about a proposition to be proved.

Within the Argument section of your trial brief, every single paragraph should begin with a thesis sentence. That's right: Every single paragraph should begin with a thesis sentence. The reason should be obvious. Each paragraph should assert one clear point. You will make it a whole lot easier for a judge to follow your argument if you tell the judge what the point of the paragraph is at the outset. The net effect will be that your thesis sentences will, together, form a skeletal outline of the argument you are presenting to a court.

Compare Example 19-bb, in which the first full paragraph uses a thesis sentence, and Example 19-cc, in which the first full paragraph does not. Notice how the thesis sentence tells the conclusion the court should reach after reading the paragraph. In doing so, the thesis sentence shapes the way the court absorbs the information provided in the paragraph.

Example 19-bb • More effective approach: The thesis sentence tells what assertion the paragraph will prove

---

.... An officer establishes reasonable suspicion to search a suspect if the officer can point to specific and articulable facts that give rise to a reasonable inference that the person might pose an immediate threat. *See State v. Ehly*, 315 Or. 66 (1993).

To establish a reasonable suspicion for a protective search, officers may rely on their knowledge that the defendant is involved in an activity associated with weapons and that the defendant associates with people who often carry weapons. For example, in *Ehly*, this court determined that officers had reasonable suspicion to conduct a protective search. *Id.* at 83. In that case, officers knew that the defendant was a drug user and that "many people who use illegal narcotics possess guns." *Id.* at 82. Moreover, the officers also knew that defendant was "running" with a person who carried weapons. *Id.* Because the defendant was rummaging through a gym bag with his hands concealed and did not respond to the officer's suggestion to dump out the contents of the bag, this court concluded that it was reasonable for one of the officers to dump the contents of the bag out on the motel room bed. *Id.* at 83.

With a strong thesis sentence, the judge knows the writer's primary assertion and what point the paragraph will prove.

Example 19-cc • Less effective approach: A paragraph with no thesis

---

.... An officer establishes reasonable suspicion to search a suspect if the officer can point to specific and articulable facts that give rise to a reasonable inference that the person might pose an immediate threat. *See State v. Ehly*, 315 Or. 66 (1993).

For example, in *Ehly*, this court determined that officers had reasonable suspicion to conduct a protective search. *Id.* at 83. In that case, officers knew that the defendant was a drug user and that "many people who use illegal narcotics possess guns." *Id.* at 82. Moreover, the officers also knew that defendant was "running" with a person who carried weapons. *Id.* Because the defendant was rummaging through a gym bag with his hands concealed and did not respond to the officer's suggestion to dump out the contents of the bag, this court concluded that it was reasonable for one of the officers to dump the contents of the bag out on the motel room bed. *Id.* at 83.

The writer omits the thesis sentence and jumps directly into application. The judge, therefore, will not get a good idea of the point the paragraph will prove.

b. The middle of the paragraph

The middle of the paragraph should, of course, relate to the thesis sentence. Although the sentences in the middle of the paragraph may not get as much attention as the first (or last) sentence of the paragraph, they are important and should support the paragraph's thesis. If you find that sentences in the middle of your paragraphs have ideas that do not relate to the thesis sentence, you may need to either move those sentences to another paragraph or create a new paragraph for those ideas.

The middle of the paragraph is a good place to put information that is less favorable to your client but that you either have to disclose (because you are ethically bound to) or that you choose to disclose (to inoculate that information). As discussed above, information in the middle gets less attention. Example 19-dd illustrates an advocate's strategy to minimize the effect of the plaintiff's elevated blood alcohol content by placing that information in the middle of the paragraph. Examples 19-ee and 19-ff illustrate paragraphs that place damaging information at the outset of the paragraph and damaging information at the end. Which is more effective?

Example 19-dd · Legal standard emphasized in conclusion at the beginning and negative information buried in the middle of the paragraph[14]

The facts in this case, even when viewed most favorably for the Plaintiff, failed to establish any "substantial evidence" of Moore's intoxication. Although Moore's blood alcohol level was .13, she did not demonstrate any outward signs of intoxication. Her speech was not slurred. She appeared to be in control of her body. She did not have the odor of alcohol. Because Moore exhibited none of these symptoms, Defendant Soto could not have known she was intoxicated.

Here, the writer must prove that the plaintiff failed to provide "substantial evidence" of the defendant's intoxication. Therefore, the writer states that conclusion at a point of emphasis—the beginning of the paragraph. The writer places another conclusion at the end. The writer also minimizes the blood alcohol content by using a dependent clause in the middle of the paragraph.

---

14. Examples 19-P, 19-dd through 19-ii, and 19-ll were adapted from class materials prepared by Professor John Korzen, Wake Forest University School of Law.

Example 19-ee · Negative information at the beginning of the paragraph and conclusion at the end

Here, although the writer starts with a dependent clause, because the negative fact is at the beginning of the paragraph, the factual argument appears overly defensive. The dual conclusions at the end are not as effective.

Although Moore's blood alcohol level was .13, she did not demonstrate any outward signs of intoxication. Her speech was not slurred. She appeared to be in control of her body. She did not have the odor of alcohol. Because Moore exhibited none of these symptoms, Defendant Soto could not have known she was intoxicated. Therefore the facts in this case, even when viewed most favorably for the Plaintiff, failed to establish any "substantial evidence" of Moore's intoxication.

Example 19-ff · Negative information at the end of the paragraph

Here, because the factual weakness is attached to the ending conclusion and not buried in the middle of the paragraph, it receives too much attention and nullifies the paragraph's effectiveness.

The facts in this case, even when viewed most favorably for the Plaintiff, failed to establish any "substantial evidence" of Moore's intoxication. She did not demonstrate any outward signs of intoxication. Her speech was not slurred. She appeared to be in control of her body. She did not have the odor of alcohol. Because Moore exhibited none of these symptoms that would support her blood alcohol level of .13, Defendant Soto could not have known she was intoxicated.

c. Final sentences

The thesis sentence tells your reader the proposition you intend to prove in the paragraph, and repeating that point at the end of the paragraph can enhance the persuasive effect. Revisiting your main point in the last sentence closes the loop by establishing that you have now proven what your thesis sentence said you would prove. In addition, and as noted above, a reader's eyes tend to rest on (and absorb) the first and last sentences of a paragraph, so that last sentence is an ideal place to remind the reader of the conclusion the reader should reach.

Look at Example 19-gg. In that example, you can see how a final sentence repeating the paragraph's thesis helps drive home the point you want to make.

Example 19-gg · Repeating assertion in the final sentence

The statement made by Adams was mere conversation, and not a stop, because Adams could not reasonably believe his liberty was ever restrained at any point during his encounter with Officer Ephgrave. Like the officer who asked for identification in *Gilmore*, here Officer Ephgrave wanted to learn if Adams was involved in the bank robbery. In addition, as in *Gilmore* where the officer only requested information but did not alter the defendant's course, Officer Ephgrave did not alter Adams's course or prevent him from leaving. Officer Ephgrave asked Adams if he was planning to leave, to which he responded that he was not. Further, Officer Ephgrave said he would move his car whenever Adams needed to leave. According to Officer Ephgrave, Adams said, "Oh, okay. No problem." Therefore, Officer Ephgrave did not prevent Adams from leaving nor did he alter Adams's course. Adams could not reasonably believe that his liberty was restrained in this case, and the statement was mere conversation.

Although having a final sentence that reiterates the original thesis is helpful, occasionally such a sentence is overly repetitive or adds length unnecessarily. In those cases, omit the final, repetitive sentences.

4. Create sentence-level persuasion

Just as paragraphs can be shaped to present your arguments more persuasively, individual sentences can be shaped to present information more persuasively, too.

a. Locate information strategically

The same location guidelines that apply to paragraphs apply to sentences. Readers tend to absorb information at the beginning and end of sentences; readers pay less attention to information in the middle.

Compare Examples 19-hh and 19-ii. Can you see how the same information in different locations is emphasized differently? Thus, think carefully about what placement is most advantageous to your client and your client's argument when you are deciding where to locate information within a sentence.

Example 19-hh • Negative information beginning of the sentence

---

Even with a blood alcohol level of .13, Moore did not demonstrate outward signs of intoxication such as such as having slurred speech or smelling of alcohol.

Here the negative information appears at the beginning of the sentence, which is a point of emphasis. Because of the location of the negative information, the writer must counter the impact of the negative fact with specific facts to minimize the impact of this weakness.

Example 19-ii • Negative information in the middle of the sentence

---

Moore did not demonstrate outward signs of intoxication consistent with a blood alcohol level of .13 because she did not demonstrate outward signs of intoxication, her speech was not slurred and she did not smell of alcohol.

Here the negative information appears in the middle of the sentence, minimizing its impact and allowing the reader to focus more fully on the lack of outward signs of intoxication.

b. Use passive voice intentionally

While you will usually prefer to clearly name "who did what," at times, clearly naming "who did what" is not to your advantage. In situations when you want to minimize "who did what," you should use passive voice. You might prefer passive voice to active voice on two occasions: (1) when

Sidebar

As discussed in Chapter 16, *Editing and Polishing*, "passive voice" refers to whether a sentence clearly states who is doing the action. In a sentence with passive voice, the main actor is no longer the subject of the sentence.

you are focused on a specific action that occurred rather than the actor and (2) when you want to minimize the role of the actor.

First, you may want to use the passive voice when you are trying to focus on a specific action that occurred, rather than the actor who took the action. Say, for example, you are defending the corporate supervisor in a wrongful termination lawsuit. An issue arises regarding whether the decision to terminate went up the appropriate chain of command at the corporation. Given the facts of the client's case, as you can see in Example 19-jj, it may be strategically beneficial for the writer to focus on the fact that an authorized termination of employment occurred, rather than focus on who provided the authorization. In that case, passive voice is appropriate.

Example 19-jj • Passive voice

Termination of the plaintiff's employment was authorized.

Second, you may want to strategically use the passive voice when you want to minimize your client's role in a situation. Example 19-kk shows two versions of a sentence. If you are representing Asha, you may want to consider using the passive voice, as in version 1, versus the active voice, when describing the accident.

Example 19-kk • Using passive voice strategically to de-emphasize client's role

Version 1: The cyclist was hit in the intersection. (Passive)
Version 2: Asha hit the cyclist in the intersection. (Active)

Although passive voice has its uses, remember that, as a general rule, active voice is easier for your reader to absorb and makes for more evocative and stronger writing.

c. Use strong verbs to emphasize an action

Another persuasive technique in sentence-level persuasion is to select strong verbs that show action. Let's take the cyclist example in Example 19-kk and rewrite it using the active voice. In that case, you may state, "The driver hit the cyclist in the intersection." However, consider using stronger action verbs to give Example 19-kk more punch. Saying the driver collided, or crashed, elevates the impact and visual image in the sentence. Take care, though, that using vivid words does not cross into a characterization of the facts.

d. Use dependent clauses advantageously

Depending on your client's goals, you may want to de-emphasize information by putting it in a part of the sentence separate from the subject and verb. Readers tend to focus on that part of the sentence that contains the actual subject and verb. Dependent clauses are a wonderful way to acknowledge less than favorable information because the actual subject and verb of the sentence are located elsewhere in the sentence. Compare the two versions of the sentence in Example 19-ll. Can you see how the emphasis of the sentence changes as information moves from the dependent clause in version one to the main clause of the sentence in version two?

> **Sidebar**
>
> A dependent clause is a group of words that cannot stand on its own because it does not express a complete thought.

Example 19-ll · The dependent clause receives less emphasis

Version 1:   Although Moore's blood alcohol level was .13, she did not demonstrate any outward signs of intoxication.

Version 2:   Although she did not demonstrate any outward signs of intoxication, Moore's blood alcohol level was .13.

Be careful, though, about putting a dependent clause in the first sentence of a paragraph. The first sentence of a paragraph is emphasized. Thus, you may undo your efforts to de-emphasize information if that information appears at the beginning of a paragraph.

e. Scatter short sentences to add punch

Short sentences add punch. Use them. Sparingly.

Example 19-mm · Too many short sentences

Officer Ephgrave pulled into the lot. He parked his car behind the defendant's car. The defendant yelled to move the car. Officer Ephgrave walked over to the defendant. He asked if the defendant was planning to leave. The defendant said, "No, I'm going to sit a little longer." Officer Ephgrave said no other parking slots were available. Ephgrave said he could move. The defendant said, "Oh, okay. No problem."

Although we love a punchy, short sentence, a short sentence has punch only when placed in contrast to longer sentences. Thus, if every sentence you use is short and punchy, your motions and briefs will have a staccato effect. The resulting read will be bumpy, like riding a bike over cobblestones. A short sentence has more effect if interspersed among longer, flowing sentences.

And remember that if you use a short sentence, place the short sentence somewhere where it will be seen. The first or last sentences of a paragraph are good places for short, strong sentences.

VII. The Conclusion

In most instances, the Conclusion of a trial brief consists of a simple request for the relief the plaintiff seeks. For that reason, the Conclusion is also called the "prayer for relief." This final section is very short, often consisting of only one sentence in which you respectfully request that the court rule in your favor on the issues presented.

Example 19-nn • Conclusion

For the reasons stated in this brief, Defendant respectfully requests that this Court grant defendant's motion for summary judgment.

VIII. Editing and Polishing Your Brief

Most judges who write about what judges want use three words: edit, edit, edit.[15] Errors and incorrect statements distract from your argument and can even result in prejudice against your client. Edit to get rid of errors, but also to have short, crisp sentences that convey your points succinctly. Your judge reader will appreciate your directness and your attention to detail. Below, we have provided a short checklist to consider when you convert your objective memorandum into a persuasive brief; however, to ensure your brief is error free, create your own editing and polishing checklist after also considering the recommendations in Chapter 16, *Editing and Polishing*. The techniques discussed in that chapter are equally applicable to persuasive writing.

Most importantly, be aware of and follow any formatting guidelines or specific court rules. At best, ignoring the technical rules makes you look sloppy or unprofessional; at worst, disregard of court rules could get your case dismissed.

---

15. Painter, *supra* note 1, at 7 ("Edit, edit, edit, and edit again. Typos, bad grammar, and misplaced paragraphs (which were not such a problem before computers) simply take away from your argument. Remember—the only time you have the full attention of [the judge] is when the judge is reading your brief.").

- Formatting
  - Does your brief meet the jurisdiction's rules for
    - Section labels (Caption, Introduction, Statement of Facts, Argument, Conclusion)
    - Font size
    - Margins
    - Page limits
- Caption
  - Have you included the proper caption on the document with the names of the parties, county, court, and type of document placed correctly and spelled correctly?
- Introduction
  - Does your Introduction contain all topics required in your jurisdiction, e.g., the nature of the case, its procedural posture, and the kind of motion before the court?
- Statement of Facts
  - Does your Statement of Facts contain the facts used in your argument?
  - Do you use an organizational structure (chronological, topical, perceptual, or a combination) that best tells your client's story?
  - Have you included negative facts but minimized their impact through strategic location, providing less detail and pairing them with favorable facts?
  - Have you cited to sources (litigation documents or the court record) that support your facts?
- Argument
  - Theme
    - Is your theme carried throughout the Argument section, i.e., across claims, and does it conform to the procedural posture or substantive law that governs the case?
  - Organization
    - Have you included only your best claims and eliminated unimportant or frivolous claims?
    - Where you have a procedural claim, have you presented it first?
    - With substantive claims, wherever possible, have you presented the strongest argument first?
    - Do your roadmaps explain the order of the claims or legal arguments that will be addressed?
  - Point Headings
    - Are the point headings formatted correctly and consistently on each level of the argument?
    - Does the first point heading for each issue contain the action or conclusion you want the court to adopt and the primary reason the court should take that action or adopt the conclusion?
    - Do the sub-headings provide the reader with an overview of the legal and factual support for the point heading's conclusion?

- Do the sub-headings work together to present an outline of the argument?
  - Conclusion
    - Is the Conclusion a short statement that focuses on the relief your client seeks?
- Other
  - Have you followed the guidelines in Chapter 16, *Editing and Polishing*?
  - Have you checked your citations?
    - Check that each citation conforms to the appropriate format for your jurisdiction and law office.
    - Check for a full cite for each legal authority the first time it is relied on and check that every subsequent mention of that authority is a short citation.
    - Use a citation manual to check citation content.
    - Check pinpoint cites.
      - Check that each case citation has a pinpoint cite.
      - Check that each pinpoint cite references the correct page.
    - Check each "*Id.*" to ensure it correctly refers to the same authority and page referenced in the citation immediately before it.

Effective Memo: Adverse Possession

MEMORANDUM*

TO: Jamie Koenig, Partner

FROM: Allison Handler, Associate

DATE: June 12, 2018

SUBJECT: Neros' Adverse Possession Claim; 08-467A

QUESTION PRESENTED

Between 1979 and 1989 Linda and Tom Nero planted and maintained a vegetable garden, built a fence enclosing the garden, and cared for an apple orchard on a piece of property they believed to be theirs. Under Oregon common law regarding adverse possession, can the Neros acquire the disputed property from the actual owners?

> The Question Presented opens the memo and provides context for the reader by describing the legal question, the facts on which the legal question turns, and the law that will control. (Ch. 13)

SHORT ANSWER

Most likely, yes. To prove adverse possession, Oregon common law requires that the plaintiffs, the Neros, show through clear and convincing evidence that they had actual, open and notorious, exclusive, hostile, and continuous possession of the disputed property for ten years. Because they built a fence and maintained the fence, a garden, and an orchard, the Neros should be able to prove each element through clear and convincing evidence. Therefore, they should be able to acquire the disputed property through adverse possession.

> The Short Answer provides a clear, concise answer to the question and describes the fundamental reasons for the answer. (Ch. 13)

---

* This memorandum is based on a fact pattern created by Diana Pratt, formerly of Wayne State University Law School.

STATEMENT OF FACTS

The first paragraph of the Statement of Facts provides context
by introducing the main players
and their problem. (Ch. 14)

Our clients, Linda and Tom Nero, purchased property in semi-
rural Oregon in 1978. The Neros recently learned that a garden and
apple orchard they had always believed to belong to them, in fact, belongs to their neighbors, Ms. Welch and Mr. Bruce. The Neros would
like to claim the garden and apple orchard as their own.

This Statement of Facts is organized topically and chronologically. The first topic is the Neros'
activities. The second topic is
the activities of the actual owners. Within each topic, however,
the facts are organized chronologically. (Ch. 14)

Before their purchase, the real estate agent toured the property
with the Neros and delineated the property lines to them. The Neros'
undisputed property lines are the ranch fence to the north, the road to
the east, and the brook to the south. According to Mrs. Nero, she and
her husband believed that the western boundary ran in a straight line
from the turn in the ranch fence to the brook and that their property
included the apple orchard. The apple orchard is on the southern end
of the Neros' property and runs along the brook from the road to the

A Statement of Facts may
include important facts that
are unknown. (Ch. 14)

purported property line. The Neros do not have a copy of the deed
and did not survey the land before they bought it.

In 1979, the Neros began pruning the apple trees in the entire orchard. Late that spring, they cleared an area 60 feet wide by 100 feet
long in the northwest corner of the property. The area was bordered
by the ranch fence on the north and by the vacant lot, then still owned
by Dot Cramer, on the west. In the area that they cleared, the Neros
planted a vegetable garden and built a two-foot-high fence made of
chicken wire to protect the garden from rabbits. The garden and fence
were visible from the vacant lot.

During most years since 1979, the Neros planted the garden during
the growing season. In 1986, Mr. Nero suffered a stroke, and although the Neros began tilling, they did not plant the garden. That
year, they also hired a woman to care for the apple trees. From 1990
through 1993, Mr. Nero fell ill again, and they were unable to plant
the garden. During this period, the Neros also took out the fence and
did not prune the apple trees. Every year that the Neros had the garden, they harvested vegetables and fruits often grown in semi-rural
Oregon. Neighborhood children helped the Neros' children weed and
water the garden. The Neros permitted their neighbors to pick vegetables from the garden and take them home. In the winter months, the
Neros allowed the garden to go fallow.

Since 1978, Ms. Cramer has lived in Wisconsin and has not visited Oregon. Recently, she sold the vacant lot to Jennifer Welch and James Bruce, both of whom are lawyers. Last week, Mrs. Nero noticed orange survey stakes in the garden and in the orchard. The survey stakes are 55 feet east of the purported property line that the Neros have observed for the last thirty years. Mrs. Nero contacted the new owners of the western lot, and they informed her that they had conducted a survey of the property and boundaries to qualify for a construction loan. The Neros were shocked to learn that the garden and apple orchard that they had always believed to be theirs was not theirs. In our interview with the Neros, Mrs. Nero exclaimed, "That's part of our land!"

> *Here, the Statement of Facts examines a second topic, the activities of the actual owners. Within this second topic, the facts are, again, organized chronologically. (Ch. 14)*

The Neros have asked the firm to examine whether they can gain legal title to the garden and the apple orchard.

> *The last sentence describes the procedural posture of the clients' case and provides a transition to the Discussion section. (Ch. 14)*

DISCUSSION

The Neros will very likely be able to gain ownership of the disputed property, including the apple orchard and vegetable garden, through adverse possession. To acquire property by adverse possession plaintiffs must prove by clear and convincing evidence that their possession of the land was actual, open and notorious, exclusive, hostile, and continuous for a ten-year period. *Hoffman v. Freeman Land and Timber, LLC.*, 994 P.2d 106, 109 (Or. 1999). Oregon Revised Statute § 105.620 (2007), prescribes these same elements of adverse possession, but also requires that the land be possessed through an honest belief that the plaintiffs owned the land. The statute applies only to claims that vested and are filed after January 1, 1990. *Mid-Valley Resources, Inc. v. Engelson*, 13 P.3d 118, 121 n.2 (Or. Ct. App. 2000). The Neros should be able to prove that their claim vested by the late spring of 1989; consequently, their claim is not subject to Oregon Revised Statute § 105.620, and a review of their potential claim should analyze only those activities on the disputed land that occurred from 1979 through 1989. The element that will be most difficult for the Neros to prove is that their possession was open and notorious; however, they should be able to prove that element and the other common law elements of adverse possession and, therefore, gain ownership of the disputed property.

> *The Discussion section opens with an introduction that maps the legal analysis ahead. (Ch. 12)*
>
> *This introduction describes the general rule that governs a claim for adverse possession. By describing the general rule, the writer also alerts the reader to the elements that will be addressed in the remaining discussion. (Ch. 12)*
>
> *Because this introduction is long, the writer restates the conclusion at the end. Restating the conclusion reminds the reader where the argument is headed. (Ch. 12)*

In this memorandum, point headings separate the arguments about each element. (Ch. 12)

A. The Neros actually possessed the land because they used the land as an owner would by maintaining a fence and harvesting fruit trees.

The first element, actual possession, is addressed with one legal argument. One legal argument includes a conclusion, an explanation of the law, an application of the law to the client's facts and a final conclusion. (Ch. 6)

Here, the initial conclusion and explanation of the law are in the first paragraph, and the application and the final conclusion are in the next paragraph.

First, Mr. and Mrs. Nero can most likely prove actual possession. Plaintiffs can establish actual possession by showing that they used the land as an owner would use that particular type of land. *Zambrotto v. Superior Lumber Co.*, 4 P.3d 62, 65 (Or. Ct. App. 2000). Courts focus on the type of use for which the land is suited and do not necessarily focus on the amount of activity. *Id.* Plaintiffs in past cases have shown that they used the disputed land as an owner would in a variety of ways. *See, e.g., Davis v. Park*, 898 P.2d 804, 806-07 (Or. Ct. App. 1995); *Slak v. Porter*, 875 P.2d 515, 518 (Or. Ct. App. 1994). In *Davis*, the plaintiffs established that they used the disputed property as an owner would by showing that they used the disputed property as they did their adjoining land. 898 P.2d at 806-07. In *Slak*, the plaintiffs built a fence and planted vegetation and, in that way, proved actual possession. 875 P.2d at 518.

Mr. and Mrs. Nero should be able to prove that they had actual possession of their land because they used the disputed property in a manner that an owner would. Like the landowners in *Davis*, the Neros used the disputed land exactly as they did their adjacent land: In both parcels of land, they planted and maintained a garden and fruit trees. In addition, like the plaintiffs in *Slak* who showed actual possession by building a fence and planting vegetation, the Neros built a fence and planted vegetation in their garden and orchard. The Neros should, therefore, be able to prove that they actually possessed the disputed land.

B. The Neros' possession was open and notorious because they built a fence and used the land extensively and openly.

The next element addressed is "open and notorious." It is a more complicated argument because open and notorious possession can be proved in two ways. The first paragraph is a mini-roadmap that describes the two ways, eliminates one of the two as unavailable to the clients, and transitions into the argument that is open to them. (Ch. 12)

After proving actual possession, the Neros will have to demonstrate that their possession of the land was open and notorious. To prove that their possession was open and notorious, the plaintiffs must prove that the owners had notice that they were asserting title to the disputed property. *Slak*, 875 P.2d at 518-19. The notice may be actual or constructive. *Id.* at 519. Owners have actual notice when they are aware that their claim of the land is being challenged. *Id.* Because Ms. Cramer was unaware that the Neros were asserting a claim to the disputed land, she did not have actual notice. Instead, the Neros must prove that they gave constructive notice of their possession.

The Neros can probably establish constructive notice because they built a fence on the purported boundary and used the land extensively and openly. A plaintiff provides constructive notice of a claim when the plaintiff's use of the property would give the owner knowledge of the use and claim. *Hoffman*, 994 P.2d at 110. Intermittent use of the land may suffice if that use is sufficient to give notice. *Id.* In *Hoffman*, occasional livestock grazing and maintaining a fence were enough activity to establish constructive notice. *Id.* at 111-12. The use does not have to be visible from the owner's land to give the owner constructive notice. *Davis*, 898 P.2d at 807. For example, in *Davis*, the plaintiffs built a fence. *Id.* The court held that the fence gave constructive notice even though the fence was not visible from the owners' land because the plaintiffs and neighbors respected it as the boundary line. *Id.*; *see also Slak*, 875 P.2d at 519 (constructing a fence was the "classic example" of open and notorious use).

The Neros can likely show constructive notice to Ms. Cramer because they used the property in more than an intermittent manner. If, as in *Hoffman*, occasional use and maintaining a fence is sufficient to show constructive notice, then the Neros can show constructive notice because they built a fence and worked the land heavily during the growing season. In addition, the Neros' fence was always visible from the western lot, even when they allowed the garden to return to its natural state. In fact, the Neros' fence was the property line respected by the Neros and all of their neighbors. Because the non-visible fence in *Davis* provided constructive notice, the Neros' visible fence should provide notice, too.

Jennifer Welch and James Bruce, the current owners, might try to argue that the fence did not give constructive notice. One court failed to find constructive notice from an irregularly maintained fence that marked a portion of a purported property line; no evidence was offered to identify who built the fence. *See Zambrotto*, 4 P.3d at 64, 66. In another case, a fence was not sufficient notice because there were no "no-trespassing" signs or other indicators that the fence marked the property line. *Rayburn v. Coffelt*, 957 P.2d 580, 583 (Or. Ct. App. 1998). Ms. Welch and Mr. Bruce may argue that because the Neros'

The discussion about the "open and notorious" element has now been reduced to one legal argument—whether plaintiffs gave constructive notice of their possession. In the discussion about constructive notice, you can again see the essential components of a legal argument.

The argument begins with a conclusion and an explanation of the law in one paragraph.

The application and final conclusion are included in the next two paragraphs.

In this argument, the application includes a counter-analysis, which describes the argument the neighbors "might try to" make. (§ 8.3)

The counter analysis is effective because it fully explains the argument that might be made, then explains why that argument is ultimately weaker, and then returns to the conclusion that is most likely to prevail.

Notice that this counter-analysis is based on additional law. Although attorneys prefer to describe all the relevant law in the initial explanation of the law, sometimes an attorney will wait to describe the law that would support a counter-analysis. Here, the attorney waited. Likely, the attorney decided that the explanation of the law was sufficiently complicated and so it was better to delay explaining the law rather than risk overloading the reader.

fence covered only part of the disputed property line and did not have a "no-trespassing" sign posted on it, the fence did not give constructive notice.

Distinguishable from *Zambrotto*, the Neros can prove through testimony that they built and maintained their fence. Moreover, their fence was even with the western edge of the orchard and these two landmarks provided a clear boundary line. Unlike the *Rayburn* case, the Neros can point to their active cultivation of the land and their neighbors' knowledge of their activity, in addition to the fence, to prove that Ms. Cramer had constructive notice of their claim. To summarize, the Neros can likely prove they possessed the disputed property openly and notoriously because they built the fence, planted the garden, and cared for the orchard. Furthermore, their neighbors were aware of all these activities.

C. The Neros' possession of the property was exclusive because they allowed access in the same manner that an owner would.

Even a very short, one paragraph legal argument has the same components: a conclusion, an explanation of the law, an application, and a final conclusion. (Ch. 6)

Next, the Neros will be able to prove that their possession of the property was exclusive. To prove exclusivity, plaintiffs need prove only that they used the land as an owner would use the land. *Hoffman*, 994 P.2d at 110. "Actual physical exclusion" of all other people is not required; plaintiffs must merely prove "use consistent with ownership." *Slak*, 875 P.2d at 519. The Neros can easily prove that they used the property exclusively. Although the Neros permitted neighbors to harvest and keep some of the garden's vegetables, exercising the right to grant neighbors permission to take some of the vegetables shows use characteristic of an owner, which shows exclusive possession. Additionally, as discussed above, the Neros kept a garden, maintained an orchard, and built a fence, just as landowners in semi-rural Oregon often do. Accordingly, they can prove they used the property as an owner would and that their use was exclusive.

D. The Neros can prove hostility under a theory of pure mistake or by their subjective intent to own the land.

This more complicated legal argument, which has two alternative analyses, is introduced with an issue statement. (Ch. 9)

Fourth, the Neros must establish that their use of the disputed property was hostile. To prove hostility, the plaintiffs must have used the disputed land intending to occupy the land as its true owners and not in subordination to the true owner. *Faulconer v. Williams*, 964 P.2d 246, 251 (Or. 1998). Plaintiffs can prove hostility in two ways. *Hoffman*, 994 P.2d at 110. Plaintiffs can establish that "possession was under an honest but mistaken belief of ownership." *Id.* at 110 n.4. This is the "pure mistake" doctrine. *Id.* Alternatively, plaintiffs can establish that, subjectively, they intended to deprive the owners of ownership. *Id.* at 110.

1. The Neros can prove pure mistake because they believed their realtor's mistaken statements about the property line.

The Neros will very likely be able to prove hostility through "pure mistake" because they honestly believed they owned the disputed property. *Hoffman*, 994 P.2d at 110 n.4. A pure mistaken belief is one without conscious doubt. *Faulconer*, 964 P.2d at 252. If plaintiffs are aware that they may not own the disputed land, conscious doubt exists, and the plaintiffs cannot prove hostility by "pure mistake." *Id.* In *Davis*, the plaintiffs proved pure mistake by establishing that they had walked the fence line before buying the land, and as a result, had honestly and reasonably believed the fence line to be the property boundary. *Davis*, 898 P.2d at 805, 806. However, a plaintiff who thought the land was "all ours" but "did not know" whether the fence was actually the boundary was not able to rely on the pure mistake doctrine to prove her possession was hostile to the owner's claim. *Mid-Valley Resources*, 13 P.3d at 122.

The Neros will be able to prove that they honestly believed that they owned the disputed property and, therefore, that their use was hostile. The Neros, like the plaintiffs in *Davis*, toured the property before making the purchase and believed from the statements of their realtor that the property line was different from where it actually was. The Neros also did not have any doubts regarding their belief, unlike the plaintiff who testified in *Mid-Valley Resources*. In explaining her problem, Mrs. Nero exclaimed, "That's part of our land!" She seemed convinced that the disputed property belongs to her and her husband. The Neros made a reasonable and honest mistake regarding the boundary line; therefore, the Neros should be able to prove that, by pure mistake, their possession of the land was hostile.

To help the reader follow the argument, the writer has provided point headings that lead the reader through the argument. (Ch. 12)

2. The Neros can also prove they subjectively believed the land was theirs.

In the alternative, if Ms. Welch and Mr. Bruce find a neighbor to testify that the Neros had any doubt during the ten-year period, then the Neros would have to prove hostility through their subjective intent to own the land. *See Hoffman*, 994 P.2d at 110 (explaining subjective intent). To prove hostility without pure mistake requires the plaintiffs to demonstrate a subjective intent to own the property without any subservience to the true owners. *Faulconer*, 994 P.2d at 251. In *Slak*, the plaintiffs proved their subjective intent to own the property by constructing a fence and planting hedges, shrubs, and other plants on the disputed property. 875 P.2d at 520. By contrast, in *Hoffman*, even though the plaintiffs maintained an existing fence, grazed cattle, thinned timber, and posted "no-trespassing" signs, the court determined that the plaintiff did not establish his subjective intent to dispossess the owner of his land. 994 P.2d at 112. The court reasoned that the plaintiffs' activities on the land were activities of mere "convenience" rather than ownership. *Id.* In particular, the court noted that the plaintiffs did not construct the fence and did not use it to establish the property line. *Id.* Rather, the fence was built simply as a "convenience," to corral cattle. As a result, plaintiffs' activities in *Hoffman* were not sufficient evidence of hostility. *Id.*

The Neros' hostile use of the land is more similar to the plaintiffs' use of the land in *Slak* than in *Hoffman*, and thus shows their subjective intent to own the land. Like the plaintiffs in *Slak* who proved hostility by building a fence and planting vegetation, the Neros also built a fence and planted a garden. The Neros' claim is distinguishable from the claim in *Hoffman*. Where the plaintiffs in *Hoffman* could not prove hostility because they had not built the fence and the fence did not run along the border of their property, the Neros built their fence, and they built it along the northwest border of their property. Building the fence on the property border shows the Neros' subjective intent to possess the land by establishing a clear property boundary.

Ms. Welch and Mr. Bruce might argue that the Neros' activity was insufficient to prove hostility. They will argue that if the activity in *Hoffman*, maintaining a fence, grazing cattle, thinning the timber and posting a "no trespassing" sign, was insufficient then the Neros' use

Effective case illustrations are detailed about the facts that triggered the court's decision and the court's reasoning. (§ 7.2)

In the *Slak* case the trigger facts are that the plaintiffs constructed a fence and planted hedges, shrubs, and other plants. The writer does not identify any additional reasoning because the court in *Slak* did not do so.

In *Hoffman* the trigger facts were that the plaintiffs maintained but did not construct a fence, grazed cattle, thinned timber and posted a "no-trespassing" sign. This case illustration does explain the court's reasoning, as the court did in the case.

An effective case comparison is carefully structured to draw out the similarity or the distinction between the client's case and a prior case. (§ 7.2)

Here, the writer uses parallel structure to help the reader see the similarity between *Slak* and the client's case.

Then, the writer uses parallel structure again to help the reader see where the client's case is distinguishable from the *Hoffman* case.

should not be considered hostile; however, the Neros' activities on the disputed land were more than activities of convenience, as were those in the *Hoffman* case. The Neros actively used the land to grow a garden and apple trees, understanding that the land was their land. Thus, the Neros can likely show hostility through either pure mistake or subjective intent.

E. The Neros held the land continuously for ten years.

Finally, the Neros must prove that they possessed the land continuously. Oregon Revised Statutes § 12.050 requires the plaintiffs to prove continuous adverse possession for a ten-year period. Seasonal use may be "continuous." *Hoffman*, 994 P.2d at 110. In *Hoffman*, cattle grazing established continuous use because the grazing was "continuous use during the pasturing season." *Id*. Similarly, use may be continuous even if the plaintiff takes a "sabbatical." *Slak*, 875 P.2d at 519-20. In *Slak*, the court determined that the existence of a fence and vegetation on an easement over a ten-year period proved continuous possession, even though the plaintiffs may have taken sabbaticals that interrupted the ten-year period. *Id*. The court explained that whether the plaintiffs took a sabbatical was "of no consequence" to the continuity of their possession because the fence and vegetation had remained. *Id*.

The Neros can prove continuous use relying on both *Hoffman* and *Slak*. The seasonal use of land for livestock grazing is fundamentally similar to the Neros' seasonal use of land to keep a vegetable garden. Any argument that the Neros cannot prove ten continuous years of possession on the disputed property because the Neros did not plant the garden in 1986 or from 1990 to 1993 should fail. Like the plaintiffs in *Slak*, the Neros maintained a fence and cared for the orchard each year from 1979 to the present, even though they did not plant the garden every single year. Thus, the Neros' choice not to plant the garden in a few years is not detrimental to their claim because the fence and orchard are further evidence of continuous possession.

CONCLUSION

The Neros have a strong claim that, under Oregon common law, they gained title to the disputed land by adverse possession. Though the Neros will likely win if they file suit, they may want to consider alternatives to filing suit, since litigation is always a gamble and usually time

In an effective memo, the topic sentences of each paragraph lead the reader through the argument. (Ch. 16)

Return to the top of the Discussion section and read just the topic sentences of each paragraph to see how the topic sentences guide the reader through the argument.

The Conclusion begins by repeating the answer to the client's overall question. This conclusion then turns to practical considerations and advises how the client ought to proceed in light of the legal analysis and the realities of litigation. (Ch. 15)

consuming. Ms. Welch and Mr. Bruce may be eager to sell the disputed property at below market value rather than face litigation since a claim against the property may stall the pending construction loan. As lawyers, Ms. Welch and Mr. Bruce are likely to recognize the strength of the Neros' claim to the land. If they refuse the Neros' offer to buy the land, the Neros should first suggest mediation before filing suit.

Appendix B

Effective Memo: Intentional Infliction of Emotional Distress

To: Carla Izaguirre

From: Barry Davidson

Date: January 10, 2018

Re: Ethan McLaughlin's claim for intentional infliction of emotional distress; Client matter 2275-09924

Question Presented

Under North Carolina's common law, which holds an actor liable for intentional infliction of emotional distress, can a person recover for emotional distress when a former relative posts to the Internet accusations of sexual and financial misconduct, causing the person to lose an important client and seek psychiatric treatment?

In this Question Presented, the writer uses the under/does/when format to establish the jurisdiction, legal question, controlling rule of law, and key facts in this case. (Ch. 13)

Brief Answer

Most likely, yes. Under North Carolina common law, the tort of intentional infliction of emotional distress includes three elements: (1) the defendant's extreme and outrageous conduct (2) that is intended to and (3) does cause the plaintiff severe emotional distress. A jury can find extreme and outrageous conduct because Dixon repeatedly, and seemingly without any foundation, publicly portrayed our client as a

In this Brief Answer, the writer sets out the rule of law — the elements of the claim — and briefly gives a reason why each element is met. (Ch. 13)

---

* The fact pattern used in Appendices B and C is based on a fact pattern obtained from the Legal Writing Institute's Idea Bank. The original author of the problem is unknown. The samples presented were based in part on memoranda by various students, but they have been significantly revised to highlight writing techniques that tend to make legal memoranda more or less effective.

sexual predator, adulterer, tax evader, and dead-beat dad. These same facts will likely show the requisite intent to harm McLaughlin. Finally, medical documentation of McLaughlin's treatment for emotional problems following the postings will satisfy the third element of severe emotional distress.

Facts

The introductory paragraph in the Statement of Facts names the players in the action and gets to the crux of the controversy. (Ch. 14)

Our client, Ethan McLaughlin, is seeking recovery for emotional damages after Sharon Dixon, his former sister-in-law, posted allegations of sexual and financial misconduct on her website.

McLaughlin is the co-owner of a marketing firm that works with clients in high-tech industries. Dixon maintains a website dedicated to sharing her sexual exploits. She generally uses pseudonyms when referring to family on her site; however, in a posting that discussed the family's negative response to her lifestyle, Dixon mentioned McLaughlin and his son by name. Soon thereafter, an important business client contacted McLaughlin with concerns about his connection to the site.

This Statement of Facts is organized chronologically; however, individual paragraphs identify distinct ideas within the chronology. For example, the writer creates a separate paragraph for each posting, the responses following each posting, and McLaughlin's conversation with the attorneys about the factual foundation for the postings. (Ch. 14)

McLaughlin then sent an email to Dixon that requested she remove references to his son from her site. Dixon complied with the request. She then, however, posted a second entry. That entry asserted that McLaughlin had sex with her 15 years earlier when Dixon was a minor, that he made sexual advances towards both Dixon and another sister, that he "cheated on his ex-wife Sue" (Dixon's other sister), and that he failed to pay back taxes and child support. The posting also included McLaughlin's home address and email address. Dixon urged those reading the posting to "let him know how you feel about what he's done."

This Statement of Facts is effective because it describes critical facts in detail. For example, review the description of the second entry on Dixon's website. Now suppose the writer had simply stated "Dixon posted derogatory information on her website about McLaughlin's relationships with her, his wife, and a sister." Such a description would leave the reader wondering "what kind of derogatory information?" and would not be sufficiently detailed to support the legal analysis below. (Ch. 14).

On the morning after Dixon posted the second entry, McLaughlin began receiving harassing emails and phone calls expressing outrage at his purported actions. That night, a brick with a death threat attached was thrown through his living room window, and McLaughlin began suffering from insomnia and loss of appetite. He also missed work and feared losing the client who was aware of the site.

McLaughlin then sent another email to Dixon asking her to please remove the postings. He described the harassment and his insomnia. He also mentioned he risked losing a client because of her postings.

In response, Dixon posted a third entry accusing McLaughlin of attempting to bribe her and characterizing him as "a potentially violent … and mentally unstable monster." After this third posting, he continued to receive harassing phone calls and emails. He calculates he has received over one hundred such emails and phone calls. He also lost the major business account.

Two weeks after the final posting, McLaughlin began seeing a psychiatrist. McLaughlin now requires daily therapy and anti-depressant medications. He has amassed almost five thousand dollars in doctor's bills and medication costs. (Copies of his medical bills are included in his file.) He reports that his insomnia and loss of appetite persist, and he is embarrassed by his ongoing need for psychiatric treatment.

McLaughlin tells us that the postings have little factual basis. He says that he never made any advances on Dixon or the sister; that he was never physically intimate with either; that he never cheated on his ex-wife; and that, although he was once late in paying his taxes and his child support, he has now paid both in full. McLaughlin believes that Dixon "had a crush on him" when they were younger and that she is still angry that he did not reciprocate her feelings.

> The last paragraph of the Statement of Facts establishes the procedural posture and transitions into the substantive issues of the memo. (Ch. 14)

McLaughlin now wants to know if he can bring a successful claim against Dixon for damages to his business and to his mental health.

Discussion

McLaughlin can most likely bring a successful claim against Dixon for intentional infliction of emotion distress. To support a claim of intentional infliction of emotional distress, a plaintiff must prove the following elements: "(1) extreme and outrageous conduct, (2) which is intended to cause severe emotional distress, and (3) does cause severe emotional distress." Woodruff v. Miller, 307 S.E.2d 176, 178 (N.C. Ct. App. 1983) (citing Dickens v. Puryear, 276 S.E.2d 325, 335 (N.C. 1981)). Mr. McLaughlin can prove each element of the claim.

> The roadmap paragraph is concise. It simply sets out the overall conclusion, the governing rule, and then the bottom-line conclusion for the whole case. Notice that the governing rule does triple-duty: It states the governing rule, identifies the elements in the governing rule, and indicates the order in which the elements will be discussed. No additional background information is necessary. (Ch. 12)

A. Dixon's public accusations that McLaughlin engaged in sexual misconduct and failed to pay taxes and child support constitute extreme and outrageous conduct.

> Notice how the writer uses "working" headings — each heading states the element and the ultimate legal conclusion of the section that follows. (Ch. 12)

A jury could find Dixon's conduct to be extreme and outrageous. To be considered extreme and outrageous, conduct must "go beyond all possible bounds of decency, and [be] regarded as atrocious, and utterly intolerable in a civilized community." Briggs v. Rosenthal, 327

> The writer's first argument begins here when she states her bottom-line conclusion. (Ch. 9)

The explanation of the law sets out the general rules for the element before going into more specific rules in the second paragraph. (§7.1)

S.E.2d 308, 311 (N.C. Ct. App. 1985) (citing Restatement (Second) of Torts §46 cmt. h (1965)). "Mere insults, indignities, threats, annoyances, petty oppressions, or other trivialities" are insufficient. Id. A court determines, in the first instance, whether the evidence could establish extreme and outrageous conduct. Hogan v. Forsyth Country Club Co., 340 S.E.2d 116, 121 (N.C. Ct. App. 1986). A jury, however, decides whether the conduct was in fact extreme and outrageous. Id.

In making the initial determination about the sufficiency of the evidence, a court will consider many factors, including the following: the offensiveness of the conduct, the persistence of the conduct, the defendant's purpose in acting, and the forseeability of injury to the plaintiff. West v. King's Dept. Store, Inc., 365 S.E.2d 621, 625 (N.C. 1988) (offensiveness, persistence, and forseeability); Briggs v. Rosenthal, 327 S.E.2d 308, 311-12 (N.C. App. 1985) (offensiveness, purpose, and foreseeability); Woodruff v. Miller, 307 S.E.2d at 178 (offensiveness, purpose, and persistence).

The explanation of the law continues with three case illustrations: Woodruff, West, and Briggs.

These case illustrations are lengthy enough that each merits its own paragraph.

Notice that each case illustration starts with a hook, which tells the reader the main point the case will illustrate. (§7.2)

When a defendant persistently distributes derogatory information for no purpose other than spite, the evidence is sufficient to establish extreme and outrageous conduct. Woodruff, 307 S.E.2d at 178. In Woodruff, the plaintiff was the superintendent of the local school system. Id. at 177. Thirty-years ago, he had participated in a college prank and been arrested. Id. The defendant, after losing two recent lawsuits to the superintendent, posted copies of the superintendent's thirty-year old arrest record on the "Wanted" board at the local post office and on bulletin boards at the local high school. Id. The defendant also showed the "Wanted" poster to at least one prominent citizen in the community. Id. A jury found that the defendant had intentionally inflicted emotional distress on the superintendent. Id. In upholding the jury decision, the Woodruff court explained that distributing derogatory information as part of a "calculated, persistent plan to disturb, humiliate, harass and ruin the plaintiff for no other purpose but defendant's own spiteful satisfaction" was extreme and outrageous conduct. Id. at 178.

Likewise, an unrelenting, unwarranted, public attack is also sufficient to establish extreme and outrageous conduct, especially when the defendant is warned that the attack is likely to cause injury. West, 365 S.E.2d at 625-26. In West, a store manager accused plaintiffs, a husband and wife, of stealing merchandise. Id. at 622-23. His accusations continued in public, for over seventy-five minutes, even though the husband and wife explained that they had bought the merchandise; presented a receipt for the merchandise; and found the cashier, who acknowledged selling the merchandise to them. Id. at 623. During much of this time, the store manager knew that the wife had recently been hospitalized and, according to her husband, "could not handle the aggravation and anxiety" of the accusations. Id. The court held that the "unrelenting attack, in the face of explanation," was sufficient to establish extreme and outrageous conduct. Id. at 625. In reaching its conclusion, the court particularly noted that the store manager continued his attacks even after being warned about the wife's delicate health. Id. at 625.

Conversely, unflattering information published to provide an "honest, sincere and sensitive portrait" of a person is not extreme and outrageous conduct. Briggs, 327 S.E.2d at 312. In Briggs, the plaintiffs were parents whose son had recently died. They sued the defendants, a journalist and a newspaper publisher, after the newspaper published an article about their recently deceased son. Id. at 309. The article described the son's drinking and anti-social behavior but, also, described the son as an "immensely substantial person, as fine, as dignified … as important as any solid citizen I ever met." Id. The Briggs court found that the article, although offensive to the parents, was "honest, sincere and sensitive." Id. at 312. The court then upheld the lower court's decision to dismiss the case. Id.

In this case, a jury could find that Dixon's conduct was extreme and outrageous. McLaughlin can present as strong a case as the plaintiff did in Woodruff. [1] To begin, Dixon's accusations were as derogatory as those in Woodruff. Accusing a person of sexual misdeeds, adultery, tax evasion, failure to pay child support, and being a "potentially violent" and "mentally unstable monster" is likely more offensive than disseminating a 30-year old arrest record that arose out of a college prank. [2] Moreover, Dixon's attacks were just as persistent as the attacks in Woodruff. The defendant in Woodruff, made his at-

---

Here, the writer had a choice about whether to include a second case illustration that shows what constitutes extreme and outrageous conduct. Although the second case is similar to Woodruff, described above, it draws out the effect of a warning, which the first case does not. Because it brings out additional information, the writer made a reasonable choice to include the second case illustration.

Notice how the writer illustrates the parameter of the rule, using two cases to show when extreme and outrageous conduct is present, and one case to show when it is not.

Notice that the client is never mentioned in the explanation of the law.

The application begins here when the writer turns to the client's case. (Ch. 8)

The comparison to Woodruff is complex. It requires three factual comparisons, labeled 1, 2 and 3. Notice that an "overt statement" of why the client's case is like the prior case begins the first two comparisons. That overt statement is then supported by specific facts. (§ 8.2) tack repeatedy available to the public by posting his "Wanted" poster in the post office and local high school and showing it to a local citizen. Similarly, Dixon made her three attacks repeatedly available to the public by posting them all to the Internet and refusing to remove them. **[3]** Finally, if they are in fact baseless, her accusations seem to have "no other purpose but … spiteful satisfaction." Because in Woodruff a jury found, and a court approved the finding, that the defendant's conduct was extreme and outrageous, a jury could also properly find that Dixon's conduct was extreme and outrageous.

McLaughlin can also establish that Dixon's conduct was as extreme and outrageous as the store manager's conduct in West. In West, the store manager could foresee that his repeated attacks were likely to cause injury because he had been warned about the wife's poor health. Similarly, here, McLaughlin told Dixon in an email that, as a result of her second posting, he was being harassed, that he could not sleep or eat, and that he worried he would lose an important client. Nevertheless, she kept her statement posted publicly on the Internet and she added the final posting describing McLaughlin as a "monster." Assuming that her postings were as unwarranted as the store manager's attack in West, a jury could also find that Dixon's conduct was extreme and outrageous because she persisted despite knowing the harm her statements were causing.

Dixon may, however, argue that her postings were warranted. Dixon may argue that she acted out of a desire to warn the public about a dangerous man. She will likely rely on Briggs to argue that simply because her postings were unflattering does not mean that a jury could find they were extreme and outrageous. Rather, she will argue that her postings are an "honest, sincere" effort to describe a person and, therefore, they are insufficient to establish extreme and outrageous conduct. If all the evidence shows that her postings were warranted, a court might hold, as a matter of law, that the postings were an honest, sincere effort to describe a person, as it did in Briggs.

All the evidence, however, does not show that her postings were warranted. McLaughlin would testify that he never made any advances on Dixon or the sister, that he was never physically intimate with either, and that he never cheated on his ex-wife. McLaughlin ad-

---

Sidebar notes:

After establishing the factual similarities to the prior case, the writer explains the legal significance of the similarities. (§ 8.2)

Notice that the application follows the same order as the explanation of the law. In the explanation of the law, the writer explains Woodruff, West, and then Briggs. The application follows that same order. (§ 8.4)

In this counter-analysis (§ 8.3), the writer explains what Dixon could argue, the legal basis for that argument, and why that argument will, ultimately, not prevent McLaughlin from proceeding to trial.

Notice that the writer explained Briggs, the basis for the counter-analysis, when he explained the other case law. When possible to do so, your reader will find it helpful if you explain at one time all the law relevant to a single element. (§ 8.3) mits that he was once late in paying his taxes and his child support; however, he states that he has now paid both in full. Given McLaughlin's testimony, a court is unlikely to hold, as a matter of law, that the postings were an honest, sincere effort to describe a person, but rather allow a jury to make that decision. Here, sufficient evidence exists for a jury to conclude that her conduct was extreme and outrageous.

B. Dixon attacked McLaughlin with the intent to cause harm.

In addition to establishing extreme and outrageous conduct, Dixon's second and third postings will likely establish she intended to cause harm. A defendant intends to cause harm if she acts "with the intention of causing emotional distress" or if she acts with "reckless indifference to the likelihood that emotional distress may result." Briggs, 327 S.E.2d at 312 (citing Restatements (Second) of Torts §46 cmt. i (1965)). Frequently, a court will rely on the same evidence to determine intent as it did to assess whether the conduct could be extreme and outrageous. See West, 365 S.E.2d at 626; Woodruff, 307 S.E.2d at 178. For example, ◄— the court in West referred back to the store manager's "unrelenting attack, in the face of explanation" and warnings about the wife's weak health to establish recklessness. West, 365 S.E.2d at 626; see also Woodruff, 307 S.E.2d at 178 (citing the same "calculated, persistent plan" as the evidence supporting each element of the claim).

Similarly, the same evidence that establishes Dixon's extreme and outrageous conduct also establishes her recklessness. As noted above, McLaughlin warned Dixon of the harm her postings had already caused and the harm they were likely to cause in the future. Nevertheless, like the store manager in West, Dixon continued with her accusations. Assuming that her allegations are without merit, a court is likely to find that her baseless, "unrelenting attack," especially in the face of warnings about the harm she was causing, is sufficient for a jury to find that she acted with reckless indifference to the likelihood she would cause McLaughlin emotional distress.

C. Dixon's attacks caused McLaughlin severe emotional distress requiring extensive medical treatment.

McLaughlin will be able to prove that Dixon's postings caused him to suffer severe emotional distress. Severe emotional distress is "any emotional or mental disorder … or any other type of severe and dis-

In explaining that "[f]requently courts will rely on the same evidence to determine intent" the attorney is making an implicit theme explicit. No court had previously stated that fact, but it is a trend that the writer saw as he reviewed the case law. By making explicit what would otherwise remain obscured, the writer adds value for his client and the attorneys with whom he is working. (§ 7.1)

In this second element, the writer does not have a parameter of the rule, but uses one case, West, to establish a threshold of behavior. (§ 8.2)

Notice how the writer re-integrates the language from the West case illustration so that the reader can see how the prior case law supports his analysis. (§ 8.2)

This explanation of the law does not include any case illustration because the writer believed that the rule was sufficiently clear without additional case law. (§7.2)

Accordingly, the application below is rule-based reasoning (§8.1) rather than analogical reasoning (§8.2).

abling emotional or mental condition which may be generally recognized and diagnosed by professionals trained to do so." <u>Waddle v. Sparks</u>, 414 S.E.2d 22, 27 (N.C. 1992) (adopting the standard used for the tort of negligent infliction of emotional distress set out in <u>Johnson v. Ruark OBGYN Assoc.</u>, 395 S.E.2d 85, 97 (N.C. 1990)). A plaintiff does not have to show physical injury. <u>Dickens</u>, 276 S.E.2d at 335-36. Claims of severe emotional distress may, however, be challenged for lack of medical documentation showing treatment for conditions related to emotional distress. <u>Waddle</u>, 414 S.E.2d at 28.

In the present case, McLaughlin can provide the necessary medical documentation to show severe emotional distress. He is receiving daily therapy and taking anti-depressant medication prescribed by his doctor. Copies of his medical bills (included in his file) show that he has amassed medical costs totaling almost five thousand dollars.

No counter-analysis is needed because the element is easily established: McLaughlin can document his emotional distress and he can show a connection between Dixon's Internet postings and his distress. (§8.3)

He can also establish that Dixon's postings caused his emotional distress. His insomnia and loss of appetite began the evening after the second posting, the same evening a brick was thrown through McLaughlin's window. He began seeing a psychiatrist, within two weeks of the third posting. Before Dixon's postings, he had never required this type of treatment. His record of medical treatment following the postings should be sufficient for a jury to find that he suffered severe emotional distress because of Dixon's postings.

Conclusion

Because McLaughlin can establish all three elements of the tort of intentional infliction of emotional distress, McLaughlin can bring a successful claim against Dixon.

Less Effective Memo: Intentional Infliction of Emotional Distress

To: Carla Izaguirre

From: Jane Malscrit

Date: January 10, 2018

Re: McLaughlin claim for intentional infliction of emotional distress; Client matter 2275-09924

Question Presented

Under North Carolina's common law, does a person recover from a former relative who posted derogatory information about him causing him loss of a business client and emotional disturbance?

Brief Answer

Yes. Our client will probably be able to prove intentional infliction of emotional distress because it is likely that the defendant's conduct was extreme and outrageous, that the defendant intended to cause, and did cause, the plaintiff severe emotional distress.

Facts

McLaughlin is the co-owner of a marketing firm, I-Tech Marketing, that works with clients in the nano-technology and pharmaceutical industries. Dixon maintains a website dedicated to sharing her sexual exploits. She generally uses pseudonyms when referring to family on her site. In postings that discussed the family's negative response to her lifestyle, Dixon mentioned McLaughlin and his son by name. McLaughlin sent an email to Dixon that requested she remove references to his son from her site. Dixon complied with the request;

The memorandum heading looks less professional because the entries are not aligned: The "C" in "Carla" should be directly above the "J" in "Jane."

This Question Presented is less effective because it does not identify the governing rule and it lists few key facts. Thus, the Question Presented fails to give a precise overview of the issue. (Ch. 13)

This Brief Answer is less effective because it does not explain the elements that need to be satisfied or explain why the elements are satisfied. (Ch. 13)

The writer jumps into detailed facts before giving the reader context. The Statement of Facts would be more effective if it opened by introducing the parties and the crux of their problem. (Ch. 14)

Notice that irrelevant details, such as the name of McLaughlin's firm and the kinds of clients he works with, will be distracting. The detail will make the reader believe the information is important when, in fact, it is not.

The postings should be described in more detail because those facts are critical to the analysis below.

however, she posted a second entry on the site accusing McLaughlin of making sexual advances on a variety of people and failing to pay back taxes and child support. The posting also included McLaughlin's home address and email address. Dixon urged those reading the posting to "let him know how you feel about what he's done."

On the morning after Dixon posted the second entry, McLaughlin began receiving harassing emails and phone calls expressing outrage at his purported actions. That night, a brick with a death threat attached was thrown through his living room window, and McLaughlin began suffering from insomnia and loss of appetite. He also missed work and feared losing the client who was aware of the site. McLaughlin then sent another email to Dixon asking her to please remove the postings. He described the harassment and his insomnia. He also mentioned he risked losing a client because of her

Notice how the lack of paragraphs makes it more difficult to read the Statement of Facts.

postings. In response, Dixon posted a third entry accusing McLaughlin of attempting to bribe her and characterizing him as "a potentially violent ... and mentally unstable monster." After this third posting, he continued to receive harassing phone calls and emails. He calculates he has received over one hundred such emails and phone calls. He also lost the major business account. Two weeks after the final posting, McLaughlin began seeing a psychiatrist. McLaughlin now requires daily therapy and anti-depressant medications. He has amassed almost five thousand dollars in doctor's bills and medication costs. (Copies of his medical bills are included in his

The last paragraph ends abruptly, without giving the procedural posture or explaining what the client would like the attorneys to do. (Ch. 14)

file.) He reports that his insomnia and loss of appetite persist, and he is embarrassed by his ongoing need for psychiatric treatment. McLaughlin tells us that the postings have little factual basis.

Discussion

The roadmap paragraph is okay. It would be more effective if the initial conclusion identified what claim will be successful. (Ch. 12)

Our client's claim will likely be successful. North Carolina follows common law guidelines to determine the presence of intentional infliction of emotional distress. The three elements necessary to establish such a claim are (1) extreme and outrageous conduct, (2) that is in-

The writer's explanation that the first element will be more difficult to establish is helpful: it helps the reader understand the relative strengths and weaknesses of the client's case. ⟶

tended to cause severe emotional distress, and (3) does cause severe emotional distress. Woodruff v. Miller, 307 S.E.2d 176, 178 (N.C. 1983) (citing Dickens v. Puryear, 276 S.E.2d 325, 335 (N.C. 1981)). In the present case, the first element, that the conduct was extreme and outrageous, will be most difficult to prove. However, our client can easily establish the second and third elements.

I. Extreme and Outrageous Conduct. ←————————————

A jury could find Dixon's conduct to be extreme and outrageous. "As to what is sufficiently outrageous to give rise to liability, the comments in the Restatement are instructive. Liability has been found only where the conduct has been so outrageous in character, and so extreme in degree, as to go beyond all possible bounds of decency, and to be regarded as atrocious, and utterly intolerable in a civilized community." Briggs v. Rosenthal, 327 S.E.2d 308, 311 (N.C. Ct. App. 1985) (citing Restatement (Second) of Torts § 46 cmt. h (1965)). "The liability clearly does not extend to mere insults, indignities, threats, annoyances, petty oppressions, or other trivialities. The rough edges of our society are still in need of a good deal of filing down, and in the meantime, plaintiffs must necessarily be expected and required to be hardened to a certain amount of rough language, and to occasional acts that are definitely inconsiderate and unkind. There is no occasion for the law to intervene in every case where someone's feelings are hurt." Id. at 311.

A court will consider many factors, including the following: the offensiveness of the conduct, the persistence of the conduct, the defendant's purpose in acting, and the forseeability of injury to the plaintiff. West v. King's Dept. Store, Inc., 365 S.E.2d 621, 625 (offensiveness, persistence and forseeability); Briggs v. Rosenthal, 327 S.E.2d 308 (N.C. App. 1985) (offensiveness, purpose, and foreseeability); Woodruff v. Miller, at 178 (offensiveness, purpose, and persistence).

In Woodruff, the plaintiff was the superintendent of the local school system. Woodruff, at 177. The defendant, after losing two lawsuits to the superintendent, posted copies of the superintendent's thirty-year old arrest record on the "Wanted" board at the local post office and on bulletin boards at the local high school. Id. The defendant also showed the "Wanted" poster to at least one prominent citizen in the community. Id. Thirty-years ago, the superintendent had participated in a college prank and been arrested. Id. At the time of the posting, the plaintiff's record was not being considered or reviewed by any person or agency for any reason or purpose. Id. No one but the defendant was interested in the plaintiff's back-

---

The point heading does not "work" because it does not tell the conclusion or the reason for the conclusion.

In addition, Roman numerals are reserved for main legal questions. An element is a sub-part of a dispositive issue, it should be designated with a capital letter, such as "A," "B," or "C." (Ch. 12)

The writer explains the rules through two long quotations. The long quotations create problems because they include more information than the reader needs; have a different voice than the writer's; and leave the impression that the writer doesn't understand the law, but merely copied rules onto the page. To be more effective, quotations should be used sparingly, with only key language quoted. (§ 7.1)

Key components of the citations are missing in each cite—the parenthetical with court and date, the pinpoint cite, and the volume and reporter.

The case illustration lacks a hook. As a result, the reader will have to guess at the point that the writer wants to make in providing this case illustration. (§ 7.2)

These facts showing that no one but the defendant was interested in the plaintiff's record are never relied on below. The writer needs to consider whether these facts are excess here or should be put to use in the application.

ground. <u>Id</u>. A jury found that the defendant had intentionally inflicted emotional distress on the superintendent. <u>Id.</u>

In <u>West</u>, a store manager accused plaintiffs, a husband and wife, of stealing merchandise. <u>Id</u>. at 622-23. He publicly accused the husband and wife even though they proved that they had purchased the merchandise. <u>Id</u>. at 623. The store manager also knew that the wife had recently been hospitalized. <u>Id.</u> The court held that the "unrelenting attack, in the face of explanation," was sufficient to establish extreme and outrageous conduct. <u>Id.</u> at 625. In reaching its conclusion, the court particularly noted that the store manager continued his attacks even after being warned about the wife's delicate health. <u>Id.</u> at 625.

By contrast, in <u>Briggs</u>, the plaintiffs were parents whose son had recently died. They sued the defendants, a journalist and a newspaper publisher, after the newspaper published an article about their recently deceased son. The article described the son's drinking and anti-social behavior but, also, described positive aspects about the son. The <u>Briggs</u> court found that the article, although offensive to the parents, was "honest, sincere, and sensitive."

McLaughlin's case is comparable to <u>West</u>. In <u>West</u>, the store manager could foresee that his repeated attacks were likely to cause injury because he had been warned about the wife's poor health. Similarly, here, McLaughlin told Dixon in an email that, as a result of her second posting, he was being harassed, that he could not sleep or eat, and that he worried he would lose an important client. Nevertheless, she kept her statement posted publicly on the Internet, and she added the final posting describing McLaughlin as a "monster." Assuming that her postings were as unwarranted as the store manager's attack in <u>West</u>, a jury could also find that Dixon's conduct was extreme and outrageous because she persisted despite knowing the harm her statements were causing.

McLaughlin can also argue that his case is like <u>Woodruff</u>. To begin, Dixon's accusations were as derogatory as those in <u>Woodruff</u> because she accused McLaughlin of sexual misdeeds, adultery, tax evasion, failure to pay child support, and being a "potentially violent" and "mentally unstable monster." Moreover, like the defendant in <u>Woodruff</u>, Dixon made her attacks repeatedly available to the public by posting

---

Margin notes:

Again, this case illustration lacks a hook. As a result, the reader will struggle to see the point the case illustrates and how this case relates to the prior case.

Also, compare the level of detail used to describe <u>West</u> here and the level of detail in the memo in Appendix B. Which illustration will help the reader better visualize why the court held the store manager's conduct was extreme and outrageous?

In addition to the problems mentioned above, the writer has forgotten to provide citations.

The application begins here. The sentence introducing the application is less effective because it does not indicate the conclusion the application will reach.

Notice that the writer applies the law in a different order than it was explained. Because an attorney assumes the explanation of the law sets out a clearly marked path for stepping through an analysis, an attorney will be surprised if the application follows a different path. Thus, your application should follow the same order as your explanation. If your application varies the path, warn your reader. (§ 8.4)

The comparison to <u>Woodruff</u> has two significant problems. First, the comparison fails to remind the reader of the key facts in <u>Woodruff</u>. Without those facts, the reader cannot see the similarities that the writer does. Second, the writer does not explain the legal significance of the comparison.

them all to the Internet and refusing to remove them. Finally, if they are in fact baseless, her accusations seem to have "no other purpose but … spiteful satisfaction."

Dixon may, however, argue that her postings were warranted. If all the evidence shows that her postings were warranted, a court might hold, as a matter of law, that the postings were an honest, sincere effort to describe a person, as it did in <u>Briggs</u>. McLaughlin would testify that he never made any advances on Dixon or the sister, that he was never physically intimate with either, and that he never cheated on his ex-wife. McLaughlin admits that he was once late in paying his taxes and his child support; however, he states that he has now paid both in full. Given McLaughlin's testimony, the evidence is sufficient for a jury to conclude that Dixon's conduct was extreme and outrageous.

This counter-analysis is less effective because it does not explain Dixon's counter-argument before explaining why the counter-argument is weak. A counter-argument should be described as fully as a primary argument so the reader can assess its strengths and weaknesses. (§ 8.3)

Notice, also, that the writer relies on facts that were not included in the Statement of Facts. This will surprise an attorney and make the writer seem less organized.

II. Intent to Cause Harm.

McLaughlin can establish that Dixon intended to cause him harm. A defendant intends to cause harm if he intends to cause emotional ← distress or acts with reckless indifference to the likelihood that he will cause emotional distress. <u>Briggs</u>, 327 S.E.2d at 312 (citing Restatements (Second) of Torts § 46 cmt. i (1965)).

Here, the failure to give a case illustration is a problem. Without a case illustration, the reader cannot visualize what intent to cause harm or recklessness looks like.

The same evidence that establishes Dixon's extreme and outrageous conduct also establishes her recklessness or intent to cause harm. As noted above, McLaughlin warned Dixon of the harm her postings had already caused and the harm they were likely to cause in the future. Nevertheless, Dixon continued with her accusations. A court is likely to find that her baseless, "unrelenting attack," espe- ← cially in the face of warnings about the harm she was causing, is sufficient for a jury to find intentional infliction of emotional distress.

Because the writer failed to provide a case illustration in her explanation of the law, her analysis here seems unsupported by the law.

The conclusion should be about the element being examined: intent. A conclusion about the overall claim of intentional infliction of emotional distress is too broad.

III. Severe Emotional Distress.

The next issue is whether Dixon's postings caused McLaughlin to suffer severe emotional distress. Severe emotional distress is "any emotional or mental disorder … or any other type of severe and disabling emotional or mental condition which may be generally recognized and diagnosed by professionals trained to do so." <u>Waddle v. Sparks</u>, 414 S.E.2d 22, 27 (N.C. 1992) (adopting the standard used for the tort of negligent infliction of emotional distress set out in <u>Johnson</u>

Introducing the client in the explanation of the law will confuse the reader. Moreover, including McLaughlin's name makes the citations to the last two sentences inaccurate: Neither the Dickens court nor the Waddle court ever mentioned McLaughlin. (Ch. 6)

The writer has omitted some of the facts that would show that Dixon caused severe emotional distress, such as his insomnia and loss of appetite. Perhaps the writer believes the relevant facts are obvious or known to the senior attorney; however, this memo acts as a record of all the facts that are relevant to each element, and so the writer should do the work of gathering all the relevant evidence in one place.

The conclusion to the client's overarching question should be in the first sentence of the paragraph where it is easy to find.

v. Ruark OBGYN Assoc., 395 S.E.2d 85, 97 (N.C. 1990)). McLaughlin does not have to show any physical injuries. Dickens, 276 S.E.2d at 335-36. However, if McLaughlin fails to provide medical documentation showing treatment for conditions related to emotional distress, his claim of emotional distress may be challenged. Waddle, 414 S.E.2d at 28.

In the present case, McLaughlin can provide the necessary medical documentation to show severe emotional distress. He can also establish that Dixon's postings caused his emotional distress. He began seeing a psychiatrist within two weeks of the third posting, and he had never before required this type of treatment. This record of medical treatment following the postings should be sufficient for a jury to find that he suffered severe emotional distress because of Dixon's postings.

Conclusion

McLaughlin can establish that Dixon caused his severe emotional distress, that she acted with reckless indifference as to whether her conduct would cause severe emotional distress, and that her conduct was extreme and outrageous. Therefore, McLaughlin can bring a successful claim against Dixon.

Effective Complex Memo: Factor Analysis in Fraud Claim

MEMORANDUM*

TO: Pendry Porten, Partner

FROM: Matthew Houston, Associate

DATE: January 20, 2018

RE: Fraudulent misrepresentation in purchase of B&B

QUESTION PRESENTED

Under the Oregon common law claim of fraud, can a buyer of a bed and breakfast, who had previously owned bed and breakfasts listed on the National Register of Historic Places, justifiably rely on a seller's misrepresentation about a property's National Historical Register status, if relevant information about whether the property was listed on the National Historic Register was available by calling or visiting the county records office?

The writer crafted this Question Presented using the "under/does/when" format (Ch. 13). Another effective option, especially when a case has many or complicated facts, would be to use the "statements and questions" format. (Ch. 13, Examples 13-K through 13-N)

BRIEF ANSWER

Most likely, no. Contracting parties are expected to use reasonable diligence to investigate a representation before justifiably relying on it. Whether a party has justifiably relied on a representation depends on the analysis of these primary factors: (1) the ability of the plaintiff to obtain sufficient information to assess the truth of the representation and (2) the relative sophistication of the parties. Courts may evaluate a third factor, the time pressure put

The Brief Answer provides a short and clear answer to the Question Presented and describes factors that the court will weigh in deciding the case along with the legally significant facts on which the court's decision will likely turn. (Ch. 13)

---

* Problem created by Hadley Van Vactor, Visiting Assistant Professor at Lewis & Clark Law School. We would also like to thank Professor Van Vactor and Professor Judith Miller (Lewis & Clark) for their instructive comments on this sample memorandum.

on the plaintiff, in relation to the other two factors. Courts evaluate these factors on a sliding scale—the more accessible the information (especially when little or no time pressure is imposed) or the more equally sophisticated the parties, the greater duty a party will have to use reasonable diligence to investigate the representation. Here, Mr. Volkova could have obtained the information from the county title office by either calling or visiting the office, and he had more than two weeks to get the information. However, even though Mr. Volkova's previous real estate transactions show him to be sophisticated, he is less sophisticated than Ms. Gilbert. On balance, the factors of justifiable reliance do not weigh in Mr. Volkova's favor, and he likely had a greater duty to use reasonable diligence to investigate the representation. Thus, Mr. Volkova is unlikely to prove he justifiably relied on Ms. Gilbert's misrepresentation.

FACTS

The first paragraph in the Statement of Facts provides context by introducing the major players and the legal controversy. (Ch. 14)

Our client, Dmitry Volkova, recently purchased a bed and breakfast from Mieke Gilbert in Portland, Oregon. Mr. Volkova thought that the building was listed on the National Register of Historic Places (National Register), based on a statement that Ms. Gilbert made to him. Because the bed and breakfast is not, in fact, listed on the National Register, Mr. Volkova wishes to sue Ms. Gilbert for fraud and either rescind the contract or get monetary damages. Had the property been listed on the National Register, Mr. Volkova would have had benefits such as better advertising and patronage, federal grants and tax credits, and a higher property value.

Notice how the writer uses legally significant facts, background facts, and emotional facts. (Ch. 14) With a complex memo, the critical facts should be described in sufficient detail, while the background and emotional facts should be limited to those necessary to the analysis or to provide adequate context for the story. As you read through the analysis, note how the writer applies all of the legally significant facts.

Ms. Gilbert and her late husband owned the Portland bed and breakfast for ten years. After Ms. Gilbert's husband passed away, she decided to sell the building. Ms. Gilbert has had a twenty-year career as a real estate agent, and she was her own listing agent for the building. She has helped clients buy or sell hundreds of homes and other buildings over the years, including at least a dozen historical properties.

Mr. Volkova has made his living by owning bed and breakfasts. He owned three of them before buying the Portland property, and he purchased each because of its unique architecture and enhanced caché from being listed on the National Register. Mr. Volkova wanted to move to Oregon from Maine, so he searched for a new building to purchase in Portland to run as a bed and breakfast. When he saw Ms. Gilbert's listing, he was excited to find the Tudor-style building, which was already being used as a bed and breakfast. It reminded him of his favorite building in Maine. The listing, however, did not specify when the building was built. Mr. Volkova contacted Ms. Gilbert, who offered to show him the building as soon as he could be in Portland. Mr. Volkova flew to Portland the following day to see the building.

Based upon the architecture and craftsmanship of the building, Mr. Volkova believed the building was historical and asked Ms. Gilbert if it was listed. She assured him that the bed and breakfast was registered on the National Register, and she promised to bring him the documentation at the closing. She did not, and could not, do so because the property was not, in fact, listed on the National Register. Because of Ms. Gilbert's reputation and past experience with historical building transactions, Mr. Volkova did not think it necessary to investigate the precise date the structure was built, nor conduct further research on the requirements for a national historic designation.

Both Mr. Volkova and Ms. Gilbert wanted to close the sale quickly. The time between their initial meeting and closing was fifteen days. During that time, Mr. Volkova did not research the building's construction date or seek to verify Ms. Gilbert's statement that the house was on the National Register. Also, because Mr. Volkova was unfamiliar with Portland's administrative procedures for real estate, he did not obtain a title report in advance of the closing. In addition, because he believed the house was on the National Register, and was not familiar with Oregon's property system or the places to obtain information—a process that can be confusing—he did not search the Oregon property registry. Mr. Volkova explained to us that because Ms. Gilbert was a seemingly trustworthy and experienced realtor and because of time constraints, he relied solely on her promise that she would provide documentation about the National Register.

At the closing, Mr. Volkova was provided with a title report, which did include the building's date of construction. Mr. Volkova, however, said that he did not see the building's date of construction. When signing so many papers, he "was focused on the financial pieces of the

The last paragraph acts as a transition between the Statement of Facts and the Discussion section where the substantive legal issues are analyzed. (Ch. 14)

transaction and didn't pay attention to the date the structure was built." Mr. Volkova learned after closing that the building was not listed on the National Register. He also learned that buildings must be at least 50 years old, among other things, to qualify for the National Register. His bed and breakfast was only forty-eight years old and thus not eligible for National Register status. Mr. Volkova has retained our law firm to bring a claim for fraud.

DISCUSSION

Mr. Volkova's claim is unlikely to be able to prove that he justifiably relied on Ms. Gilbert's promise to provide documents relating to the National Register. To prove fraud, a plaintiff must prove the following elements: (1) the defendant made a material misrepresentation, (2) the defendant knew it was false, (3) the defendant intended the plaintiff to rely on the representation, (4) the plaintiff justifiably relied on the representation, and (5) the plaintiff suffered damages as a result. *Murphy v. Allstate Ins. Co.*, 284 P.3d 524, 530 (Or. Ct. App. 2012). As you requested, this memo will address only whether Mr. Volkova justifiably relied on Ms. Gilbert's promise to provide National Register documents.

In this case, Mr. Volkova cannot prove that he justifiably relied on the seller's statement that the house was listed on the National Register. In a fraud claim, a party has a duty to use reasonable diligence to investigate the truth of a representation before relying on it. *Murphy*, 284 P.3d at 530. Whether a party used "reasonable diligence" usually depends upon two circumstances: (1) the ability of the plaintiff to obtain sufficient information to assess the truth of the representation, and (2) the relative sophistication of the parties. *Id.* at 530-31. Courts may also evaluate a third circumstance of whether pressure was exerted on the plaintiff to enter into the contract quickly. *Id.* Courts evaluate these factors on a sliding scale—the more accessible the information, the more equally sophisticated the parties, and the less pressure to execute the transaction quickly, the greater the duty a party will have to use reasonable diligence to investigate the representation. *Id.*

Courts will thus consider whether, under the totality of the circumstances, the plaintiff conducted sufficient due diligence to

Because this memo is more complex, the roadmap consists of several paragraphs. Notice how the writer moves from general rules to specific rules. The first paragraph provides the governing rule and then focuses the reader on the "justifiable reliance" element of the rule—the only element at issue. The second paragraph provides the overall rule for analyzing justifiable reliance and introduces the factors or circumstances that the court will weigh in analyzing such a claim. The remaining paragraphs in the roadmap provide a description about how the courts will weigh and analyze the factors, as well as the writer's bottom-line prediction regarding the likelihood of success of the claim (Ch. 12).

Factor analyses can be arranged in different ways. (Ch. 4 & Ch. 12) The writer could have chosen to discuss all three factors simultaneously by organizing the discussion as a single CREAC, with multiple paragraphs of rules and explanations followed by multiple paragraphs of analysis. The writer might also have chosen to analyze each factor separately.

Here, the writer discusses two factors jointly (factors that rely on many of the same facts), and then analyzes the last factor separately. Look at the details of the writer's organization:

R/E: Combines the rules and explanations for the factors of **accessibility** and **time pressure** because the courts often integrate that analysis

Continued on next page

justifiably rely on the misrepresentation. *Or. Pub. Employees Ret. Bd. v. Simat, Helliesen & Eichner*, 83 P.3d 350, 360 (Or. Ct. App. 2004); *see Murphy*, 284 P.3d at 530. In reaching a conclusion about whether a plaintiff has justifiably relied, courts seek to balance competing concerns: On the one hand, "a person who intentionally deceives another should not be allowed to profit from the deception[;] on the other hand . . . the person deceived, as an autonomous individual, should be responsible for protecting his or her own interests." *Murphy*, 284 P.3d at 530. When forced to choose, however, Oregon courts have adopted the policy that it is better to protect the person deceived than to protect the deceitful. *Johnson v. Cofer*, 281 P.2d 981, 985 (Or. 1955).

In this case, however, because the information was accessible within the allotted time frame and because of Mr. Volkova's business sophistication, a court will likely conclude that Mr. Volkova had a higher duty to use reasonable diligence to investigate the truth of Ms. Gilbert's representation. He, therefore, did not justifiably rely on the representation and cannot meet the elements of fraud.

A. Because Mr. Volkova could easily obtain the information that would have revealed the truth of Ms. Gilbert's statement and had ample time to investigate, these factors will not weigh in his favor.

Mr. Volkova could have easily accessed information that would have revealed the truth about the building's status on the National Register. To determine whether the information was accessible to the plaintiff, courts consider the circumstances surrounding the transaction. Two important circumstances are (1) the extent to which the information was in the defendant's control and (2) whether the pressure to enter the contract precluded the plaintiff from investigating the truth of a representation. *Murphy*, 284 P.3d at 530. Although one court, the *Murphy* court, examined pressure as an independent factor, *id.*, prior courts examined time pressure when assessing the extent to which information was accessible, *see e.g., Miller v. Protrka*, 238 P.2d 753, 759 (Or. 1951). Because the ability to obtain information often turns on the amount of time available to investigate, this memo examines these circumstances together.

A court is less likely to conclude that a plaintiff has justifiably relied if relevant information is easily accessible. *Id.* at 758-59, 761. In

A: Combines analysis for factors of **accessibility** and **time pressure**

C/A: Counter-analysis for both factors

R/E: Next addresses rules and case explanations for **sophistication** factor

A: Analysis for **sophistication** factor

C/A: Counter-analysis for **sophistication**

C: Overall prediction of claim's success and recommendations for client

Because factor analyses can be organized differently, think about the most effective organization for your assignment. The most effective organization may depend upon how the courts have analyzed these issues, as well as how the factors are implicated by the facts of your client's case.

Notice how the writer uses working subheadings to introduce the accessibility and time factors. (Ch. 12)

Although factors are often analyzed separately, here, because the circumstances of accessibility and time pressure rely on similar facts and law and because the courts' analyses are often integrated in the case law, the writer discusses these factors together rather than separately. This strategic choice helps avoid repetition for the reader, and allows the reader to understand more precisely how the courts use a "sliding scale" analysis that considers accessibility and time pressure in tandem — the more accessible the information is to the buyer, the less time will be reasonably needed for the buyer to investigate.

When constructing a case explanation, sometimes the writer has to decide how to refer to the individual players in the previous cases. Using proper names in a case explanation may not be helpful because a reader could be confused by multiple names. That confusion is even more likely later in the application paragraphs when the actions of individuals in the prior cases are compared to the actions of the individuals involved in your client's case. To avoid this confusion, consider designating individuals by the roles that they play in the factual story (for example using "buyer" and "seller"). If the parties' roles will not work, you may use the players' status in litigation ("plaintiff" and "defendant"). (Ch. 7).

Miller, the plaintiffs bought a motel from the defendants. *Id.* at 755-56. Before the purchase, the defendants, through their realtor, had provided an "Estimated Income" statement, which asserted the motel was "taking in $56,000 a year." *Id.* at 756. After purchasing the motel, the plaintiffs concluded that the motel was not, in fact, "taking in $56,000 a year," and they alleged fraud. *Id.* In considering whether the plaintiffs had justifiably relied on the "Estimated Income" statement, the court noted that the business records "permitted an easy determination of exactly the true condition of the business for any given fiscal year." *Id.* at 757. The plaintiffs, however, had failed to look at those books. *Id.* at 756. The court noted that "the [plaintiffs] were not refused an opportunity to look at the books, which were all on the premises" when the plaintiffs inspected the motel. *Id.* at 761. Accordingly, the ease with which the buyers might have inspected the books weighed against the buyers when the court considered whether the buyers had justifiably relied on the "Estimated Income" statement.

Even when all the relevant information is not accessible, if a purchaser has *enough* information to assess the truth of a statement, he is obligated to take "reasonable precautions to protect his own interests." *Vukanovich v. Kine*, 342 P.3d 1075, 1083 (Or. Ct. App. 2015). In *Vukanovich*, the plaintiff, a property developer, partnered with the defendant, another developer, to purchase a property. *Id.* at 1080. When their joint offer fell through, the defendant told the plaintiff he was no longer interested in the property. *Id.* Relying on the statement that the defendant was no longer interested in the property, the plaintiff was slow to submit another offer, and when he did, he offered a low price. *Id.* Meanwhile, the defendant put together a competing bid and ultimately bought the property. *Id.* The court noted that at the time the plaintiff made his low offer, the plaintiff knew that the joint effort had ended, the market was competitive, the defendant was a competitor who had previously acted alone to purchase the property, and that plaintiff distrusted the defendant's business practices. *Id.* at 1083. Although the truth of the defendant's intentions was in the exclusive control of the defendant, plaintiff had access to enough relevant information to assess the truth of the defendant's statement. *Id.*

If a seller actively impedes a buyer's efforts to obtain relevant information, a court is more likely to conclude that the buyer justifiably relied on the seller's assertion. *Johnson*, 281 P.2d at 985. In *Johnson*, the plaintiffs agreed to take over a lease for a rooming house with thirty-two rooms. *Id.* at 984. The person selling the lease knew the city intended to shut down the rooming house due to building code violations; however, when the plaintiffs asked about permits, explaining they wanted to continue running the building as a rooming house, the seller assured the plaintiffs the building could continue to be used as a rooming house. *Id.* at 982-83. When the plaintiffs saw a fireman talking with the seller and discussing permits, the plaintiffs again asked whether the seller had the proper permits. *Id.* The seller assured the plaintiffs that the fireman simply had a personal prejudice against the seller and that the building was properly licensed as a hotel. *Id.* Six days after the deal closed, city officials ordered the plaintiffs to bring the building up to code or vacate within 30 days. *Id.* at 984. The seller's conduct, which the court described as a "steady course of action [intended] to dissuade the plaintiffs from making contact with the city," contributed to the court's decision that the plaintiffs justifiably relied on the seller's words. *Id.* at 985.

As a second circumstance, courts may look at the time pressure put on a plaintiff to enter a contract; the greater the time pressure, the less reasonable diligence a plaintiff must demonstrate to prove the justifiable reliance element. *See Murphy*, 284 P.3d at 530. Thus, if the necessity to enter a contract precludes a plaintiff from investigating the truth of a representation, a plaintiff is more likely to have justifiably relied. *See id.* at 529, 531. In *Murphy*, the plaintiff had suffered extensive water damage to his home. *Id.* at 531. The plaintiff met with the insurance adjuster and the insurance company's chosen contractor, both of whom told the plaintiff that the repair work would not require a building permit, which was false. *Id.* The contractor also told the homeowner that he needed to sign the contract immediately—that day in fact—to prevent further damage to the home, and the insurance adjuster agreed. *Id.*

In assessing whether the information was accessible, the court noted that the information was available because the homeowner could have "easily" asked a city building inspector about the need for a permit; however, the court also noted that the information might have been difficult to obtain quickly, perhaps involving "a complex or difficult search." *Id.* at 531 (relying on *Soursby v. Hawkins*, 763 P.2d

With this hook, the writer is focusing on the second factor in the analysis. The writer uses the term "circumstance" instead of "factor" to track the language the courts use.

725, 730 (Or. 1988)). The court found that the insurance adjuster and contractor exerted pressure on the plaintiff to sign the work authorization quickly so they could prevent further water damage. *Id.* at 531. Based on that pressure, the court determined a jury could infer that even if the information was readily available, "plaintiff simply could not be said to have had any opportunity to conduct an independent investigation before signing the contract." *Id.*

On the other hand, if the time pressure is not great, the plaintiff's duty to investigate with reasonable diligence will not be excused. *Miller*, 238 P.2d at 587-88. In *Miller*, explained previously, the plaintiffs (buyers of a motel) had three weeks between the property inspection and the transaction's closing date to review the hotel's books and discover the accuracy of the defendants' statements regarding the motel's financial viability. *Id.* at 588-89. As part of the court's assessment on the accessibility of the information, the court reasoned that three weeks' time was a sufficient time period for the buyers to have inspected the books. Accordingly, when the time pressure is a matter of weeks, not days, and the necessity to enter a contract is not so immediate, time pressure will not alleviate the plaintiff's duty to investigate with reasonable diligence.

On balance, a court is likely to conclude Mr. Volkova had the ability to obtain relevant information and that no time pressure alleviated his burden to use reasonable diligence in investigating. The information here was available and accessible with minimum effort. This case is like *Miller* because an examination of readily available information would have revealed the truth of the seller's statement. Just as the records in *Miller* "permitted an easy determination" of the true condition of the motel's business, Mr. Volkova could have found the age of the bed and breakfast and the criteria for a building to be listed on the National Register. A simple online search reveals the criteria necessary for a building to be listed on the National Register. The title information for the bed and breakfast, acquirable at the county recorder's office and presented to Mr. Volkova at the closing, would have revealed that the bed and breakfast was less than 50 years old and was unlikely to be on the National Register.

Even if Mr. Volkova did not have all the necessary information available to him, Ms. Gilbert will argue that he had *enough*

Notice how the writer illustrates the parameter of the rule by setting forth case illustrations of both *Murphy* and *Miller*. This choice gives the reader a more complete picture of the spectrum of the rule. (Ch. 7.2)

In this analysis, the writer uses analogical reasoning techniques to effectively compare and contrast the facts of this case with those of prior cases, such as *Miller* and *Vukanovich*.

information to know he needed to act to protect his interests. Mr. Volkova is similar to the plaintiff in *Vukanovich* who knew that he was working in a competitive market and that his former partner was now a competitor. Likewise, Mr. Volkova knew—or should have known—that Ms. Gilbert was working in her own interest to sell her own property. Although Mr. Volkova did not have any indication that the Ms. Gilbert would act fraudulently, he knew that the sale was an arm's length transaction. Thus, like the plaintiff in *Vukanovich* who should have acted to protect his own interest from a competitor, Mr. Volkova should have acted to protect his own interest.

Further, Ms. Gilbert did nothing to impede Mr. Volkova from obtaining the relevant information. Unlike the defendant in *Johnson* who repeatedly lied to the buyer about whether the hotel was licensed and attempted to "dissuade the plaintiffs from making contact with the city," Ms. Gilbert made her representation once and never said anything further about the building's National Historic status. Moreover, she did not dissuade Mr. Volkova from obtaining accurate title information or researching the home's history. Thus, this case is distinguishable from *Johnson*.

In addition, the court is unlikely to find time pressure a circumstance that lessened Mr. Volkova's duty to investigate. Mr. Volkova had ample time to obtain the relevant information because, even though both parties wanted to close the deal quickly, they had more than two weeks to finish the transaction and no exigent circumstance demanded immediacy of action. This case does not present the same immediacy as in *Murphy*, where the homeowner had no choice but to enter the contract at once, lest he incur more water damage. A judge might determine that entering a contract within one day is reasonable when the plaintiff needs to act to prevent further property damage, but less reasonable when the only pressure is that both parties want to complete a transaction quickly. Similarly, although time pressure was not explicitly discussed as a separate factor in *Miller*, the court nonetheless recognized that because the transaction took several weeks, no time pressure affected the plaintiff's duty to investigate. The plaintiffs in *Miller* had at least three weeks to investigate the finances of the motel, which the court noted was ample time. Similarly, Mr. Volkova had two weeks to investigate whether the

This paragraph provides the reader with a more nuanced understanding of the rule. Specifically, the previous paragraph focuses on the availability of the information, and this paragraph focuses on the amount of information Mr. Volkova had.

Notice how the author uses straightforward topic sentences to guide the reader through the discussion. This technique can help the reader understand and retain the information more easily. (Ch. 16)

building was on the National Historic Register. For these reasons, a court is likely to conclude that the information needed to assess the truth of Ms. Gilbert's statement was accessible and that Mr. Volkova had time to obtain it.

Mr. Volkova's best argument is for the court to adopt the analysis in *Murphy*, and hold that the complexity of obtaining specific information, coupled with the short time frame for the transaction, made the information insufficiently accessible. In *Murphy*, the court noted that, although information about whether permits were needed was available, the information would have been difficult to obtain, possibly involving a "complex or difficult search." Mr. Volkova, who lived in Maine, was arguably not familiar with Oregon's property system or the places to obtain information, making the search more difficult. In addition, Mr. Volkova could argue that, like the plaintiff in *Murphy* who was under pressure to sign the contract to avoid additional water damage, Mr. Volkova was also under pressure to complete the sale quickly. Ms. Gilbert expressed a desire to complete the sale of the bed and breakfast quickly, and a competitive market always puts pressure on a buyer to complete a sale quickly. Thus, even though the information was available, it was not sufficiently available due to the pressure and complexity of the search for someone not familiar with Oregon's property system. However, Mr. Volkova's argument may not be persuasive to the court because the facts indicate that the transaction was expedited solely because *both* parties wanted a quick closing. Many businesspeople wish to complete transactions quickly, and a court is unlikely to excuse the duty to conduct reasonable diligence simply because a businessperson wants to close a deal quickly. Accordingly, these factors will likely weigh against the conclusion that Mr. Volkova justifiably relied on the representation.

Here the author analyzes the remaining circumstance considered by the courts — the parties' relative business sophistication.

B. Although Mr. Volkova had experience with commercial real estate transactions, he was less sophisticated than Ms. Gilbert on the specific property and the requirements for a National Register listing.

The second factor, which addresses the parties' relative sophistication, also weighs against the conclusion that Mr. Volkova justifiably relied. When a court assesses the relative sophistication of the parties, it considers the extent to which each party is capable of evaluating facts about a representation. *See Murphy*, 284 P.3d at 530; *Vukanovich*, 342 P.3d at 1082. When parties have similar levels of business sophistication, each party is expected to use reasonable diligence to evaluate the truth of a representation made by the other party. *Miller*, 238 P.2d at 758-59.

Parties have comparable sophistication, and thus a greater duty to use reasonable diligence to investigate, when they are generally in the same line of business. *Id.* at 759-60. In *Miller*, discussed above, the court concluded that in a deal to sell a rooming house, the plaintiffs and defendants were "engaged in a generally similar business, that is, selling living accommodations to the public." *Id.* at 759. The plaintiffs owned and operated an apartment house. *Id.* at 761. The defendants operated the 30-unit rooming house, which was for sale. *Id.* at 755. The court noted that the plaintiffs had been successful enough in their business venture to make a cash down payment of $25,000 (in 1955 dollars). *Id.* Accordingly, the court concluded that the plaintiffs were sophisticated enough to evaluate the facts available to them regarding the representation of the motel's annual revenue. *Id.* at 759, 761.

In assessing the relative sophistication of the parties, a court will also consider whether one party has less knowledge or experience regarding the specific subject matter, and a less sophisticated party has less of a burden to ascertain the truth of a representation before justifiably relying on a statement. *Murphy*, 284 P.3d at 530. In *Murphy*, an insurance company's claims adjuster, and a contractor hired by the insurance company, informed the plaintiff that a permit was not required to repair water damage to the plaintiff's property. *Id.* at 527. The plaintiff had worked in construction for most of his life and knew construction work required permits. *Id.* at 531. The court concluded that a reasonable jury could come to opposite conclusions: a jury could infer that "plaintiff's construction experience makes him a sophisticated party . . . or it could reach the opposite inference based on the fact that nothing in the record suggests that plaintiff ever had to assess the need for building permits or had to obtain them as part of his construction employment." *Id.* Under those circumstances, the facts were sufficient for a jury to conclude that the plaintiff was the less sophisticated party.

Here the author adds case support with this explanatory parenthetical. Because the *Johnson* case adds a bit more nuance to the rule in *Murphy*, but does not support the direct proposition, the author uses the signal "see also." This signal introduces the legal proposition in *Johnson* (regarding how the sophistication of the parties affects the duty to disclose) and how that proposition supports the *Murphy* court's analysis on the same topic.

Id.; see also Johnson, 281 P.2d at 985 (explaining that the more sophisticated seller in a transaction has "a duty to fully disclose" relevant facts to avoid deceiving less experienced purchasers).

A court could conclude that although Mr. Volkova is sophisticated, he is less sophisticated than Ms. Gilbert in both knowing the requirements of a National Registry listing and in buying and selling historical properties. Thus, his duty to use reasonable diligence to investigate the representation was not as great. First, even though Mr. Volkova had bought three historical properties previously, he was not in the same line of business as Ms. Gilbert. Ms. Gilbert was an active real estate agent, and her business was helping clients buy and sell homes. By contrast, although Mr. Volkova had previously bought three historical buildings, his business was running bed and breakfasts. Thus, unlike the plaintiffs in *Miller,* whose level of sophistication gave them a higher duty to evaluate the seller's representations about annual revenue because they were in the same line of business, Mr. Volkova's relative sophistication is not equal to or greater than that of Ms. Gilbert. Thus, even though Mr. Volkova had limited familiarity with buying historical properties, he was not in the same line of business and consequently had far less experience in such transactions.

Second Mr. Volkova could also argue that Ms. Gilbert had a duty to disclose relevant information to him because she knew more about the specific subject matter than he did. As a real estate agent, she was presumably familiar with criteria used to designate a building as historical, and as the listing agent for her own property, she knew more about this particular house and whether documentation proving that it was listed on the National Register of Historic places actually existed. Moreover, Ms. Gilbert had extensive experience with this type of transaction. In more than a decade of business, Ms. Gilbert had sold hundreds of properties, at least twelve of which were historical properties. Mr. Volkova, by contrast, had bought only three historical buildings, all of which had been listed on the National Register before he purchased them. Mr. Volkova has never sought an historical designation for a building, nor has he ever had to verify such a designation. Like the buyer in *Murphy* who had been in the construction business but had never been in charge of assessing the need for work permits, Mr. Volkova had never had to assess whether a building was, in fact, on the National Register. Further, just as the seller in *Johnson* had a duty to disclose that the building was not permitted to function as a hotel when the buyers "were inexperienced," Ms. Gilbert had a duty to disclose that the bed and breakfast was not listed on the National Register. Thus, a jury could conclude that Mr. Volkova was the less sophisticated party because Ms. Gilbert knew more about the specific subject matter at issue.

Because the parties are not in the same line of business and because Ms. Gilbert had far more knowledge of the subject matter in the transaction, Mr. Volkova likely has less sophistication than Ms. Gilbert. Thus, Ms. Gilbert had a duty to disclose the age of the building and its ineligibility for National Register listing. Consequently, a court's concern for protecting the deceived rather than the deceitful might weigh in favor of concluding that the more sophisticated party, in this case Ms. Gilbert, had a duty to disclose relevant information to the less sophisticated party, Mr. Volkova.

C. On balance, the factors probably weigh against concluding that Mr. Volkova justifiably relied on Ms. Gilbert's statements.

While Mr. Volkova has a viable argument for the sophistication factor, on balance, the court is likely to conclude that Mr. Volkova did not justifiably rely on Ms. Gilbert's assertion that she had documents proving the bed and breakfast was on the National Register. Courts will consider whether, under the totality of the circumstances, the plaintiff conducted sufficient due diligence to justifiably rely on the misrepresentation. *Or. Pub. Employees Ret. Bd. v. Simat, Helliesen & Eichner*, 83 P.3d 350, 360 (Or. Ct. App. 2004); *see Murphy*, 284 P.3d at 530. The three factors of accessibility of information, time pressure, and sophistication of the parties, when evaluated on a sliding scale, weigh against Mr. Volkova. As explained above, the relevant information was accessible to Mr. Volkova, and he had ample time to access it. In addition, although he may be less sophisticated than Ms. Gilbert, his general sophistication balanced with the accessibility of the information and the lack of time pressure, mean that Mr. Volkova had a higher duty to investigate Ms. Gilbert's statement with reasonable diligence. Because he did not use reasonable diligence to investigate

Here, the writer weighs all three factors (accessibility, time pressure, and sophistication) as they relate to the facts of Mr. Volkova's case and predicts the most likely outcome of a claim. (Ch. 12)

the representation, he did not justifiably rely on it. Thus, Mr. Volkova will not likely be able to bring a successful fraud claim.

RECOMMENDATION

Because the writer gave the reader a bottom-line prediction in the previous paragraph, the writer uses this last paragraph to recommend the next practical steps for the client. (Ch. 15)

We should inform Mr. Volkova that he will have difficulty proving that he justifiably relied on Ms. Gilbert's misrepresentation. If he wishes to proceed, we will need to gather more facts relating both parties' experience with sales of historical properties, what our client actually knew about the property, and whether our client made any effort to verify the property's designation on the National Register of Historic places. If the client does want to bring a claim, Ms. Gilbert might be willing to settle the matter to avoid lengthy and expensive litigation.

Glossary

ALWD Manual. The common name for the *ALWD Citation Manual: A Professional System of Citation*, which sets out a system for citing authority in legal documents.

Analogical Reasoning. Reasoning by which an attorney argues that a client's case is similar enough to a previous case that the outcome in the previous case should control the present case or that a client's case is different enough from a previous cast that the outcome of the previous case does not control.

Analysis. The process of evaluating the law on a particular topic.

Background facts. Facts that provide context for understanding the underlying problem in a legal conflict, but that are not necessary to resolve the legal issue.

Balancing test. The evaluation of a governing rule composed of factors.

Bluebook. The common name for *The Bluebook: A Uniform System of Citation*, which sets out a system for citing authority in legal documents.

Brief Answer. In a memorandum of law, the Brief Answer provides the bottom-line answer to each Question Presented discussed.

Caption. The part of a court document that identifies the parties, the court in which the case is being heard, the docket number, and the title of the document.

Case illustration. An explanation of how a rule was applied in a prior case. An illustration will usually include a hook, trigger facts, the court's holding, and the court's reasoning.

Case law. Any judicial decision rendered by a court, whether construing a statute or common law. (Compare to **common law.**)

Citation. A reference to a specific legal authority or source that gives all identifying information about that source.

Code. A compilation of statutes, legislative acts, regulations, or ordinances, usually arranged topically.

Common law. A subset of case law referring to decisions created solely by the judicial branch without reference to statute, regulation, or any other law from the legislative branch. (Compare to **case law.**)

Critical reading. A reading process in which one actively engages information and questions it rather than passively accepting every word as written.

Dicta. Assertions or statements in a judicial opinion on points that are not necessary to address an issue presented by a party.

Element. A requirement that must be met before a governing standard can be established.

Elemental analysis. The analysis of a governing rule composed of elements.

Emotional facts. Facts not necessary to resolve a legal issue but that help the reader understand what motivated the parties to act or react in a particular way.

Enacted law. Law that has been passed and put into effect by a legislature.

Executive order. A directive from the executive branch that implements or interprets a statute, a constitutional provision, or a treaty.

Factor. A condition that a court considers when determining whether a governing standard is met.

Finding. A determination of fact a court makes in a judicial opinion.

Governing rule. The standard for a particular legal issue which tells people what they must or can do, what they must not or should not do, or what they are entitled to do under certain conditions. The governing rule can come from a statute or common law or from a combination of both sources.

Headnote. A one-paragraph or one-sentence summary for each point of law presented in a case, found at the beginning of a judicial opinion. Because headnotes are publishing tools and not legal authority, they should not be cited.

Holding. The court's answer to a particular legal question in a case that includes both the controlling rule of law and the specific facts of the case pertinent to the legal question.

Hook. The first sentence of a case illustration that states the legal principle that the illustration will clarify and prove to be true.

Jurisdiction. The area of authority over which a governing body has authority.

Legal argument. An analysis of a legal question that includes a conclusion or issue statement, an explanation of the law relevant to a client's problem, an application of that law to the client's facts, and a conclusion.

Legally significant facts. Facts in a client's case that a court will likely rely on to make its legal decision.

Legislative history. The record that develops as an idea for a law evolves into a statute.

Mandatory authority. Legal authority from a governing body within a jurisdiction that a court must follow. Mandatory authority is always primary authority.

Memorandum. A document used to communicate a legal analysis.

Mini-roadmap. An introductory section to a legal argument that sets out the governing rule for one element or factor, tells the reader the parts of that rule that will be discussed, the order the discussion will follow, and the conclusion for that discussion.

Objective analysis. A neutral assessment of a legal problem that overtly discusses both the strengths and the weaknesses of a client's legal position and predicts the most likely outcome. (See also **predictive analysis**.)

Persuasive authority. Non-binding law or commentary that a court may consider when deciding a case. Persuasive authority may be primary or secondary authority.

Point heading. A statement in a legal discussion that separates or introduces individual legal arguments. A point heading can include all or a combination of the following parts: the ultimate conclusion for a legal issue, the rule of law governing the issue, and the key facts supporting the conclusion. Point headings should be a complete sentence.

Policy. The underlying purpose or reason for a law.

Precedent. A prior judicial decision that establishes a basis for a similar case or similar question of law arising later. Binding precedent must be followed; persuasive precedent need not be.[1]

Predictive analysis. A neutral assessment of a legal problem that overtly discusses both the strengths and the weaknesses of a client's legal position and predicts the most likely outcome. (See also **objective analysis**.)

Primary authority. Any law created and published by a governing entity within a jurisdiction.

Prong test. An evaluation of whether a standard is met by using a multi-part inquiry. A prong test can be an element analysis, a balancing test, or a series of questions.

Question Presented. In a memorandum of law, the Question Presented sets out each dispositive legal question the discussion will analyze and answer.

---

1. Bryan A. Garner, *A Dictionary of Modern Legal Usage* 680-81 (2d ed. 1995).

Red flag words. Words that proscribe action, inaction, limitation, causation, entitlement, or consequence. (See also **special operative words**.)

Regulation. A law created by an executive branch agency that implements or expounds on a statute.

Reporters. A series of books that collects and publishes cases in chronological order.

Roadmap. An introduction to a legal analysis that tells the reader the legal question being asked, the governing rule for the question, the applicable parts of the question the analysis will discuss, the order in which those parts will be presented, and the ultimate conclusion to that legal question.

Roadsign. A signal to the reader alerting attention to an important part of the analysis.

Rule of the case. A point of law a judicial opinion will represent to future cases.

Rule-based reasoning. Direct application of a rule to the facts of a client's case to predict an outcome.

Secondary authority. Commentary about the law from sources such as legal encyclopedias, law review articles, or treatises, which explain how the law works. Secondary authority can be persuasive authority, but not binding.

Special operative words. Words that proscribe action, inaction, limitation, causation, entitlement, or consequence. (See also **red flag words**.)

Stare decisis. Part of the phrase, *stare decisis et quieta non movere,* which means "to stand by things decided and not disturb settled points." Stare decisis is a principle in American jurisprudence that requires a court to follow its prior decisions when the prior decision addresses the same issue.

Statute. A law enacted by the legislature. (See also **enacted law**.)

Synopsis. A brief summary of a case explaining the most basic issue, the underlying facts, and the dispositions by the lower courts and the current court. It is found right after the caption of a judicial opinion. Because a synopsis is a publishing tool, not legal authority, do not cite it.

Synthesis. The process of combining or blending parts to create a whole.

Test. An examination to determine whether a standard set out in a governing rule is met.

Topic sentence. The first sentence of any paragraph that clearly identifies the point that paragraph will prove.

Totality of the circumstances test. An evaluation of all relevant facts, together, to determine whether the standard set by a governing rule is met.

Trigger facts. The facts of a prior precedential case that triggered the court's decision on an issue. Trigger facts can also be called "critical" or "key" facts.

Index